THE
GERMAN CENTER PARTY
1870–1933

A Study in Political Catholicism

By Ellen Lovell Evans

SOUTHERN ILLINOIS UNIVERSITY PRESS
Carbondale and Edwardsville
1981

LIBRARY OF CONGRESS CATALOGING IN PUBLICATION DATA

Evans, Ellen Lovell, 1930–
    The German Center Party, 1870–1933.

    Bibliography: p.
    Includes index.
    1. Germany—Politics and government—1871–1918.
2. Germany—Politics and government—1918–1933.
3. Deutsche Zentrumspartei—History.   4. Catholic
Church in Germany—History.   5. Kulturkampf. I. Title.
DD221.E93   324.24302   80–27668
ISBN 0–8093–0997–1

CONTENTS

Contents

PREFACE

The Center party has received little attention from American historians, and this informal survey is intended partially to fill this omission. I hope that a study of the political representation of Germany's Catholic population will contribute to the understanding of an aspect of the country's past which is less familiar than most.

Some periods in the Center party's history are better known than others, particularly the years of the *Kulturkampf*; the final years from 1930 to 1933; and the years from 1890 to 1914, well covered in two recent monographs by John K. Zeender and Ronald J. Ross. My doctoral dissertation, completed in 1956, concentrated on the less-examined years of 1924 to 1930, and the present book reflects that emphasis. I have also continued to pursue my original interest, which was to try to explain how the policies and actions of the Center were affected by its Catholic affiliation. Hence the books deals with some issues, such as education, church-state relations, social policy, and corporativism, at much greater length than would be usual in a straight political history. On the other hand, topics such as foreign policy, tariff policy, and the activities of individual Centrists as cabinet ministers, have been dealt with lightly, because they seemed to me to be less relevant to my main theme.

Sections of several chapters have appeared in two published articles: "The Center Wages *Kulturpolitik*: Conflict in the Marx-Keudell Cabinet of 1927," *Central European History* 2 (1969): 139–58; and "Adam Stegerwald and the Role of the Christian Trade Unions in the Weimar Republic," *Catholic Historical Review* 59 (1974): 602–26.

My research on the Center party was begun twenty-eight years ago at the University of Wisconsin under the guidance of Professor Chester V. Easum, at that time chairman of the Department of History. I continued the project at Columbia University, where I had the privilege of participating in a seminar with the late Professors Franz Neumann, Hajo Holborn, and Henry L. Roberts. My dissertation was directed initially by Professor Roberts and then by Professor Fritz Stern. I am deeply grateful and appreciative to all of these scholars for their assistance and encouragement.

More recently, I have been helped in the preparation of this book by Dr. Arnold H. Price of the Library of Congress and Professor John K. Zeender of the Catholic University. Important eleventh-hour assistance has been rendered by Professor Margaret L. Anderson of Swarthmore College.

I also owe a debt of gratitude to several of my colleagues in the history department at Georgia State University, in particular to Gerald H. Davis, who first read and criticized the manuscript, and most especially to my friend and former chairman Joseph O. Baylen, whose encouragement and support have been invaluable.

Finally, this book could never have been written without the help of my housekeeper Mrs. Marie Stinchcomb.

Atlanta, Georgia   ELLEN LOVELL EVANS
October 1980

PROLOGUE

It is the intent of this study to provide a brief analysis and history of the Center party, the political organization of Germany's Catholic population, from its origins to its dissolution in 1933. Continuing themes which will be traced through the years of the party's existence are the effects of Catholic-clerical influence upon the parliamentary functioning of the Center; the relationship of the Center to other political parties, in opposition and in coalition; and the efforts of the party's leaders to balance and to satisfy the diverse interest groups which it represented.

The founding of the Center party in the 1870s as a defensive "tower" for German Catholics has sometimes been described as the intrusion of an unnatural element into the parliamentary arena, where political parties are customarily based upon class or economic interests. Bismarck's assertion that a confessional party is by definition dangerously divisive has been echoed by many historians, who see the Center as an almost accidental by-product of the Prussian *Kulturkampf*, continuing to exist after the ending of that episode more from inertia than from any discernible need. Such an interpretation cannot adequately explain the role of the Center in German political life. The Center was organized in response to a particular German situation, but comparable Catholic parties were also formed and continue to exist today in France, Italy, Belgium, Austria, and, in strikingly exact parallel to Germany's experience, Switzerland, and the Netherlands. In the latter two countries, confessional Protestant parties exist alongside the Catholic. Although some of these Catholic parties were identified with certain class interests, others represented as broadly diverse social and economic strata as the Center did. Critics of confessional parties often fail to consider that European parties based primarily upon social or economic platforms have frequently professed philosophies incompatible with Catholic belief. In the German spectrum, the

ix

liberal and Socialist parties were in the past strongly anticlerical, secularist, and freethinking, while the conservative parties were closely identified with the established Protestant state churches (though never so explicitly as their Swiss and Dutch counterparts). Thus the existence of a Catholic party in Germany was really no more unnatural than any other constellation if attention is focused upon each group's intellectual underpinnings rather than upon its economic platform; indeed, since the Center was the last of the major German political parties to be formed, it might be considered a very natural response to the already existing grouping which offered no welcome to those seeking to represent the Catholic viewpoint. The settlement of the *Kulturkampf* did not alter the philosophy of any party nor of the Prussian administration, and hence it did not constitute an invitation to supporters of the Center to disband and align with other parties according to their class interests.

Furthermore, the Center party was originally concerned not only with the defense of Catholic interests but also with the representation of a demographic minority which had specific grievances and demands unrelated to religion. In addition, the Catholic minority was not evenly dispersed within Germany but was concentrated in the southern states, in Alsace-Lorraine, and in the Prussian provinces of the Rhineland, Silesia, West Prussia, and Posen, all areas with historical reason to be unhappy with the Prussian government and with the results of German unification. The Center was therefore never simply the political arm of the Catholic church but a party reflecting a variety of causes, all opposed to the dominant leadership in Prussia and the Reich. In the 1870s the events known as the *Kulturkampf* acted as a catalyst to unite these interests into a powerful political movement. As a consequence of the conflict, a section of the population whose leadership was traditionally conservative and even allied with reaction developed a political party allied, for many purposes, with the Left, "a brother to bourgeois liberalism and the Socialist workers' movement,"[1] with an ideological base flexible enough to encompass a strong civil rights platform, a relatively high concern for social welfare, an oppo-

1. Karl Buchheim, *Geschichte der christliche Parteien in Deutschland*, (Munich, 1953), p. 23.

sition to militarism, and even, by the opening of the twentieth century, a tentative embrace of democracy.

Because of this flexibility, the Center was able to come through the revolution of 1918 and the transition to parliamentary democracy in the Weimar republic remarkably smoothly. The party was successful in achieving most of its old goals through the new constitution and republican institutions. But after the initial crises had been weathered, the republican years saw increasing division within the party and a steadily declining support for it from German Catholics. Its very success in carrying out its program meant that too few common interests remained to hold together the diverse elements among the membership and the electorate. At the end of the 1920s, the Center's leaders retreated into a narrow clericalism of the type which the party had consistently repudiated throughout its previous history. Since the only remaining clerical goals proved impossible to achieve within the republican parliamentary system, and since the Vatican no longer placed much confidence in Catholic political parties, this change in policy only led to further decline and disintegration. In spite of substantial continued support from its voters, the Center capitulated to National Socialism in a distinctly unheroic manner. The "end of the party"[2] in 1933 was not followed by a revival after 1945 but by the creation of an entirely new organization, the Christian Democratic Union. After sixty-three years, the Center, which originally had possessed great vitality and performed a necessary and important role in German political life, had outlived its usefulness.

2. Erich Matthias and Rudolf Morsey, *Das Ende der Parteien*, (Düsseldorf, 1960); phrase taken from the title.

THE GERMAN CENTER PARTY
1870–1933

I.
THE YEARS BEFORE 1850

The fragmentation of Germany into several hundred autonomous states in the medieval Holy Roman Empire was perpetuated in the sixteenth century by the effects of the Protestant Reformation, which reinforced political division with sectarian division. "For a long time thereafter practically two Germanys existed side by side, and new political divisions followed the religious rift."[1] The separation of the population into Protestant and Catholic denominations, each claiming the allegiance of roughly half of the German-speaking people, became a permanent factor in German history. With the secularizing influences of the eighteenth century and the shift of international attention from religious controversy to more material concerns, the denominational division ceased to have great political significance; a balance had been achieved. But the upheaval of the French Revolution and the Napoleonic Wars, while bringing about a desirable reduction in the number of German states, had also the effect of disturbing this balance. The peace settlement for Germany worked out by the victors after the defeat of Napoleon completely altered the relationship of the Catholic and Protestant denominations to one another. The full consequences of the change did not become apparent until the international revival of the Catholic church in the 1850s and 1860s, when a definite political consciousness emerged in the German Catholic population. Earlier in the century, however, there were several events which prefigured such a consciousness.

Before the French Revolution, a high proportion of German Catholics lived in states within the Holy Roman Empire which were officially Catholic. Most of these states were autonomous bishoprics or archbishoprics: the archbishoprics of Trier, Mainz, Cologne, Salz-

---

1. Hajo Holborn, *A History of Modern Germany*, 3 vols. (New York, 1967–69), 1:vii.

burg, Trent, the bishoprics of Münster, Fulda, Augsburg, Regensburg, Freising, Würzburg, Hildesheim, Liège, and others. These were governed by prelates (several with plural holdings) who maintained intricate dynastic ties with the larger Catholic states of Austria and Bavaria; Habsburg and Wittelsbach bishops were numerous in the eighteenth century, and the Electoral Archbishop of Trier, on the eve of the Revolution, was a member of the Catholic dynasty of the Protestant state of Saxony. These ecclesiastical states were politically and militarily weak in spite of these dynastic connections, but they actually comprised sizable aggregations of territory and population in the west and south of the old empire.

A number of the fifty-one free cities of the empire were also Catholic in population: Aachen, Cologne, Dortmund, and Augsburg were the largest of these. There were, it is true, very few Catholic princely states apart from the extensive holdings of the Austrian Habsburgs, which included, as well as the eastern provinces, several small enclaves on the Upper Danube (the Breisgau and Burgau being the largest.) After the loss of Lorraine to France, the Electoral Duchy of Bavaria was the only other Catholic principality of significant size, and it was only half the size of the nineteenth-century Bavarian state. The Rhenish Palatinate and Jülich-Berg had Catholic rulers at the end of the eighteenth century but were of mixed denomination in population.

The largest Catholic minority in a Protestant state before the French Revolution was in Prussia. It had been acquired by Prussia in the conquest of Silesia in 1740 and the annexation of West Prussia, Posen, and the Bishopric of Ermland in the three partitions of Poland. Certain legal accommodations for the Catholic church and its members had been made upon the acquisition of these lands, but there had been no modification of the Protestant nature of the state and its administration.

It is indisputable that the ecclesiastical states, free cities, and tiny principalities were inefficient forms of government and handicaps to the formation of a modern state. This was recognized even in the eighteenth century. But the final outcome of the Napoleonic Wars in Germany meant not only the disappearance of these anachronistic survivals but also, in the process, the transference of nearly the entire population of west and southwest Germany to Protestant administrations.

This was not the intention either of the French occupation or the great powers at the peace conference, but it was the result of their decisions. The people of nineteenth-century Germany were still of two denominations, Catholic and Protestant, but the states were no longer so evenly divided between them.

All of the Catholic free cities were absorbed into larger states, and all of the ecclesiastical states were divided among the princes, most of these divisions taking place even before French armies penetrated east of the Rhine. Liège passed out of Germany altogether, becoming part of the kingdom of the Netherlands in 1814, later of Belgium, and Salzburg, Trent, and others were incorporated into Austria. Würzburg and Bamberg and parts of others were taken by Bavaria, and all of the rest were shared among Protestant states. Of the Catholic princely states, only Liechtenstein, the two Hohenzollerns (annexed to Prussia in 1850), and the greatly enlarged Bavaria were left. Prussia became more than one-third Catholic; Bavaria, with the Rhenish Palatinate, became more than one-fourth Protestant. Württemberg, Baden, the Hesses, and Hanover all acquired large Catholic minorities. In many cases, mediatized Catholic princes in compensation for their loss of independence were given seats in the upper parliamentary chambers of those states which enacted constitutions. The endowments of the church had been lost and the new states were not disposed to restore them. Under French rule, however, Napoleon had decreed that there should be equal rights for minority sects in the Confederation of the Rhine; and the Left Bank of the Rhine, when it was joined to France, had been dealt with by the French government in accordance with the terms of the Concordat of 1801. The Treaty of Vienna of 1815 guaranteed equal rights for all Christian churches and the German princes themselves saw the Catholic church as a force for conservatism and stability and, hence, did not contemplate its impoverishment but, instead, adopted the pattern of state support which had prevailed in Lutheran states since the Reformation.

Pius VII and his agent Cardinal Consalvi worked out arrangements with Bavaria in the Concordat of 1817, and similar agreements with other states were concluded by 1827. The agreement with Prussia was included in the papal bull *De salute animarum* of 1821. In all of these arrangements, dioceses were redrawn to coincide as closely as possible with the new state boundaries, and financial support, legal recognition, and a full range of religious activities were assured. Political influence and participation were not.

In Prussia, the Catholics' goal of "parity," that is, equal representation in the civil service, universities, and other public institutions, was never realized. From the time of Frederick the Great, the exclusively Protestant character of the administration had been maintained in Prussia. When Silesia was annexed in 1740, Protestant officials had been installed there, and the same policy had been followed after the Polish partitions, with the additional motive here of replacing Polish with German personnel. When the territories of the Rhineland and Westphalia were added in 1814, they too were administered by Protestant officials. In 1819, Prussian Minister for Religion and Education (*Kultusminister*) Karl, Freiherr von Altenstein, wrote, in a memorandum outlining the goal of his office, that the Prussian state "is a Protestant state" and that the government should "care for the Protestant church with love; care for the Catholic church out of duty. The Protestant church must be favored. The Catholic church should not be slighted. It will be conscientiously cared for in its best interests."[2] Gen. Leopold von Gerlach wrote later that the Prussian state should "Germanize the Poles and Protestantize the Romans."[3] Mass conversion was of course never seriously considered, but neither was a genuine parity, which increasingly became the Catholic demand. On the other hand, the obtaining of a genuine parity would have been made difficult because of the existing substantial inequalities of wealth and education between the two denominations, so that compliance in the civil service and the faculty of the universities, for example, would not have been practical because of the relative shortage of qualified Catholics. This was the argument against parity put forth by the government later in the century, and one which had some validity well into the middle of the twentieth century.

Two incidents in the 1830s served to unite Catholics in Prussia, and in all of Germany, in their first show of political self-consciousness: the famous "Cologne troubles" (*Kölner Wirren*) and a similar case in the east. The two incidents both involved the resistance of Catholic archbishops to state regulations concerning civil marriage

2. Karl Bachem, *Vorgeschichte, Geschichte und Politik der deutschen Zentrumspartei, 1815–1914*, 9 vols. (Cologne, 1927–32), 1:159.
3. Ibid., p. 160.

ceremonies and mixed marriages. According to canon law, priests could not assist at mixed marriages unless the couple promised to raise all of the children in the Catholic faith. The civil ceremony itself had been accepted by the Vatican in 1830, providing other conditions had been fulfilled. In the late eighteenth and early nineteenth centuries, a great many German bishops had been accommodating in such matters, ignoring the strict wording of the canon law, and up to the middle of the century there are many examples to be found of Catholic prelates in Germany and elsewhere subservient to their rulers and unwilling to take the ultramontane position. Count Ferdinand August von Spiegel, archbishop of Cologne before 1837, was one of these. But the revival in international Catholicism and the increased prestige of the papacy after Pius VII was beginning to produce a generation of men who took their obligations to doctrine and church law more seriously, and in doing so came into conflict with governments and rulers, both Catholic and Protestant. In 1837, the new archbishop of Cologne, Clemens August von Droste-Vischering, began his term of office by purging the theological seminary in Bonn of professors who taught the principle of state supremacy over the churches and he defied the state regulations on mixed marriages (which decreed that sons be brought up in the father's faith and daughters in the mother's). He was thereupon imprisoned, and Cologne remained without an archbishop until 1845, with the duties being taken over by the cathedral chapter, which remained loyal to the state.

The following year, Archbishop Martin von Dunin of Posen-Gnesen, in the eastern part of Prussia, was imprisoned for ten months for the same reason. These events roused strong feelings of unity and protest in the Catholic population of all of Germany, and they foreshadow rather strikingly the later course of the *Kulturkampf*. The tendency of the Prussian state to regard the Catholic clergy as a potentially subversive element, the immediate willingness to use force against it, and, most significant, the passive acceptance of this by the non-Catholic population are all suggestive for later civil rights issues not only in the *Kulturkampf* but also in actions against other "subversive elements" such as Socialists, Poles, Alsatians, and Jews.

In response to the "Cologne troubles," Joseph von Görres, the leading Catholic intellectual and German patriot who had been forced to leave his native Rhineland because of his outspoken journalism and was now settled in Munich, wrote a widely circulated pamphlet, *Athanasius*, which protested the imprisonment of the archbishop and demanded freedom of action for the church and parity for Catholics in the civil service and universities. The next year Görres and his circle at the University of Munich began publication of the *Historische-politische Blätter für das katholische Deutschland* in order to represent the political views of Catholicism. The very phrase "Catholic Germany" expressed for the first time a common national cause.

The death of Frederick William III of Prussia and the accession to the throne in 1840 of the romantic medievalist Frederick William IV seemed to promise a change for the better for Catholics and other opponents of the authoritarian state. Liberal hopes were soon disappointed, but conservative Catholics actually did experience a marked improvement in their status, within the limits of the reactionary outlook of Frederick William. He and his *Kultusminister*, J. A. F. Eichhorn, were determined to impose a rigid orthodoxy upon the Protestant Evangelical church (a Prussian union of the Lutheran and Calvinist Reformed churches effected in 1822) and hoped to complement this with a partnership with the presumably equally rigid and orthodox Catholic hierarchy. To this end, Archbishop von Dunin was reinstated in his diocese of Posen-Gnesen, and Archbishop von Droste was released from prison (though never reinstated). Full concessions were made to the Catholic position on mixed marriages. Any solution in favor of the state position would have meant the introduction of the civil marriage ceremony as the sole legal requirement for marriage, and this Frederick William was determined to prevent. His concept of society was quite compatible with the idea of equality between the two denominations, provided that each was loyal and obedient to his notion of monarchy. His plan to organize the Protestant consistories, however, was never implemented, and so that idea of direct communication with the two churches was abandoned in favor of a plan to add to the Prussian *Kultusministerium* special Catholic and Protestant departments which would act as mediaries between the state and the churches. These departments were organized and continued in operation until 1871.

Frederick William also permitted the modification of the *placet*, the necessity for royal approval of church appointments, promising instead to appoint as bishops only those men in whom the pope expressed confidence, concerning which decision the historian Treitschke wrote: "Thus the authority whose function it was to maintain the supremacy of the Prussian crown vis-a-vis the Catholic church, was to consist of persons thoroughly satisfactory to the curia!"[4] Treitschke's indignation was increased by his belief that "most of the measures of the Catholic Department [in the ministry] were prepared in the Radziwill palace," i.e. by machinations of the Polish nobility.[5]

Under Frederick William IV, religious education in the schools was intensified for both denominations (the public schools were organized separately for the two, as they were throughout Germany) and, as an especially romantic and conciliatory gesture, work was begun on the completion of Cologne cathedral. Ironically, the see of Cologne was not only still vacant when this work was begun but was again vacant for a similar reason when the work was completed in 1880.

Charges made by Protestant critics that Frederick William favored his Catholic subjects over the others were unfounded, but it is undeniable that the position of the church as an institution, if not that of its adherents, was greatly improved in the 1840s. This is made clear by a comparison with the other German states which had substantial Catholic population. In none of these, including Catholic Bavaria and Austria, did the church have such freedom of action over its own affairs as it did in Prussia.

Baden, Württemberg, and Hesse-Darmstadt were the three Protestant states which contained the largest number of Catholic subjects after the Vienna settlement. Baden was nearly two-thirds Catholic, the other two, slightly over one-quarter. The dioceses of these states and two other districts (Hesse-Kassel, Nassau-Frankfurt) were reorganized in the papal bull *Provida Sollersque* of 1821 and placed under the archbishop of Freiburg, in Baden. The civil service in all three states continued to be predominately Protestant in spite of government declarations of intent toward parity, as in the Baden constitution of 1818 and the Württemberg constitution of 1819. On the other hand, the upper houses of the legislatures of these states were heavily Catholic, be-

---

4. Heinrich von Treitschke, *A History of Germany in the Nineteenth Century*, 7 vols. (New York, 1915–19), 7:30.
5. Ibid., p. 31.

cause seats had been allotted to the mediatized princes of small principalities and former imperial knights of the Holy Roman Empire.

All three states issued official edicts establishing the principle of state supremacy over the churches immediately after the publication of the papal bull. Neither clergy nor laymen protested this at the time, and the two archbishops of Freiburg before 1842 acquiesced in all state controls, including, in Baden, the introduction of the German liturgy and permission for Catholics to eat meat on Friday. Just as the southwest of Germany was the most liberal region, so was its Catholic population the least self-conscious and the most likely to share in the liberal secular outlook. For example, the German Catholic movement (for separation of the church from Rome) founded by the Silesian priest Johannes Ronge in 1844 met with an initial favorable response in the southwest and was officially approved by the Baden Parliament in 1845. This movement paralleled the several secessions from Protestantism which took place in the 1840s in the direction of deism and rationalism. The German Catholics never obtained much numerical support, even in Baden, and disappeared into political byways in 1848, the revolutionary Robert Blum being their best-known adherent. The same motivations and outlook were to reappear in the Old Catholic movement in the years after the Vatican Council and the promulgation of the dogma of papal infallibility.

In Bavaria, the status of the church was more favorable in many ways, for example, in the freedom of monastic orders to organize; Bavaria was the only German state in which all of the male orders were permitted. But the royal administration was as firm a believer in state supremacy as the governments of Baden, Württemberg, and Hesse, and the political influence of the ultramontane interest was slight until late in the century. The Concordat of 1817 was very generous to the church but was effectively contradicted by the terms and spirit of the constitution of 1818 which established official parity among the three Bavarian denominations, Catholicism, Lutheranism, and Calvinism (Reformed church). A special Religious Edict of 1818 confirmed this and provoked the opposition of Pius VII and the Bavarian hierarchy, after which a few modifications were made. But Bavaria did institute a far greater degree of parity for Protestants in the civil service and universities than existed for Catholics in Prussia, and the Palatinate remained an exclusively Protestant enclave in the state. In the problem of mixed marriages, the Bavarian government refused to endorse the canon law provision about the upbringing of children, and the *Landtag* upheld this in 1831.

Maximilian I (elector 1799–, king 1806–25) had been strongly influenced by Austrian Josephine teachings and the views of the Enlightenment regarding toleration of Protestantism and the principle of state control over education. Laws for the toleration of minority sects and state supremacy over the churches had been effected in the ministry of Maximilian von Montgelas, the ruler's chief adviser until 1818. The next king, Ludwig I (1825–48) continued to follow the precepts of Montgelas. He had a Protestant mother and wife, and his sister was married to Frederick William IV of Prussia and eventually converted to the Evangelical faith. His determination to maintain state supremacy disappointed the ultramontane faction in Bavaria, but Catholics all over Germany benefited from Ludwig's generous support of the University of Munich, which became a center of Catholic scholarship. Görres, Franz von Baader, Johann Adam Möhler, and Ignaz Döllinger all served on the faculty of the university at some time. For the most part their work upheld the revived internationalism of the church, although some, notably Döllinger, changed their position in later years.

Dr. Döllinger also represented the Catholic interest as university delegate to the lower house of the Bavarian *Landtag* in the years 1845–48. Several of these Catholic professors led the protest in the 1840s against the influence of Ludwig's controversial friend Lola Montez and were consequently dismissed from office. Throughout Ludwig's reign, his personal piety, respect for the papacy, and encouragement of Catholic scholarship were at all times balanced by his firm belief in a Josephine state supremacy, which decisively prevailed in 1847–48. In fact, according to one authority, the good relations between his government and the Vatican in his reign are to be attributed to the unusually tolerant and conciliatory position taken by the papacy toward Bavaria in comparison to other German states, rather than to the lack of potential reasons for conflict.[6]

In Austria, the policies of state supremacy, including the introduction of civil marriage, had been the rule since the time of Joseph II and

---

6. Rupert Hacker, *Die Beziehung zwischen Bayern und dem heiligen Stuhl in der Regierungszeit Ludwigs I (1825–1845)* (Tübingen 1967), pp. 150–52.

were fully maintained until after the revolution of 1848, in spite of the growth in court circles of a "pious party" anxious to improve the position of the church.

In general, there is very little evidence, before 1848, of the existence of an active political Catholicism in any part of Germany except Prussia. In liberal Baden and in conservative Bavaria and Austria, educated Catholics in and out of government accepted the idea of state domination over the church either out of conviction or from the belief that the interests of state and church were for the most part in harmony. In Prussia, on the other hand, both "liberal" and conservative Catholics had already begun to feel somewhat threatened by state domination in a state which was both Protestant and authoritarian.

In another part of the German-speaking world, in Switzerland, a rather differently oriented Catholic minority did take decisive political action in the 1840s. When the northern, largely Protestant urban cantons of Switzerland began to lead the majority in the federal Diet in the direction of greater centralization and unity, the more economically backward rural central and southern Catholic cantons organized resistance to change, strongly backed by Austria. Their promotion of their common interests, most notably their invitation to the Society of Jesus to return to Switzerland, provoked the liberals of the Protestant cities to more radical proposals in favor of national unity and the secular ideal. This conflict culminated in the Catholic organization of the *Sonderbund* ("particularist league") for military defense and the brief civil war of November 1847.

There was keen interest expressed in Germany concerning the events in Switzerland. Expansion of the war was a possibility, with Austria, Prussia, and perhaps France supporting the *Sonderbund*, but the campaign ended too quickly for outside intervention, with an overwhelming victory for the centralists over the *Sonderbund*. This was a microcosmic prelude to later events in the unification of Germany. It should perhaps be noted, however, that the degree of centralization attained in Switzerland as a result of this war was great only in comparison with the earlier confederation. The amount of self-determination remaining to the cantons after the reforms of 1848 was far greater than that prevailing at the provincial and local levels in Prussia, for example. Catholics received in defeat in Switzerland what Catholics in Prussia would have regarded as the rewards of victory.

In Switzerland, the causes of national unity and of liberalism were visibly linked with the Protestant faith, and this connection was to influence the course of events in Germany in the years of unification. In the revolutions of 1848, however, there was no clear-cut division of interest between Catholics and liberals. On the one hand, the *grossdeutsch* position taken by most Catholics, which necessarily involved maintaining a high degree of state autonomy in Germany, could, by analogy with Switzerland, be identified as reactionary. On the other hand, in another matter of liberal concern, the question of individual civil rights, liberals were supported by Catholics who considered themselves restricted by regulations in nearly all of the states. Freedom of speech and the press were strongly supported by the Catholic delegation to the Frankfurt Parliament from Prussia, as well as the more predictable freedoms of religion and education.

The Catholic activists elected to Frankfurt who met in the Catholic Club in the *Steinernen Haus* were actually only a small percentage of the delegates who were Catholic in personal affiliation. There were, for the last time in Germany, a large number of participants in the 1848 events whose Catholic birth was simply irrelevant to their political activities. This was even more true of the Berlin Parliament than of Frankfurt, for there there was no special fraction or club for Catholics at all, although many prominent members, for example the liberal Ludolf Camphausen, were Catholic. It is true that thirty-nine members of the Berlin Parliament were priests, including the newly instated Archbishop Johannes von Geissel of Cologne; and thirty-four priests, including four bishops, went to Frankfurt, compared to fourteen Protestant pastors.[7] This seems to have been more because of the personal prestige and habits of leadership of the Catholic clergy among their congregations than because of any desire to present a homogeneous bloc, and, in fact, differences of class background within the clergy were often as significant as differences between clergy and laymen in determining policies and voting patterns.

The president of the Catholic Club in Frankfurt was Gen. Joseph von Radowitz personal friend of Frederick William IV and president also of the extreme conservative group which met in adjacent, but

7. Frank Eyck, *The Frankfurt Parliament, 1848–1849*, (New York, 1968), pp. 97–98; Bachem, 2:76.

separate, quarters in the *Steinernen Haus*. Radowitz was far from being a liberal, but like many Catholic statesmen he had a concern for social problems and had even urged Frederick William to alleviate social distress in Prussia by the imposition of a progressive income tax and increased poor relief. He supported a *grossdeutsch* union of Germany but favored leadership of such a union by the king of Prussia, in which lead he was not followed by the rest of the Catholic Club, all but two of whom voted against Frederick William as constitutional monarch of a united Germany.

Among the younger Catholic delegates in Frankfurt were August Reichensperger, Wilhelm, Freiherr von Ketteler (a young priest), and Dr. Döllinger from Munich, men who were to play important roles in political Catholicism in future years. Reichensperger was a legal councillor from the Rhineland, appellate court councillor in Cologne after 1849, and delegate to the new Prussian *Landtag* in 1851. His brother Peter was also a legal councillor, in Koblenz, and was a delegate to the Berlin Parliament in 1848. Peter Reichensperger set something of a record in parliamentary membership by being returned to the Prussian *Landtag* every election after 1849 and to every session of the North German and German Reichstag until his death in 1892. Freiherr von Ketteler was a clergyman of dynamic personality, shortly to be named bishop of Mainz. His brother, a conservative landowner, sat with the Right at Frankfurt, but Wilhelm associated with the republican Left. He made a national name for himself as speaker at the first Catholic Congress for all of Germany, held that October in Mainz. Here he spoke of his belief that Catholicism "has nothing to fear from freedom" and of his concern for social welfare. Dr. Döllinger was one of the few Bavarian delegates who attended the Catholic Club; most associated themselves with the liberals or other purely political factions.

The Catholic Club in Frankfurt was in no sense a political party, and very few of its members wanted it to become one, although Ketteler urged the idea. It was decided that the members should work for Catholic rights from within many different political factions. Apart from defense of their religion, the only common interests they had were those of civil rights and a preference for the *grossdeutsch* position. In the latter issue they were greatly handicapped by the underrepresentation of many Catholic districts in the German Confederation. Bavaria and Austria had interpreted the *Vorparlament*'s instructions on election procedures very narrowly in determining those who were sufficiently "independent" to be voters, and, in addition, many parts of Austria either did not send representatives or sent representatives of non-German nationality, especially Italians and Poles. The German-speaking Tyrol, on the other hand, sent a full delegation which proved hostile to *any* proposals of change, whether *grossdeutsch* or *kleindeutsch*. This was one reason for the low number of votes for inclusion of Austria in a German union, and another reason was the steady attrition of conservative Catholic delegates, *grossdeutsch* in sympathy, in the months before the exclusion of Austria became an issue. Many left as early as October 1848, and many others, including Ketteler, left before the final votes were taken on the constitution and on the presentation of the crown to Frederick William. According to one statistical analysis, about 70 percent of those delegates known to be Catholic who did vote opposed the exclusion of Austria, and 85 percent opposed Frederick William as hereditary emperor of a united Germany.[8]

There was also concerted Catholic action on the question of civil rights. The Cologne election platform, used as a model in much of western Germany, had called for German citizenship without discrimination, complete freedom of education (including the education of clergy outside Germany, at that time not permitted), freedom of the press and of speech, the rights of petition, assembly, association (including religious orders), and travel. The platform was based upon the clauses relating to church-state relations in the Belgian constitution of 1831, which represented the ideal legal status to European Catholics. The Catholic Club was cautious about specifically requesting a restoration of the Jesuit order throughout Germany, perhaps recalling the Swiss precedent.

Many of these demands coincided with liberal goals, but not all. The desire for the independence of the church did not at all imply the desire for loss of state financial support or for any kind of true separation. A Catholic bill for "independence" of the churches was heavily defeated by the assembly. Such a measure, it was felt, even though it was to affect all denominations, would in its results have aided Catholics at the expense of the established Protestant churches in most parts

8. Eyck, pp. 361–65.

of Germany. Catholic demands for church control of schools were also decisively defeated when the assembly voted in October 1848 to put all schools under state supervision.

Defeat on such crucial issues led many conservative Catholics to feel that their usefulness was at an end, and the reduction of their numbers, especially among the clergy, dates from these votes. On the other hand, the demand for freedom of worship, supported by Catholics even though it would have included non-Christians and breakaway groups like the German Catholics (of whom there were several at Frankfurt) was readily upheld, being opposed only by the intransigent Austrian Tyrol delegation.

In October 1848, while the Frankfurt Parliament was still in session, the first Catholic Congress was held in Mainz. Although this gathering, which was to become a tradition, was religious rather than political, the very fact of its attendance by Catholics from all parts of Germany was itself of political significance. Twenty-three delegates from Frankfurt attended the congress, among them Ketteler, who delivered a powerful speech on the social question. As yet, his recommendations for its solution lay in the realm of charity and personal conscience; later he was to advocate legal measures and worker organizations.

The chairman of the Mainz Congress was Professor Franz Joseph Buss of Baden, a delegate to the *Vorparlament* and the Frankfurt Parliament. He was an outspoken clerical who had single-handedly represented that point of view in the overwhelmingly liberal Baden Lower House. Significantly he too, though so very conservative in most ways, had made a name for himself on the social issue. In 1837 he had sponsored a bill in the Baden *Landtag* for the passage of a factory police regulation to insure against injuries or losses connected with factory industry, to be paid for by the worker, the employer, and the state. He had described factory conditions as a "sickness in the body of society" and recommended education of workers in vocational schools and the establishment of savings and loan associations, the elimination of child labor, and the restoration of mandatory Sunday rest.[9] His bill was defeated and his suggestions ignored in Baden. In Germany as in Great Britain, the early years of the Industrial Revolution saw concern for

9. Bachem, 1:274.

the new class of factory workers coming more from political conservatives like Buss than from liberals committed to a laissez faire policy. Such concern was backward-looking in those years, bound up with an obsolescent way of life, but at a later date it would provide a broad popular base for the otherwise conservative Center party in Germany and pose a challenge to classical liberalism.

The events of 1848 in Bavaria are often appended to accounts of the revolution as a ruefully humorous footnote, since the uproar over Lola Montez resulted in the victory of conservative clerical opinion over the relatively liberal policies of Ludwig I and his protégée. Yet the days of the revolution in Munich saw crowds as large and as passionate as in any other revolutionary center, and, as elsewhere, the arbitrary will of the monarch was challenged by public opinion. In the process, institutional changes were demanded and obtained which would prevent arbitrary rule—however enlightened—from being exercised in the future. Bavaria in 1848 is an example of the paradox so evident in Germany during the *Kulturkampf*: although liberalism and Catholic ideology were in conflict, Catholics could benefit their own cause by recourse to liberal methods. The advent of the democratic suffrage proved eventually to be of far more practical use to the Catholics of Germany than to the liberals.

The 1840s in Bavaria had seen a determined effort on the part of clericals in the state to undo the parity arrangements and to prevent further expansion of Protestant influence. They were supported in their efforts by Minister of the Interior Karl von Abel. Changes were made in the schools, returning history classes to instructors of religion. The universities of Würzburg and Munich were altered in faculty and curriculum with the purpose of "re-Catholicizing" them.[10] Ludwig at first acquiesced in the changes, but even before the advent of Lola Montez he had begun to reverse the trend by removing religious affairs from Abel's jurisdiction and placing them in a separate ministry. It was by no means Lola's influence alone that led the king to act against the ultramontanes. Her significance lies not so much in her own actions as in the fact that she provided the opportunity to the clericals to achieve their will through massive public support.

Abel's ministry was dismissed in February 1847, after it had sent

10. Michael Doeberl, *Entwicklungsgeschichte Bayerns*, 3 vols. (Munich, 1931), 3:132.

a memorandum to Ludwig in the name of the entire cabinet refusing to approve his wish to make Lola a Bavarian citizen in order to make her eligible for the title of Countess Landsfeld. Six Catholic-clerical professors at the University of Munich, including Dr. Döllinger, were dismissed a few days later on similar grounds, Görres being permitted to remain because of his eminence and advanced age (in fact he died in January 1848). Protests over the dismissals and over the composition of the new cabinet (changed twice in the course of 1847) grew louder and in January 1848 erupted into violence, after student demonstrations against Countess Landsfeld, as she now was, and her followers. But during the month of active revolution, the demands of the rioters coalesced into much more than the desire to get rid of the countess, and, perhaps inevitably, took on the appearance of a liberal platform: responsibility of ministers, a modern electoral law, introduction of the jury system, and abolition of censorship. At the same time, peasants in the countryside, however much they may have been morally outraged by the king's favorite, did not neglect to include in their demands an end to the burdensome manorial obligations, which were duly canceled or commuted to money payments in March by the *Landtag*.

The resulting broader suffrage for the *Landtag* (still with indirect voting) and the introduction of ministerial responsibility meant that the Bavarian legislature became less doctrinaire-liberal and more responsive to clerical opinion than it had been before. But the new king Maximilian II, who succeeded to the throne when his father, overwhelmed by the events of the revolution, abdicated, was a man of liberal views, who in his youth had even had thoughts of uniting the three religious denominations of Bavaria into one. By the time he inherited, he had returned to a conventional Catholicism in his personal life, but he resumed the state supremacy position of his predecessors and it was not until after his death, in 1864, that the ultramontanes were able to alter government policies in the state.

It is clear that the events of 1848 were neither particularly significant nor favorable for the growth of a Catholic political consciousness. One important consequence of the revolution, however, was the rapid development of a Catholic press, made possible by the relaxation of censorship laws in the German states. Some of these newspapers were:

the *Rheinische Volkshalle* (becoming the *Deutsche Volkshalle*), the *Mainzer Journal* in Hesse, the *Deutsche Volksblatt* in Stuttgart, and the *Kölnische Blätter,* called after 1869 the *Kölnische Volkszeitung,* a powerful voice for Prussian Catholics.

2
THE UNIFICATION OF GERMANY

From 1848 until the middle 1860s it is possible to trace a slowly widening gap between the liberal and the Catholic viewpoints in the German states, but it is clear from election records and other evidence that a large number of Catholic laymen still continued to support liberal platforms. In Prussia, a "Catholic fraction"[1] was formed in the newly created House of Deputies, but it did not by any means include all Catholic representatives, some of whom sat with liberals, others with the conservatives of the *Kreuzzeitung* fraction, assisting in the reactionary revision of the constitution. The Catholic fraction was organized by the Reichensperger brothers and Hermann von Mallinckrodt, a tall, distinguished-looking conservative from Dortmund in Westphalia, whose Catholicism was the more devout from having been instilled in a household of mixed Catholic and Protestant parentage. These three men really wanted to drop the name "Catholic" and develop a full political program for their party but were dissuaded from doing so by the other members, who wanted a clearly recognizable title to attract voters. The title was finally changed, on the accession of Prince William as regent in 1858, to the *Fraktion des Zentrums*, but with the words "Catholic fraction" in parentheses after it.

The fraction was not really needed in these years to protect Catholic interests, since the Constitution of 1850 gave ample protection, and the upper chamber of the *Landtag*, the *Herrenhaus*, was always active in preventing liberal innovation, as when it vetoed legislation for civil marriage and the easing of divorce laws. On other issues, there was a lack of consensus among the members of the *Zentrum*. Their

---

1. The English word "fraction" will be used in this work as the most convenient equivalent of the German *fraktion,* meaning the parliamentary delegation of a political party.

grossdeutsch orientation was expressed in such lukewarm terms as to disappoint many of their former supporters, and their approval of the controversial army budget led many of their previous voters to desert the party for the Progressives, or to abstain from voting altogether in the elections of 1866. The fraction was reduced by half in 1863 and cut down to only fifteen men in 1866. At that time it was disbanded and its few delegates were simply classified as *Wilde*, independents, in the House of Deputies. It was not until 1870 that another Center was founded, after events had profoundly altered the political situation.

Anticlerical liberalism continued to rule in both Baden and Württemberg in the 1850s and 1860s. Attempts to negotiate concordats with the Vatican failed in both states. Laws were indeed passed guaranteeing the independence of the church and eliminating the need for state approval of appointments, but these laws did not satisfy the more ardent Catholic leaders because they did not include the free establishment of religious orders and did not cover the increasingly sensitive subject of the schools. In Baden, in fact, the "school war" which began in 1864 really marked the beginning of a *Kulturkampf* in that state.

The climate in Hesse-Darmstadt was somewhat more favorable to Catholicism in this period because of its Grand Duke Ludwig III, who was married to a Catholic princess of the Bavarian Wittelsbach dynasty, and his reactionary Minister of the Interior Reinhard, Freiherr von Dalwigk, not a Catholic but a friend to Austria and a stalwart supporter of the *grossdeutsch* position. The democratic suffrage introduced in 1849 into Hesse was revised under Dalwigk into a version of the Prussian three-class system, which actually hurt Catholics in terms of their representation in the lower house of the legislature, but in the upper house, where many mediatized Catholic nobles sat, and in appointments to government office, Hesse offered more opportunities for Catholic influence than its neighbors in the southwest or Prussia.

The presence of Bishop von Ketteler, bishop of Mainz since 1849, naturally affected Hessian clerical affairs also, especially when he sat for some years in the upper house of the legislature himself. He was successful in having the Mainz seminary reopened for the training of priests and in readmitting both male and female orders, including the Jesuits, into the state. However, the written convention he negotiated with the Vatican was never accepted as law in Hesse-Darmstadt.

In Bavaria, ironically, the victory of the clericals in ousting Ludwig I had resulted in the accession to the throne of another state supremacist in the person of Maximilian II. He was actively interested in achieving equality for Protestants in the state and refused to remove the *placet*, the necessity for state approval of church appointments.

Part of the impetus behind the efforts of Catholics in the southern states to obtain concordats with the Vatican (or, in the case of Bavaria, to negotiate more favorable terms than were included in the Concordat of 1817) was provided by the conclusion of the Austrian Concordat of 1855, an extremely generous, though as it turned out, short-lived concession to Catholic demands. In the aftermath of the 1848 revolution, Franz Joseph had abandoned the Josephine position of his predecessors and agreed to the urgings of the "pious party." The Society of Jesus was readmitted to the empire. Minister-President Felix von Schwarzenberg, whose brother was a cardinal, then reversed the liberal religious clauses of the 1849 constitution by issuing two imperial rescripts in 1850 which abolished the *placet*, established free communication between the papacy and the episcopate, removed all restrictions on the publication of papal bulls and encyclicals, left the disciplining of clergy to the church, and stated that the emperor would henceforth "take advice" from the pope on appointments of bishops and other officials. The concordat, signed three years later in the Bach administration, confirmed these rescripts and in addition, gave complete control of the education of Catholic children into the hands of the church, established church censorship of books, rescinded civil marriage, and guaranteed the "sacrosanct" nature of church property, even granting compensation for earlier confiscations of property. Such was the goal of the most ardent Catholic extremists in the rest of Germany, never to be attained. Resentment of liberals in Austria was so intense that a reversal was inevitable, and here, as in Baden, a conflict between church and state began at an earlier date than in Prussia.

The ideological conflict between a revived militant Catholicism and liberal anticlericalism forms only one strand in the complicated pattern of events leading to the *Kulturkampf* and the building of the Center party. The consequences of the wars of German unification were at least as significant.

The boundary changes after the Napoleonic Wars had left most

German Catholics outside Austria as minorities within officially Protestant states, but their numbers in the confederation as a whole were still slightly in the majority. The expulsion of Austria in 1866 not only reduced their numbers to approximately one-third of the population (about the same as in Prussia) but also branded them as somehow less than true Germans, potential subversives in the new state, even including, by association, those large numbers of educated Catholics who had supported liberal candidates in elections. It is difficult to pinpoint exactly at what time the position of supporting a federal solution including Austria ceased to be a respectable, though conservative, position and became suspect. It is equally difficult to determine at which point *grossdeutsch* became synonymous with Catholic, and of course it never did so entirely. Certainly the victory of the clericals in Austria may have helped to identify the two, and perhaps, by analogy, the opposition of the papacy to the unification of Italy; the Swiss experience was also remembered. In any case, it seems clear that by the 1860s *grossdeutsch* had become, for most Germans who so described themselves, an attitude of mind, not a platform for action.

The principal organization formed to counter the National Union of the liberal *kleindeutsch* party, was the Reform Union, established in Frankfurt in the autumn of 1862. It met with little popular response and had less than two years of active life. Among its leaders were Julius Fröbel and the von Gagern brothers, Heinrich and Max, southwestern liberals who had been participants in the 1848 Frankfurt Parliament. The chairman, Gustav, Freiherr von Lerchenfeld, was a Bavarian conservative, typical of the aristocrats from the small and middle states who hoped to retain local autonomy and resist northern domination. Prominent Catholic leaders in the union were Eduard Jörg, the Bavarian conservative and particularist, Buss of Baden, who combined reactionary clericalism with a kind of democratic social-mindedness, and Rudolf Probst, a thoroughgoing democrat from Württemberg. Democratic and extreme conservative viewpoints were uneasily allied in the *grossdeutsch* movement. Protestant and Catholic cooperation was equally fragile. Although the leadership of the Reform Union was predominately Protestant, the membership as a whole was heavily Catholic. This fact dissuaded many interested Protestants from joining and especially hindered the growth of local branches. Any discussion of program was always restricted by the clerical issue, and the editor of the union's weekly newspaper had to be taken to task for making derogatory mention of the Austrian Concordat and other anti-Catholic remarks. In general the union tried to avoid the issue: as Lerchenfeld said, "We need the Catholics and want them, yet we ought not to hold the Catholic standard too high; so— away with any clerical discussion!"[2]

Even on economic questions it proved difficult to reach consensus. The Tübingen professor Albert Schäffle was the union's economic expert and served on its executive committee. He supported the *grossdeutsch* position as a means toward his goal of one great common market stretching from the North and Baltic seas to the Adriatic. But many southern particularists did not really want to break down all economic barriers with the Austrian Empire, and Schäffle left the union in 1863 after quarreling with other members on the subject. He later served in the Austrian cabinet. The only program subscribed to by the union as a whole seems to have been that of instituting common currency and weights and measures, strengthening the executive of the confederation, and establishing some sort of national representative body.

In Austria itself, so essential to the success of any *grossdeutsch* plan for union, there was practically no interest in the Reform Union outside Franz Joseph's ministry. In Saxony the union also failed to take root; here the political antagonisms between liberals and conservatives proved too great. Hanover, on the other hand, was a major battleground for the two opposing unification programs and the Reform Union and the National Union were both active. There the local branch of the Reform Union was originally called the George Union, after the king, and stressed Hanoverian patriotism and anti-Prussian propaganda. Many of the Hanoverian members were Catholic, but the best-known Catholic statesman in Hanover, Ludwig Windthorst, took very little part in local union activities, though he was a member of the national organization. He felt that the parliamentary arena was a better place to carry on the work of the *grossdeutsch* program and was skeptical of the union's chances of success.

2. Willy Real, *Der deutsche Reformverein: Grossdeutsche Stimmen und Kräfte zwischen Villafranca und Königgrätz* (Lübeck, 1966), pp. 69–70; see also Nicholas Martin Hope, *The Alternative to German Unification: The Anti-Prussian Party: Frankfurt, Nassau, and the Two Hesses, 1859–1867* (Wiesbaden, 1973).

The Bavarian Reform Union was also active, but its branches were dominated by conservative Old Bavarian particularists and handicapped by internal quarreling between democrats on the one hand and aristocrats and clericals on the other. In Württemberg there were many union branches, though more in the northern districts, and little support in the capital city of Stuttgart. Foreign Minister Friedrich Freiherr von Varnbüler was closely involved with *grossdeutsch* politics but held aloof from the union, apart from serving on its executive committee. The membership in Württemberg was of both denominations, but there was some feeling among Protestants there that the ultramontanes were overactive in the cause. In neighboring Baden, stronghold of the National Union and anticlerical liberalism, the Reform Union's branches were almost entirely Catholic and led by the clergy. The union's largest membership and greatest proportion of Protestants was in the two Hesses, the Duchy of Nassau, and the city of Frankfurt; even here, denominational differences created problems.

Prussia proved to be as poor soil for the growth of the union as Austria. The only interest shown there was among Catholics, and that was expressed with great discretion and considerable pessimism. August Reichensperger rejected membership, even in the national organization, as politically unwise for a deputy in the *Landtag*, and felt that it was not appropriate for clergy and civil servants to be active in such an undertaking, while "business people and rentiers seldom concern themselves with such questions."[3] Local Prussian branches were never formed, though it is clear that there was much covert sympathy with the union's viewpoint in the Catholic western provinces of Prussia.

It has recently been suggested that one of the reasons for the failure of the Reform Union was its reluctance to take advantage of widespread favorable public opinion in the working classes, artisans and peasants who might have supported its goals.[4] Dr. Schäffle wrote that "the *grossdeutsch* party cannot and does not want to make propaganda and retain influence through ideologies which inflame the masses."[5] Reluctance to make full political use of the lower strata of society

3. Real, p. 82.
4. Theodor S. Hamerow, *The Social Foundations of German Unification 1858–1871*, 2 vols. (Princeton, 1969), 1:394.
5. Ibid., p. 336.

remained a characteristic of many Catholic politicians until after the First World War. In this instance, however, it is doubtful if the potential mass public opinion represented anything more than a vague sentimental preference. In any case, the *grossdeutsch* proponents preferred to work through decorous legal channels and this led only to humiliation and defeat.

Julius Fröbel's energies had been directed not only to the organization of the Reform Union but also to the personal persuasion of Franz Joseph and his ministers to his plans for strengthening the confederation. Franz Joseph invited the German princes to a conference in Frankfurt in 1863 under Fröbel's influence, but the plans for union presented at this time in the *Reformakte* were less liberal and more weighted toward Austrian supremacy than his original program. The terms appeared to be designed to put Prussia in a position where she would be permanently outvoted by combinations of other states, while at the same time obliging her army to defend all parts of the Austrian Empire. Even the staunchly anti-Prussian Eduard Jörg wrote as editor of the *Historische-politische Blätter* that the specific proposals were defective, though he hailed the Princes' Conference as "a day of incalculable significance" and a return to the glorious traditions of the Holy Roman Empire.[6] Heinrich von Gagern and Lerchenfeld were also hopeful and approving.

The conference opened in August 1863, with an impressive solemn ceremony, and passed the Reform Acts with a large majority. But the absence of William I of Prussia, engineered with difficulty by his minister-president, Bismarck, effectively made their execution impossible, since the smaller states were not prepared to consider a closer union without Prussia.

The failure of the Austrian program presented at Frankfurt is usually considered to have marked the end of any chance of implementing a *grossdeutsch* reform of the confederation. Austrian prestige was actually far more seriously injured by that government's conduct in the Schleswig-Holstein crisis and the events following the Danish War. *Grossdeutsch* supporters naturally expected to see Schleswig-Holstein admitted to the confederation as a separate state after the expulsion of

6. Real, pp. 148–49.

the Danish army. They were angry and disillusioned by the Gastein Convention dividing the hitherto indivisible duchies between Austria and Prussia. Lerchenfeld wrote to Reichensperger: "The events of the last weeks have destroyed all our expectations and hopes, and instead of the consolidation of Germany, there is more serious disintegration than ever. The unfortunate interpretation of the question of the duchies by Austria and Prussia and their conduct resulting from it, the agreement between them, are occurances of a significance which should by no means be overlooked."[7] The Reform Union broke apart during the course of 1864; its leaders resigned and its newspaper ceased publication.

The Catholic Center party in Prussia joined the southern states in opposing the Gastein Convention and strongly supported the claims of the duke of Augustenburg to the duchies. The Prussian party, already greatly reduced in size by the elections of the 1860s, had even refused to vote war credits for the Danish War. This stand reinforced the argument, heard more and more frequently in the 1860s, that Prussian Catholics were unpatriotic. Southern Catholics who championed the interests of Bavaria or Württemberg were not, on the other hand, called patriots for doing so, but labeled "particularists." It could be plausibly argued that it had been the Prussian government's "particularism" which had prevented reform of the confederation during the past fifteen years, but the term with its pejorative connotations was always used in reference to *Kleinstaaterei*, never to Prussia.

As war between Prussia and Austria became probable in 1866, opposition to Bismarck's course became more and more the unpatriotic stance. General gloom and sorrow characterized the now isolated Catholic population in Prussia and its political representatives, rather than an overt refusal to accept the war, in which Catholic soldiers served without protest in Prussian forces. Their gloom was deepened by the quick defeat of Austria and the realization that the *grossdeutsch* ideal was dead. Demoralization and a lack of long-term goals are noticeable among Catholic political leaders in the years 1867–70.[8] August Reichensperger had lost his seat in the House of Deputies in

7. Ibid., pp. 185–86.
8. See George C. Windell, *Catholics and German Unity, 1866–1871* (Minneapolis, 1954), for a description of the prevailing mood.

1863 and did not seek to regain it in 1867; he gave up politics altogether (temporarily, as it turned out) and returned to an avocation in art history.

One understandable reason for Catholic dismay was that the victory of Prussia over Austria was widely hailed in Germany as a victory for Protestantism over Catholicism, a true completion of the Reformation. Catholics did not have to be paranoid to feel that they were about to be Protestantized as well as Prussianized.

The only delegates to the North German Confederation Reichstag of 1867 from the former Center fraction were Peter Reichensperger, who sat alone, and Hermann von Mallinckrodt, who joined a small Federal-Constitutional Union largely composed of delegates from outside Prussia. Mallinckrodt departed from his usual quiet, courtly demeanor by giving a speech in the opening days of the session in which he called Prussia the aggressor in the recent war and asserted that this interpretation of events was believed not only outside Germany but by many Prussian citizens themselves. His allusions to Prussia's aggressive role in German history were countered by Bismarck who pointedly blamed Germany's division upon the thirteenth century "Guelphs and ultramontanes."[9]

Mallinckrodt and Reichensperger were joined in sympathy and in debate by Ludwig Windthorst, who sat as a member of the Federal-Constitutional Union from Meppen in Hanover, now incorporated into Prussia. Windthorst had served in several legal positions in Hanover and had been the first Catholic to enter the state's government, serving as minister of justice from 1851 to 1853. He had something of a reputation as a democrat, as well as being known as a Hanoverian patriot and supporter of Austria, and his dismissal from the ministry had come about partly as a result of intervention by the Prussian government. Bismarck had counseled Otto von Manteuffel in 1853 that a change in the Hanoverian ministry was essential, "at least the resignation of Minister Windthorst, who is considered decidedly the Left in the ministry."[10] Now, added to Bismarck's earlier suspicions of Windthorst's democratic tendencies was the fact of his passionate refusal to recognize the legitimacy of Prussia's annexation of Hanover. Bismarck

9. *Stenographische Berichte über die Verhandlungen des Reichstages des Norddeutschen Bundes im Jahre 1867* (Berlin, 1867) pp. 156–58.
10. Eduard Hüsgen, *Ludwig Windthorst* (Cologne, 1811), p. 45.

appears to have felt a personal resentment against Windthorst on this score, in contrast to William I, who had more respect for Windthorst's loyalty to the unfortunate George V than for the conversion to Prussianism of his fellow Hanoverians Rudolf von Bennigsen and Johannes Miquel.[11] Bismarck more than once said that he believed Windthorst to be a better Guelph (i.e., Hanoverian) than ultramontane; that he had really "no religion at all"; and that he received an annual pension from the Guelph dynasty to continue championing its cause.[12] Certainly it is hard to understand his position if it is considered to be motivated by a sentimental attachment to the dynasty, because the diocese of Osnabrück which was Windthorst's home had only been annexed to Hanover in 1815, and the royal family had never been particularly friendly to its Catholic subjects nor, indeed, to Windthorst himself. It is more likely that his stand was based upon his feeling that the annexation to Prussia was an unlawful act of force, and upon a basic dislike of Prussianism.

The accusation that Windthorst had "no religion at all" is absurd and contradicted by much evidence to the contrary; it was perhaps based upon his independence of the clergy and his refusal to take direction from the papacy in political matters. He never traveled to Rome at any stage of the great church-state conflict, a surprising fact which is not adequately explained by the excuse that he spoke no Italian and poor French,[13] and he antagonized representatives of the Vatican by expressing his opinion that the Catholic church in Germany would be better off with complete separation of church and state, as in the United States.[14] Although Windthorst's personal piety is unquestioned, his actions do not seem to have been directly motivated by religious considerations. He was originally drawn to the Catholic political cause through learning of the restrictions on officeholding by Catholics in the city of Osnabrück, and by reading Görres's pamphlet circulated at the time of the "Cologne troubles."[15] He dedicated his life to the defense of Catholic interests, sacrificing several opportuni-

11. Ibid., p. 61.
12. Erich Foerster, *Adalbert Falk: Sein Leben und Wirken* (Gotha, 1927); p. 539, Bachem, 5:213–14, 225.
13. Bachem 4:33–34.
14. Margaret Anderson, *Windthorst: A Political Biography* (Oxford, 1981), pp. 122, 144, 278–79, 294–95; Rudolf Lill, *Die Wende im Kulturkampf* (Tübingen, 1973) p. 273.
15. Bachem, 5:225–30.

ties of high position and wealth, because he wanted to rectify injustice and to restore the Catholic people of Germany to that position, not only of equal rights but of status and dignity, to which he felt them to be entitled. As for the pension from George V, if it existed it must have been an extremely small one, for Windthorst and his family lived in very modest circumstances.

Windthorst, Mallinckrodt, and Reichensperger all voted against the constitution of the North German Confederation, soon to become, with slight modification, the constitution of united Germany. Mallinckrodt and Reichensperger had tried, without success, to persuade the Reichstag to include in the constitution the clauses for religious freedom from both the Frankfurt Bill of Rights of 1848 and the Prussian constitution of 1850. The practical result of such inclusion at that time would have been to have forced a change in the laws in Protestant Saxony and the Mecklenburgs, where Catholics still did not have complete freedom in their religious activities; if the southern states had then joined the confederation, as seemed eventually probable, the clauses would have forced changes in the more state-supremacist laws of the south.

Windthorst had not supported the inclusion of these clauses because he believed that it would increase the power of the central government and reduce that of the states.[16] It is true that in this case the usual Catholic stand for the rights of individual states was reversed in favor of making use of central government to change an unfavorable situation in a state. It was an inconsistency which can be seen in Center party policy throughout its history. On the other hand, it is unlikely that the liberal vote against the inclusion of the clauses was motivated by a desire to preserve states' rights to denominational exclusivity. Pressure for anticlerical legislation was growing in liberal circles. Its effect would be, not to persuade the smaller states to imitate Prussia by limiting state control over religion, but to persuade Prussia to imitate the smaller states by increasing it.

The votes against the constitution furthered the image of political Catholicism as one of intransigent opposition. At least one prominent Catholic spokesman, Bishop von Ketteler of Mainz, came out strongly in favor of reconciliation after the Austrian War. In his pamphlet

16. Anderson, p. 112.

Deutschland nach dem Kriege he urged Catholics to accept the result of the war and to work toward the entry of the southern states into the North German Confederation. His prompt acquiescence was not universally applauded, however, and August Reichensperger said that he should at least have allowed for a year of mourning.[17]

In the matter of the future of the four southern states left out of the new confederation, the idea of a league of the south, or *Südbund*, received very little support from anyone because of the great decline of respect for and confidence in Austria after the debacle of the Seven Weeks War. Bavarian leadership of such a league, another alternative, was unthinkable for Württemberg and Baden, where army officers threatened to resign and join the Prussian army rather than submit to such an eventuality. The prolonged negotiations for a French alliance carried on by Austria did not meet with much response from the south either; "anti-Prussian" was not to be interpreted as "pro-French," and French assistance in the formation of a Southern League was out of the question for them. Minister-President Ludwig von der Pfordten of Bavaria, who had sought French mediation, though not an alliance, lost his reputation with both the pro-Prussian and the anti-Prussian Bavarian parties for doing so. The situation was not unlike that in 1919, when an indigenous movement for the separation of the Rhineland from Prussia within Germany was doomed to failure because it was ineradicably linked with French attempts to set up the Rhineland as an independent state. Southern Catholics who contemplated any sort of dealings with the major Catholic powers of France and Austria between 1866 and 1870 were presenting to their opponents the association of Catholicism with lack of German patriotism. The defeat of Austria, followed by the defeat of France and of the papacy in 1870, seemed to symbolize the downfall of international Catholicism and placed German Catholics, however they felt as individuals, collectively on the defensive.

The Reichstag of the North German Confederation was elected by manhood suffrage and its members also formed part of the larger *Zollparlament* which included the south because it dealt with the affairs of the common market of which the southern states (though never Austria) were a part. Southern delegates to the *Zollparlament* were to

17. Bachem, 3:10.

be elected by the same suffrage, and the results of these elections were the first direct expression of mass public opinion in the southern states. Middle-class liberal voters for the first time were joined by peasants and artisans who had not met the property qualifications for the state elections, and the conservative Catholic cause was in general helped by this, although its leaders were not altogether anxious to extend the democratic franchise to the states. In the Bavarian and Württemberg elections to the *Zollparlament* the particularists won surprising victories which appeared likely to postpone indefinitely the entry of these states into the confederation. Even in pro-Prussian Baden, where in the *Landtag,* elected by an indirect, limited franchise, only one man cast a vote against the defense treaty with Prussia, six delegates to the *Zollparlament* were Catholic-clerical and *grossdeutsch* in sympathy.

In these years the Catholic-particularist party in Bavaria, calling itself the Patriotic People's party (a forerunner of the Bavarian Center party) was able to increase its strength in the *Landtag* and to challenge the liberal government of Ludwig II. In Bavaria the former *Mittelpartei* of moderate liberals had been completely polarized by the events of 1866 and its membership had split between the more doctrinaire Left-liberal Progressive party which favored Bavarian entry into the North German Confederation, and the new Patriots' party, which of course did not.

To replace the discredited Pfordten, Ludwig II had appointed as minister-president Prince Chlodwig von Hohenlohe-Schillingsfürst, a man of Catholic family and brother to a cardinal, but liberal in sympathy and with a generally pro-Prussian program. A clash between him and the lower house was inevitable, and clashes in fact occurred over not one but several issues. The adoption of the Prussian military system after the conclusion of the defense treaty was vehemently opposed by the Patriots' party; a bill for the introduction of state supervision and lay inspection of schools was bitterly contested; and there was resentment about the letter which Hohenlohe circulated to European governments warning them of the dire effects of the anticipated pronouncement of the dogma of papal infallibility by the Vatican Council. The ministry's economic policies of freeing trade and restricting the powers of the guilds were also opposed by the Patriots. Hohenlohe was forced to rely upon the support of the Progressives who, ironically, were working for a much greater degree of parliamentary rule than was desired either by Hohenlohe or the conservative Patriots.

The *Landtag* was dissolved in the spring of 1869 after having been in session for six years. The elections which followed showed a decisive gain for the Patriots, giving them half the seats in the lower house. This produced a stalemate. The subsequent new elections in the fall increased their numbers to 80 out of 154 seats, a clear majority, against only 63 Progressives, and the upper house was also in their control. The Patriots drew their support from a coalition of aristocrats, peasants, and inhabitants of small towns. The Farmers' Union organized in 1869 was helpful to them, as was the "casino" movement of Catholic youth clubs. The new party was led by Dr. Jörg, the fierce and eloquent anti-Prussian. He succeeded in defeating the school bill and forcing out of office the ministers of the interior, of religion and education, and finally, Hohenlohe himself, in February 1870, after some attempt by Ludwig to retain him with minority support. Hohenlohe chose his own successor, Count Otto von Bray-Steinburg, and there was no abrupt change in government policy; on the contrary, the administration held to a liberal and anticlerical line throughout the 1870s. This was possible because the electoral laws and districting disproportionately favored the urban middle classes. But the potential strength of Catholic opinion had been demonstrated in Bavaria in 1869, as it had earlier in the revolution of 1848.[18]

As war between the North German Confederation and France appeared imminent in 1870, the antimilitarist stand of both the southern Catholic parties and the Catholic leadership in Prussia added yet another element to the charge of lack of German patriotism, though it was certainly not the case that German Catholics favored France in this conflict. In Prussia, in the south, and very noticeably in German Austria, there was strong support for the war and much rejoicing in the victory. It was true that in the Rhineland, the local election platforms of the explicitly Catholic candidates had, like their colleagues in Bavaria, opposed a rise in expenditures of tax money for armaments and other military needs (as illustrated in the Münster program as late as June, 1870). But in the famous Soest Program of October 1870, when

18. Doeberl, pp. 450–95.

elections to the Prussian *Landtag* were about to be held and the war was already under way, there was no direct reference to military matters but simply a demand for general economies (number seven in the program). The Soest Program was later designated by the Center party as its founding platform. It was signed by fifty candidates and their supporters, of whom eighteen were clergy and eight were noblemen.[19] The nine points of the program were as follows:

1. Maintenance of the constitutionally recognized independence and rights of the church.
2. Practical furthering of equality among the recognized religious confessions.
3. Protest against any attempt to dechristianize marriage.
4. Maintenance and support of denominational schools.
5. A federal state [*Bundesstaat*] for the entire German fatherland which provides unity in essentials but which in all other matters leaves untouched the independence and free self-determination, as well as the constitutional rights, of the federal states.
6. Decentralization of the administration on the basis of the self-determination of political bodies in the municipality, county, and province.
7. Limitation of state expenditures, as far as possible, and of taxes and imposts, and their just and equitable distribution.
8. Balancing of the interests of capital and landed property, as well as of capital and landed property on the one hand and labor on the other, by means of the maintenance and support of a strong middle class in the independent ranks of farmers and small businessmen [*Bürger- und Bauernstände*].
9. Freedom for all legally based efforts toward a solution of the social problem; legal elimination of such evil conditions as the worker being threatened with moral or physical ruin.[20]

Most of these points continued to be important to the Center party platform until the party's demise in 1933. It is significant that the program's emphasis upon a decentralized "federalism" for the whole of Germany is matched by equal emphasis upon decentralization within the state of Prussia. It was the consistent desire of the Center to obtain more autonomy for the Catholic provinces of the

19. Hüsgen, p. 79.
20. J. Meerfeld, *Die deutsche Zentrumspartei* (Berlin, 1918), pp. 21–22; Bachem, 3:113.

Rhineland, Westphalia, and Silesia, as well as for the Polish districts. The goal was not reached, however, until after the Second World War, and then only under the direction of Allied occupation forces, in the process of redividing Germany altogether.

The decisive defeat of France in the Franco-Prussian War and the loss of Rome by the papacy produced among Prussian Catholics an increased consciousness of being a minority on the defensive, and this was undoubtedly a factor in the elections of the autumn of 1870, since candidates running on explicitly Catholic platforms were again successful in winning votes, in contrast to their total eclipse in 1866. Forty-eight delegates were returned to the House of Deputies, and they decided to form a separate party there, although Windthorst continued to sit as a "fraction of one" from Meppen until 1871.

The name of the new party was a matter for considerable deliberation, and the problem of the name reflected the problem of the nature and purpose of the party, which was never fully resolved throughout its history. If the word "Catholic" were included in the name, as in the suggested "Catholic People's party" (a name actually used later by an Austrian party) this would automatically imply an exclusion of potential Protestant supporters. But any program for the protection of the rights of Catholics must defend those of all denominations, and it was felt that these should not therefore be excluded. The delegates decided not to use the word "Catholic" in the name of the party, even though in so doing they lost the support of a good many voters. The next decision concerned the directly political implications of the name. The party was conservative and opposed to doctrinaire liberal ideology; hence the titles "Conservative People's party," "Christian-Conservative People's party" and even "Anti-liberal party" were considered. But here the risk was that of alienating the large number of German Catholics who had shortly before been affiliated with liberal parties of various shades. If the party was to be Catholic, it could not be exclusively conservative, and if it was to be "Christian" and concerned with a variety of social and political issues it could not be exclusively Catholic. The old, noncommittal name of *Zentrum*, the Center, was consequently chosen again for the Prussian fraction, and in 1871 applied to the new Reichstag fraction. A few Protestants, less than a dozen initially, joined the new party, Leo von Gerlach being the best known of these. Silesian candidates in the 1870s continued to pledge themselves "convinced and loyal Catholics."[21]

In the Reichstag elections of 1871, with the democratic franchise, fifty-seven Centrists were elected, winning 18.6 percent of the vote in united Germany (considerably less than the approximately 32 percent of the population which was Catholic.) The Center fraction in the Reichstag was composed of delegates from all states having significant Catholic population, but the states themselves were slow in forming local parties under the name of Center. Baden's Catholic People's party became the Baden Center party in 1870, and Hesse's Catholic party took the name in 1872, but the Bavarian Patriots' party did not call itself the Bavarian Center party until 1887, and Württemberg did not adopt the name until 1894–95. Alsace-Lorraine had a Center fraction in its *Landesausschuss* after 1907, but its delegates to the Reichstag always kept themselves separate from the Center fraction there. The Polish Party and the Hanoverian Guelphs sat with the Center also, but kept their organizations separate.

Although Center party organization was extremely loose, in fact for many years virtually nonexistent, the personal cohesion of the parliamentary fractions was considerable, and more Centrists were members of both the Prussian and the national legislatures than was the case in any other party. Twenty served simultaneously in both houses in the 1870s and the same party leaders served on the executive committees of both fractions. Karl Friedrich von Savigny, a devout Catholic though of Protestant ancestry, formerly a Prussian representative to the Confederation Diet before 1866 and a friend of Bismarck's in those years, was head of the Center's Prussian fraction from 1870 to 1873 and head of the Reichstag fraction from 1870 until his death in 1875. Mallinckrodt, Peter Reichensperger, and Windthorst served in both houses. Leader of the Prussian fraction from 1873 until 1890 was Burghard, Freiherr von Schorlemer-Alst, a Westphalian nobleman who founded the Westphalian Agrarian League. August Reichensperger returned to political life again after his temporary disillusionment and served in the Reichstag from 1875 to 1888 and from 1890 to 1891. Karl Prince zu Löwenstein from Baden served on the Reichstag executive

21. The Catholic exclusivity of the Silesian Center was approved by Windthorst as a means of disarming other parties which might be allies in elections (Anderson, p. 262).

committee for many years. All of these men were conservative and many of them were aristocrats, hardly of the type to be considered rebels against authority. Yet within two years they were called that and other names and linked with radicals, Socialists, and other "enemies of the state." The experience of the *Kulturkampf* had a lasting effect on political Catholicism and guided it in surprising directions.

3
BACKGROUND OF THE *KULTURKAMPF*

The diplomatic events and the wars of the previous decade had by 1871 created a defensive, yet belligerent, self-consciousness among the former *grossdeutsch* Catholics in Germany. Even more conducive to such a mood were the events within the church itself: the attempts of the papacy under Pius IX to reassert its spiritual authority, from the Syllabus of Errors in 1864 to the Vatican Council of 1870 and the dogma of papal infallibility. The uncompromisingly antiliberal position of the Syllabus, with its flat assertion that "it is an error that the Roman Pontiff can and ought to reconcile himself to, and agree with, progress, liberalism, and civilization as lately introduced," and its negation of the supremacy of the nation-state in an age when national passions were most inflamed, were embarrassments to the many Catholics everywhere who had joined liberal and national movements, but doubly so to those whose form of national allegiance had been branded as "unpatriotic" and condemned to failure. The once-reasonable hopes of seeing Germany united with Austria had given way, inexorably, to the total exclusion of Austria. The hope of seeing Italy united in a federal state in which the temporal power of the papacy could be preserved had given way to the prospect of the total elimination of the temporal power, and conceivably, of the papacy itself.

Many German Catholics were dismayed to learn of the pope's plan to submit the infallibility dogma to the council. Bishop von Ketteler felt that the timing was unfortunate. Windthorst, Mallinckrodt, and Peter Reichensperger notified the Vatican of their opinion that the dogma was ill timed and would place a burden on German Catholics; in fact their objections were substantive as well, and they feared a possible schism in the church.[1] The editors of the *Kölnische Volkszei-*

---

1. Anderson, pp. 126–29.

tung expressed strong opposition also. Yet these men all rallied to accept the dogma after it was proclaimed, not only from religious conviction but also because of the exaggerated rhetoric coming from anticlerical circles concerning the disastrous effect the proclamation of the dogma would have. Such very different personalities as Bismarck and William E. Gladstone were predicting serious defiance of national authority. Prince Hohenlohe's circular letter to the European governments, sent in April 1869, expressed equal alarm about the possible political effects of the dogma. This letter was composed in close collaboration with Dr. Döllinger, theologian at the University of Munich.

Döllinger had abandoned his earlier orthodoxy after the 1859 Italian War and a subsequent trip to Rome, and had now become an outspoken critic of papal policy. As early as 1863 he had opposed the stand taken by the Bavarian hierarchy and had proposed the end of the temporal power of the papacy. In 1870 Döllinger became convinced that dire consequences would ensue if the dogma were accepted. He wrote to Hohenlohe that the Syllabus of Errors of 1864 would itself become dogma and that the bull of Paul IV (1555–59) ordering that princes not of the faith be deposed (referring to Queen Elizabeth I of England) would become current doctrine; that demands would again be made for the immunity of clergy from taxation and secular jurisdiction; and similar excesses.[2]

Döllinger tried to build an antidogma party at Rome, and when the dogma was nevertheless approved, refused to submit and was consequently excommunicated in April, 1871. His position in Bavaria and that of the Old Catholics (with whom Döllinger was never officially connected) posed an acute problem which became a key issue in the opening rounds of the *Kulturkampf.*

Although a great many German and Austrian clergy, including bishops attending the council, were at first opposed to the dogma, nearly all of them, and nearly all Catholics in general, accepted it in the end. Hohenlohe summed up the situation well when he wrote that the Old Catholics, the secession of those Catholics who had refused to accept the dogma, would not be successful because "interest in dog-

---

2. Chlodwig von Hohenlohe-Schillingsfürst, *Memoirs*, 2 vols. (New York and London, 1906), 1:333.

matic subtleties no longer exists. There are only believers, who wish at all costs to remain Catholics, and who would remain so were the Pope to declare himself the Dalai Lama and introduce the Buddhist praying wheel, and the indifferent, who in general have little belief, and will not violate their reason. The latter will not throw themselves with enthusiasm into a fight against the dogma of infallibility, which obliges them to adhere to all the other dogmas, which they have long ceased to believe, or of which, at most, they only believe a part."[3] The second position surely better characterized Hohenlohe himself than his earlier exaggerated concern over the dogma's international consequences. However, although Catholic laymen, including politicians, may have fit into one of these two categories, the small number of theologians, clergy, and other academics who like Döllinger *did* take an "interest in dogmatic subtleties" became important out of all proportion to their numbers because they so frequently were, in one capacity or another, state employees.

The first such case occurred in the summer of 1870, when the archbishop of Breslau asked the Prussian government to carry out punitive action against Joseph Hubert Reinkens, professor of Catholic theology at the University of Breslau, who had published writings opposing the dogma (and who later became the first bishop of the Old Catholic church.) Prussian Minister of Religion and Education von Mühler attempted to smooth over the affair but refused to remove Reinkens from office, which set a precedent for subsequent similar cases.

The Prussian *Kulturkampf* of the 1870s stemmed partly from the decisions of the Vatican Council and partly from the effect of the defeat of the Catholic *grossdeutsch* movement in German unification. In the southern states, a conflict between church and state began some years before 1871; in fact, events in Prussia followed the lead of the south, rather than, as is sometimes said, persuading the south to follow the Prussian example. Among German-speaking states, it was in Baden first, then in Switzerland, Austria, and Bavaria, and finally in Prussia that liberal state action against the Catholic church took place. On the other hand, only in Prussia was the emotional intensity

3. Ibid., 2:49.

of the conflict such as to warrant the use of the dramatic phrase "culture-struggle."

The government of Baden, like that of Prussia, was confronted in the 1860s with a strong liberal majority in the lower house of the *Landtag*. In 1864, in reaction to the publication of the Syllabus of Errors, the liberal party began a campaign to introduce lay supervision of the schools and to make it possible to combine local Protestant and Catholic elementary schools into *Simultanschulen*, schools for students and teachers of both denominations, with separate classes only for religious instruction. The resulting law for lay supervision was drawn up by a councillor in the Interior Ministry, Julius Jolly. Jolly was descended from a family of French Huguenot refugees, and had been a jurist at the University of Heidelberg. His convictions were more Josephine than Calvinist, however, as he believed that "the church in the state must be subject to the state." His success with the liberals in the legislature resulted in his being named minister of the interior and minister-president in 1866. Jolly has been called "much more the minister of the *Kulturkampf*" than Adalbert Falk of Prussia, and he became, in fact, Falk's model and adviser.[4]

The Catholic population of Baden had not previously shown any separate political consciousness, but the school supervision law of 1864 providing for the election of local lay school boards produced for the first time a wave of resentment against the dominant liberal bourgeoisie in the state. At first this resentment was expressed through the formation of "casinos," Catholic social clubs (later introduced into Bavaria and Austria), which became centers of protest against the school measures and threatened a boycott of the new school boards. The government responded by imposing fines upon those who refused to serve on the boards. Only one man, Jakob Lindau, represented the Catholic view in the lower house of the *Landtag*, and his was also the only vote cast against the military alliance of Baden with Prussia in 1867.

The anticlerical campaign intensified in 1867, when Jolly and the liberals obtained the passage of a law requiring all clergy (Catholic and Protestant alike) to pass a state examination on educational qualifica-

---

4. Josef Becker, *Liberalerstaat und Kirche in der Aera von Reichsgründung und Kulturkampf (1860–1876)* (Mainz, 1973), pp. 7; 75–76.

tions, the *Kulturexamen*, before holding office. The following year, after four years of agitation, a law was passed permitting the establishment of "simultaneous" schools, although only a few were actually created at this time. The system of mixed schools was made general and obligatory in 1876; it was also introduced into Hesse-Darmstadt in the 1870s and became an ideal, albeit an unattainable one, for liberal reformers in other parts of Germany.

Catholic indignation at these new laws enabled Lindau to organize for the first time a specifically political instrument, the Catholic People's party, founded in 1869 and later renamed the Baden Center party. The party attracted supporters from all those social and occupational groups which were antagonistic to the dominant Protestant liberal bourgeoisie of the big cities: farmers, artisans, shopkeepers, a few noble landowners, and of course, clergy. Its platform denounced the entire range of recent liberal reforms, including the abolition of guilds, the introduction of freedom of occupation and movement, the emancipation of Jews, and, in general, the incursion of modern urban values into the traditional rural and small-town life in the state. The school reforms, which included a broadening and modernization of the curriculum, were just one part of the whole liberal package, but one which finally served as a catalyst to unite the Catholic population to action. Interestingly, the party's proposed solution to the clerical conflict was local self-government and complete separation of church and state on the American model, rather than the Belgian model favored by Catholics elsewhere in Germany.[5]

The People's party was antimilitarist and demanded a free press, direct voting, the secret ballot, and reapportionment of the seats in the *Landtag*, a move obviously suggested by the favorable results of the *Zollparlament* elections in February 1868. In these demands as on other issues the party allied with the Left-democrats in the legislature, which later provoked the accusation of "ultramontane communism" from its majority-liberal opponents.[6] The secret ballot and a degree of reapportionment were obtained during the 1870s, to the slight benefit of Catholic representation, but the direct vote was not achieved until 1904.

5. Ibid., pp. 143–47, 214–15.
6. Ibid., p. 234.

The party's first members elected to the *Landtag,* an embattled group of four men, were known as the Quadrilateral, in reference to the Austrian fortresses in northern Italy, and, like the fortresses, they fell before the liberal onslaught, with the passage in 1869 of a law for compulsory civil marriage and a law declaring all educational and charitable foundations to be inherently secular and putting them under the administration of communal and state authorities. In September 1870, the Baden government prohibited the publication of the dogma of infallibility in the archdiocese of Freiburg.

The aged but vigorous archbishop of Freiburg, Hermann von Vicari, forbade his clergy to take the required state examination and condemned all of the anticlerical legislation. Upon his death in 1868 at the age of ninety-four, it proved impossible for the cathedral chapter, the Vatican, and the government to agree upon a successor, because Jolly rejected most of the names proposed by the church and insisted that the candidate take a special oath to uphold the laws. An acting archbishop was finally named and the diocese remained officially unfilled until 1882, after Jolly's dismissal.

Throughout these years, Jolly's motives, and those of Grand Duke Frederick of Baden whose government he headed, were by no means the same as those of the liberal party in the *Landtag,* whose bidding they seemed to be carrying out. Jolly and the grand duke were determined to keep Baden in Prussia's camp and at the same time to keep policy-making in their own hands and out of Parliament. Playing the anticlerical card enabled them to distract the legislature from lingering anti-Prussian or antimilitarist sentiments and to maintain the initiative. In a letter written at the height of the conflict, in 1870, Jolly said: "Our sole support lies in anticlerical policy. . . . At this time, in our state there is no other basis for a national government than a sharply anticlerical one."[7]

To the south of Baden, the Swiss engaged in what was certainly the longest-lasting, if not the most bitterly fought, of all the *Kulturkämpfe* in the German-speaking world. The result of the *Sonderbund* war had been the total victory of the liberal party. Although the constitution of 1848 left matters of church-state relations to the individual cantons, liberals had succeeded in including in the constitution

7. Ibid., pp. 268–69.

the prohibition of the Jesuit order from the entire confederation. In 1859 the Federal Assembly unilaterally broke the connections of southern cantons with the dioceses of Como and Milan in Italy, leaving them without episcopal affiliations. The imprudent decision of Pius IX in 1864 to authorize a Catholic bishop for the Geneva area brought about a crisis when outraged liberals and Calvinists united in refusing to allow Bishop Mermillod to carry out his duties, forcing him to flee to France, where he launched a series of diatribes against the situation in Switzerland and Germany. Geneva passed a law in 1872 decreeing that ministers of all denominations must henceforth be elected by their congregations. A similar law was passed in Bern canton. The Old Catholic church, in Switzerland called "Christ-Catholic," replaced the official Catholic church in a number of cities, including Bern and Zurich. Bishops who protested were expelled from the country. The Federal Council suspended the papal nunciature in 1873. The new Swiss constitution of 1874 strengthened the powers of the federal government, which had actually overstepped its former authority in the religious conflict.

Some degree of peace was obtained in the Swiss conflict when Leo XIII in 1883 transferred the controversial Bishop Mermillod to the vacant diocese of Lausanne and ended the Genevan bishopric; Leo tacitly accepted the Geneva law of elections, which remained on the books. In Basel and Bern, a real settlement was not reached until the 1920s, and the papal nunciature was not resumed until 1920.[8]

In Austria, the new Reichsrat was the scene of a concerted attack by liberals on the Concordat of 1855. If there were any German Catholics who still had hopes of an eventual *grossdeutsch* victory after 1866, they must have had their spirits dampened by Franz Joseph's acquiescence in anticlerical legislation and reversion to the Josephinism of his ancestors. In the drawing up of the constitutional laws in 1867, Count Friedrich von Beust had returned to the state supremacy principles of the years before 1848. By 1869, specific laws to this effect had been accepted by the German-liberal Reichsrat, causing indignant bishops to leave the upper chamber in protest. "Wild anticlerical demonstrations" were held in Vienna, and the city was illuminated, on the

8. Georg Franz, *Kulturkampf* (Munich, 1954), pp. 158–64, 242.

occasion of the reinstitution of a civil marriage law.[9] The upper house refused to make civil marriage compulsory, however. Lay supervision of schools and the equality of all denominations before the law followed, including rights for "freethinkers" with no church membership and also easy transferal of membership from one denomination to another.

The Austrian government hoped that Pius IX would declare that in the light of these changes the concordat had been broken, but he limited himself to strong denunciation of the laws. When the dogma of papal infallibility, which German-Austrian and Hungarian prelates had accepted only with great reluctance, was published in Austria-Hungary, Beust declared in an imperial rescript that the concordat had thereby been nullified. Many clergy carried on passive resistance to the new laws, but the government did not attempt the repressive measures later used in Prussia; only one cleric, Bishop Rüdiger of Linz, was sentenced to a prison term, not for disobeying the laws but for "incitement to disturb the peace" and he was pardoned by the emperor before serving his term.

A very important factor in this surge of anticlericalism was the feeling among German Austrians that the Catholic church in Austria favored the Slavic nationalities and supported the idea of a federal organization for the empire rather than German-Magyar dualism. Many believed that the proportion of Slavic clergy was far higher than was justified by the percentage of Slavs in areas of mixed populations: that bilingual Czech, Polish, and Slovene priests were converting Germans to federalist ideas and preventing the transformation of Slavic children into German-speakers in the public schools. Statistics from Styria, Carinthia, and the Sudetenland appear to bear out this claim.[10] Such arguments were also to be used later in Prussia about the influence of Polish clergy in the eastern provinces and, to a lesser extent, about French-speaking clergy in Alsace-Lorraine.

The most bitter resistance to the Austrian anticlerical legislation, however, did not come from the mixed Slavic-German districts, but from the Tyrol, where both German- and Italian-speaking representa-

9. Arthur May, *The Hapsburg Monarchy, 1867–1914* (New York, 1968), p. 47.
10. Erich Schmidt, *Bismarcks Kampf mit dem politischen Katholizismus* (Hamburg, 1942), pp. 149–50.

tives denounced the laws. It was many years before this resistance could be effective, because in Austria as in Bavaria and the southwest of Germany, suffrage laws and apportionment of seats kept the representation of rural and small-town Catholics disproportionately low in the Parliament. Until this situation was altered, the building of a strong Catholic political party in Austria was not possible. Bishop Rüdiger urged the creation of a political bloc but attracted mainly clergy and nobility. The modern Christian Social party was not formed until the end of the 1880s.

In Bavaria, curtailment of church power came after a period of vigorous assertiveness in the 1850s under the leadership of Archbishop Reisach of Munich-Freising. His goal was to combat the state supremacy policies of Maximilian II and fully implement the favorable Concordat of 1817. "Für das Konkordat—das ganze Konkordat—nichts als Konkordat!" was the slogan, and his followers demanded a lifting of the *placet* and unlimited freedom for the church in the administration of its property and the education of its clergy.[11] Maximilian rejected the demands, making only a few concessions, and Reisach was compensated for his failure by being made a cardinal, moving permanently to Rome. After the Austro-Prussian War the Bavarian government, now in the reign of Ludwig II, introduced a program of anticlerical legislation under the continuing advice of Dr. Döllinger. Although Hohenlohe fell as a sacrifice to the Patriots' party majority in the lower house, and the new minister-president was moderate on the church issue, the dominant figure in the cabinet was a determined anticlerical, Johann Freiherr von Lutz, minister of justice from 1867 to 1871, *Kultus* minister (for religion and education) after December 1867, and finally minister-president from 1880 to 1890.

Lutz was a self-made man, the son of an elementary-school teacher, and had only recently been granted the title of "Freiherr." His initial attempt to put through a bill for lay supervision of the schools failed, as had a previous effort under his predecessor, because of the hostile majority in the lower house. Consequently, measures were next tried which could be carried out by administrative action without submission to Parliament. Lutz refused permission to publish the infallibility dogma in Bavaria, and his government consistently refused

11. Doeberl, 3:544.

44

to dismiss Old Catholics from state employment. A number of Catholic parishes in the state converted to Old Catholicism, and many Old Catholics continued to hold positions on the faculties of Bavarian universities (although the total membership in the sect was only a few thousand). Much excitement was aroused in the state over the question of the Old Catholics' legal status, but a four-day debate in the lower house resulted in a 76-to-76-vote deadlock, and the problem remained unresolved. The state never extended financial support to the new sect as such, except in the form of salaries for individuals continued in state employment. Ludwig II upheld Döllinger even after his excommunication in 1871 and named him president of the Academy of Sciences.

Lutz became so angered at resistance to government policy among the Bavarian clergy that he resolved to take punitive measures against them. He prepared a draft for a law to prohibit "abuse of the pulpit" (that is, speaking against state laws in the churches) and submitted it to the Federal Council of the Reich in December 1871, for addition to the German criminal code. This was the so-called *Kanzelparagraph* ("pulpit paragraph," or "Lex Lutz"); it was modeled upon a similar Italian law passed a few months earlier. Although the offense at which the law was aimed was probably already covered by existing laws, the mood of the delegates to the Federal Council was such that they quickly approved the draft. Reich Chancellor von Bismarck gave hearty encouragement to Lutz and personally asked Adalbert Falk, a Prussian judicial councillor, to help defend the bill before the Federal Council.[12]

In 1873, Lutz again approached the school question, attempting to achieve by administrative decree what could not be got through the Parliament; he announced through a government order that a school statute dating back to 1810 and the days of Montgelas was now to be interpreted in a new way. The statute had originally been intended to make possible in unusual circumstances the mixing of denominations in a single school. It had never been implemented. Lutz proposed a complete reorganization of school districts which would result in at least a few cases in the establishment of simultaneous schools similar to those in Baden. This offered financial advantages to local commu-

12. Foerster, pp. 70–72.

nities which could in this way combine two small schools into one, and it was not compulsory. But the order created a storm of protest from conservatives of both denominations who saw in it the first step toward the abolition of denominational schools. By 1883, Lutz was forced to abandon his plan, in the face of such opposition, and returned to the previous status, maintaining the denominational system intact. His ideological defeat was made complete three years later when, under the influence of the Regent Luitpold (taking over from the insane Ludwig II) all government recognition was withdrawn from the Old Catholics. He remained in office until his death in 1890, however, receiving steady encouragement from his patron Bismarck.

It is significant that throughout the years of the Bavarian equivalent of the *Kulturkampf* the Concordat of 1817 was never abrogated, and membership in religious orders actually increased; the national law against the Jesuit Society was interpreted in the state as narrowly as possible, permitting related orders to continue to exist. The primary goal of Lutz's policy seems to have been not to diminish the role of the church in the state but to prevent the control of the ministry by a clerical majority in the *Landtag*. His motives were the same as Jolly's in Baden: to use the church-state conflict as a distraction and to delay the inauguration of true parliamentary government in the state.

In Württemberg, Catholics had hoped to secure a concordat to safeguard the interests of the church, but they were obliged to settle for a state law, passed in 1862, which effected compromise on several issues. The government kept the *placet*, but with modifications in its use. The education of the clergy and state citizenship requirements for clergy were to be regulated by the state, but much leeway was allowed the church in the field of education.

On a personal level the state was free of belligerent warriors on both the doctrinaire-liberal and the ultramontane-clerical sides and so was spared a "culture-struggle" altogether. Catholics and Protestants worked together amicably in the Democratic party which dominated the lower house of the legislature, while the upper house had a permanent majority of Catholic aristocrats which could block offensive anticlerical measures there. The minister-president of Württemberg in these years, Freiherr von Mittnacht, was a Catholic himself, and he and King Karl (1864–91) refused to follow the Baden government in exploiting religious issues for political ends.

In Hesse-Darmstadt a liberal attack on the privileges of the church was difficult so long as the particularist Minister-President von Dalwigk remained in office, though some steps had been taken in this direction in 1863 when the *Landtag* had voted to regulate the education of theology students and to forbid religious orders to operate within the state. Dalwigk resigned in 1871, after intense pressure from Bismarck upon the Grand Duke Ludwig IV. The new ministry heeded the urgings of the majority liberals in the *Landtag* and sponsored a series of anticlerical laws. In Hesse, unlike the rest of the south and the southwest, the campaign was a conscious imitation of the Prussian *Kulturkampf,* with its April Laws of 1875 echoing the Prussian May Laws of 1873. A school law introduced simultaneous schools on the Baden model, as a compromise with the liberal demand for secular schools.

Bishop von Ketteler protested the laws and tried to work out some sort of compromise in their execution, which was not as rigorous as in Prussia. He managed to escape imprisonment, but when he died in 1877 there was no agreement between the state government and church officials on the choice of a successor, and the diocese of Mainz remained vacant until 1886.

In Saxony, only about 5 percent of the population of the state was Catholic and a large number of them were members of a Slavic minority, the Sorbs, or Wends. This might have provided a parallel with the Polish-Catholic situation in Prussia, but the Sorbs were mostly poor peasants without a political voice and had traditionally been protected by Saxony's Catholic dynasty, so there was no significant conflict in the state during the years of the *Kulturkampf,* in spite of some attempts by liberals to promote one.

The relative tardiness of events in Prussia in comparison to the southern states can be explained by two circumstances: first, the continuing tradition of Frederick William IV in the upper reaches of the administration, and particularly in the Ministry of Religion and Education itself, in the policies of the Minister Heinrich von Mühler and the head of the Catholic Department, Adalbert Krätzig. Since 1840 the parity state might not have been achieved, but the ideal had been recognized. Queen Augusta, in her letters during 1870 to the king, frequently recalled the tradition in her pleas to William that he intervene to help the pope in his difficulties. On September 18, for example, she wrote: "The Austrian emperor's speech [in defense of the pope] is colorless; the parity situation [*paritätische Stellung*] of Prussia could be so much more effective."[13] She felt that Prussia's failure to come to the aid of Pius IX might change the opinions of south German Catholics about joining the North German Confederation. "Your blessed father [Frederick William III] restored the temporal power in 1815, your blessed brother [Frederick William IV] offered protection to the pope in his difficulties; how can you now in justice refuse to act regally as always in this favorable moment which will not recur, when there are no confessional barriers for the patriotism, self-sacrifice, and bravery of your soldiers, and when important new elections are at hand?"[14] William did not do as Augusta wished, in this, nor in the later events of the *Kulturkampf*, but neither was he anxious to initiate action against the church within or outside of Prussia.

The second factor retarding moves against the Catholic church in Prussia was the feeling in liberal political circles that such moves might prevent the adherence of the southern states to the Confederation, as the queen had suggested. In 1868 and 1869, parliamentary committee recommendations had been made for secularizing education and curtailing the authority of religious orders to run educational and charitable organizations. Peter Reichensperger, Mallinckrodt, and Windthorst had tried to bring the recommendations to debate, but they had been deliberately shelved by the majority. Similarly, in August 1869, when there had been particularly unpleasant mob violence directed against a religious order in the Berlin suburb of Moabit, a full airing of the matter was avoided by the liberals, and Eduard Lasker of the Progressive party acknowledged that this was a postponement of the issue.[15] Consequently, when the newly elected legislatures of the imperial Reichstag and the Prussian House of Deputies convened in 1871, there was a tense atmosphere of confrontation evident from the beginning between the liberal majorities and the embattled, defensive Center. Now that the south was securely included in the Reich, the campaign could begin.

The Center's numerical strength was increased, but its patriotic

13. Adelheid Constabel, ed., *Die Vorgeschichte des Kulturkampfs: Quellenveröffentlichung aus dem Deutschen Zentralarchiv* (Berlin, 1957), p. 29.
14. Ibid., p. 37.
15. Bachem, 3:42.

credentials still more discredited, by the presence in its ranks of "guests" (*Hospitanten*) and allies consisting of Hanoverian Guelphs, Danes, and Poles (and after 1874, Alsace-Lorrainers.) They formed a parliamentary opposition which was seen by their opponents as a national opposition. As Johannes Miquel of the National Liberal party (himself a Hanoverian by birth) said: "Germany has come into existence against the will of these gentlemen; they are now the defeated party."[16]

At the very beginning of the legislative session the mood was set for the anticipated conflict by an altercation over the wording of the Reichstag's address to the throne. Rudolf von Bennigsen's proposed draft for the address included the sentence: "The days of intervention in the internal life of other peoples will, we hope, under no pretext and in no form, return." This was interpreted by the Center as a reference to German Catholics' desire to restore Rome to the papacy, and hence as a deliberate provocation. Peter Reichensperger proposed an amended motion which omitted the offensive passage. During the ensuing debate, Windthorst asked what the liberals really intended by the sentence and pointed out that "in no form" might be said to exclude even a verbal gesture of sympathy with the pope's predicament, a gesture which might do much to conciliate Catholic opinion in Germany. The original version of the address was nonetheless accepted by a large majority of the Reichstag.[17]

Two days later, Reichensperger made a motion to include the Prussian constitutional guarantees on religion (clauses 15 and 18) in the Reich constitution. This was also defeated by an overwhelming majority, thus continuing to ensure that the favored position of the Catholic church in Prussia would not be extended to the smaller states. In April, acting separately from the Center, the Polish deputies moved that their territories be excluded from the borders of the new Reich.

Bismarck then took the offensive in June, with letters to two newspapers linking the Center with the Progressive radicals because of its civil rights stand, and conjuring up a "Red-Black alliance." He believed that the party contained a "strong and active" revolutionary

16. Windell, p. 290.
17. *Stenographische Berichte über die Verhandlungen des deutschen Reichstags*, 8:52–65 (30 Mar. 1871), 10:61–62 (27 Mar. 1871), 10:73–74 (28 Mar. 1871).

wing, and blamed it for a recent outbreak of violence in Königshütte in Upper Silesia, where the Polish-speaking miners had gone on strike and sent petitions to the ministry.[18] Bismarck implied that Center party agitation had stirred up the miners. Although he linked the party with the Progressives at this time, as the *Kulturkampf* progressed, Bismarck was able to suppress the Progressives' concern with civil rights by appealing to the anticlericalism which was also basic to their platform. In fact, his charge of a Red-Black coalition between Center and Social Democrats in later years had more substance than this odd coupling of doctrinaire liberalism with doctrinaire antiliberalism.

The association of the Center with the support of non-German national groups was more typical of Bismarck's approach at this time. Mention was made on several occasions in the records of the Prussian cabinet in 1871 of the connection between the Catholic church and the Slavic nationalities: for example, on October 13, Minister President Bismarck advised that there had been "too much forbearance against ultramontane, anti-Prussian efforts in West Prussia, Posen, and Upper Silesia. There is a Slavic ultramontane and reactionary propaganda from the Russian border to the Adriatic Sea, and it is necessary to defend our national interest and our language against such hostile efforts." Again, from the cabinet sitting of November 1: "The influence of local clergy hinders the use of the German language, because Slavs and Romans in alliance with ultramontanism seek to uphold barbarism and ignorance and fight everywhere in Europe against Germanism, which seeks to spread enlightenment."[19]

Before the anticlerical campaign desired by Bismarck and the liberals could be effectively launched, however, changes had to be made within the Ministry of Religion and Education. Bismarck found opportunity to do this during the last half of 1871, after a controversy involving the acceptance of the infallibility dogma in Prussia.

For some months there had been difficulties in the state universities and secondary schools because of the unwillingness of some of

18. Erich Schmidt-Volkmar, *Der Kulturkampf in Deutschland, 1871–1890* (Göttingen, 1962), p. 42. This book is a continuation of the author's earlier work published under the name of "Erich Schmidt," cited above. The tone of the second, published during the time of a Christian Democratic government, is very different from that of the first, published under National Socialist auspices.

19. Constabel, pp. 128, 137.

the teachers, all state employees, to accept the dogma. The case of a teacher of religion at the Catholic *gymnasium* in Braunsberg, East Prussia, Dr. Wollmann, became a test in Prussia of the relative powers of bishop and state over the schools. Wollmann had refused to read the dogma in the school church as ordered by the bishop of Ermland, and refused to teach it to his students. The school director supported Wollmann because he did not want the dogma read aloud either and feared that it would cause a general walkout of the faculty. The archbishop of Breslau eventually appealed to Minister von Mühler either to order Wollmann to comply or to dismiss him. Mühler refused to do either, as had all of the lower authorities before him.

Actually, Mühler's personal attitude was conciliatory and mild. He was a conservative, a devout Protestant, and concerned to maintain the denominational school system intact. He had worked closely with Adalbert Krätzig, the head of the Catholic Department in the ministry, since 1866. Krätzig was not only a Catholic but also an active member of the Center party, sitting for Silesia in the Reichstag until 1873. He sympathized with the bishop and archbishop and felt that the teachers should make their peace with them. Krätzig had approved the publication of the dogma in Prussia and criticized the refusal of the Baden and Bavarian governments to do so. Bismarck believed, or said that he believed, that Krätzig belonged to a family which had been serfs of the Radziwill family and that he was leader of a clique in the ministry which sought to favor the Poles; he was also a personal friend of the Empress Augusta.[20] Bismarck resolved to get rid of Krätzig, and four days after the excommunication of Dr. Wollmann, in July 1871, the entire Catholic Department in the ministry was abolished. Krätzig was compensated with a position elsewhere. (Mühler's suggestion that he be moved to the Justice Department was rejected by Bismarck because of his Centrist affiliations.) The cabinet justified the elimination of the department to the king with the argument that the merging of the two departments into one, with a Protestant at the head, was essential for the impartiality of the state.[21] The new combined department contained ten Protestants and two Catholics.

Mühler continued to seek a compromise in the Braunsberg case.

20. Bachem, 3:223; Adalbert Wahl, *Deutsche Geschichte*, 4 vols. (Stuttgart, 1926), 1:144.
21. Wahl, 1:148.

He agreed that it was awkward for the parents who wanted to continue their children's education but were forbidden by the bishop to allow them to attend Wollmann's classes. He suggested a suspension of religious instruction altogether for those students (a solution also proposed in the House of Deputies by Peter Reichensperger). The decision of the cabinet as a whole, however, was that students must attend the classes or leave school. A final disposition of the Wollmann case was not made until the ministry of Dr. Falk the following year.

Bismarck appears to have grown increasingly impatient with Mühler's slowness to act, and in October 1871 he asked the minister for a precise statement on the subject of measures to strengthen Protestantism in relation to Catholicism in Prussia. If this was designed to provoke Mühler's resignation it was unsuccessful, because he responded with a written program very much like that later put into effect by Falk. This program (marked "strictly secret") called for, on the negative side, measures such as: the right to break off church membership, the introduction of civil marriage, lay supervision of schools, the reintroduction of the *placet*, prohibition of the Jesuits; and on the positive side, a reorganization of the Evangelical church, including the establishment of regular synods and endowments as promised by Frederick William IV in the 1840s, and the forging of close connections among the different state churches under Prussian leadership. Mühler even pointed out, in a later memorandum, that it would be quite possible to force compliance from the Catholic church, in such matters as excommunicating a subject without state permission, by the withholding of financial support. But he doubted if it would be wise to do this "and thereby inaugurate a full-scale state of war with the Catholic church or with an individual diocese."[22] To Mühler's conservative mind, even though he personally agreed with the principle of state supremacy, a "state of war" was by definition undesirable. Bismarck and other members of the Prussian cabinet had come to consider it a necessity. Yet Mühler would not resign to give way to a more active combatant. In the end, his resignation in January 1872 came only after he was explicitly told by William I that he had lost confidence in him over a trivial issue concerning a museum ap-

22. Constabel, p. 163.

pointment. An article in the Berlin paper, the *Vossische Zeitung*, said at the time of Mühler's resignation that there was conflict between the two ministers about the schools in Alsace-Lorraine: that Bismarck wanted to secularize them, against the wishes of the local clergy, and that Mühler had sought to prevent this. The article said "We need a *Kultusminister* who is capable of rising to the objective heights of the Reich chancellor."[23]

The replacement of Mühler by Adalbert Falk in January 1872 and the rapid pushing-through of the *Kanzelparagraph*, or Lex Lutz, in the Federal Council in December 1871, may fairly be said to have been the opening shots in that "state of war" so dreaded by Mühler and welcomed by Bismarck and the liberals. Falk's defense of the "pulpit paragraph" in the Federal Council may well have decided Bismarck on his fitness to replace Mühler. The law was sent on to the Reichstag where it was hastily passed. The law's obvious abridgement of the right of free speech was an embarrassment to some liberals, and twelve Progressive deputies and one National Liberal (Lasker) joined the Center in voting against the bill.

Falk's nomination as minister of religion and education on Bismarck's urgent recommendation represented something of a departure in Prussian cabinet appointees, for he was a liberal who had been close to, though not actually a member of, the National Liberal delegation in the Reichstag of the North German Confederation. Yet his past record had much in it that differed from doctrinaire liberalism and made him acceptable to Bismarck and, equally important, to William I. He was the son of an Evangelical pastor in Silesia, a province with a majority of Catholics and many Polish-speaking districts. (His father was an old friend of Mühler's and disagreed with his son about denominational schools.) Falk had spent the first four years of his legal career in Lyck, in the region of Masuria, near the Russian border. He had then served in the Prussian *Landtag* from 1858 to 1862, sitting on the Polish Commission and the Budget Committee. His speech on the Polish question revealed a suspicious attitude toward this minority, which coincided with Bismarck's feelings; he spoke of the Poles' "mendacity and exaggeration" regarding their linguistic grievances and refused to

---

23. Ibid., p. 169.

acknowledge the Masurians as Poles, thus denying their claims for recognition as a linguistic minority.[24] On the Budget Committee Falk had been one of the few liberals to support the army reforms of 1861 and his speech on this occasion, though not convincing to the majority, caused Bismarck to exclaim "*Wohlauf zur Falkenbeize!*" ("Cheers for falconry!"—a play on the name Falk which means "falcon.") Here was a falcon to help him in his present hunting.

The only opposition to Falk's appointment in government circles came from the Empress Augusta, who behaved with extreme coldness to Falk whenever they met and who at one point tried to influence his actions by appealing to his wife to win him to tolerance. Frau Falk reported that she simply replied to the empress that the subject was "not a matter for women," which was about the same response that Augusta got from William I in her persistent defense of the Catholic cause.[25]

Falk's instructions from Bismarck were "to restore the rights of the state in relation to the church, and naturally, with as little fuss as possible." This he was well disposed to do. A fuss nevertheless occurred, and the reason for this lay more with Bismarck than with Falk.

24. Foerster, p. 37.
25. Ibid., p. 86.

4
THE *KULTURKAMPF*

In recent years, most discussion of the long conflict between the Prussian state and the Catholic church known as the *Kulturkampf* has focused upon the question of Bismarck's motivation and the extent of his responsibility for the legislation. Although in his memoirs he disclaimed personal responsibility, the evidence is clear that all of the laws and the entire punitive program were known, approved, and in some cases, urged by Bismarck. He had no sympathy with the secularist ideals of the liberals but was more concerned with using the anticlerical campaign as a means of combating the nationalist strivings of the Poles and the anti-Prussian sentiments of the Rhinelanders; he feared an alliance between Social Democracy and the Center party and fought the church in order to destroy the party. In addition to these considerations, it seems clear that Bismarck also exploited the conflict in order to forestall or prevent the growth of parliamentary independence in Prussia and the Reich, following the example of Jolly in Baden and Lutz in Bavaria. It has often been suggested that the entire *Kulturkampf* was used by Bismarck as a "diversionary policy in the grand manner": that the liberals were kept occupied with religious issues in a conscious effort to distract them from political and constitutional issues.[1] On the other hand, it has also been suggested that the liberals used the *Kulturkampf* as a means of keeping Bismarck dependent upon them.

Whatever the conscious or unconscious intentions of the chancellor may have been, it is surely equally interesting and significant that the *Kulturkampf* was immensely popular in Germany.[2] Most of the

1. Michael Stürmer, *Regierung und Reichstag im Bismarckstaat, 1871–1880* (Düsseldorf, 1974), p. 87, is a recent example of this interpretation.
2. See Ronald J. Ross, *Beleaguered Tower: The Dilemma of Political Catholicism in Wilhelmine Germany* (Notre Dame, Ind., 1976), p. 13.

legislation, both the original laws instituting state supremacy and the punitive laws which followed, passed the Parliaments with large majorities and with astonishing speed. Passionate public enthusiasm marked the first years of the campaign, and Minister Falk was feted and cheered by crowds of thousands during his tour of the Rhineland in the summer of 1875. The deep and lasting impression which the events of the *Kulturkampf* made upon the Center party was not created simply by the parliamentary struggle against Bismarck and his officials, but by the obvious enthusiasm for anti-Catholic measures shown by the Protestant population of Germany.

Falk prepared to carry out Bismarck's injunction to draw up a program of legislation "with as little fuss as possible" but discovered that Bismarck himself did not really wish to avoid a public confrontation, and that the Center party was ready to debate each and every government action with enthusiasm. It was in these early months that Ludwig Windthorst came into his own as a superb verbal duelist. He seldom spoke from notes (in fact his eyesight was too poor) and gave his speeches standing from his seat rather than from the speaker's rostrum; because of his small stature he also stood up to listen to any speech of particular interest to him, which could be disconcerting to the speaker. His debating tactics are best summed up by his own often-quoted remark: "When I see a locomotive coming at me, I don't stay in its way, but jump on board and travel with it."[3] He delighted in turning the emotional energy and the logic of his opponents' arguments against them.

His diminutive body and large head presented an irresistible subject for newspaper cartoonists, pitted against the tall, imposing figures of Falk and Bismarck. Falk himself noted his first impression of Windthorst: "The head was huge, the face really ugly [*recht garstig*], the whole appearance extraordinary."[4]

In January of 1872, Bismarck began his campaign with a parliamentary speech aimed at the Center in which he used the famous phrase "a mobilization against the state" and denounced the idea of a confessional party as dangerous and divisive. Many commentators, in-

3. Bachem, 5:242.
4. Foerster, p. 63.

cluding some otherwise antipathetic to Bismarck, have agreed with this particular judgment and have described the Center as an unnatural wedge driven into the normal political order, where parties are based upon platforms representing social and economic interests. Although there is much justice in this criticism, it should be pointed out that the Center party in its final form was organized after existing parties had defined, or redefined, themselves in terms which specifically excluded Catholic interests; that is, the liberal parties by 1872, unlike their precursors in the 1840s and 1850s, had become belligerently anticlerical (as were also the Social Democrats) while the Conservatives remained closely tied to the Protestant faith and issued no welcoming invitations to ultramontanes in search of a home. This self-definition changed very little in the years following the *Kulturkampf* or in the Weimar period, and when tentative efforts were made by Centrists to break out of the confessional mold they met with absolutely no response in either Protestant or liberal circles. The fact that the other parties were also based upon socioeconomic interests tends to obscure the fact that they were not hospitable to participation in their ranks by conscientious Catholics.

In this same speech of January 26, Bismarck took up the subject of parity, the persistent demand of the Center that Catholics should have representation in government proportionate to their numbers in the population. Mallinckrodt had protested that the abolition of the Catholic Department in the Ministry of Religion and Education violated the principle of parity established under Frederick William IV, and Windthorst had cited the Netherlands as a good model for Prussia to follow in this respect. Bismarck made fun of the notion by imagining a perfect statistical parity in which not only Evangelical Protestants and Catholics but also Reformed church members and Jews would be proportionally represented. This witticism aroused laughter in the House, and yet it brought out a concept of which the Center's leadership was acutely aware: the need to recognize the rights of other sects. Mallinckrodt said in response "We stand up for the freedom and independence of the Evangelical church with the same determination as for our own, and we have defended and protected the rights of Jews and Dissenters [*Dissidenten*] insofar as it concerns free circulation of their points of view. Refute me! [directed to the Left, where sounds of remonstrance had come] and if you cannot refute me then concede to us that we know what parity is."[5]

Windthorst further countered Bismarck's sarcasm on the subject with the serious consideration of parity for Jews, and in later years when there was considerable pressure from some Center supporters in rural areas for the party to adopt an anti-Semitic program, Windthorst prevented this by a reminder that defense of minority rights for all sects was necessary to justify efforts on behalf of Catholics. On the other hand, the Center never extended this concern to the rights of the Old Catholics, who were seen by the party as usurpers of the legal position of the Catholic church in the state.

In February, the bill for state supervision of the schools was introduced in the House of Deputies and a stormy debate began. The bill was to permit, though not require, the nomination of lay inspectors to replace the clergy who had until now carried out all school inspection. This was a demand basic to the liberal program, but as has been shown, Bismarck's special concern was to eliminate the influence of Polish clergy who sought to prevent the Germanization of Polish children through the schools. His speeches violently attacked the clergy, calling Germany the only country where priests were "international" and claiming that they sought to advance the ambitions of the Polish nobility (though only a month before he had castigated the Center and its clerical supporters for having "appealed to the passions of the lower classes").[6]

It proved to be somewhat more difficult to enlist support for the school inspection law than for the other laws of the *Kulturkampf*, partly for the practical reason that its implementation promised to be very costly, the clergy having performed the duty without salary, and partly because it was opposed by Protestant conservatives, particularly in the House of Lords, who felt that it would be injurious to the rights of the Evangelical church and the rights of local patronage of Prussian landlords. Bismarck and Falk sought to allay concern on both counts by implying that the law would be carried out very selectively, primarily in Polish-speaking districts, and that it only "permitted" lay-

5. Hüsgen, p. 82.
6. Ibid., pp. 119, 107.

men to be chosen, did not require them, and "in most cases it would prove advisable on practical grounds to choose clergymen." In fact, by 1880, laymen had been nominated in only 179 of 705 school districts, nearly all of them in Catholic districts in the Rhineland and in the eastern provinces with Polish population. Even with such concessions, however, it was necessary that ten new peers be created in order to obtain a majority in the *Herrenhaus* for the school supervision law.[7]

Minister Falk himself was interested in more far-reaching changes in the Prussian educational system and was able to accomplish part of his goal of a modern, secular, liberal school system without recourse to parliamentary legislation. By administrative order he was able to prohibit religious orders from teaching in the schools and to insist that the German language be used in religious instruction classes as well as in the rest of the curriculum (they had previously been exempt from this stricture). His ministry also reinterpreted the original Prussian school ordinance of 1849 to permit the establishment of some schools of mixed denomination, mostly in areas of sparse population where two small schools could efficiently be merged into one. (Such schools already existed in Nassau and the city of Frankfurt, annexed to Prussia in 1866.) Several hundred of these schools, resembling the *Simultan-schulen* of Baden and Hesse, were created, but Falk's ambition of crowning these piecemeal changes with a comprehensive new school law was never achieved, partly because of strenuous objections from Evangelical church spokesmen (including William I) and partly because of the great outlay of revenue it would have entailed. His draft for such a law was completed in 1877 but never brought before the *Landtag*; it proved to be the first in a series of efforts, all failures, from 1877 to the late 1920s.

Shortly after the passage of the school inspection law, Falk settled the still-outstanding Braunsberg school case through administrative action. In his usual painstaking legalistic fashion, he decided that Wollmann should not be dismissed from a state position simply because of condemnation and excommunication by the bishop, and that to dismiss him, in fact, would mean that the state would be deciding for itself the question of whether Wollmann was or was not a real

7. Foerster, p. 109; Wahl, 1:163–64; Stürmer, pp. 78–81.

Catholic, which would be interference in spiritual matters. However, students should not be forced to attend Wollmann's classes. Both Wollmann and the school director were soon transferred to less controversial posts.[8]

On the other hand, Falk came to the conclusion that the excommunication of Wollmann by Bishop Krementz of Ermland was not entirely a spiritual matter, did seriously affect his civil rights, and should not have been done without state permission. It was frustrating to find that there was very little that the state could do about this in order to force the bishop to rescind the order, but, as punishment for his making it, Falk thought that the stopping of financial support to the diocese (*Temporaliensperre*) should be effective. His recommendation to this effect was made in June, and for the next three months there followed an exchange of letters between William I and the bishop. William hoped that Bishop Krementz would make sufficient gesture of submission to make punishment unnecessary.

Bismarck was anxious to make a test case of the incident and urged that the bishop be required to state explicitly that he should not have issued an excommunication decree without the foreknowledge of the government.[9] Krementz refused to do this, and his financial support was terminated in September. The move was greeted with praise from the liberal press and, of course, with protests from the bishop's supporters.

The same conflict of interest illustrated by the Wollmann case occurred in the case of Bishop Namszanowski, the highest cleric in the Prussian army. The post of *Feldpropst* which he held, whose duties were to supervise the religious welfare of all Catholic personnel in the army, was a new one, created only in 1868 after long negotiations with the Vatican. Namszanowski had incurred the anger of Minister of War von Roon when he had forbidden Catholic services to be held in an army-owned chapel. The chapel was normally available to both denominations, but the bishop objected to the fact that Old Catholics had been permitted to hold services there as well. In addition, he had

---

8. Wollmann was sent to a teaching post in Cologne; the director, Dr. Treibel, was transferred to the post of head of the Berlin Institute for the Deaf and eventually converted to Protestantism (Wahl, 1:146).

9. Foerster, p. 133.

removed an Old Catholic from office as an army missionary-priest. Roon solved this problem by suspending the bishop and abolishing the office of *Feldprobst*: this naturally angered the pope. Many military chaplains found themselves, like other state employees, caught in this dilemma of conflicting authorities.

If Pius IX was offended by the Namszanowski affair, he was positively insulted by the abruptly announced nomination that spring of Cardinal von Hohenlohe to the position of Prussian ambassador to the Vatican. To appoint any man to this delicate post without private soundings as to his acceptability beforehand was unusual. To appoint a cardinal to such a post was unprecedented. But to suggest Hohenlohe, an outspoken opponent of infallibility at the council, an enemy to the Jesuits, and a brother of the anticlerical Bavarian statesman, was unthinkable.[10] Whether or not Bismarck persuaded King William to make the nomination in order deliberately to provoke the pope into rejecting it is not known, but the rejection gave the Prussian government an excuse for eliminating the position of ambassador to the Vatican altogether.

The highly popular law disbanding the Society of Jesus in Germany and exiling its members was passed by the Reichstag with great rapidity and enthusiasm in July 1872. Although the law affected only a few hundred men (the Center claimed only two hundred, but other sources cite figures of up to nine hundred), the civil rights issue was very clear-cut: without due process of law or any stated cause other than their membership in the society these men were deprived of their rights of residence in Germany. On these grounds, Eduard Lasker of the National Liberal party opposed the bill, and the Progressive party was divided, with eleven votes opposed, fifteen abstaining, and nine supporting the bill. August Bebel, the sole Social Democratic deputy, voted against the bill but carefully dissociated himself from the Center. Bismarck justified the law by his statement to Rudolf Delbrück that "We are acting in self-defense and cannot restrain ourselves with liberal phrases about citizens' rights."[11] The administration had not

10. The nomination has sometimes been called a propitiatory move by Bismarck as "an attempt to make peace with the Vatican" (George O. Kent, *Arnim and Bismarck* [Oxford, 1968], p. 85), but this interpretation is difficult to credit.
11. *Verhandlungen des Reichstags*, 14:1123–50 (19 June 1872); Statement to Delbrück from Schmidt-Volkmar, p. 110.

actually proposed the bill itself but had left it to be done by the National Liberal party.

Bavarian influence in the Federal Council had prevented an even more severe bill from being presented, which would have deprived the Jesuits of their German citizenship altogether and included with them several other related orders. It may be noted that Switzerland and a number of German states including Württemberg, Baden, Saxony, and Bavaria had already prohibited the order, at least on paper. Austria, on the other hand, though undergoing a wave of anticlericalism itself and officially discouraging entry of Jesuit emigrés into the empire, quietly permitted them to take refuge there.

Although the Bavarian government participated in drafting the final version of the anti-Jesuit law for the Federal Council and the Reichstag and was, as has been shown, equally as active as Prussia in limiting the authority of the church in its own territory, the state balked at any further attempt to legislate on religious and educational matters on a national scale. Hence the campaign had to be continued solely on the Prussian state level, and in August 1872 the famous May Laws of the succeeding year were first drawn up by the Prussian *Kultus* ministry. No Catholic personnel in the ministry were present at the drafting.[12] The subsequent denunciation of the 1872 measures by Pius IX in December gave an added propaganda advantage to the Prussian government, but was in no way a reason for the May Laws, whose origin can be traced back even before August to Bismarck's correspondence with Mühler in 1871.

In April, the government prepared the way for the proposed laws by putting before the *Landtag* a revision of articles 15 and 18 in the Prussian constitution which granted to the churches the right to independent management of their own affairs. Minister Falk felt that the articles were irrelevant to the proposed legislation, that they referred to purely clerical matters, and that consequently revision was neither necessary nor desirable. Both Bismarck and the majority leadership in the House of Deputies believed, however, that it added legitimacy to the proceedings to amend the articles by attaching qualifying statements. The original wording of Article 15, based upon a similar article in the Belgian constitution, was as follows: "Every religious organiza-

12. Foerster, p. 145.

tion regulates and administers its affairs independently and remains in the possession and enjoyment of its appointed institutions, endowments and foundations for its spiritual, educational, and charitable purposes." In the amended version, the clause "but remains subject to state laws and the lawfully regulated supervision of the state" was inserted after the word "independently." Article 18 originally read: "In appointments to clerical offices the right of nominating, proposing, electing, and confirming is suspended insofar as it pertains to the state and not to the individual patron or to particular legal titles. This stipulation does not apply to the appointment of the clergy by the army or by public institutions." The amended version added the further qualification that "In other respects the law determines the authority of the state with regard to the education, appointment, and dismissal of clerical and religious officials and establishes the limits of clerical powers of discipline."[13] There was so much opposition to these amendments in the conservative House of Lords that it was necessary for the king to create new peers in order to obtain the required majority for them.[14] The amendments were passed only a few weeks before the May Laws won final approval. Two years later the constitutional articles themselves were abolished with equal speed.

The four May Laws, or Falk Laws, of 1873 were those concerning 1) "the training and employment of the clergy," 2) "clerical disciplinary power and the establishment of a royal court for clerical matters," 3) "legal limits to the use of clerical punishment and corrective measures," and 4) easy withdrawal from church membership. These were all passed in four days, May 4 through May 11. The second and third laws affected the Catholic church almost exclusively and dealt with such matters as the powers of excommunication. Falk thought them necessary in part in order to protect the lower clergy from the severe judgment of their superiors. The first law was originally intended to apply only to seminaries for the Catholic priesthood and stressed instruction in the German language and German culture as a weapon against the employment of Polish and other foreign clergy. The ministry decided in the course of drawing up the bill that it was more politic to make those clauses dealing with education of the clergy ap-

13. Ernst Rudolf Huber, ed., *Dokumente zur deutschen Verfassungsgeschichte*, 3 vols. (Stuttgart, 1961), 1:402–3.
14. Wahl, 1:180.

plicable to all denominations and the draft was altered to this effect. This law also restored the *Anzeigepflicht* or *placet,* the necessity for state approval for the appointment of clergy to offices, which the constitutional Article 18 had suspended.

The fourth law was clearly intended to facilitate departure of the Old Catholics from Catholic church membership. In its long-range effects, however, it hurt the Protestant denomination more than the Catholic, because far more Protestants took advantage of its provisions for easy withdrawal from church membership than did Catholics. It is interesting that Mühler himself had favored easy separation because it would permit each church to remain conservative and closely bound to the state while relieving specific areas of controversy. Peter Reichensperger agreed, and said in the House debate on the law that the seceder should not have to pay the stipulated fee but should on the contrary be paid for his service to the cause of church solidarity!

All of these laws remained permanently on the books, though they were less rigorously enforced after the years of the *Kulturkampf.* Their publication was promptly followed by their condemnation by the assembled German bishops' conference in Fulda on May 26. Open defiance naturally heightened the conflict. One hundred and eighty-four prominent Catholics, including the Hohenlohe family, countered the bishops' pronouncement with a State Catholics' Address to the king on June 14, but most German Catholics backed the bishops and the Center party, as the November election results made clear.

The elections to the lower house of the Prussian *Landtag* reveal that public opinion had been aroused in both camps. Both of the belligerent parties gained, the Center increasing from 60 to 89 seats, and the National Liberals from 123 to 174. The Conservatives, on the other hand, whose delegates, especially in the House of Lords, had been reluctant to support the anticlerical legislation, but had not consistently opposed it either, lost substantially. The Center had effectively mobilized Catholic opinion by means of pamphlets (often written anonymously by leading Centrists) and popular "associations" (*Vereine*) such as the one in Cologne which had organized mass meetings in that city. Police supervised the meetings and the other activities of the associations closely, and Falk and Bismarck on several occasions considered laws to ban them, but they were never fully suppressed.

The effect of the publication of the Prussian May Laws in Baden was to stimulate demands from liberals there that the Baden regulations for examination of the clergy be stiffened, and that legal penalties be imposed for failure to obey them. Minister President Jolly acceded to these pressures and penalties were duly imposed, but their enforcement was milder than in Prussia.[15] Thus the anticlerical fervor which had spread from south to north was returned with renewed vigor to the south again.

During the actual passage of the May Laws, Bismarck had been replaced as minister-president of Prussia by Roon, formerly minister of war, and in later years Bismarck used this fact to minimize his own role in their promotion, but as has been shown, the laws were prepared long before his resignation in January 1873. Roon, ironically, had originally been critical of the anticlerical program. He retired in November, and Bismarck returned as minister-president.

Roon's resignation did not precipitate a general resignation of the cabinet, as would have been usual in a truly parliamentary regime, and Windthorst made use of this fact to take the offensive in the opening days of the new *Landtag* session. He accused Bismarck of wanting to turn the office of minister-president into a replica of that of Reich chancellor and thereby to reduce the status of the other Prussian ministers to that of state secretaries. He also introduced a motion for the liberalization of the Prussian three-class voting system, which embarrassed the liberal delegates, who supported the intent of the motion but not its sponsors; as one speaker said, "the motion offers a gift from a hand from which we can accept nothing." The motion was tabled. As in Baden, the division between clericals and anticlericals effectively prevented the development of parliamentary government in Prussia, a consequence of the conflict which was surely not overlooked by Bismarck.

Windthorst played the liberal card again the next month when the Center brought a bill to abolish the stamp tax on newspapers. The party felt that its own newspapers had been consistently harassed and illegally censored. The previous December the government had tried, for example, to prevent the publication of the papal allocution against the 1872 laws, and this had aroused much indignation. The Ministry

15. Becker, p. 330.

of the Interior had said then that this was only a "warning" that the papal message contained libelous material.[16] In the debate in December on the subject of government censorship and the use of the official press for proadministration election propaganda, a delegate for the Free Conservatives defended the unconstitutional treatment of the Catholic press by stating that "a political party in this house which has its center of gravity outside Germany has no right to be judged by the same standards with which the other parties are judged."[17] Most members of the liberal parties could not agree with that, perhaps seeing that in this particular instance, at least, the curtailment of rights for one group could lead to similar inroads upon their own freedom. The House voted both to abolish the stamp tax and to ban the use of official publications for election propaganda.

The year 1873 brought the greatest success for the Old Catholic movement in Germany, which had been responsible for so many of the early clashes between the Catholic church and the Prussian government since the Vatican Council. There had been an international congress in Munich in September 1871, but it was not until June 1873 that the German Old Catholics chose Joseph Reinkens as their first bishop (after three other nominees had refused the post).[18] The government of Baden provisionally recognized Reinkens as a Catholic bishop in the state, and the *Landtag* passed a law the following year permitting the sect to make use of Catholic church buildings in any parish which agreed to declare itself Old Catholic (though legally the parish and the buildings were considered by the state to be Catholic). There were two and one-half times as many Old Catholics in Baden as in Bavaria, and eight times as many as in Prussia; eighteen of fifty National Liberal party members in the *Landtag* were Old Catholics. The total number in the state, however, numbered no more than seventeen thousand out of approximately a million Catholics.[19]

A Swiss denomination of Old Catholics was also organized that year, and several Swiss cantons, including Geneva and Bern, recognized the new church as the official Catholic institution. No German state did this, and Bismarck and Falk both rejected all such sugges-

16. Hüsgen, p. 134.
17. Ibid., p. 176.
18. Foerster, p. 214.
19. Becker, pp. 331–39.

tions, hoping to avoid the possibility of state financial aid being granted to three denominations instead of two. Their position, as noted, was simply to maintain state employees in their jobs without attempting to decide whether or not they were "real" Catholics.

Ardent liberal supporters of the Old Catholics in Prussia did put through a law in 1875 (modeled on the Baden law and not sponsored by the cabinet) to give them legal recognition and to give individual parishes which adopted the new sect the right to the use of Catholic church property and income. But by that time, the movement was already foundering. Most of the Old Catholics were either clergy or professors involved in theological questions, or secularists not really concerned with founding a new church but simply with making a stand against Rome. The entire membership has been estimated as no more than about thirty thousand to forty thousand of whom most were middle-class professionals. Reinkens himself resigned as bishop in 1878, disappointed with the lack of real religious concern in the membership and especially dismayed at the marriage of his clergy. The church had agreed that year to permit its clergy to marry in exceptional cases, but within six weeks of the decision, seven priests had become engaged (one to a Vienna opera singer "of the lowest rank") and an eighth had proposed but been turned down.[20] There is no doubt that the *Kulturkampf* had the effect of greatly increasing the sense of solidarity among German Catholics and of killing any chances the Old Catholic movement may have had of becoming a permanent institution.

By the spring of 1874, intransigence on the part of the Catholic clergy in refusing to obey the May Laws, and adamancy on the part of the administration in enforcing them, had led to many situations where priests and bishops were no longer recognized by the state. Archbishop Miecislav von Ledochowsky of Posen-Gnesen had been imprisoned for encouraging the continuation of religious instruction in the Polish language in his diocese. Paul Majunke, the editor of the militant Centrist newspaper *Germania*, had been arrested in spite of the fact that he was supposed to have immunity as a member of the Reichstag.

A particularly awkward situation had been created in regard to

20. Foerster, p. 271.

the legal status of marriages performed by clergy who were no longer recognized by the state. Although an emergency civil ceremony was available, many Catholics simply continued to have marriages performed by unauthorized priests. Falk insisted, over the objection of the rest of the cabinet and especially of William I, that a Prussian law for obligatory civil ceremony was essential. Falk tried to explain to the king that a voluntary or optional plan, which the latter favored, would hurt the Evangelical church far more than an obligatory plan because it would make each marriage an occasion for a conscious choice between state and church; whereas if a civil ceremony was an automatic requirement, there could still be occasion for a religious service. Many Centrists agreed on this point and felt that if civil marriage had to come, obligatory would be more advantageous for the Catholic church than optional; but of course the party opposed the measure in the *Landtag*.

Falk also pointed out to the king that cases in which the church refused to sanction a marriage, because of a previous divorce or some other obstacle, would now be greatly simplified. William finally approved the bill, with reluctance, and it passed into law in March 1874. The following year, a more comprehensive Reich law was passed which included state responsibility for the registration of births and deaths. In the long run, civil marriage, like the law for easy withdrawal from church membership, hurt the Evangelical church more than the Catholic, and the number of religious weddings and baptisms among Protestants steadily declined. It has been estimated that by the 1880s in Berlin, 80 percent of Protestant marriages were outside the church and 40 percent of babies were unbaptized. As Court Chaplain Rudolf Kögel said at the General Synod of 1879, "Rome was the target but Wittenberg was hit."[21]

Civil marriage, the repeal of the constitutional clauses, and most especially the separation law, also produced the first adverse reaction to the *Kulturkampf* from Germany's Jewish community. Originally, Jewish opinion had been strongly favorable to the liberals' campaign, regarding it primarily as an intellectually enlightened movement, and not as an increase in the power of the state and the Protestant estab-

21. Karl Kupisch, *Die deutschen Landeskirchen im 19. und 20. Jahrhundert* (Göttingen, 1966), p. 77.

lishment. The strong support given by many Jewish spokesmen to the initial *Kulturkampf* legislation unfortunately had the effect of reinforcing anti-Semitic prejudices among German Catholics. But by 1874, some Jewish leaders were protesting the National Liberals' claim to the state's "sovereignty over religion and nationality" and decrying the Law of Separation which left Jews without any identification with their faith if they simply chose to drop their affiliation with their particular synagogue.[22] The anticlerical campaign had produced some unexpected and unforeseen results.

The new May Laws of 1874 were punitive in nature. These were the law "concerning the prevention of unauthorized exercising of clerical offices," or Expatriation Act, providing for the exiling of recalcitrant priests; the law for the "administration of vacant Catholic dioceses"; and the law defining and extending the terms of the act for the education of the clergy passed the previous year. Like the Jesuit law, the Expatriation Act clearly violated the civil rights of German clergy, but only a few Progressive delegates in the liberal camp opposed it. It is interesting that the Center in nearly all of the deliberations over the laws of the *Kulturkampf* could count on the support of a few other delegates in the House, in some cases from Protestant Conservatives, in other cases from radical Progressives, but never from both of these groups at once, consequently always finishing in the decided minority of the vote.

The law for the "administration of vacant Catholic dioceses" provided for the choosing of a priest by the local community or by a "patron." It remained on the books, but proved to be a dead letter, as no community ever made such an independent choice. Only a few priests offered their services to fill vacant offices and most of these substitute *Staatspfarrer* went to Polish-speaking districts, motivated by German nationalist feeling. The substitutes were duly excommunicated by the pope.

Soon after these punitive measures were put into effect, an attack was made on Bismarck's life by a young Catholic journeyman-cooper named Kullmann. This gave the government excuse to close down many of the Catholic "associations" in Berlin and elsewhere and to

22. Uriel Tal, *Christians and Jews in Germany: Religion, Politics and Ideology in the Second Reich, 1870–1914* (Ithaca, N.Y., and London, 1975), pp. 96–115; quote from Bennigsen, pp. 104–5.

keep an even closer supervision over the Catholic press. Bismarck reserved the the full propaganda use of the Kullmann case for the opening session of the Reichstag some months later, when he launched an attack on the Center party, blaming it for the attempted assassination. "Try as you will to renounce this murderer, he is hanging firmly to your coattails!" He claimed to have had a private interview with Kullmann in which the boy had said to him "You have insulted my fraction." When Bismarck had asked "Which is your fraction?" he had answered, "The Center." The anecdote provoked great laughter in the house, and the coattail image inspired several newspaper cartoons. Naturally the Center delegation became incensed. Windthorst objected to Bismarck's manner and also pointed out that such an interview with the accused by the victim was hardly according to standard criminal-law procedure. "The *Herr Reichskanzler* has involved and concerned himself in this matter in a way which never should have occurred." Since there were no witnesses to the interview and no notes were taken of it, Windthorst was implying not only that it was improper for the chancellor to have acted in this way but also that there was a likelihood that the conversation had never actually taken place. Bismarck was convulsed with rage at these remarks and the episode must certainly have contributed greatly to his perception of Windthorst as the man he loved to hate.[23]

Within this one year of the conflict, the older leaders of the Center died, Mallinckrodt in May 1874 and Savigny in February 1875. Savigny had served as chairman of both the Reichstag and the Prussian *Landtag* fractions, but after his death the offices were divided; the Bavarian Georg, Freiherr von Franckenstein, was chosen chairman in the Reichstag, in an effort to bind Bavaria more closely to the national party; and the conservative Freiherr Dr. von Schorlemer-Alst became chairman of the Prussian fraction. Windthorst himself remained active in both houses and did more to hold the party together and to provide moral and tactical leadership than any other person, but his failing eyesight made it impossible for him to take care of much party business; he was unable to read or write or to get about without assistance.[24] He also felt that his Guelph loyalties made him an inappro-

---

23. *Verhandlungen des Reichstags* 24 (4 Dec. 1874): 485–90; Hüsgen, p. 157.
24. Bachem, 3:296; Anderson, pp. 16, 27, 244.

priate party head, and that a nobleman lent more prestige to the office. He kept in close touch with all party activities, however, and particularly with the rapidly expanding Catholic press, of which he made good use. Although Windthorst never followed Bismarck's practice of writing signed or anonymous articles to be planted in the papers, he was in close communication with his friend Joseph Bachem, publisher of the *Kölnische Volkszeitung*, and Theodor Stahl, the lead writer for *Germania*, the nearest equivalent to an official party organ that the Center had. He also made frequent use of the *Frankfurter Zeitung* (a Progressive paper) and was a friend of August Stein, its Berlin representative. His good relations with *Germania* did not extend to its first editor in chief Paul Majunke, a Silesian cleric who, Windthorst felt, harmed the party by his polemical and frequently inaccurate journalism. Majunke also served in the Reichstag and Prussian House of Deputies and later wrote a highly colored history of the *Kulturkampf*. He left the editorship of the Berlin paper in 1878, partly through Windthorst's influence, and was succeeded by the less flamboyant Dr. Franz.[25]

The Catholic press and the church hierarchy together waged an active campaign against the May Laws, fully encouraged in this by Pope Pius IX, who in February 1875 issued an encyclical condemning them as "invalid since they are completely contrary to the God-given institutions of the church" and excommunicating all those "state-priests" who had agreed to serve in vacant parishes. Windthorst and the Reichensperger brothers defended the encyclical in the legislatures and tried to mitigate its effect by arguing that it was not issued *ex cathedra* and did not mean that the laws were "invalid" (*ungültig*) in a legal sense but only "morally not obligatory." They cited the Latin version to try to prove their doubtful point. Falk and Bismarck took the encyclical literally and seriously, and its uncompromising defiance was the direct reason for the third series of laws put forward that spring. The government tried to prevent the publication of the encyclical, but a Center deputy read it aloud in the Prussian lower house, thus ensuring its reprinting as a constitutional right.

Bismarck also proposed at this time a "purification" of public of-

---

25. Ursula Mittmann, *Fraktion und Partei: Ein Vergleich von Zentrum und Sozialdemokratie im Kaiserreich* (Düsseldorf, 1976), pp. 211–41; 246; Bachem, 5:198.

ficials, a purge of civil servants, in particular, the *Landräte*, who were not enforcing the anti-Catholic laws with sufficient zeal. Falk rejected the idea and thought the suggestion of an oath of loyalty from Catholic officials to be "completely useless."[26] Bismarck's preference for administrative enforcement of laws, and for state coercion of officials responsible for enforcement, later went to the extraordinary length of his asking the *Kultus* ministry in November 1877 whether the pope himself might properly be considered subject to the May Laws as the "highest Catholic church employee . . . naturally only within the territory of the Prussian state." The ministerial councillor who responded to this suggestion felt that the law in question "had not really been intended for foreigners" and would not be possible to apply in practice to the pope![27]

In this instance, Falk's legalistic approach prevailed over Bismarck's preference for administrative measures and resulted in the three additional punitive laws passed in the spring of 1875: the law concerning "the suspension of income from state sources for the Catholic dioceses and clergy," or Breadbasket Law; the law permitting the administration of church income by the state (somewhat resembling the controversial French Law of Associations which was rejected by the French church in 1906); and the law prohibiting the existence of all Catholic religious orders in Prussia. Of these laws, the first was unused after the ending of the conflict, and the third was considerably modified as a consequence of the peace settlement between church and state, but the second remained in effect until 1918, not without some benefits to the church in terms of financial efficiency.

The Orders Law involved 296 different branches and several thousand men and women. Their property was taken by the state. Their disbanding by the police was the occasion of much public protest, and caused William I and Augusta more distress than any other aspect of the struggle.

Outcry over the Orders Law and the Breadbasket Law, and the contention that they violated the Prussian constitution, merely convinced Bismarck that the constitutional clauses guaranteeing the independence of the churches, even as recently amended, were an ob-

26. Foerster, p. 249.
27. Rudolf Morsey, "Bismarck und der Kulturkampf," *Archiv für Kulturgeschichte* 39 (1957): 267–69.

stacle to the government. Falk felt that they were "harmless" and that it would be a mistake to insist upon their deletion, but nevertheless the government rapidly carried through the nullification of articles 15, 16, and 18, with the first two readings being hurried through in one day. (Article 16, which had not been amended in 1873, read as follows: "Communication of religious organizations with their supporters is not to be obstructed. Public announcement of clerical instructions is subject only to those limitations which apply to all other publications."[28] Justification for the suppression was that the Catholic Church had been interpreting the clauses too broadly. It was hoped, mistakenly, as it turned out, that the Protestant churchmen would not raise objections because, as Falk put it, the clauses "had not been of the slightest use" to the Evangelical church![29] The usual large majority was obtained in the *Landtag* for this facile abrogation of constitutional rights.

Windthorst rose to his greatest heights of eloquence in the debates over these four laws and pointed out some rather obvious flaws in the government's reasoning. When Bismarck jeered that the Breadbasket Law would not result in starving clergy, since the pope and the Jesuits had plenty of money, Windthorst asked what could in that case be the purpose of the law, if economic pressure was not expected to be effective? On the question of absolute state supremacy he suggested that the Prussian state might not always be controlled by authoritarian conservatives and that a Social Democratic state might make use of the principle of absolute supremacy in very different ways.

Rejection of the supremacy of the state was the justification for the rejection of specific laws which expressed it. Windthorst here presumed a right of passive resistance for which Prussian history gave him little precedent: "one must recognize that according to the Christian-Germanic conception of life, as opposed fundamentally to the state-absolutism of classical antiquity, cases can occur which make it an individual's duty to withhold obedience to the laws of a state which oversteps its bounds, even at the risk of becoming a martyr to his convictions."

Windthorst discounted any suggestion that a peace settlement de-

28. Huber, 1:403.
29. Foerster, p. 257.

pended on the pope's taking the initiative, or on changes in the *Kultus* ministry, and placed the responsibility solely upon the chancellor: "Prince Bismarck is the only person who can possibly restore peace and he will restore it on the day when he is convinced that he is on the wrong track. (Laughter from the house.) And this conviction *will* come to him, believe me, gentlemen, even though he may as yet have no suspicion of it."[30] Though this prediction was greeted with incredulous laughter, it proved to be accurate. The parliamentary opposition which Bismarck had hoped to kill off in its earliest beginnings, had become sufficiently strong to persuade him within the next decade to offer conciliation and a peace settlement.

The cancellation of the constitutional articles was the first of the laws that seems to have seriously disturbed the leadership of the Prussian Evangelical church. Until that time the Protestant church had not identified its own situation with that of the Catholics except on specific issues like school supervision and civil marriage. In fact, several members of the Evangelical High Church Council, the top administrative body of the church, were actively involved in the preparation of the government's program. Two of them, Emil Friedberg and Paul Hinschius, were on Falk's commission which drew up the May Laws. They justified their actions on the grounds that the Catholic church had obtained too many privileges in the 1830s and 1840s and had upset the proper balance between church and state, as established by the *Allgemeine Landrecht* of 1794. Some Protestant churchmen, for example, General Superintendent Wilhelm Hoffmann, went even further than this and approved of the goal of the Protestant Union of merging the two denominations into one national German church.[31]

On the other hand, the Evangelical church leadership had not always shown the enthusiasm for the *Kulturkampf* that liberals would have liked. Bismarck himself, characteristically, thought that as a branch of the Prussian state, the church should be more active in support of the state's position, and in April 1875 he wrote a memorandum to the cabinet inquiring about the possibility of encouraging prayer in Protestant churches for the "ending of the rebellion of the Catholic clergy." That was, he felt, the way it would have been done during the

30. Hüsgen, pp. 169–71; Bachem, 3:311.
31. Robert W. Lougee, "The *Kulturkampf* and Historical Positivism," *Church History* 23 (1954): 223–29.

Reformation. "It seems to be wrong, and suggests indifference, if not cowardice, that the Evangelical church as such cannot at least enthusiastically set to work to bear witness against the attack which the papal militancy expresses in every clerical act." Bismarck believed that the Evangelical church and the conservative *Kreuzzeitung* party had "left the government in the lurch."[32]

The Evangelical clergy were thus divided in their attitude toward the campaign against "papal militancy." They were equally divided in their reactions to Minister Falk's efforts in these years to reorganize the Evangelical church and make it more responsive to its congregations, and ironically, it was these efforts which finally led to Falk's dismissal by the king in 1879. All of the popularity and support which Falk won from liberal circles could not make up for the lack of backing from the court and influential conservatives; only Bismarck's determination lent him security, and when the chancellor decided to change course, Falk's eclipse was inevitable.

That possibility still seemed remote in the summer of 1875 when Falk made a triumphant tour through the Rhineland. Cheering crowds and special deputations of teachers and members of the German Association (founded in response to the local Catholic associations) greeted him, and the *Oberbürgermeister* of Cologne gave him the honorary title of *Praeceptor Germaniae*. A poet composed verses to him in the local dialect, and many complimentary puns were made on his name.[33] Whether this welcome was given to the Noble Falcon because of his liberal educational reforms and his attempt to reorganize and democratize the Evangelical church or for the anti-Catholic campaign is not clear, but certainly there was little sign of public sympathy that year with the Catholic resistance.

32. Foerster, p. 240.
33. Ibid., pp. 284–85.

5
THE DISMANTLING OF THE *KULTURKAMPF*

The year 1875 marked the high point of the *Kulturkampf*. In February of that year the newspaper *Frankfurter Zeitung* published a list of fines, arrests, and other acts of enforcement, enumerating the arrests of 241 priests, 136 editors, 210 Center party members (in addition to those included in the first two categories) and 55 other persons; 20 confiscations of newspapers; 74 house searches; 103 expulsions and internments; and 55 dissolutions of meetings and organizations. Another source estimates that 989 parishes were without priests at the height of the controversy and numbers imprisonments at 225. Five Prussian bishoprics were vacant by judicial removal (archdioceses of Posen-Gnesen and Cologne, dioceses of Breslau, Münster, and Limburg) and four others were vacant where the bishop had died and had not been replaced (Fulda, Trier, Osnabrück, and Paderborn). Theology students had been reduced in number by one-half. The Vatican had sent apostolic delegates secretly into Germany to carry out essential functions in the vacated parishes, but this kind of clandestine operation not only could not fully compensate for the loss of the official clergy but also had resulted in constant tension and suspicion within the congregations.[1]

These deplorable consequences had had the predictable effect of strengthening Catholic unity and providing the moral armament of martyrdom. The Center was acquiring ever more electoral support and the Catholic press was taking full advantage of the situation to rally public opinion. Windthorst's masterly management of press and party had made him the undisputed leader of German Catholics. The *Kul-*

1. First set of figures from Bachem, 3:303; second set of figures from Schmidt-Volkmar, pp. 168–69; apostolic delegates from Anderson, p. 178.

turkampf had had the effect, however, of making the defense of church interests not only an important goal of the party but also, or so it seemed, its only goal, in contradiction to the original expectations of its founders. Bismarck on his part had feared the Center originally because of its potential role in the development of a truly parliamentary regime in Germany and because of its defense of dissident regional interests. Now, although the party made more use of parliamentary weapons than ever, these seemed to be used primarily in the defense of the church. If the *Kulturkampf* could be ended and the church appeased, there was a good chance that the party itself might lose its reason for existence, particularly if the peacemaking were accomplished by direct negotiation with the Vatican rather than through parliamentary action. On the other hand, if the party did not disintegrate, it might be won for the government if the religious issue were resolved. These considerations were certainly part of Bismarck's rationale for deciding to "dismantle" the *Kulturkampf*.

There were other reasons too. William I was becoming restless because of the continued activities of Minister Falk, not solely because of their proven effect on the Catholic church but also because of their threatened effect on the Evangelical church. He had already clashed with Falk and was likely to insist upon his resignation and replacement by a man of more conservative outlook. Bismarck would then be obliged either to direct the continuation of the anti-Catholic campaign himself, a distasteful prospect, or to accede to its modification.

In addition, the government's decision to abandon a free-trade policy for the Reich in favor of a move toward protective tariffs was certain to lose it the parliamentary support of many in the liberal parties and thus to make the support of the Center essential. In 1876, Windthorst had introduced a motion in the Reichstag to extend the duties on pig iron, which were due to be phased out in that year. Although the motion failed, it had impressed Bismarck with the possibility of future Center cooperation on this issue.

To be dependent on the liberal parties was burdensome in other ways as well. If the *Kulturkampf* gave Bismarck opportunity to distract liberals from their concern with parliamentarization, it also gave them opportunity to distract the chancellor from his program. Bennigsen's compromise proposal for the septennate for the army budget in

April 1874 might not have proved acceptable to Bismarck if he had not needed liberal votes for the punitive May Laws of that year.[2]

Finally, if foreign policy considerations had been important in Bismarck's decision to begin the struggle, they were no longer relevant. Of the two Catholic adversaries of 1871, republican France had by 1879 begun its own anticlerical campaign with the passage of the Laic Laws, and Austria-Hungary was engaged in negotiations for an alliance with Germany, which would be aided by a modification of the *Kulturkampf*. Russia had not responded as favorably as Bismarck had hoped to the course of events in Prussia and was attempting to work out a *rapprochement* with the Catholic church in Russian Poland. Even antipapal Italy could by this time be kept within the German orbit without this particular bond, and all his efforts to engage Italy in a direct conflict with the Vatican in conjunction with Prussia had ended in failure.

Even before Bismarck initiated a reconciliation in Prussia, the government of Baden had begun steps to end the conflict there, thus providing a model for the larger state to follow as it had in the opening stages of the *Kulturkampf*. In Baden, it was Grand Duke Frederick, son-in-law of Empress Augusta, who wearied of the campaign. He had not liked the severity of the Prussian laws and was worried about the effects of the Old Catholic law and other legislation upon the social and political stability of his state. He planned to dismiss Jolly and hoped to prevent the passage of a liberal bill for obligatory *Simultanschulen*, but he found, as Jolly had, that liberal pressure on this issue was too strong to withstand. Consequently the school bill became law, but Jolly was asked to resign in September 1876. His successor was also an anticlerical with ties to the National Liberal majority in the lower house but was committed to a modification of the conflict. After 1876, parish churches were no longer made available to Old Catholics and the *Kulturexamen* was removed by 1880, resulting in the filling of 416 vacant parishes. The grand duke made some attempt to mediate between Prussia and the Vatican, but was frustrated in this by Bismarck.[3]

The death of Pius IX in February 1878 and the accession of the

2. Anderson, p. 187.
3. Becker, pp. 346–68.

conciliatory Leo XIII were the determining events which began the slow retreat of the Prussian government. On the day of his election, Leo sent a friendly message to William I. William's answer included a frigid request that the new pope advise German Catholics to obey the law, but he was nevertheless impressed with the gesture and with later marks of favor from Leo, such as a note of sympathy after the attempted assassination of June 1878 and congratulations on his golden wedding anniversary in the following year.

These early overtures and the negotiations that summer between Bismarck and the papal nuntius in Munich were unproductive because the Vatican asked a return to the legal status of the years before 1870 and, specifically, a restoration of the Prussian constitutional guarantees; whereas Bismarck wanted to keep the existing legal status and ameliorate the position of the church through administrative "discretionary powers" in enforcing the laws. Neither side consulted the Center leadership, and there was a coolness between Rome and the party because of the latter's refusal to vote for the law against the Social Democrats in 1878 and its cooperation with Social Democrats in some districts in the Reichstag elections of that year. By mutual agreement between the Vatican and Bismarck, the Center party was to be excluded from participation in the bargaining throughout the dismantling period.[4]

The nuncio, Aloisi-Masella, seems to have accepted Bismarck's explanation of the origin of the conflict as an aggressive attack by the Center party and the Polish clergy upon the Prussian government. He and the state secretaries at the Vatican paid little attention to lengthy messages from Windthorst and Franckenstein explaining the situation in Germany. Aloisi and Leo XIII did not see the conflict as one of constitutional principle, as the Center's leaders did. Efforts at mediation were made by Archbishop Melchers of Cologne and the democratic Reichstag deputy Canon Moufang, both of whom described Bismarck as insincere and his government as repressive, but Aloisi remained distrustful of the Center and would not sanction any legislative efforts. Windthorst then traveled to Vienna to talk with the papal nuncio there, Ludovico Jacobini, in order to find out the Vatican's priorities so that he could draft a bill expressing them and fight for it in the House

4. Lill, p. 236.

in full publicity. His arguments were ignored and he was told simply to press for total repeal of the *Kulturkampf* laws and to refrain from parliamentary maneuvers.[5]

Although the Center was thus to be excluded from the slow-moving negotiations ending the *Kulturkampf*, Bismarck did not wish to exclude the party from his plans to alter the economic policies of the Reich, plans which depended upon the Center's support. He opened this separate campaign in May 1879 by inviting Windthorst to his parliamentary soiree, and all Berlin was astonished to hear of the exchange of pleasantries and the drinking of May wine by the two antagonists. The matter of tariffs was probably not touched upon that evening but had been broached earlier, in March. The platform of the Center had never been free-trading, and its influential agrarian wing strongly favored a return to a protectionist policy, so that Windthorst's decision to vote for the tariff bill was not, as suggested by liberal critics, a "deal" undertaken in exchange for concessions in the *Kulturkampf* but a genuine following of party interest. Moreover, the insertion of the "Franckenstein clause" in the tariff bill, providing that any surplus revenue would revert to the individual states, was a victory for the federalist program of the Center. Nevertheless, the atmosphere was favorable for proceeding with concessions in the religious field, and the resignation of Falk in the same month as the passage of the tariff bill was universally believed to be Bismarck's token of gratitude to Windthorst.

Falk had been in continuing difficulties with the king since 1877 because of his attempts to reorganize the Evangelical church and his support of the new Protestant Union, which William considered to be a hotbed of radicalism.[6] Falk's new constitution for the Evangelical church gave it a unified structure for the eight older Prussian provinces, though not for the whole of the state, and introduced a far greater degree of congregational self-government. This entailed a weakening of the old patronage system which had given much influence to the local aristocracy and ultimately to the king. William protested several times to Falk about these changes and was also incensed when the minister overruled him and denied seats on the church ad-

5. Ibid., pp. 246–76.
6. Foerster, pp. 372–73.

ministrative council (*Oberkirchsregierungsrat*, or OKR) to the king's court chaplains Adolf Stöcker and Rudolf Kögel. Falk actually submitted his resignation on this issue as early as May 1878.

Just at this time, William was attacked by a would-be assassin. He asked Falk to withdraw his resignation, expecting that the attack would help the minister to see the connection between Protestant reform and red revolution which was so clear to him.[7] However, the quarrel over the OKR appointments continued, and Falk might well have been obliged to resign that year had it not been for the fact of the king's being seriously wounded in a second shooting and unable to carry on government business for some months; the regent, acting for him, was Crown Prince Frederick, who was friendly with Falk and approved of his policies. Falk's relations with Bismarck seem to have remained good until the conversations between the chancellor and Windthorst in the spring of 1879. Falk agreed to resign as early as May but postponed a public announcement until July in order not to detract from the king's golden wedding celebration. He did not oblige Bismarck by becoming inconspicuous after his departure from office but continued to defend his former policies while sitting as a member of the two legislatures.[8]

Whether or not Falk's departure was part of a definite bargain between Bismarck and Windthorst, it was certainly taken to be one by both liberal and Catholic observers. It was not immediately followed by further steps of reconciliation. But Falk's successor as *Kultus* minister, Robert von Puttkamer (a family connection of Bismarck's), was a conservative man who put a stop to any further consolidation of denominational schools into simultaneous schools and interpreted the educational supervision regulations in a less rigid way than Falk had done. Priests began again to give religious instruction in Catholic schools everywhere except in Posen. Puttkamer's policies in this respect were continued by the next minister, Gustav von Gossler. Liberal academics like Professors Rudolf Gneist, Rudolf Virchow, and Heinrich von Sybel, active *Kulturkämpfer* earlier, protested the change in the spirit of the laws, but the new course was approved by

---

7. Ibid., pp. 474–75.
8. Ibid., pp. 635–37. Michael Stürmer, pp. 265–79, believes that Falk's resignation, like that of the ministers of agriculture and finance, was necessitated by the shift away from liberalism at the time of the tariff law.

the *Landtag*. William's court chaplain Stöcker and other Evangelical Conservatives joined the Center in upholding Puttkamer and Gossler.

That same summer of 1879, negotiations between Bismarck and the Vatican continued in Vienna, carried on by Prince Reuss, the Prussian ambassador to Austria-Hungary, and State Secretary Jacobini, soon to be made a cardinal. (Bismarck had suggested the possibility of a papal nuncio being assigned to Berlin, but Windthorst had rejected the idea as a further encroachment upon the Center's sphere of action.) The Vienna talks resulted in continued stalemate, for the most part, but did persuade Leo XIII to concede the *placet* for certain lower positions in the clergy, which were at first not precisely defined. Windthorst was greatly distressed to learn of the pope's concession; he excitedly offered his resignation, exclaiming that he had been "shot down!" and tried to prevent publication of the news in *Germania* while he appealed urgently for a retraction.[9] Leo XIII not only did not retract his concession but promised more extensive application of the *placet* if specific demands of the church were met: for example, the reinstatement of the deposed bishops and priests. Bismarck responded with the first of three "modification laws" (*Milderungsgesetzen*). These laws did not alter the May Laws, but did give consistency and legislative sanction to the discretionary powers already being exercised by the government in modifying the effect of the May Laws.

The first modification bill was passed by the Conservatives with the help of a number of National Liberals, after a struggle within the ranks of the latter party. The Center had offered amendments and revisions, but when these had been rejected, its delegation voted against the bill. Windthorst did not believe that the modification law was sufficient reward for the pope's concession. In opposing the bill he was criticized by some of the more conservative Centrists, notably by August Reichensperger (soon to retire, to Windthorst's relief). The Center press was more sympathetic to the party's stand, and the *Kölnische Volkszeitung* called the use of "discretionary powers" an inadequate and unreliable remedy.[10]

In spite of its rejection of the modification law, the entire Center

9. Schmidt-Volkmar, p. 260; Bachem, 4:413; Lill, pp. 694–97.
10. Lill, pp. 697–704.

fraction was probably happy to see it passed, but the party continued to oppose the government's policies by refusing, in the next few months, to support either the renewal of the law against the Social Democrats or the septennate for the army budget. Bismarck had hoped that the Vatican's urgings would have prevented this; he never ceased to hope, against experience, that the Center would pay as much attention to the interests of Rome as its liberal opponents accused it of doing. As he wrote to Prince Reuss in April 1880: "Of what use to us is the theoretical position of the Roman See against the Socialists, when the Catholic fraction in the state, while loudly avowing its devotion to the will of the pope, gives public assistance in all its votes to the Socialists, as [it does] to every other subversive tendency?"[11]

Windthorst had several reasons for this continuing intransigence. First, he and his followers opposed the anti-Socialist law and the septennate on real, substantive party principle. Exceptional legislation like the anti-Socialist law was a contradiction of the civil rights guarantees that the Center supported, and really had to support, in its own interests. Windthorst objected to the septennate because the Reichstag was thereby deprived of its proper role in finances. A number of Centrists did not entirely agree with his position on these measures, but his leadership prevailed. Second, tactical considerations certainly reinforced these voting patterns and led to the rejection of the modification law. Windthorst hoped to achieve the repeal of the May Laws, not their amelioration. Third, though this can only be surmised, Windthorst was probably concerned to maintain a clear, independent line separating party political action from papal authority, for the survival of the party as a political force was as much at stake now as in its first years of existence. "Discretionary action" on the part of the government was no substitute for an active parliamentary defense of Catholic interests, and any change in attitude by the ministry could reverse the favorable trend without any recourse, as Windthorst repeatedly explained to State Secretary Jacobini. The death of William I and accession to the throne of the crown prince might well result in the dismissal of Puttkamer and the reversal of the ameliorative policy. Jacobini was urged to take to Rome assurances of the Center's loyalty

11. Bachem, 4:9; see also Lill, pp. 705–8.

and its anti-Socialist convictions and to plead for recognition of the party's need for complete independence.[12] Seven years later, Windthorst's view of the nature of the relationship between party and Vatican was to triumph in the struggle over the next septennate bill.

The mood in the two legislatures, the Prussian *Landtag* and the Reichstag, changed rapidly in the early 1880s and the deputies themselves showed a greater willingness to take steps to undo their previous work than was shown by either Bismarck or the Federal Council. In 1882 and again in 1884 the Reichstag voted to annul the Expatriation Law of May 1874 (the motion being rejected on both occasions by the Federal Council) and the following year supported a Conservative resolution urging an "organic revision of the May legislation." During the 1882 debate, a Progressive deputy, Dr. Albert Hänel, representing the wing of his party which remained faithful to the anticlerical position, made reference to the changed atmosphere:

> At that time . . . [in the 1870's] it was considered necessary, correct and patriotic, yes, even a condition of being acceptable in higher society, that a person *"kulturkampfed"* (laughter); you had to categorically support, blindly, all demands which the government, the Conservatives, made in connection with church legislation, or else you were politically somewhat disreputable. Gentlemen, what is it like now? Now . . . I am continually asking myself, for heaven's sake, just who really were the *Kulturkämpfer* at that time? Now all of a sudden no one wants to have been one (laughter). And if you ask somebody, "yet, didn't you make *Kulturkampf* speeches at that time?" he says "that's true, but privately I always said, nothing can come of the *Kulturkampf"* (much laughter).[13]

Perhaps partly to forestall independent legislative initiative, the Prussian government re-created the post of ambassador to the Vatican and appointed to it Kurt von Schlözer, a close friend of Bismarck's and an experienced diplomat. Schlözer's arrival in Rome was promptly followed by the government's second modification bill, of May 1882, extending the temporary provisions of 1880 and in addition allowing discretion in the application of the examination requirements for clergy.

---

12. Lill, pp. 714–22.
13. *Verhandlungen des Reichstags* 57 (12 Jan. 1882): 562–63.

This law, which was reluctantly supported by the Center in fear that it might not otherwise pass, also suspended the necessity for the *placet* temporarily, in order to permit the naming of bishops to empty dioceses. Its provisions were continued and extended in the third modification law of July 1883.

Several important bishoprics had been filled even before 1882: Limburg and Münster (by the return of the former incumbents), Osnabrück, Paderborn, Trier, and Fulda. Funds were released for all dioceses except Posen-Gnesen. The filling of the Trier post was a considerable victory for the Vatican, as William I consented to the naming of Michael Felix Korum, a French-speaking Alsatian of anti-Prussian reputation. The choice for Fulda, Bishop Georg Kopp, was also significant, as he was to play an important role in the dismantling of the *Kulturkampf.* The most difficult cases to settle were those of Archbishop Melchers of Cologne and Archbishop Ledochowsky of Posen-Gnesen, whose reinstatement would not be tolerated by the Prussian government. Leo XIII defended them for some time but finally indicated his acceptance of their permanent exclusion by appointing Ledochowsky (cardinal since 1875) as secretary of papal briefs in Rome, in 1881, and similarly calling Melchers to Rome as a resident cardinal in 1885. Bishop Krementz of Ermland was then named archbishop of Cologne. This came five years too late for the solemn ceremony held at the completion of the construction of the cathedral, which was carried out without the presence of an archbishop and, indeed, with very little Catholic participation of any kind.

Posen-Gnesen proved to be the most obstinate problem because Leo understandably wanted to appoint a Polish candidate, but the Prussian ministry rejected thirteen Polish names one after the other. The pope eventually approved a German for the post, Julius Dinder, a man who knew some Polish but did not succeed in winning the confidence of the local population.[14]

The new mood of reconciliation in the legislatures was evident in 1881 when Georg, Freiherr von Franckenstein, of the Bavarian Center was elected first vice-president of the Reichstag, the first time that the

---

14. Lech Trzeciakowski, "The Prussian State and the Catholic Church in Prussian Poland, 1871–1914," *Slavic Review* 26 (1967): 628–32; Wahl, 2:237; Bachem, 4:79.

position had been won by a Centrist. Bismarck and Franckenstein worked amicably together, but the chancellor's hopes of dividing the party by appealing to its right wing (Franckenstein, Schorlemer-Alst, and the Reichenspergers) and of replacing Windthorst in the leadership, were not realized.

In 1884, Franckenstein led a large minority of the fraction in voting for the extension of the anti-Socialist law. Windthorst as spokesman for the majority of the Center, continued to argue as he had on numerous occasions earlier, that the law constituted "exceptional legislation" of the same type used against Catholic clergy and was thus unacceptable to the Center. It is possible that the split on the vote may have been deliberately planned in order to ensure the bill's passage and so avoid a serious confrontation with Bismarck.[15] Certainly the party was relieved to be able to support with good conscience the chancellor's social insurance laws of the 1880s. Bismarck's new sponsorship of government action to solve the social problem was far more congenial than his previous commitment to liberal laissez faire principles.

Catholic social policy since the beginning of modern machine industry in Germany had been motivated by feelings of repudiation of capitalism and Manchester School liberalism. In the early part of the century the only remedies proposed were those of private charity and the work of men like Adolf Kolping, the founder of the Catholic journeymen's associations. The real transition to modern solutions for modern problems occurred in the 1860s with the writings and exhortations of Bishop von Ketteler. Ketteler's concern was originally confined to voluntary work among industrial laborers and the attempt not only to protect them from the exploitative effects of capitalism but also to educate them to form an independent, self-reliant *Stand* in society. His ideas were first set forth in his book *Die Arbeiterfrage und das Christentum* (1864).

By the end of the 1860s, Ketteler had come to realize that voluntary action was not sufficient, and he began to urge the passage of laws regulating working hours and conditions and granting Sunday rest, with state inspection to enforce them. He also recommended the for-

15. John K. Zeender, *The German Center Party, 1890–1906* (Philadelphia, 1976), p. 11. For a contrary view, see Anderson, p. 462, n. 52.

mation of workers' cooperatives and other associations, although stopping short of advocating actual labor unions. His later views were incorporated in the book *Die Katholiken im Deutschen Reich* of 1873.

The Center party delegations in the legislatures of the newly formed German Reich were too much concerned with the pressing problems of unification, the Roman question, and the advent of the *Kulturkampf* to devote much attention to social problems in the early 1870s. Windthorst himself was not inclined to take a personal interest in the subject, and he delegated it to other members of the party. In the 1880s he persuaded two rather unlikely men, the young intellectual priest Franz von Hitze, and the university professor Georg von Hertling, to become the Center's *Sozialpolitiker*. Hertling transferred his interest in later years more to academic and political matters, but Hitze became a dedicated speaker, writer, and organizer in the Catholic social movement.

The party's first venture into practical legislation for social reform was in 1877 when Count von Galen brought the first motion for workers' protection to the Reichstag. There was some existing Reich legislation limiting child labor, derived from earlier Prussian state laws, but there was need for additional protection. The Center's motion included most of Ketteler's program: for Sunday rest, the raising of the legal age limit for work from twelve to fourteen years, and protective measures for female workers; it also recommended the establishment of corporative organizations for industry, reminiscent of the guild system so recently ended in Germany. Perhaps because of the latter provision, and the insistence on Sunday rest, the motion was labeled "medieval" by liberals and Social Democrats (who were, however, inspired to produce motions of their own on the subject).

This first motion was not passed by the house, although it found some support among the Conservatives. The following year, a similar Center motion was passed by the Reichstag and again in 1882, 1884, and virtually every year after that. Until Bismarck's resignation, the matter got no further than the Reichstag. Bismarck justified his refusal to sanction protective legislation of this sort by claiming that it would be impossible to enforce and that it would be a financial imposition upon industry. In 1884, when the motion was made, he challenged the Center to explain how the reforms were to be implemented without "killing the hen that lays the eggs."[16] The motion was buried in committee, but the party's efforts did lead to an investigation by the Reichstag into the actual conditions of labor in the country.

Bismarck presented his own solution to the social problem with the series of insurance laws carried through between 1884 and 1889. The Center had some reservations at first: for example, the party did not favor extension of the provisions to agricultural workers, claiming that a "patriarchal relationship" was still existent on the land and would be disturbed by the insurance program. The party also objected to the compulsory nature of the provisions and worked to amend the bills for sickness and accident insurance to eliminate direct state subsidies and to provide for administration of the laws by local rather than national institutions.[17] Reservations and revisions notwithstanding, the Center in the final readings voted for all of the insurance laws. The chancellor on his part reciprocated the gesture by taking further steps toward ending the religious conflict, though without altering his stand against parliamentary initiative in this matter.

Bismarck's brilliantly creative decision, at the end of 1885, to ask Leo XIII to mediate in the Caroline Islands dispute between Spain and Germany is often credited with leading the dismantling of the *Kulturkampf* into a more productive stage. Certainly the pope was pleased to be addressed as a reigning head of state on this occasion, and he presented Bismarck with an impressive decoration. William reciprocated by awarding Cardinal-State Secretary Jacobini with the Order of the Black Eagle. But equal credit should be given Bishop Kopp of Fulda who was named to the Prussian House of Lords in 1886 and thenceforth became chief mediator between the government and the Curia. Kopp's role was clearly intended by Bismarck to move the negotiations to the legislative arena while still continuing to bypass Windthorst and the Center party.

Kopp's outlook was far more accommodating than Windthorst's, and he set to work determined that concessions be made on both sides. This involved the sacrifice of many of Windthorst's hopes, and he did not hesitate to criticize the "peace laws" inaugurated by Kopp. Many disappointed Centrists protested the elevation of Kopp to archbishop

---

16. *Verhandlungen des Reichstags* 73 (15 Jan. 1884): 630–32.
17. Bachem, 4:99–100.

of Breslau in 1887, calling him a "court-Catholic" and "state-Catholic," and succeeded in delaying, but not preventing, the appointment.[18]

The result of Kopp's labors was the drawing-up of the first of two peace laws, which went beyond the "discretionary powers" formula and made concrete revisions of the May Laws, eliminating the examination for the clergy, allowing full use of the seminaries, abolishing the special clerical courts, in addition to other minor changes. After the bill had been assured of passage in the House of Lords, Leo XIII responded by granting the full *Anzeigepflicht*, or *placet* (with some reservations, removed two months later in an effort to win acceptance of the bill in the lower house). This was the concession most desired by Bismarck in order to avoid the accusation that the Prussian government had arrived at Canossa. It was regretted by Windthorst and many of the German bishops, who expressed their disappointment at the Fulda Bishops' Conference in August 1886.[19]

The Prussian lower house passed the first peace law in May 1886 by a vote of 280 to 180, the National Liberals opposing but the Free Conservatives and Progressives both split on the issue. Windthorst did not feel that the benefits of the Peace Law, which the Center unenthusiastically supported, needed in any way to be "paid for" by the party's future backing of government measures, and he made this clear a few months later during Reichstag committee discussions of the new septennate for the military budget. While conceding to the government "every man and every penny" that it requested for the army, Center members of the committee voted to recommend a bill granting the money for three years instead of seven, and the Reichstag then approved this change, infuriating the chancellor, who denounced what he called a "Polish majority" and precipitously dissolved the Reichstag on 14 January 1887.

Bismarck was angry because he had obtained a promise of assistance from the Vatican in securing the passage of the septennate and had expected it to deliver the Center's vote. Cardinal-State Secretary Jacobini had sent a note, dated January 3, informing the Center of the pope's wish that the (unamended) bill be passed. The famous note (actually composed, according to one source, by State Secretary Luigi

18. Rudolf Morsey, "Georg Kardinal Kopp," in Rudolf Morsey, ed., *Zeitgeschichte in Lebensbildern* (Mainz, 1973), pp. 17–18.
19. Schmidt-Volkmar, pp. 313; 321–22.

Galimberti, a more worldly and less sympathetic personality than Jacobini)[20] was sent to the papal nuncio in Munich, who passed it on to Franckenstein, the party's fraction head. Franckenstein revealed its contents only to Windthorst and the Centrist members of the budget committee, not to the other members of the fraction or the party press.[21]

Franckenstein replied to the note, explaining the party's action in opposing the septennate and asking if the Holy See believed that the existence of the Center party was still necessary; that if it did not, then he and his colleagues would resign their seats, but that if a party was to exist, it must make its own political decisions. Jacobini (or Galimberti for him) then sent a second note, dated January 20, assuring the Center of its continuing importance and of its freedom to act independently as a political party—but again asking for its support for the septennate after the Reichstag elections. Jacobini was very ill at this time and died in February. Galimberti took over the cardinal's post temporarily. He was at home in court circles, friendly to Bismarck, but not to Windthorst, and it was presumably through him that Bismarck came to know of the content of the second note, which was leaked to the press and published in the Rhineland area on February 4, in the midst of the election campaign.

The campaign had opened with much angry rhetoric on both sides, with the Boulanger adventure in France providing the government with an effective propaganda weapon against the "unpatriotic" opposition. The Center was again attacked on the old grounds of being pro-Alsatian, pro-Polish, collaborator with Social Democrats, and in general, a danger to the fatherland. Some prominent Catholics publicly dissociated themselves from the Center and spoke in favor of the septennate. Windthorst was traveling by train to Cologne preparing to speak at the congress of the Rhenish Center party, when he was told of the publication of the second papal note. His eyes were too weak to make out the newspaper article himself, but he had it read aloud twice as he considered how to deal with this unexpected blow. His early excitement and threat of resignation were succeeded by a calm determination to transform disaster into triumph.[22]

20. Bachem, 4:166–68.
21. Mittmann, p. 153.
22. Hüsgen, p. 234.

The second note was actually far less damaging to Windthorst's position than the first would have been, if published at that time, because it contained words of praise and appreciation for the work of the Center party and acknowledged its political independence. Windthorst's masterful speech at the party congress stressed these points and only then tackled the main issue. He admitted that the pope wanted the septennate passed, but not because of the bill's contents, which did not properly concern him, but for tactical reasons. The Center party leadership, closer to the issue and better informed about it, had felt that these same tactical goals would be better achieved by opposition. This had been a clear case of its exercising that political independence which the pope himself had specifically acknowledged.[23]

The Rhinelanders applauded throughout the speech, which was surely the greatest of Windthorst's career, though something of a tour de force. The future of the Center as a political organization separate from church interests was assured on that day. Although the election results brought a great increase of support for government candidates, the Center delegation lost only one seat, and the total number of its votes actually increased slightly.

Both the liberal and the conservative press criticized the "disloyalty" of Catholic politicians to their religious leader, and Windthorst was dubbed the "Guelph antipope" by one liberal paper, the *Kölnische Zeitung*. Yet unquestioning obedience to the pope had been a supposed characteristic of the Center condemned by opponents as a fatal flaw in that party's makeup; a papal note urging opposition to a government measure would have called forth equal indignation, as it had in the days of Pius IX.

After this climactic scene in Cologne, there was a prolonged debate within the party leadership as to whether or not the party should persist in opposing the septennate, and whether it should approve, reject, or try to amend the proposed bill for a second peace law, which appeared to be the government's final offer for a settlement. The election results had guaranteed Bismarck his majority for the septennate, and most of the party's leaders felt that continued opposition would not only be futile but would look like a calculated flouting of the pope's wishes. Similarly, the conservative wing led by Schorlemer-Alst

23. Ibid., pp. 235–41. The entire text of the speech is reproduced here.

and the Reichenspergers urged acceptance of the peace law without objections or amendments. The Center therefore abstained in the Reichstag vote on the septennate (with seven deputies including Peter Reichensperger actually voting for it) and supported the Prussian peace law. This law repealed several more sections of the May Laws, most importantly those forbidding the activities of the contemplative religious orders, and marked the final legislative dismantling of the *Kulturkampf* in Prussia.

Windthorst had represented the minority on both issues and remained bitterly disappointed that the chance was now lost for restoring the protective clauses in the constitution and for repealing the Reich's anti-Jesuit law. He was not cheered by the pope's solemn declaration in May 1887 that the *Kulturkampf* was officially ended. To him it was not ended unless the status quo ante were restored. Bishop Kopp's method of compromise and conciliation had achieved a great deal; it will never be certain whether Windthorst's method of continued intransigence could have accomplished more.

Thus it was the church hierarchy, and not the Catholic political party, which brought the struggle to a close, but the strength and determination of the party had been a powerful factor in Bismarck's decision to conclude a peace.

A judgment on church-state relations after the conclusion of the *Kulturkampf* would give the final victory to the church, although its position was never again so favorable as in Prussia in the years before 1870. State supervision of the public schools, civil marriage, and easy withdrawal from church membership were permanent realities, not even challenged in the Weimar period. Several other laws remained in force until the end of the Second Reich: some parts of the anti-Jesuit law, in spite of persistent attempts to repeal it; the law for the administration of the finances of Catholic parishes (*Vermögungsgewaltunggesetz*) and the *Anzeigepflicht*. The religious orders remained somewhat restricted until 1918 (no male orders were permitted in Posen or in East or West Prussia, for example). Other laws remained on the books but were either no longer enforced or became dead letters: the "pulpit paragraph," the Expatriation Law (repealed in 1890,) the law for the administration of vacant bishoprics, the Old Catholic law. Many buildings and funds appropriated by the Old Catholics were returned to the church. The Catholic *Feldpropst* was reinstated in 1888. The constitutional guarantees were never restored but were replaced by similar guarantees in the constitution of the Weimar republic.

Altogether the permanent legacy of the liberal program was meager, strikingly so when compared with the anticlerical successes in France and Italy. State financial support of the church, the denominational school system, and religious instruction in the schools survived unimpaired to the end of the empire and through both world wars.

However, the poisoned atmosphere between Protestants and Catholics engendered by the *Kulturkampf* was unfortunately not dissipated by the favorable peace settlement but continued well into the twentieth century, moderating only after the events of the National Socialist regime produced an altered German consciousness in this as in so many matters. In 1886, at the time when the Prussian government was abandoning its anti-Catholic policy, Prussian Protestants were forming the Evangelical League "for the defense of German Protestant interests" against "false parity and tolerance concepts" to bring "more light into the Roman darkness which still lies over fully a third of our people."[24] The league took an active part in election campaigns and other aspects of public life both under the empire and in the Weimar republic. Catholic counterattack began with the formation of the *Volksverein für das katholische Deutschland* in 1890, conceived by Windthorst as not only a defensive propaganda organization but as a much broader social and educational agency. Integration of Catholics into German national life proceeded steadily but slowly, with frequent rearguard clashes between the denominations in the years after the old antagonisms of the Reformation had been so unnecessarily revived.

Several recent historians of the *Kulturkampf* have pointed out basic divisions and contradictions in the forces behind the anti-Catholic campaign.[25] On the one hand, there was a conservative attempt to strengthen and extend the Prussian concept of state supremacy and control, already existing for the Evangelical church, to the Catholic church; and on the other hand there was a liberal attempt to introduce the separation of church and state and the ideal of a secular society.

24. Kupisch, p. 78.
25. For example, Heinrich Bornkamm, "Die Staatsidee im Kulturkampf," 2 pts., *Historische Zeitschrift* 170 (1950): 41–72; 273–306; and Franz, *Kulturkampf.*

The two forces could ally only in negative acts of repression and punishment but could never agree upon a positive solution to the problem of state-church relationship.

Within each camp, moreover, there were internal contradictions. The conservative view entailed a belief in the necessity of a Christian society, yet the specific repressive legislation clearly undermined the importance of religion in education and community life. The liberals on their part fought in the cause of enlightenment and the free development of the individual, yet they were led through this same legislation to most illiberal restriction of freedom and the imposition of stringent state controls. Paradoxically, the Catholic forces during the course of the struggle were able to appear more conservative than the conservatives in their principles and more liberal than the liberals in their actions.

In the political sphere, the *Kulturkampf* unquestionably had an injurious effect upon the development of responsible parliamentary government in Germany. This may well have been Bismarck's primary intention in his promotion of the campaign, since he by no means agreed with the anticlerical doctrines of the liberal parties. The example of Baden, where Jolly successfully staved off transition to parliamentary rule by stirring up the passions of both clericals and anticlericals and deflecting them from political issues, must certainly have influenced Bismarck. A recent historian comments: "The chancellor imagined himself a 'political chessplayer,' 'holding together the divergent inclinations of the liberal parties in the Reich by means of a slogan appealing to wide circles, a sort of outcry against popery,' in order to corrupt liberalism, the strongest parliamentary force, through the *Kulturkampf* and to divert it from its constitutional-political goals."[26] The game proved to be equally corrupting for the Center, because it permanently alienated Catholic parliamentary forces from those parties which might have become, and had been in the past, their natural allies. For the next forty-six years, the wedge driven between Catholics and liberals during the *Kulturkampf* continued to make cooperation difficult among the parties of the middle.

26. Becker, pp. 375–76; see also Stürmer, "Konservatismus und Revolution in Bismarcks Politik," in Stürmer, ed., *Das kaiserliche Deutschland: Politik und Gesellschaft 1870–1918* (Düsseldorf, 1970), p. 149.

6
THE CENTER PARTY ORGANIZATION
BEFORE 1914

The events of the year 1887 determined that the Center party was not an appendage of the Catholic church but an independent organization which could survive and flourish even in a time of peace between church and state. The *Kulturkampf* was ended, yet the Center continued to grow, becoming the largest party in the national and Prussian legislatures until 1912. It should be said, however, that conditions of adversity for the Catholic population of Germany had by no means been ended by the conclusion of the *Kulturkampf,* and that the party derived great strength from a defensive position. The much more satisfactory legal and social status obtained in the Weimar republic had a detrimental effect upon the party's unity and support and contributed indirectly to its final dissolution in 1933.

Ludwig Windthorst continued to lead the party after his triumph of 1887 and lived to see the fall of Bismarck. After his death in March 1891, the Center never again had a single leader of the sort that he had been; the only man who attained even comparable status was Heinrich Brüning, under very different circumstances. For many years before the First World War the party suffered acutely from a lack of any strong central leadership, partly because of a propensity of its politicians to regard their work in Berlin as part-time and to spend long periods of time in their home districts. A very high proportion of Reichstag delegates were also members of state legislatures and lived in their home states, or home provinces in Prussia, rather than in Berlin. The still rudimentary organization of the party could not overcome this centrifugal tendency.

For a long time the Center continued its tradition of choosing an aristocrat as titular head of the Reichstag fraction, and this was another handicap in developing effective central leadership, as these men were neither the most able nor the most representative of the membership. Until his death in 1890, the fraction was headed by the Bavarian Count Franckenstein, whose most useful contribution was the formation of closer bonds between the Bavarian and the national Center. His successor in 1890 was the wealthy Silesian landowner and industrialist Count Ballestrem, a member of the extreme right wing of the party, who resigned from the post in 1893 as a protest against the party's rejection of the Caprivi military budget. He later rejoined the fraction and also served as president of the Reichstag from 1898 to 1906. He presided over the house with impartial dignity, even to the extent of ignoring the Center's interests,[1] and led a special memorial service on the occasion of Bismarck's death. It is difficult to realize that this same Count Ballestrem, now an accepted and conventional figure of the Reich, had been imprisoned in 1873 for his ardor in electioneering for the Center and had created a sensation in the Reichstag for shouting "Pfui!" at Bismarck in a particularly heated debate during the *Kulturkampf.*

The Center lost the presidency of the Reichstag after the 1907 elections and Ballestrem retired at that time. His successor as fraction head in 1893 was Count Hompesch, a genial man who spent much of his time in convivial sessions at a convenient beer hall; this and his advanced age precluded any vigorous leadership from him. After his death at the age of eighty-two in 1909, the next fraction head was also a nobleman, Georg, Freiherr (later Count) von Hertling, a professor at the University of Munich, and an able man, but one who had never before spent much time on Berlin affairs. When Hertling left to become minister-president of Bavaria in 1912, the party for the first time chose a man of middle-class origins for head, Peter Spahn, a jurist from the Rhineland then serving as a higher court justice in Holstein, who held the office until 1917.

The Prussian *Landtag* fraction shows a similar pattern of noblemen holding the title of chairman, backed up by younger and more active colleagues of middle-class birth. Freiherr von Schorlemer-Alst was chairman until 1889 (clashing frequently with Windthorst); Klemens, Freiherr von Heeremann, held the office from 1889 to 1900.

The most effective politician in the party after Windthorst was not

1. Mittmann, p. 35.

any of the fraction chairmen, but Dr. Ernst Maria Lieber, member of both the Prussian and the national legislatures from 1871 until his death in 1902. Lieber was an outspoken democrat from Nassau, unforgivingly anti-Prussian, and actively concerned to reduce the influence of the landowning aristocracy in the party and keep it on the path favored by Windthorst. Lieber had more cosmopolitan interests than most Centrists; he traveled several times to the United States and was keenly interested in maintaining ties with overseas German Catholics there and in Germany's new colonies.[2] His particular specialty was finance.

When Lieber died, there was no single man in the party who possessed both the ability and the will to devote sufficient time to the task of leadership. The prominent figures of the next period, Hertling, Peter Spahn, Adolf Gröber, were all preoccupied with regional and professional concerns of their own. It was for this reason that the young, ambitious Matthias Erzberger, living in Berlin and occupied solely with politics and political journalism, managed to win such a following in the party in spite of total lack of sympathy from the official leadership.

Although the pre–World War I Center party is sometimes described as having been extraordinarily well organized and united, such unity as it possessed before the turn of the century was functional rather than organic. The Reichstag and *Landtag* fractions for many years provided the only contacts between the various local branches of the party. The party relied heavily on Catholic *Vereine* and on the clergy to rally votes. Choice of a candidate was left to temporary election committees in the voting districts, and the leadership of these committees was in the hands of local clergy and other notables, with no attempt at democratic representation; especially in rural districts the committees were run in patriarchal fashion and nominations by the leadership were usually approved by acclamation. Once elected, a Reichstag or *Landtag* deputy could be certain of renomination, except in cases where the deputy departed radically from party policy, as in the "nationalist" secessions of 1887 and 1893. The party had a higher percentage of safe seats than any other in Wilhelmine Germany.[3]

2. Zeender, p. 23; Bachem, 5:330–32.
3. Thomas Nipperdey, *Die Organization der deutschen Parteien vor 1918* (Düsseldorf, 1961), pp. 266–74.

The southern branches of the party were earlier than the Prussian Center in creating state organizations to coordinate and direct these local committees, but here even the question of adopting the name of "Center" proved to be a controversial one, so that for a long time any further amalgamation of the state parties was impossible. The Bavarian Patriotic People's party changed its name to the Bavarian Center party after the septennate crisis of 1887 and, except for secession moves in 1893 and 1898, overcome by its leadership, remained closely linked with the national party fraction until after the war. In that state, the party leadership was an odd mixture of clergy, professors, noblemen, and farmers. The legal profession and the civil service, which provided by far the largest occupational group in the Prussian party leadership, were, in Bavaria, whether Catholic by birth or not, completely identified with the liberal ideology of the state government. (Minister von Lutz, who steadfastly opposed the Center and its program, was born a Catholic.) The Center's representation in the lower house of the Bavarian *Landtag* hovered for decades either at the frustrating halfway mark or at a bare majority, in spite of the large Catholic population in the state. Reapportionment of seats and a change in voting methods improved the position somewhat after 1906.

After the retirement of Eduard Jörg in 1881, the state party was headed by Dr. Balthasar Daller, a prelate of the church and a university professor, who held the office until 1911. Dr. Georg von Orterer, a teacher at a *gymnasium*, was prominent in both the state and national fractions. Dr. Franz Joseph Schädler, a priest and teacher, represented the Bavarian Palatinate, a less parochial region than the rest of the state, and was most active at the national level, providing a liaison between state and national parties. Dr. Georg Heim was the strident leader of the Bavarian Christian Farmers' Association (*Christliche Bauernverein*). He was a consistent advocate of separation of the Bavarian party from the national Center and led the secession move of 1893. After the war he accomplished his goal when he created the independent Bavarian People's party in a split from the Center which proved to be permanent.

At the other end of the social scale in the Bavarian party were the Franckensteins, father and son, Prince Karl zu Löwenstein, who eventually became a member of the Dominican order, and his son Aloys, hereditary member of the upper houses of Bavaria, Württemberg,

Baden, and Hesse-Darmstadt. In addition to their defense of particularist interests, the representatives of the Center from Bavaria were noted for their opposition to military, naval and colonial expenditures, and a fiercely protective attitude in all matters concerned with the production or sale of beer.

In Hesse, as in Bavaria, the Catholic People's party adopted the name of "Center" at the time of the septennate elections of 1887. No national personality after Bishop von Ketteler (who died in 1877) emerged from this state, where the party was of minimal influence.

In Baden and Württemberg, in contrast, the state parties were much later in joining the national organization and in building internal structures of their own. In Baden the cleric Franz Lender who had been one of the earliest and most radical defenders of Catholic interests in that liberal state had by the 1880s lost most of his combative spirit, and his Catholic People's party was virtually inactive. A younger, more militant priest, Theodor Wacker, accused Lender of oversubmissiveness toward the grand duke and his government and split the party leadership, causing further demoralization and eclipse in the next *Landtag* elections. In 1887, the Catholic People's party won only seven out of sixty-one seats in the *Landtag*, although the population of Baden was two-thirds Catholic, and the liberals swept all before them.

Windthorst was disturbed by this lack of activity in the state, where the legislation of the *Kulturkampf* survived almost intact, and he arranged that the annual German Catholic Congress be held in Freiburg in 1888. He gave a speech at the congress exhorting Baden Catholics to greater effort and suggesting ways of achieving particular goals: uniting the Catholic People's party with the Center, expanding the Catholic press in the state, finding suitable Protestant allies, and appealing to the grand duke's presumed practical desire for religious peace.[4] The two latter goals were never really attained, but a Baden Center party was organized in the months following the congress, and a number of Centrist newspapers were founded. Wacker reentered politics on the strength of these developments and served as head of the *Landtag* fraction from 1891 to 1903, modeling himself upon Windthorst. The Center's seats in the lower house rose to a maximum of

4. Bachem, 8:115–16.

twenty-three, and the party also captured a higher percentage of the twelve Reichstag seats from Baden.

Grand Duke Frederick, however, looked with suspicion on Father Wacker's activities, which seemed to introduce an unnecessary element of discord into the liberal monopoly which had prevailed so long, and his government put constant pressure upon the archbishop of Freiburg to disapprove the political agitation of his subordinate. Evidently this pressure was the reason for Wacker's suddenly resigning his *Landtag* seat in 1903. He continued as state party chairman, however, until his retirement in 1918. His successor in the *Landtag* fraction was Konstantin Fehrenbach, who later transferred most of his attention to the national party.

The role of the Center in Baden was largely one of unsuccessful opposition to the anticlerical liberal majority in the *Landtag* and government, and this was necessarily a conservative role; in Berlin politics these same Baden Centrists formed part of the party's more democratic wing.

The history of the Center in Württemberg is particularly instructive because it demonstrates how much the party depended for its existence upon a defensive position and a situation of adversity and conflict. Württemberg has been described as an oasis of calm amid the turbulent denominational strife and church-state conflicts of the rest of Germany. The *Kulturkampf* was never introduced there, and the Catholic population in the state lived peaceably with the three-quarters Protestant majority. Catholics were concentrated in the less-prosperous rural areas of the state; for many years they accepted the leadership of the dominant Progressive party.[5]

King Karl (1864–91) was sympathetic to Catholic interests and generous with financial arrangements for the church. The Protestant minister of religion and education was assisted by a Catholic Church Council (similar to the Catholic Department in Prussia abolished in 1871) which mediated between government and church. The lower house of the *Landtag* was liberal, as in Baden, but the upper house had a permanent majority of hereditary seats occupied by Catholic noble-

---

5. David Blackbourn, "The Political Alignment of the Centre Party in Wilhelmine Germany: A Study of the Party's Emergence in Nineteenth-Century Württemberg," *Historical Journal* 18 (1975): 821–50.

men, and the upper house had consistently made anticlerical legislation impossible. Catholics who were elected to seats in the lower house sat with various parties, most with the Progressives, or Democrats, but quite a few with the government State party.

No real reason existed for the creation of a specifically Catholic party, and much Catholic opinion in the state was opposed to the idea, including that of the influential Bishop Hefele of Rottenburg. With no perennial challenge like the state supremacy principle of Bavaria, the liberal bureaucracy of Baden, or the "Protestant Calling" of Prussia, Catholics had no incentive to separate political action.

A Württemberg Center was finally organized, but only after outside impetus was given by the national party, making use of an artificially inflated issue. As in Baden in 1888, the device was used of holding a Catholic Congress in Ulm in 1890. Huge crowds attended the *Land* Congress and were roused to enthusiasm over the issue of the continued prohibition of male religious orders in Württemberg. This was the only grievance to be found and seems to have been deliberately used to win public support for a new party. Rudolf Probst, formerly a prominent member of the Progressive-Democratic party, announced his support for a state Center organization (although he himself gave up politics shortly thereafter) and was seconded by an obstreperous young politician, Adolf Gröber, who had been sitting as an independent in the *Landtag* and had held a seat in the Reichstag since 1887.

The organizers were helped by the increasing discontent with the economic policies of the Progressives among the occupational groups in which Catholics predominated: the small farmers, artisans, and shopkeepers. The Center's defense of *Mittelstand* interests appealed to these groups in contrast to the consumerist program of the Progressives and the Social Democrats in the state. Pressures from the farmers, particularly, pushed the Center in later years more and more into partnership with the Württemberg Conservatives.[6]

After nearly three years of agitation, the official "founding day" of the new Württemberg Center party was 11 July 1894; in the next state elections it won eighteen of the sixty-three seats in the lower house.

6. Blackbourn, "Class and Politics in Wilhelmine Germany: the Center Party and the Social Democrats in Württemberg," *Central European History* 9 (1976): 232.

No progress at all had been made in obtaining permission for the male orders, but the issue had served its purpose.

All of the southern states had perfected their organizations before a state structure was completed for Prussia. The first real party apparatus in Prussia was in Cologne, put together at the end of the 1880s by Karl Trimborn and Carl Bachem, the future party historian. It was soon extended to the whole of the Rhine province, with Trimborn serving as its chairman for many years. In the Rhineland organization, large assemblies representing the election districts met to choose a committee which in turn elected a board of directors (*Vorstand*) for the province. Similar provincial organizations were created in the 1890s for Westphalia and Silesia. In Silesia the board of directors was chosen directly by the large assembly, without an intermediary body, and could also co-opt some of its members. Selection by the mass meeting tended to mean in practice approval of the local notables, the *Honoratioren*, by acclamation. The Rhineland party was thus slightly more democratic than the Silesian and open to influence from below, through the intermediary committees, which met twice a year, but the boards in all the provinces held the initiative and continued the patriarchal, rather authoritarian tradition of earlier years. The provincial boards took over the responsibility of choosing candidates, and very few candidates were nominated without their approval.[7]

Only after the difficult elections of 1907 were steps taken toward the formation of a Prussian State Committee, which was finally established in 1908 after a careful apportionment of power and positions among the particularist provincial organizations. Although the Rhineland, Westphalia, and Silesia naturally predominated, proportional representation on the State Committee was included for the tiny party branches of Hesse-Kassel, Nassau, Hanover, East Prussia, and (Prussian) Saxony. The presiding officers were also selected according to their regional affiliations: Felix Porsch, head of the *Landtag* fraction and of the Silesian party, became State Committee chairman, with Karl Herold of Westphalia and Karl Trimborn of the Rhineland as his deputies.

The Prussian party leadership had a relatively high proportion of

7. Nipperdey, pp. 269–70.

large landowners, not only in the honorary posts but in policy-making positions. Count Ballestrem and Count Praschma of Silesia, Count Galen and Count Landsberg of Westphalia, all held important posts for many years, and many Centrist nobles were succeeded almost in dynastic fashion by their sons (as for example the Ballestrems, Praschmas, Galens, and the Bavarian Franckensteins). Herold, though not a nobleman, was the owner of a large landed estate. The great Silesian magnates were in many ways the counterparts of the Polish aristocratic landowners who dominated the Polish party in the legislatures until after the turn of the century. Only in the Rhineland did nonaristocratic names predominate.

Within the state and local organizations of the Center, members of committees contributed fixed dues to help pay party expenses, and members of the boards of directors paid proportionately more, but the Center continued to obtain most of its financing from voluntary contributions from wealthy sympathizers (for example, Ballestrem, and Richard Müller).[8] In addition, the intricate network of auxiliary Catholic institutions affiliated with the party took care of many election expenses which might otherwise have been borne by the party itself. The Center complained frequently about the lack of stipends for Reichstag members, before they were introduced in 1906, but did not use party funds to support its own members.[9]

The need for a Reich organization became increasingly obvious in the years of the great controversy over the nature of the party, the *Zentrumsstreit* of 1907–14, but it took many years of negotiation before a National Committee was established. The chief obstacle to be overcome was the independence of the southern state parties and their fear of being dominated by the Prussian party. At the end of 1911, statutes were finally approved for a National Committee, but it was not until February 1914 that its first meeting actually took place. As in the Prussian organization, no region of the country was slighted, and some representation was given even to the states of Oldenburg and Saxony, where the number of Catholic voters was very small. Actually, in such areas, known in Germany as the Catholic "diaspora," the loy-

8. Ibid., p. 276.
9. Mittmann, pp. 24–25.

alty of Catholic voters to the Center was consistently much stronger than in areas of heavy Catholic population density, so that it was important that they not be neglected.

Peter Spahn, the head of the Reichstag fraction at that time, became first chairman of the National Committee, with Porsch of Prussia and Heinrich Held of Bavaria as his deputies.

In addition to its official party structure, so delayed in its development, the Center depended upon a number of affiliated leagues, clubs, associations, and a wide network of newspapers, all of which helped greatly in rallying voters during elections and in keeping the lines of communication open. The largest and most effective of the affiliated organizations was the *Volksverein für das katholische Deutschland*. This had been founded in 1890 with the intention that it should be a defensive and counterpropaganda weapon against the Evangelical League, but at the urging of Windthorst its mission was defined in much more positive and constructive terms. The bylaws of the *Volksverein* stated its object to be "the opposition of heresy and revolutionary tendencies in the social-economic world as well as the defense of the Christian order in society." This translated into the attempt to educate German Catholic workers in social and economic matters as well as religious so that they might better withstand the pressures of Social Democracy. The *Volksverein* was originally based in Mainz but after a few years found permanent headquarters in München-Gladbach (now spelled Mönchengladbach) near the heart of the Rhenish industrial complex. Among its other activities, the *Volksverein* gave a series of courses on the economy at its school in München-Gladbach. Although Windthorst was its first president, his role was largely an honorary one, and the actual direction was carried on by Franz Brandts, a factory owner, until his death in 1914. General director and most active leader was the cleric August Pieper.

The *Volksverein*'s largest membership was in the Rhineland and in the southern areas of mixed denominations, that is, in Baden, Württemberg, and the Bavarian Palatinate; it was less active in the rest of Bavaria and was not significantly active at all in Silesia or the Berlin area before the war, because of hostility from the local church hierarchy. By 1914 the *Volksverein* had a membership of more than eight hundred thousand, but the Weimar years saw its steady decline.

The *Volksverein* has been called the "social and civic conscience of the Center party" but as is often the case with consciences, its opportunity for practical accomplishment was limited. It could do little besides public relations work without the cooperation of the Reichstag fraction and the result was chronic frustration among the party's *Sozialpolitiker* who dreamed of reforming the social structure. When released from the confines of the Wilhelmine authoritarian government, the idealistic Catholic social leaders of the *Volksverein* were forced to face the reality that the party as a whole had no intention of supporting social experiment, and the organization became less and less relevant as a result of these inner contradictions.[10]

Two other organizations affiliated with the Center were the Görres Society "for the encouragement of scholarship in Catholic Germany" founded in 1876 by Hertling (the future Reich chancellor) and the publisher J. P. Bachem; and the youth organization, the Windthorst League. Of the very many Catholic youth clubs in Germany, the Windthorst League was selected to be the one closest to the Center, to train political leaders and to "educate the more politically active elements."[11] By 1910 the League had 162 branches with about 11,000 members. There was also a Catholic Women's League, founded in 1903, headed after 1912 by Hedwig Dransfeld, who became one of the few women to sit for the Center in the Reichstag and Prussian *Landtag* in the Weimar years. Before the war, the Women's League membership was only about 36,000 and was pretty much restricted to middle-class, educated women.[12] When the Reich Associations Law of 1908 recognized the right of women to take part in public meetings, the league worked actively for the party in the elections of 1912, but the party leadership did not particularly welcome this, and in general was

10. Ibid., pp. 177–81. Mittmann believes the *Volksverein* leaders themselves never had serious intentions of changing the social and economic bases of society. Morsey agrees with this in "Die deutschen Katholiken und der Nationalstaat zwischen Kulturkampf und Erstem Weltkrieg," *Historische Jahrbuch* 90 (1970): 58. For a particularly hostile, Marxist view of the *Volksverein*, see the article of that name in Dieter Fricke, ed., *Die Bürgerlichen Parteien in Deutschland*, 2 vols. (Berlin, 1968), 2:810–34.
11. Jürgen Bertram, *Die Wahlen zum deutschen Reichstag vom Jahre 1912* (Düsseldorf, 1964), p. 27.
12. Walter Ferber, "Hedwig Dransfeld," in Morsey, *Zeitgeschichte*, p. 136.

not anxious to see women involved in politics, in spite of the fact that in the years after 1919, well over half of the votes for the Center were cast by women.[13]

Although they were not permanent organizations, the Catholic congresses, held each year in a different city in Germany, were extremely useful to the Center as public forums to heighten popular enthusiasm for particular issues. Members of the Center's Reichstag fraction served as presidents of the congresses in twenty-three out of thirty-four years, and the fraction was very active not only in providing speakers for the congresses but also in formulating its resolutions.[14] These resolutions were usually of a relatively noncontroversial and general nature, but the political potential of the congresses was recognized by government authorities; in 1890 the government of the Bavarian prince-regent forbade the congress to meet in Munich as planned, because of a fear of political agitation. On this occasion a new meeting place was hastily found, in Koblenz, and the annual congresses were not interrupted.[15]

Newspapers supporting the Center were sometimes referred to as a "party press," sometimes as the "Catholic press"; in fact, there was a considerable overlapping of the two categories and there were always Catholic papers and magazines which did not support the Center in all of its policies. Papers which did consistently reflect party policy—and sometimes created it—were united in 1878 to form the Augustine League. Their combined circulation at that time was about 300,000. By 1912 the Augustine League contained 446 papers, mostly appearing in the Rhineland, Bavaria, and Westphalia, with a readership of two and a half million. The most important continued to be the *Kölnische Volkszeitung* (an organ of the J. P. Bachem publishing concern) and *Germania* of Berlin. The latter was the more conservative of the two in the prewar period, but the more republican in the postwar period. Others were the *Düsseldorfer Volksblatt* (edited by Dr. Hüsgen, the biographer of Windthorst), *Tremonia* of Dortmund, the *Deutsche Volksblatt*, and the *Katholische Sonntagsblatt* of Stuttgart. Most of

13. Johannes Schauff, *Die deutschen Katholiken und die Zentrumspartei* (Cologne, 1928), p. 75.
14. Nipperdey, pp. 283–84; Mittmann, pp. 119–20.
15. Bachem, 8:14–15.

the Catholic papers, however, were small-town organs of very local circulation.

Magazines which could be considered as, in the main, Centrist were: the *Historische-politische Blätter, Stimmen aus Maria-Laach,* and *Hochland. Stimmen aus Maria-Laach* was a Jesuit publication founded in 1864 and named after a Jesuit *Studienhaus.* It was published by the Herder Press in Freiburg and appeared monthly after 1871, but its editors were obliged to live outside the country, in Belgium and Luxemburg, during the years when the Jesuit law was in force. The magazine was moved to Munich in 1914 and at that time adopted the name of *Stimmen der Zeit,* continuing to appear monthly except for the years 1941 to 1946.[16] *Hochland* was founded in 1903 as a monthly covering "all areas of knowledge, literature and art" with the goal of helping Catholic culture emerge from "the ghetto." It was not much concerned with politics in the prewar years, but later its editors became much more outspoken; its position toward the Center party in the Weimar republic was ambivalent and has even been labeled pro-Fascist. Like *Stimmen der Zeit, Hochland* was suppressed by the National Socialist regime in 1941 but reappeared as a bimonthly in 1946.[17]

In addition to the party's connections with the periodical press, the Center and the *Volksverein* were avid distributors of pamphlets on all kinds of subjects. Of some forty-five pamphlets, with millions of copies, in circulation at the time of the 1912 elections, typical titles were: "Forward into the Red Swamp" (a derogatory reference to the Social Democratic paper *Vorwärts*), "Christendom, Center and Social Democracy," "Struggle over World-Outlook," "The Reich Taxes of 1909." Production of this kind of propaganda suffered from much regional competition and lack of central coordination.[18]

The Center party was thus only one unit in a complex network of Catholic political, social, and cultural organizations, and its structure is difficult to compare to that of other German parties for that reason.

---

16. Oskar Simmel, S.J., *"Stimmen der Zeit," Staatslexikon,* 8 vols. (Freiburg, 1957–63), 7:727.

17. Franz Josef Schöningh, *"Hochland," Staatslexikon,* 4:113–14; Richard van Dülmen, "Der deutsche Katholizismus und der Erste Weltkrieg," *Francia* 2 (1974): 355–67.

18. Bertram, pp. 76–77.

A more unified party structure was achieved after the war, but this had the eventual effect of disturbing the unity of the network as a whole.

The Center party was a party for the representation of Catholic interests and membership in the Catholic faith was the single factor uniting the leadership and the voters, who were otherwise extremely diverse. The possibility of Protestant membership in the party and the attracting of Protestant voters were important theoretical issues to the party but were of no practical significance either before or after the war. In the Second Reich, about one-third of the population was classi-fied as Catholic, and the Center's electoral support never approached 100 percent of that number. But it should be noted that all persons in Germany at that time were recorded officially as either Catholic, Prot-estant or Jewish; there was no category known to government records of those who were indifferent or unbelieving. Even professed atheists were irrevocably Protestant or Catholic or Jewish according to their birth records and those of their parents and grandparents. Conse-quently the question "how many German Catholics supported the Center?" is not the same as the question "how many practicing Catho-lics supported the Center?" A statistical analysis reveals that those Catholics who attended at least the Easter service were much more likely to support the Center than the general "Catholic" population, and this was even more true of those who attended services regularly.[19] During the years of the *Kulturkampf* there was almost unanimous support of the party by practicing Catholics. This tended to decline slightly in the years from 1890 to the war, and more steeply after the first crisis year of the Weimar republic.

To equate Catholic membership by birth with Centrist affiliation would be an error but to equate practicing Catholics with the party electorate would seem to be an accurate generalization. The chief ex-ception to this rule was to be found among the most highly educated persons, those who were closer to the social and governmental estab-lishments in their states, and most especially those who were ambi-tious for high political office. Windthorst once remarked that the meeting room of the Reichstag fraction should have a sign above the door reading "abandon hope, all ye who enter here," because Centrist

19. Schauff, p. 66.

affiliation was such a barrier to government appointment.[20] A large proportion of the government officialdom in Bavaria was Catholic by birth but shunned Centrist connections, and the same is true to some extent in Baden and parts of Prussia. Occasionally there would be a more extensive secession from the party, as in 1893 in indignation over the Center's rejection of the army budget, or in the 1907 elections when a group of "national Catholics" was formed and entered candidates of its own, again over the question of patriotism. These temporary secessions of upper-class, educated Catholics foreshadowed a permanent exodus in 1919 and 1920.

A statistically larger group of non-Centrist Catholics was the Prussian Polish population. The Poles are always cited as allies and partners of the Center in the legislatures, but it is worth noting that they organized themselves as a distinct party throughout the period. It would be more correct to say that the Center supported Polish interests than to say that the Poles supported the Center, and in fact on several occasions (again the 1893 army bill) they went their separate way. Polish political leadership in the years before 1900 was in the hands of Catholic clergy and landed aristocrats who had much in common with the Centrist leaders, but in the twentieth century leadership passed to more militant nationalists who were often not particularly concerned with Catholic issues as such, and the relationship with the Center grew less close. In the last elections before the war, Polish candidates actively opposed Center candidates in Silesia and won seats from the party. To some extent this was the consequence of the hostile policies of Cardinal Kopp, who sought to eliminate Poles from membership in the Silesian Center.[21]

Similarly, the majority political party in Alsace-Lorraine, though Catholic and using the name of "Center" in its provincial organization, kept itself aloof from the national party and never merged with it in spite of repeated invitations to do so. A few men in the Reichstag delegation were finally persuaded to join the national Center fraction in 1907, but shortly after that, when Alsace-Lorraine was granted its own constitution and a degree of self-government, the Alsace-Lorraine Center party was formed, and these men left the national party to join

20. Bachem, 4:288.
21. Anderson, p. 380; Bachem, 7:381; on Kopp, Trzeciakowski, p. 630.

the new organization. After 1911, relations between the two groups became strained.[22] Common membership in the Catholic faith was never sufficient grounds for unity, and the Reich government saw to it that it had little opportunity to become so by its consistent policy of appointing only Protestant officials to administer the *Reichsland*.

The Guelphs, the third regional group which sat as *Hospitanten* with the Center, were the Hanoverian fraction, those few deputies representing the still unreconciled feelings of hostility toward Prussia in that state after its forcible annexation in 1866. Unlike the Poles and the Alsatians, the Guelphs represented a population largely Protestant, and it is to be assumed that it was the personality and abilities of the old Guelph Ludwig Windthorst which bound them originally to the Center, but the interest of both parties in local and regional autonomy within the state of Prussia was another reason for the connection. The Center's leadership was proud of the adherence of the Guelphs because it provided a concrete example of the nonconfessional nature of the party.

In elections, Centrists and Guelphs never contested the same seats; on some occasions the Center supported the Guelph candidate and at other times the Guelphs supported the Center candidate (as it did Windthorst in his seat for Meppen). The partnership revealed a basic anti-Prussian philosophy in both parties. "For Bismarck, the problems with the Guelphs, particularists, and Ultramontanes were all closely intertwined."[23]

As the years passed, the defense of the Guelph dynasty against the predatory Hohenzollern became less and less urgent. In 1892, Ernst August, the heir to Georg V, the last king of Hanover, was finally permitted to receive the interest from the notorious "Guelph fund" formed from the confiscated property of the dynasty, after he affirmed that he would not undertake any moves against the Reich. He did not go so far as to renounce his claim to Hanover, and in fact, claimed the inheritance of Brunswick as well, after the death of the regent in that state in 1906. But this continued awkwardness was ended in 1912 when Ernst August's son married Kaiser William II's daughter and was

22. Dan P. Silverman, *Reluctant Union: Alsace-Lorraine and Imperial Germany, 1871–1918* (University Park, Pa., 1972), pp. 147–50.
23. Steward A. Stehlin, *Bismarck and the Guelph Problem, 1866–1890* (The Hague, 1973), p. 114.

allowed to take up the claim to Brunswick. The dynastic issue thus appeared to be amicably settled, but even though the original reason for the formation of a separate party became less valid, and then disappeared altogether after the 1918 revolution, the strong regional feeling of resentment against Prussia remained, even leading to an unsuccessful secession attempt in 1924.[24]

The Guelphs' relationship with the Center was interrupted by the *Zentrumsstreit*, the controversy over the nature of the party, and the possibility that the party might be transformed into one of exclusively Catholic composition and interests. Their deputies refused to work with the Center in the election of 1912 and sat apart from the party in the legislatures for several years, but during the war and in the Weimar years this breach was healed and the accustomed relationship was resumed.

The Center's opponents called it "priest-ridden" and it was true that members of the clergy had from the beginning played a major role in the party, though it became a tradition not to have a cleric at the head of either the Reich or the Prussian party. Most of the best-known clerical Centrists before 1918, except for those active in social organizations like the *Volksverein* and the workers' associations (Hitze, Pieper, Brauns) were from the southern states: Daller and Schädler in Bavaria; Lender, Wacker, and Schofer in Baden; Moufang and Ketteler in Hesse. In the list of the party founders who signed the Soest Program of 1870, nineteen of the fifty signers were ordained priests. In an analysis of the occupations of Reichstag deputies, 20 percent of the Center's deputies after the 1903 elections were priests, but the percentage dropped to about 11 percent in 1912.[25]

As in other German political parties, a large percentage of the leadership was traincd in the law and employed in private practice or, much more commonly, in the ranks of the civil service at the state or local level. In the early years, Windthorst, Mallinckrodt, and the Reichensperger brothers; in the later years, Lieber, P. Spahn, Gröber, Porsch, Roeren; and still later, Marx, Trimborn, Fehrenbach, were all in this occupational category. After 1900, about 10 percent of the Reichstag Center deputies were in civil service positions (including

24. Ibid., pp. 154–55; 210–19.
25. Bertram, p. 162.

the judiciary) and about 5 percent in the private practice of law. University professors provided 4 percent to 8 percent (Jörg, Hertling, Daller). The landowning aristocracy formed an important pressure group in the prewar Center, especially in Prussia and Bavaria: Franckenstein and Löwenstein in Bavaria; Schorlemer and Heereman from Westphalia; Hompesch and Loë from the Rhineland; Huene, Praschma, and Ballestrem from Silesia. The landowners, particularly those from Silesia, were more apt to differ from official party policy than any other occupational group, notably in the matter of grain tariffs. The Soest signers of 1870 included, out of fifty, eight noblemen, and in addition, four calling themselves landowners and four calling themselves farmers. In the analysis of Centrist Reichstag deputies, an average of 18 percent from 1900 to 1914 were landowners.[26]

Commerce and industry were of secondary importance in the party before and after the war, since even in the most highly industrialized parts of the Rhineland, the number of Catholic-owned factories and businesses was always low in proportion to the number of Catholics in the population. But there were a few Centrist industrialists (Brandts, of the *Volksverein*, Ballestrem, Richard Müller the finance expert) and many representatives of the crafts, shopkeepers, and small industries. Like the industrial laborers, however, the artisans and shopkeepers did not provide many party leaders until after the 1918 revolution. Of the prewar deputies, 7 percent are listed as being from "commerce and industry" and 5 percent to 6 percent from industrial labor unions.[27] The best known of the older prewar labor leaders were priests and factoryowners, not workingmen, but the next generation, men like Giesberts, Joos, and Stegerwald, were themselves from the working class and were to take a much more important place in the party ranks after 1918.

Even in the prewar years, the majority of Center voters, as opposed to the leadership, consisted of industrial workers, small farmers and winegrowers, artisans and shopkeepers. The party electorate formed, as has often been said, a microcosm of German society.

With its following so diverse, the Center's party platform had to avoid many of the social and economic issues that contributed the

26. Ibid.
27. Ibid.

most important planks to the platforms of the other German parties. There were nevertheless a number of common principles apart from the defense of Catholic interests upon which the party could consistently unite. Ideological aversion to laissez faire "Manchester-school" liberalism and the practical fact of the relative unimportance of manufacturers and industrialists in the party made it possible for the Center to support a program of social reform. Solving the "social question" but at the same time combating Marxist Social Democracy played as great a role in the Center's public relations activity as did Catholic issues.

Federalism, that is, the defense of states' rights and of local and regional autonomy continued to be an important plank in both the national and state platforms until 1919, although with little practical result; the party's interest in and talent for finance tended to work toward increasing centralization in this area in spite of federalist rhetoric. Furthermore, whenever an important religious goal was at stake (as in the case of the Jesuit law and the Tolerance Motion) federalist principles were totally forgotten.

Somewhat related to the principle of federalist states' rights was a consistent opposition in the Center to the Prussian militarist tradition. This was especially apparent in the first twenty years of the party's existence, but it never completely disappeared. It was a *grossdeutsch* heritage and carried with it the same stigma of lack of patriotism. This was something about which the party membership felt acutely sensitive, and there was always a painful conflict between the antimilitarist philosophy and the desire to be considered wholly German and patriotic. Opposition to the army budgets, begun partly as a tactical weapon in the *Kulturkampf* and continued until after 1893, was often explained by the party leadership as simply a matter of economy, of the need to avoid excessive expenditure, but it was patently something more than that.

After the great fight over Caprivi's army budget of 1893, finally passed over the votes of the Center after new elections, the growing number of crises in international relations persuaded the party that support of increased military expenditure was unavoidable. Even the seven- or five-year duration of the army budget was no longer contested, since the trend after 1900 seemed to be such that a yearly budget would have meant an even more rapid rate of increase. But the antagonism to militarism still existed and revealed itself in 1906 in the defeat of the colonial budget for the war in Southwest Africa, which once again placed the Center in the position of being excoriated for lack of patriotism. The unpleasant experience of the election campaign of 1907 following this crisis seems to have convinced the Center's leadership that any stand against army demands was too much of a political liability, and there was no more open resistance to militarism in the last years of the empire.

Foreign policy was the least exploited issue for the Center, which was handicapped by the lack of experience and knowledge among its leaders. The party had few links with the Foreign Office or the diplomatic corps and, until the last months of the war, had no source of information on the subject other than the government's official channels of communication.

An issue which might have become a plank in the party platform and, unfortunately, might have become a popular one with many voters, was anti-Semitism. The endemic antagonism felt toward the economic role of Jews in some rural regions of Germany, combined with the more recent resentment against the active role played by the "Jewish" Berlin liberal press in waging the *Kulturkampf*, could have led to the same propaganda usage of anti-Semitism that was characteristic of the Christian Social party in Austria in this period. Catholicism, antiliberalism, anticapitalism, and anti-Semitism formed powerfully effective ingredients in Karl Lueger's Christian Social movement and they might have done the same for the Center, leading it away from its democratic civil rights stand down the path toward authoritarianism and bigotry taken by the Austrian party. In 1880 when the Anti-Semite League was founded in Germany there was considerable interest in Centrist circles in joining forces with it. Schorlemer-Alst urged such a move (as founder of the Westphalian Farmers' Association he was doubtless aware of the potential value of finding a scapegoat with which to bind the peasant population more closely to the landowners), and he was supported by the majority of the Prussian *Landtag* fraction; but they were argued down almost singlehandedly by Windthorst, who felt as strongly as ever that exceptional treatment of any minority group threatened the security of Catholics, and that toleration could not be demanded for themselves and rejected for others.

A few party members made speeches in the Prussian house favoring the anti-Semitic movement at about this time, and *Germania*, especially during the *Kulturkampf*, published articles denouncing the "Jewish" press, but by and large the party avoided the issue and continued throughout its history to shun it. Windthorst's successor Dr. Lieber was equally vehement on the importance of the avoidance of anti-Semitism in word or deed. In response to a motion by the Anti-Semite party demanding expulsion of foreign Jews from the Reich, Lieber, besides of course rejecting the motion, expanded his remarks to comment on the entire anti-Semite program, pointing out that one exceptional law against alien Jews would undoubtedly lead to others against German Jews and making sympathetic comments about the historical pressures and difficulties for the Jews in their participation in German economic life. He concluded: "We don't want any exceptional laws, against particular classes of our fellow citizens, or against political or economic parties, nor do we want exceptional laws against certain confessions or—as people like to elegantly express it—against certain races . . . we . . . can't turn our hand to forging weapons today against the Jews, tomorrow against the Poles, day after tomorrow against the Catholics."[28]

Not all of the Center were as enlightened as Lieber and Windthorst, and on a number of occasions in the 1880s and 1890s there were verbal outbursts against the economic activities of Jews, especially in the Rhineland where there was much friction between Catholic retailers and artisans and their Jewish competitors. But the political consequences of these mutterings were slight. The Anti-Semite party seldom ran candidates in areas of heavy Catholic population and never succeeded in winning a seat in a Catholic district.[29]

The Center's platform was not anti-Semitic; neither was it anti-Protestant. It might even be said that a consistent part of the party program was the active defense of Protestant interests. This is not really surprising, when it is understood that the only possible way in which Catholic interests could be defended in a country two-thirds

28. *Verhandlungen des Reichstags* 140 (6 Mar. 1895): 1285–87.
29. Zeender, p. 14; Richard S. Levy, *The Downfall of the Anti-Semitic Parties in Imperial Germany* (New Haven and London, 1975), pp. 186–87; Peter G. J. Pulzer, *The Rise of Political Anti-Semitism in Germany and Austria* (New York, 1964), p. 277. All three authors attribute the Center's avoidance of anti-Semitism to the personal influence of Windthorst and Lieber. For a more critical view of attitudes of German Catholics toward the Jews, see Tal, pp. 87–93.

Protestant was by defending the interests of all organized religions. In the fight to retain denominational schools and to continue receiving state financial aid for the church, an alliance with serious Protestant leadership was essential (though cooperation was often meager and halfhearted from the Evangelical church.) Thus the Center always supported legislation for increments for the Evangelical church in Prussia and the other states. Especially in the years of the Weimar republic, the party would have welcomed a far stronger political representation of Protestant interests than actually existed, but the search for a Protestant conservative partner met with no real success until the formation of the Christian Democratic Union in 1945.

7
THE EARLY YEARS OF THE WILHELMINE
PERIOD 1888–1900

The Center had no ties to the Hohenzollern dynasty nor any special reason for loyalty to it, but through the years, German Catholics had come to feel a sentimental affection for William I and his consort and had never identified them with the excesses of the *Kulturkampf*. His successor, Emperor Frederick, was regarded with more reserve, since he had the reputation of being a liberal and an anticlerical. But the young William II was an unknown quantity. When he began his reign his public pronouncements acknowledged the interests of his Catholic subjects and frequently stressed the importance of Christian principles in government in a manner highly acceptable to German Catholics. Yet gradually it became clear to the more knowledgeable among them that in private conversations and correspondence William revealed strong anti-Catholic, anti-Jesuit, and anti-Centrist prejudices.[1] In the clash between William and Bismarck, it was not at all obvious whose victory would be to the Center's advantage.

In any case, in the drama of Bismarck's fall from power, the party was in no position to be more than a passive onlooker. Ludwig Windthorst was rumored at the time to have engaged in complex intrigue, plotting either the downfall of Bismarck or else his continuation in office. Such rumors were encouraged by Bismarck himself after the collapse of his own complex intrigues. The most recent investigations into the reasons for his dismissal appear to bear out completely the insistence of Windthorst and his followers that the Centrist leader

1. This is attested to in numerous examples from many sources, including Michael Balfour, *The Kaiser and His Times* (London, 1964); Bernhard von Bülow, *Memoirs*, 2 vols. (Boston, 1931); John C. G. Röhl, *Germany without Bismarck* (Berkeley, 1967); and Johannes Ziekursch, *Politische Geschichte des neuen deutschen Kaiserreiches*, 3 vols. (Frankfurt am Main, 1925–30).

played no active role in events. According to these accounts, the famous interview between the two men in March 1890 was initiated by Bismarck, not by Windthorst, in the hopes of forming a Centrist-Conservative alliance in the Reichstag to replace the *Kartell* which had fallen apart because of the desertion of the National Liberals. Windthorst accepted the idea and agreed to support a modified anti-Socialist law; he naturally made some conditions, still hoping in the long run for a return to the religious status quo before the *Kulturkampf*, but in the short run asking simply for repeal of the anti-Jesuit law and consideration of a favorable Prussian school bill. Windthorst urged Bismarck to remain in office, but privately thought there was little chance of it.[2]

This was the beginning and the end of Windthorst's part in the affair. His own comment to the press about the visit is characteristic: "The newspapers are concerned about the visit which I am supposed to have paid to Prince Bismarck. Now, if I had really seen him, it would certainly be impossible to betray a single word of what was said. But if I had not seen him, it would be to my advantage quietly to let people think that I *had* seen him. So, I'm saying nothing, although I have been told that the editor of an enterprising Berlin morning newspaper has an interview with me about the matter already in print."[3] News of the meeting was in fact spread not by Windthorst but by Bismarck. The chancellor's enemies in court circles (Philipp Eulenburg, Friedrich von Holstein, Paul Kayser) were adamantly opposed to the idea of a Centrist-Conservative coalition and the turn toward parliamentary government which it implied; Eulenburg especially feared the repercussions in Bavaria, where the liberal regime might fall and be replaced by the Catholic "separatists," thus endangering the unity of the Reich. As one of them put it, "Saving the Reich with the aid of the Jesuitical Guelphs is really the limit!"[4] They convinced the kaiser, with little difficulty, that Bismarck was betraying him with Windt-

---

2. Anderson, p. 386–87; Zeender, p. 18; Röhl, "The Disintegration of the *Kartell* and the Politics of Bismarck's Fall from Power, 1887–1890," *Historical Journal* 9 (1966): 60–89.

3. Bachem, 9:100.

4. Röhl, "Staatsstreichplan oder Staatsstreichbereitschaft?" *Historische Zeitschrift* 203 (1966): 610–24; see also Norman Rich, *Friedrich von Holstein*, 2 vols. (Cambridge, Mass., 1965), 1:230–32.

horst, and a few days after the interview, William demanded Bismarck's resignation.[5]

The Center party was on the whole restrained in its reception of the news of the resignation, and the *Kölnische Volkszeitung* printed an editorial which was almost kindly in its tone. The future was uncertain, and Bismarck, who had brought the *Kulturkampf* to an end, was to be preferred to many possible alternatives. Windthorst's death a year later, in March 1891, was a second shock to the party: a great opponent and a great leader had between them united diverse elements to create the Center party, and it was not clear that it would remain united in their absence.

The new chancellor, General von Caprivi, was anxious to govern with the cooperation of the Reichstag and made a conscious effort to conciliate the Center. He wrote in a letter to Eulenburg, "As the move to crush the Catholic Church has failed—and no-one would now wish to repeat it—the only course left is to grant to Catholic subjects of His Majesty the same position in the State and the same pride in public life as that enjoyed by Protestants."[6] In return for Center support for the army bill of 1890, the chancellor promised concessions in Prussian education policy and government backing for the party's program of social protective legislation, which had been for so long discouraged by Bismarck.[7] In his February Edict of 1890, William II had indicated an interest in the same sort of protective legislation for labor that the Center had been advocating (Sunday rest, a raising of the age limit for working children, special protection for women), and he aroused great hopes for reform by sponsoring an international conference on labor in Berlin, to which he invited Franz Hitze, the Center's expert on social policy. The result of the conference was a comprehensive government bill for labor protection which was prepared by the Federal Council and passed by a large majority in the Reichstag, where its details had been worked out under Centrist chairmanship in committee. The bill became law in 1891, fourteen years after Count Galen's original "me-

---

5. Röhl, "Disintegration of the *Kartell*," pp. 60–89. This account accords in all important respects with earlier accounts by Bachem (9:85–110) and Hüsgen (pp. 268–72), although Röhl gives the date of the interview as March 12 and Bachem as March 10, five days before Bismarck's resignation.

6. Röhl, *Germany without Bismarck*, p. 80.

7. Zeender, pp. 18–19.

Galen's original "medieval" proposal. Unfortunately, William's interest in positive social reform was short-lived and so was his toleration of Caprivi's policy of concessions to the Center party.

The Prussian government had suffered defeat in 1890 on an education bill because of the Center's opposition, and Caprivi resolved to win the party to his support by promoting a state educational policy which would conform to its interests. The difficulties inherent in this plan proved to be insurmountable, however, and led to its defeat, which in turn lost him the support of the Center. The contest over the Prussian school bill of 1892 is deserving of closer attention, since it was the first of a series of confrontations which do much to explain the failure of the Center to function successfully in parliamentary coalitions.

The subject of education was always one which could be counted upon to produce heated emotional debate in Germany, in the 1950s as surely as in the 1890s. The insistence upon the maintenance of confessional schools and of religious instruction in those schools was basic to the program of the Center party; the demand for a secular or interdenominational public-school system was basic to the programs of both the liberal parties and the Social Democrats. The conflict of viewpoints was total, and time was working against the Catholic party, as the strength of the Socialists steadily increased and that of its only allies, the old-fashioned Protestant Conservatives, declined. Because the two sides were so evenly matched, neither could ever achieve a victory. Although repeated efforts were made to pass first a Prussian and then a national school law, none was ever passed from the time of the founding of the Reich to the 1960s. The Center party and its post–World War II successors fought a remarkable delaying action through the years to prevent the relatively favorable status quo from being altered in any way inimical to their interests.

When the German states first established public elementary schools, religion was an essential part of the curriculum, and separate schools were provided for the major denominations as a matter of course. Denominational school systems of this sort remained undisturbed in most of the smaller northern states and in Bavaria and Württemberg until 1918, but in a few areas of mixed population (Baden, Hesse, Nassau, Frankfurt-am-Main) "simultaneous" schools serving both Protestant and Catholic children were introduced. In

Prussia, the constitution of 1850 provided for separate confessional schools and extensive religious instruction conducted by clergy, for the basic elementary schools, the *Volksschulen*. The constitution also stated that "a special law regulates the entire educational system," but no such law had ever been passed. Prussia's annexations of territory in 1866 left the school systems of these areas unaffected, including the simultaneous schools of Nassau and Frankfurt. During the *Kulturkampf*, the government had introduced lay supervision into the schools and had temporarily been able to convert some small denominational schools into simultaneous schools, but Falk had not been able to put through his plan for a comprehensive school law in 1878, partly simply because of the great expense which would have been involved.

In the 1880s Bismarck had let the school question rest and had halted the formation of simultaneous schools. After his dismissal in 1890, the Caprivi government took up the subject again. The *Kultusminister* Gustav von Gossler drafted a bill to regulate the *Volksschulen* which was actually a modified and less expensive version of Falk's liberal plan. It increased state control over the curriculum and anticipated the formation of interdenominational schools. The Center managed to kill the bill in committee and Gossler was forced to resign, since Caprivi depended upon Centrist support in the legislatures.

The next minister of education and religion, Count Robert von Zedlitz-Trüzschler, a conservative Protestant from Silesia, was assigned the task of producing a school bill which would be acceptable to the Center. The Zedlitz bill, brought to the Prussian House of Deputies in January 1892, was all the party could have hoped for, and more: it maintained the denominational system and specified that not only the student body but also the teachers and the teacher-training institutions must be exclusively of one denomination or the other. Any new *Volksschule* built was to be of one denomination or the other. Religious instruction was to be given by clerics, normally the local priest or pastor. Private schools could easily be founded (these were desired by Catholics for areas where not enough Catholic children lived to justify a separate public school for them). The bill also eliminated all fees for the *Volksschule*, greatly improved the financial condition of teachers, and set up a more efficient organizational structure.

Chancellor Caprivi was satisfied with the bill and hoped that its passage would persuade the Center to vote for upcoming military appropriations. He presented the issue as a choice between Christianity and atheism, which outraged the liberal parties in the House of Deputies, who vigorously opposed the bill. Opposition was also strong from the liberal press and the universities. But the bill seemed assured of passage by a narrow majority of Center and Conservatives, in spite of reservations in Conservative ranks, when its progress was abruptly halted by a decisive change of mind by the kaiser. He had apparently become convinced, perhaps by the Finance Minister Johannes Miquel, that the extreme hostility of the National Liberals should not be ignored, and he may also have been influenced by Count Philipp Eulenburg, Prussian ambassador to Munich, who had warned him and Caprivi that pandering to the Center would, among other bad effects, weaken the liberal establishment in Bavaria and even somehow lead to a breakup of the federal union.[8] Zedlitz resigned, Caprivi also resigned (though was persuaded to keep the chancellorship), and the new Prussian minister-president, Botho Eulenburg, withdrew the school bill.

This was a blow to the Center, especially when in later years it was realized that there would never again be so favorable a parliamentary makeup. Only in 1927 were chances to be so good for passage of a favorable school bill, and the attempt that year was also a failure. On the other hand, the Center was always able, as the case of the 1890 Gossler bill shows, to prevent a liberal bill from being passed.

Caprivi had seen, as Bismarck had seen in 1890, that a government coalition of Conservatives and Centrists would work as well or better for his purposes as the old *Kartell* of Conservatives and National Liberals, but the school bill incident showed that the conciliation and concession necessary to transform the Center into a government party was intolerable to the small group of men who actually controlled the decision-making in Prussia and the Reich. Thus the royal and imperial governments deliberately rejected support and assistance from a basically conservative source in order to keep German Catholic political representation in a subordinate role.

After the failure of the clerical school bill, the Center's leaders saw no reason to be cooperative about the Army Bill of 1893, and Lie-

8. J. Alden Nichols, *Germany after Bismarck: The Caprivi Era, 1890–1894* (New York, 1968), pp. 76–81.

ber directed the party in its old antimilitarist stand against the bill. This produced a serious internal crisis, because Lieber was less effective than Windthorst had been in enforcing party discipline among the landowning nobility, some of whom wanted to support the government on this issue. Karl, Freiherr von Huene, a personal friend to Caprivi, led a secession from the party of twelve aristocrats (most of them from Silesia) including Count Ballestrem who resigned the chairmanship of the Center Reichstag fraction. Cardinal Kopp, Cardinal Ledochowski, and Archbishop Stablewski of Posen all spoke out in favor of the army bill, hoping to use it to extract concessions for the church. Kopp even persuaded Pope Leo XIII to suggest compliance to the Center,[9] in spite of the precedent of 1887. Church intervention convinced the Polish delegation to vote for the bill but had the opposite effect on Lieber and the majority of the Center fraction, who remembered the crisis of 1887 and were determined to maintain an independent stand on what was clearly a political rather than a religious matter.

Moreover, a vote for the bill, which involved a rise in beer and brandy taxes, would have brought about a secession of the Bavarian delegation of the Center, a threat more alarming than the walkout of a handful of aristocrats; in fact the bill was unpopular among wide circles of the Catholic population in the country. Consequently, the party rejected the bill (except for the secession of twelve), which therefore failed to pass, and Caprivi dissolved the Reichstag and called for elections.

The government's election campaign of 1893, unlike that of 1887, did not present the issue as one of German patriotism versus subversion and treason, and so did not further alienate the Center and its voters. The party lost ten seats, dropping from 106 to 96 in the Reichstag, but Huene and the other renegades were not reelected. The resubmitted army bill passed the new house with a bare majority, the Center rejecting, the Poles again supporting it.

The next year was one of continued division in the party fraction over the question of whether or not to continue in opposition. There was first a split over Finance Minister Miquel's proposed tax reforms. Lieber supported them but most of the fraction were opposed, because

9. Zeender, pp. 32–33; Nichols, p. 251. According to Rich, 1:398–99, Holstein planned to offer a bribe to Leo XIII in the expectation that the pope would persuade the Center to vote for the bill, but the plan fell through.

they believed these measures would decrease the influence of the states upon Reich finances and probably also because they resented Miquel's part in killing the school bill in 1892. In this instance, Lieber lost the argument and the Center helped to defeat the tax reforms.

Lieber's chief opponents in this conflict were the Rhineland Centrists and, especially, the Bachem family which controlled the *Kölnische Volkszeitung* and its publishing concern. He seems to have been suspicious of the role of the press and to have feared a "palace revolution," showing, according to one account, "the oversensitivity of a man still insecure in his position of leadership."[10] The Bachemites, led by Julius and Carl Bachem and their friend the editor Hermann Cardauns, believed themselves to be following the Windthorst tradition of popular opposition, while Lieber, though evidently personally more democratic in his views than they were, wanted to see the Center accepted into the governing circles of Germany.[11]

The next party division occurred over the issue of Caprivi's commercial treaties regulating the grain trade with Russia and Rumania. In this instance Lieber, in line with his policy, led the majority in supporting the treaties, but the protectionist agrarian representatives deserted the party en masse. The fraction's vote on the Russian treaty was 46 in favor, 39 opposed, and 11 either abstaining or absent. Until the end of the world agricultural crisis of the 1890s the landowners and farmers put their economic interest ahead of party discipline, in the Center as in the Conservative party. By 1894, however, both Lieber and the Bachem faction had returned to a policy of wary cooperation with the government.

The appointment of Prince Hohenlohe as chancellor after Caprivi's resignation was not regarded by the Center as an improvement. A practicing, devout Protestant like Caprivi was greatly preferable to an indifferent, freethinking, Jesuit-hating Catholic like Hohenlohe, and Centrists had neither forgotten nor forgiven the role which the prince had played in the early stages of the *Kulturkampf*. But through the mediation of the Reich State Secretary for Foreign Affairs Marschall von Bieberstein, who had succeeded in cultivating a good relationship with Dr. Lieber, the Center was persuaded to accept the new

10. Mittmann, pp. 253–54.
11. See Zeender, pp. 35–47.

chancellor after he agreed to include in his first speech to the Reichstag a statement amounting to an apology for the events of the past.[12] After this reconciliation, relations between the party and Hohenlohe were amicable, and Lieber tried for the next five years to transform the Center from an opposition party into a pillar of government, with the goal of attaining full respectability and an influence on public affairs commensurate with its numerical strength in the legislatures. Unfortunately for Dr. Lieber, his efforts were thwarted on two sides, by the continued distrust of government by important sections in the Center and by the blatant prejudices of the kaiser.

William's personally sponsored "revolution bill" of 1895 provoked a crisis within the party.[13] On the one hand, the bill sought to repress Socialist revolutionary tendencies which had consistently been condemned by the party; the Vatican was sympathetic to the bill's content and many Catholics even favored an expansion of its provisions to include a broader interpretation of "revolutionary" ideas. On the other hand, the bill was clearly yet another of those exceptional laws which Windthorst had led the party to oppose on principle, and it threatened to injure the nascent Catholic labor movement. The Reichstag fraction was under pressures from Catholic public opinion on the issue and divided as to the correct course to pursue. Lieber on his part did not wish to offend the kaiser by a direct attack on the bill. Several younger members of the fraction found a solution to the dilemma.

In the past, Centrist speakers had frequently said that "Godless socialism" represented a spiritual sickness in society and that the most effective weapons against it would be spiritual ones. Under the direction of Adolf Gröber from Württemberg, the Center members of the committee considering the revolution bill proceeded to "clericalize" it until it was altered beyond recognition. In addition to the punitive clauses against union activity and revolutionary propaganda, the committee included prison sentences for those who "publicly or in print attack the existence of God, the immortality of the soul, or the religious and moral character of marriage."[14] Gröber declared the teachings of liberal professors like Ernst Haeckel to be as subversive

---

12. Röhl, *Germany without Bismarck*, p. 132.
13. For a detailed description of the Center's reaction to the Revolution Bill, see Zeender, pp. 50–54.
14. Wahl, 3:583–84. For a satirical cartoon of the Center's maneuvers on the *Umsturz*

to the Christian state as those of Socialist and anarchist agitators, and said that they should logically be regulated in the same way. As he had anticipated, such tactics of *reductio ad absurdum* produced a wave of anticlerical fervor in liberal circles and united them with the Left in opposition to the bill. Conservatives also rejected the committee's version of the bill, and in its final reading it received support only from the Center, thus failing to pass. In this ingenious fashion the party was able to follow its current policy of support of the government while at the same time ensuring the defeat of another exceptional law.

Soon after this crisis had been surmounted, the Prussian Center fraction was presented with a similar problem, the so-called little Socialist law of 1897. In this case Prussian Minister of the Interior von der Recke hoped to win the Center's vote for the bill by rescinding an existing ban on political meetings; but the bill canceled out any benefit from this by giving police the right to break up any meetings which "endangered public peace or the security of the state." With such flexible wording the "little Socialist bill" could lead to the same violation of civil rights as Bismarck's laws, including moves against political meetings of non-Socialist parties. It was defeated in the House of Deputies by the votes of the Center and the liberal parties.[15]

Still another attempt at repressive legislation was made, at the request of the kaiser, in 1899 with the introduction of the bill officially titled "for the protection of the workers' free will" but popularly called the "penitentiary bill" from the severity of the penalties it proposed for labor organizers. The bill was directly aimed against union activities and by this date the Center represented a labor union movement of considerable importance. The party consequently denounced the bill, which found general lack of support in the Reichstag and was not even sent to committee.

The "penitentiary bill" was the last overt act by the kaiser and his ministers to crush the Socialist movement, and the abandonment of the attempt was a great relief to the Center. The party's stand on the repressive laws had been a definite hindrance to Lieber's plan to achieve status and respectability in government circles. It had con-

---

law, see Ernst Dolm et al., eds., *Zentrums-Album des Kladderadatsch, 1870–1910* (Berlin, 1912), p. 179.

15. Karl Erich Born, *Staat und Sozialpolitik seit Bismarcks Sturz* (Wiesbaden, 1957), p. 139.

firmed William in his dislike of Catholics and of Lieber personally (as revealed on an occasion when he refused to speak with him and said that "the swine should be kicked in the behind").[16]

Two incidents illustrate the precarious nature of the party's position in the 1890s. In the spring of 1895, friends of Bismarck in the Reichstag proposed an ovation in honor of his eightieth birthday. The Center fraction decided, because of the ex-chancellor's continuing active participation in current affairs, that the proposal was a political act with ulterior motives, and so refused to support it. As he had threatened to do in such a case, the president of the Reichstag, Conservative Albert von Levetzow, resigned, and so did the National Liberal second vice-president. The evident intent to bring parliamentary business to a standstill was frustrated, however, when the Centrist First Vice-President Rudolf, Freiherr von Buol, calmly took over direction of the house. In the next election for president, Buol was elected by default when both conservative parties and the National Liberals abstained, and he served without incident until 1898. The first vice-presidency went to the Progressives and the second to the Centrist Peter Spahn who, ironically, represented the Reichstag at Bismarck's funeral. The kaiser was incensed at what he took to be a calculated insult to Bismarck in the failure of the birthday tribute, and he was dissuaded only with difficulty from ordering a dissolution of the Reichstag.

A similar parliamentary crisis occurred in 1897 when it became known to the Reichstag that the kaiser had referred to its members as "scoundrels without a fatherland." Lieber could not stomach this and wanted to bring it up for debate and to prepare an interpellation, but Hohenlohe persuaded him against a move which might well provoke a dissolution and the dismissal of himself and Marschall.[17]

In spite of such demonstrations revealing how great the distance still was between the Catholic politicians and the imperial establishment, by the end of the decade the Center had made advances in respectability. The party worked constructively to complete a new civil law code for the Reich, the *Bürgerliche Gesetzbuch für das Deutsche Reich*, or BGB. There had been a delicate problem with the code at

16. Röhl, *Germany without Bismarck*, p. 133; see also Rich. 2:491.
17. Röhl, *Germany without Bismarck*, pp. 223–24.

first, when the Vatican had sent instructions forbidding the party to vote for anything contrary to Catholic marriage laws. The Centrist members of the parliamentary committee, led by Lieber and Spahn, felt that positive cooperation was more useful than opposition; they managed to make a number of changes in the draft, for example, changing the word "marriage" to "civil marriage" and including provision for legal separation as well as for divorce. After detailed explanations of their work were relayed back to Rome, the Vatican sent instructions to the party leadership to use its own judgment, which it did, asking the fraction to vote for the completed draft of the code in its entirety.[18] This was the last direct intervention from Rome in a matter of political judgment, and the outcome ensured that Windthorst's policy of independence was to be maintained after his death.

The real test of the Center's patriotism and reliability, as Lieber was well aware, was of course its position on military and naval appropriations. Lieber hoped to find favor with the kaiser by offering wholehearted support for his new naval building program, but initial reaction in the Center to the first major naval bill in 1898 was decidedly negative. It was not certain until the last reading of the bill that it would receive enough Center votes to pass. The Bavarian delegation resisted all efforts at party discipline and simply threatened secession if coerced on the issue. Opponents of the bill in the Rhineland as well as in South Germany complained that no compensations or concessions to the party or the church were offered in exchange for their vital votes. Lieber, Spahn, and Hertling worked in committee to alter the method of financing the fleet expenditures, including a provision that any further funding should be obtained by state income taxes; they were then able to convince most of the fraction, though not the Bavarians, to vote for the final version of the bill. This hard-won victory for Lieber's policy made the desired favorable impression on the kaiser and his Navy Secretary von Tirpitz.[19] It remained to be seen, however, whether their recognition would be followed by any concrete advantages to the Center or by its admission into the imperial ruling circles.

Those party leaders who had been reluctant to vote for the naval appropriations had warned of a loss of public support if the Center

18. Wahl, 3:587–95; Bachem, 5:431–46.
19. Zeender, pp. 70–72. For liberal reaction to the "love affair" between Lieber and Tirpitz, see Dolm, *Zentrums-Album*, pp. 192–93; 209.

abandoned its antimilitarist stance without practical rewards. They were pleasantly surprised by the outcome of the elections of June 1898, which increased the party's Reichstag delegation from 96 to 102 seats. The party now held a commanding position in both the national and Prussian legislatures; no feasible majority could be formed without its votes, yet for several more years the government continued to hope to receive them without the need for compensation. Repeated consultations were held between Lieber and Hohenlohe, Miquel, and the new imperial secretary of the interior, Arthur von Posadowsky-Wehner, to try to obtain government backing for specific Centrist demands: for repeal of the law banning the Jesuit Society; for payment of salaries or daily stipends for Reichstag deputies; for legal recognition of labor unions and extension of labor protection legislation; for reform of Prussia's communal suffrage requirements; and for the appointment of more Catholics—and Centrists—to positions in the civil service. None of these requests was met with anything more than vague promises of future action, and several were rejected out of hand.

A lack of prompt attention to the demand of the Rhineland Centrists for reform of Prussian communal suffrage cost the government one of the kaiser's pet projects, the canal bill of 1899, which would have joined the agricultural areas of eastern Prussia with the industrial west. On this issue William was deserted by the Conservatives, who felt that the bill would be injurious to the interests of landowners in the east. Center representatives of Silesian landowners also opposed the bill for the same reason, but Lieber expected to deliver enough Center votes from western districts to put the measure through. The delegates from the Rhineland, however, led by the Bachem interests, insisted upon electoral reform as a prerequisite for their cooperation, and when it was not forthcoming, followed the Silesians in defying party discipline and thus defeated the canal bill.[20] William was not persuaded by the incident to appease the Center but instead decided upon further appeasement of the Conservatives, in spite of his anger at their defection.

A few months later, William, rather suddenly and impetuously, offered to sponsor a total repeal of the Jesuit law if the Center Reichstag fraction would agree to vote for the upcoming second naval appro-

20. Wahl, 3:609–12; Zeender, p. 80; *Zentrums-Album*, pp. 204–5.

priations bill. The offer was regarded with skepticism, because his sincerity was doubtful, and the terms of the bill were as yet not even known. As Lieber said, "We are ready to do everything for the sainted Ignatius's order that is possible, but not fatally dangerous political stupidities."[21] When the terms of the naval bill were completed and brought to the Reichstag in the spring of 1900, nothing more was heard of the kaiser's offer. The government apparently counted upon the heightened international tensions resulting from the Boer War in South Africa and the Boxer Rebellion in China to produce a wave of patriotic fervor which would carry through the appropriations.

This time Dr. Lieber's struggle to please both the government and the increasingly outspoken dissidents in his party brought on a permanent breakdown of his health.[22] His collapse and subsequent death two years later left the Center without effective leadership and sharply divided as to the correct strategy to pursue on the naval bill. On the one hand, Catholic public opinion in the country was, as always, opposed to additional military expenditures; on the other hand, it appeared that refusal to pass the bill might result in unwelcome new elections or even a coup d'état restricting the suffrage and weakening the Reichstag.[23] In order to make the bill more acceptable to the fraction, Center committee members, led by the party's financial expert Richard Müller-Fulda, sought to ensure that the revenues necessary to implement the bill would not include additional taxes on consumer goods. Their decisions determined the final form of the bill: "whichever kind of funding was finally chosen depended exclusively upon the Center." This represented a significant increase in Reichstag participation in the preparation of legislation.[24] However, there was still much dissatisfaction and indecision in the ranks of the Center, and this was reflected in the second reading of the bill in June 1900. The fraction delivered enough favorable votes to ensure its passage, and only nine opposed it, but fifty-six Centrists were absent when the vote was taken.[25]

---

21. Bachem, 9:313.
22. Zeender, p. 82.
23. See Röhl, *Germany without Bismarck*, pp. 220–22; 250–51.
24. Manfred Rauh, *Föderalismus und Parlamentarismus in Wilhelminischen Reich* (Düsseldorf, 1973), pp. 220–41.
25. Zeender, pp. 83–84.

The government's victory was thus accompanied by a clear demonstration that the Center would have to be managed with care in the future if it was to be relied upon for continued support. After six years, Hohenlohe had not succeeded much better than Caprivi in harnessing the party's strength for imperial purposes.

His successor as chancellor, Bernhard von Bülow, had the confidence to believe that it could be done and the intelligence to see that it must be done, if the existing constitutional relationships were to be maintained. The crucial role which the Center had played in finding financial resources for the naval bill had revealed the possibility that the Reichstag might seize the initiative altogether and attempt to carry out a parliamentarization of the Reich government through the full use of its financial powers. The kaiser's response to that would surely be a reversion to his plans to stage a coup, a possibility as undesirable to Bülow as parliamentarization.[26] The obvious solution to the dilemma was to win the Center to the government's side by a friendlier approach and, more important, by the granting of specific concessions. This was to be the policy of his government during the following six years.

26. Röhl, *Germany without Bismarck*, p. 221.

8
THE CENTER IN ALLIANCE WITH THE GOVERNMENT 1901–1906

Bernhard von Bülow had already achieved a good relationship with the leaders of the Center before he took office. Of all the chancellors of the era, he was the most acceptable to the Center because he did not share the ingrained prejudice against Catholics of most of the administration, and his Italian wife, who was something of a liability to him in his dealings with the court, was a distinct advantage to him in understanding and dealing with the Catholic politicians. He himself had no doubts of his talent in this regard: in 1898 he had written to Phillipp Eulenburg, "Today I shall work on five Center deputies in favour of the [naval] bill: It is a kind of spiritual massage."[1]

Bülow's desire to govern through the Reichstag by cooperating with the Center was shared by the Reich secretary for the interior, Posadowsky-Wehner. Posadowsky had originally been appointed to his post by William II to carry out a policy of strict repression of the Social Democrats and he had sponsored the unsuccessful "penitentiary bill" of 1899, but during the debates on that bill he had become convinced by arguments from the Center that socialism would be more effectively combatted by a policy of social reform and conciliation of non-Socialist labor organizations, in particular the Christian trade unions affiliated with the Center party. Posadowsky also had in common with the Center his concern for the maintenance of the denominational school system; he was a member of the General Synod of the Prussian Evangelical church.[2] Bülow and Posadowsky both hoped to enlarge the sphere of the Reich government and reduce that of the Prussian min-

1. Röhl, *Germany without Bismarck*, p. 250.
2. Born, pp. 140; 163–66; 171.

istry, bypassing the Federal Council (which was generally guided by the Prussian ministry) and making more use of the Reichstag. Cooperation of the Reichstag in this plan depended upon winning the large bloc of Center votes, and that in turn depended upon a substantive response by the government to the needs and wishes of the party. Such a policy diverged sharply from the original conception of the Reich constitution and might have led to parliamentarization of the Reich, but there was little interest in the Center for encouraging the trend toward parliamentary government. The party leadership, divided after Lieber's illness and death, was only concerned to maintain the existing rights of the Reichstag and to carry out as much as possible of its own partisan program.[3]

Discussions were opened early in 1901 to secure the Center fraction's support for an important agricultural tariff bill. In return for its votes, the party was promised the repeal of at least the most onerous sections of the law against the Jesuit order and the immediate consideration of social reform legislation which had been neglected since the early years of the reign of William II. Bülow had an unexpectedly hard time fulfilling the first promise, but Posadowsky was prompt in attending to the second.

The social reforms which were sponsored and carried through the Prussian and Reich legislatures by Posadowsky and the Center were of two kinds: laws for the protection of workers' health and safety and laws extending basic civil rights of association and organization to the working class. None accomplished anything very remarkable, yet taken together they represent the high point of social welfare legislation for the Wilhelmine period and compare favorably with legislation in other industrialized states at this time.[4]

A prerequisite for the reforms was the repeal of existing restrictions on workers' associations (which were also in conflict with clauses in the new civil law code.) This was done in December 1899, when Hohenlohe was still chancellor, and helped to smooth the way for Centrist approval of the 1900 naval law.[5] The repeal law acquired the name "Lex Hohenlohe," but the initiative came from Posadowsky.

3. Rauh, pp. 249–50; 350–51.
4. Born, pp. 179; 249–51.
5. Ibid., pp. 164–65.

Removal of the former prohibitions on association was intended to be followed by a more positively worded associations law, but this was not completed until 1908.

Between 1900 and 1905, laws were passed to establish factory councils and similar councils for commercial employees; to regulate labor conditions for sailors; to extend the ban on child labor to household industries; and to provide public funds for the construction of workers' housing. In 1905, after a widespread but orderly miners' strike in the Ruhr, in which the Center-affiliated Christian trade unions took part, a law was passed for the improvement and regulation of labor conditions of Prussian miners. Each of these measures was put through with the aid of the Center and was either opposed or accepted with great reluctance by the Conservative party and the kaiser.[6]

While Posadowsky wooed the Center with labor legislation, Bülow attempted to help the party to obtain repeal of the Reich law forbidding the Society of Jesus to establish itself in Germany and permitting the internment and exile of its individual members. He had only limited success, however, and injured his own reputation at court in the attempt.

The continued resistance in government circles to repeal is difficult to understand. One cannot read an account of the long struggle without feeling that the issue was one of great symbolic importance for both sides. It was as important for the state governments represented in the Federal Council to maintain this last remnant of the *Kulturkampf*, the concrete evidence of the subordination of the Catholic church to the state, as it was important to the Center to be able to use the issue to rally votes and to bargain with the government when deciding its stand on proposed legislation.

Opposition in the Federal Council to repeal of the Jesuit law ostensibly came not from the Prussian government or the Bavarian government (which had originally sponsored the law) but from the combined votes of nearly all the other states. It is difficult to believe, however, that the Reich chancellor and the Prussian cabinet could not have used their influence to obtain a favorable vote if they had wished one. Evasions and delays lasting several years at a time were the most

6. Ibid., pp. 183–88.

usual means of effective rejection, with occasional ameliorations or modifications of the Law.

The campaign for repeal began in 1890, when the anti-Socialist law was allowed to lapse. As long as the activities of Marxists were also condemned as dangerous to the state, the opponents of the Jesuits could cite the law as part of a general legal principle of restraint. But after 1890, when Socialists of all degrees of radicalism could (at least according to the law) speak and assemble with relative freedom, the position of the few hundred members of the Society of Jesus became glaringly anomalous, and the Center felt that its case could be effectively presented. It was able to round up considerable majorities for repeal from a combination of Centrists, Social Democrats, Poles, Alsatians, and a few individuals from the Conservative and Radical-Progressive parties. Seven times between 1890 and 1914 the Center drew up motions for repeal, and five times these were voted upon favorably by the Reichstag, but the Federal Council refused to confirm the votes.[7] When the Reichstag passed the repeal for the first time in 1893, the Federal Council did act to permit the reestablishment of the Redemptorists and other related orders, but rejected repeal of the law as such. The motion was passed by the Reichstag again in 1895, 1897, and 1898, with no further results. Cardinal Kopp attempted to use his personal friendship with William II to win approval for the measure, but both the kaiser and Chancellor Hohenlohe had long-standing prejudices against the order and saw no need to act. William's impulsive offer early in 1900 to obtain repeal in exchange for the Center's vote on the second navy bill was not interpreted by anyone as a serious gesture.

A new approach was tried by the party in 1900 with the Tolerance Proposal, a more general motion to establish complete freedom of religious activity in the Reich, for individuals and for institutions. The first part of the motion dealt with individual rights of religious affiliation, and the second with the rights of church organizations to establish themselves and operate freely anywhere in Germany. As one German historian has noted, this was completely in contradiction to the

---

7. For a detailed and sometimes wearisome account of this sustained effort, see Bachem, vol. 9, chap. 7.

Center's usual stand on states' rights.[8] The party's arguments ignored this inconsistency and cited as precedents for Reich legislation on religious matters the Jesuit law and the pulpit paragraph, both dating, of course, from the *Kulturkampf*! The Reich constitution was indeed very unclear about the delimitations of national authority.

The *Toleranzantrag* recalled the Center's bid in 1871 to extend the Prussian constitutional guarantees to all parts of the Reich. One of its effects would have been to have admitted the Catholic church to a position of equality with the Evangelical state churches in the smaller Protestant states, such as Saxony, Brunswick, and the Mecklenburgs, where it was still handicapped in many irritating ways, including not only restrictions on the number of clergy in the state, or on the frequency of services, but in the right to erect steeples, ring bells, and so forth. Since the motion specified *all* religious organizations, it was heartily supported by representatives of the "dissidents," the small Protestant sects such as the Old Lutherans and the Baptists, who were also restricted by the anachronistic monopoly of the Evangelical state churches.

The question of the status of minority sects in these smaller states was becoming less of a purely academic one, because, as in any industrialized country, there was growing mobility of the population in Germany, and colonies of Catholics had sprung up in many places which were previously exclusively Protestant. This was especially true in the large cities. For example, the population of Mecklenburg increased from being less than 3 percent Catholic to 4.5 percent by 1910, and the population of Brunswick from less than 3 percent to 7 percent Catholic, while, conversely, the Protestant population increased steadily in the south and in the Rhineland. (The Catholic population of Berlin was eight times greater in 1910 than in 1870.)[9]

Besides affecting the small Protestant states, the motion, if passed, would also require the Bavarian government to give up its *placet*, and the Prussian government to give up its remaining restrictions on religious orders. One short and simply worded article, number 10, would have permitted all the orders full rights of establishment anywhere in

8. Wahl, 3:650. The author thinks the bill a "crazy" idea.
9. Bachem, 7:365.

the country. Specific repeal of the Jesuit law would no longer be necessary if this motion succeeded. Of course it did not. Only the first part, relating to individuals, passed a poorly attended session of the Reichstag; the second part did not come to a vote, and the Federal Council ignored the vote on the first part. Chancellor Bülow, in fact, had stated from the outset that the government would never even consider approving the measure. The *Toleranzantrag* was brought forth again in 1904, without success. The work put into drafting this quixotic motion was not in vain, however, for in addition to being an excellent piece of propaganda for the Center, the motion was incorporated almost word for word into the final draft of the Weimar Constitution.

Though Bülow would not countenance the *Toleranzantrag*, he did promise to seek relief for the Jesuits, and early in 1903 he expressed in a speech to the Reichstag his personal belief that a repeal of Article 2 of the Jesuit law was desirable. This was the part of the law which most flagrantly violated civil rights by permitting the internment and exile of anyone shown to be a member of the order. Bülow found it impossible to obtain a majority in the Federal Council even for this.

The chancellor's policy of bypassing the constitutional role of the Federal Council, creating a new "Reich government" of himself and the state secretaries, and appealing directly to the Reichstag had angered the governments of the smaller states, and the Jesuit law was the issue on which they decided to assert their rights. Bülow had been assured of Prussian and Bavarian support for repeal of Article 2 and had ignored the other delegates; they retaliated by combining to prevent a majority.[10] (In his memoirs Bülow does not mention the constitutional issue but blames the prejudices of the princes, particularly the king of Saxony, a Catholic himself, who bent over backward to ensure the dominance of the established Evangelical church in his state.)[11]

Upon confessing failure to Spahn and the rest of the Center fraction, Bülow was informed that unless at least Article 2 was repealed, the party would not support a forthcoming Reich financial reform.

10. Rauh, p. 255.
11. Bernhard von Bülow, *Memoirs*, 4 vols. (Boston, 1931–32), 2:12–14.

Bülow was put in the humiliating position of having to go begging to each and every one of the delegates of the smaller states, some of which would stand to benefit from the financial reforms, to win votes for repeal. A horse trade was finally arranged with Baden. The grand duke, hitherto adamant in refusing consideration of repeal, offered to abstain from voting his three Federal Council votes against repeal of Article 2 if the Center in return would support Baden's special interests in the financial measures. The fraction was angry and divided over what response to give this rather insulting offer. The deal was made, but with conditions: Baden must vote yes for repeal, not simply abstain; other votes necessary for a majority must be secured in advance; and the passage of repeal must be ensured before the financial measures could be approved. After much bargaining and delay, the Federal Council voted for repeal of Article 2, with a narrow majority composed only of Prussia, Bavaria, Baden, Hamburg, and two tiny states under Prussian influence. Hamburg had reluctantly agreed to vote yes if its sister states Lübeck and Bremen agreed to abstain rather than to oppose.[12]

This very grudging and halfhearted gesture provoked public demonstrations of protest and was condemned not only by the Evangelical League, which was to be expected, but also by the Evangelical *Oberkirchenrat* in Prussia.[13] Bülow was subjected to harsh criticism for his part in the concession (his wife received ugly anonymous letters), and it may well have been the reaction to this episode which later persuaded him that a break with the Center would be expedient for his personal career.

As for the Center, the repeal of Article 2 was hardly a triumph, because individual Jesuits had in practice been able to live and work in most parts of Germany for some time, and their situation was little improved, since police regulations interpreted "activities of the order" so broadly that no Jesuit could teach or lecture without danger of harassment. The regulations, absurdly, permitted speeches or teaching on any subject except those having to do in any way with religion. (Another absurdity of the law was that after 1900, all religious orders including the Jesuits could pursue their activities freely in any Ger-

---

12. Bachem, 9:328–33; Rauh, pp. 255–62.
13. Wahl, 3:660; see *Zentrums-Album*, pp. 228–29.

man colony, yet Jesuit missionaries had of necessity to be educated and trained entirely outside the Reich.)

The party's continuing campaign on behalf of the Jesuits, its insistence on the maintenance of denominational schools, and its vigilance to uphold a particular concept of Christian values comprised an area of *Kulturpolitik* which divided the Center from both Socialists and liberals and prevented the formation of enduring parliamentary partnerships with either group, in spite of many mutual interests. An incident in 1900 illustrates the divergence of views. The Center was normally an ardent supporter of a free press and free public expression, but the party was tempted too greatly by a government proposal that year to amend the criminal code to include various crimes of sexual immorality, and it launched a short-lived crusade for extensive censorship. The contents of the government's bill were greatly expanded in committee by the Centrist members to go far beyond the original provisions concerning prostitution and obscenity to include a broad censorship of literature, advertising, and the theater. Most of the arguing of the Center's case was done by Deputy Hermann Roeren, later a leader of the integralist faction in the *Zentrumsstreit*.

The expanded bill naturally provoked a wave of protest from artists, theater people and intellectuals, and public petitions were presented to the Reichstag signed by well-known persons. The liberals and Social Democrats took up the cause of freedom in the arts and vowed to kill the bill; parliamentary obstructionism from the Left created an impasse, until a compromise was worked out. The final draft when approved by the majority omitted entirely the provisions pertaining to the theater and most of those concerned with literature: in other words, it was a return to the original government bill.

The incident of the Heinze Law (so-called after the pimp whose activities had prompted the government to act) was of little importance in itself, but it is worth noting because it was this kind of issue, involving a paternalistic guardianship of public morals, that so often divided the Center from the parties of the Left and middle and, like the issue of public education, created a mutual antagonism which prevented cooperation in other matters.

A Catholic interest which had nothing directly to do with religion was that of the elimination of alleged discrimination against Catholics in government positions: the demand for "parity." In return for its transformation into a government party, the Center expected Bülow and the Reich and Prussian administrations to provide for Catholics an entree into their own circles. But this problem proved even more intractible than the Jesuit law because of the complexity of the reasons for the existing lack of parity; and Bülow's contribution toward a solution was minimal, of token significance only.

Ideally, full parity would be attained when the proportion of Catholics in every rank of government would approach the proportion of Catholics in the population. For national positions, this would mean approximately 34 percent, but for local positions in heavily Catholic areas like the Rhineland and Silesia, a much higher percentage. Obviously, this goal was never even remotely approached in the period of the Second Reich. All sources are agreed that Catholics were underrepresented, especially at the higher levels of government.[14] The facts are clear, but the reasons behind them are less easy to determine. As in every case of employment discrimination based upon religion, sex, or race, there were other factors involved beside direct prejudice at the level of appointment.

First, government officials in imperial Germany were chosen from a narrow range of social backgrounds, from the aristocracy and the more or less professional bureaucratic class, and relatively few Catholics were included in these social classes, particularly in Prussia. The reason for this lies far back in the past history of the country since the Reformation. Neither William I nor William II showed any inclination to increase the size of the Catholic aristocracy in Prussia, and only 7 percent of their new creations of nobles were Catholic.[15]

Second, opponents of the Center claimed that the small number of appointments at the top merely reflected the smaller numbers of Catholics in the lower ranks of government; that this reflected the correspondingly low numbers of Catholics attending the *Gymnasien* and universities; and that this in turn reflected the inferiority of the exclusively Catholic schools at the elementary level. There is cer-

14. See, for example, Röhl, "Higher Civil Servants in Germany 1890–1900," *Journal of Contemporary History* 2 (1967): 109: "Catholics were virtually excluded from holding high office either in the Reich or in the Prussian bureaucracy."
15. Lamar Cecil, "The Creation of Nobles in Prussia, 1871–1918," *American Historical Review* 75 (1970): 757–95.

tainly some truth in this line of reasoning. In the 1960s, German Catholics were finally beginning to acknowledge that the denominational school system, or its side effects, had held them back for generations.[16]

It is also true, however, that appointments to civil service positions in imperial Germany (as in England at that time, and elsewhere) were very much based upon personal knowledge of a candidate's background and upon a pervasive Old Boy network. Former members of the university "corps" or military clubs were favored, and after them, members of the originally liberal fraternities, the *Bürschenschaften*. But Catholics were rarely members of either of these types of university fraternities, especially after the rise of Catholic consciousness in the 1850s, most importantly because of the church's prohibition against dueling. Catholic students increasingly organized themselves in separate Catholic student clubs, which were unconnected with the web of influence controlling appointments.

Finally, there is a distinction to be made here between religious prejudice and political prejudice. Much discrimination in government appointments was not against Catholics but against Centrists; and conversely, the Center party's constant agitation for parity for Catholics was a concealed effort to obtain a position in the administration for itself commensurate with its numbers and strength in the legislatures. "When the critics said 'Catholic' they meant 'Centrist,' . . . they were seeking party parity and patronage behind the facade of religious parity." It was possible for Catholics to rise in government service if they held themselves aloof from the Center party, particularly if they joined the Conservative party. Quite a few Catholics were appointed to the important office of *Landrat* in heavily Catholic districts, but not a single one of them before 1918 was affiliated with the Center party.[17] Since one of the duties of a *Landrat* was understood to be that of supporting government programs in elections, this is not surprising. Before the unification of Germany and the *Kulturkampf*, the percent-

16. Frederic Spotts, *The Churches and Politics in Germany* (Middletown, Conn., 1973), pp. 220–28.
17. Lysbeth W. Muncy, "The Prussian *Landrat* in the Last Years of the Monarchy: A Case Study of Pomerania and the Rhineland in 1890–1918," *Central European History* 6 (1973): 327–29.

age of Catholic officials in the Rhine Province was much higher than at any time afterward until World War I.[18] The grievance of the Center was a real grievance, but it was as much a political as a religious one.

The Center kept close records of appointments of Catholics and in 1897 and 1899 actually prepared elaborate memoranda on the subject, which were sent to the chancellor and other high officials. These memoranda were updated until the end of the empire in 1918. At the ministerial level in Prussia and the Reich, only three prewar Prussian cabinet ministers (aside from Minister-President and Chancellor Hohenlohe) were Catholic, holding the portfolios for Justice, Railways, and Agriculture. None was a Centrist, of course, although Freiherr von Schorlemer, minister of agriculture from 1910 to 1917, was a son of the former Center fraction-head in the Reichstag. Only two Catholics served as state secretaries for the Reich, one for Justice and one for the Treasury. At the next highest level of ministerial director in the ministries, the percentage of Catholics was everywhere low, but conspicuously lowest in the Prussian Ministry of Religion and Education and the Ministry of the Interior, the very departments of most concern to Catholics: the first for obvious reasons, the second because the Ministry of the Interior controlled appointments to the lower ranks of government service. The *Kultus* ministry had two permanent positions reserved for Catholics, which dealt exclusively with Catholic affairs, but no other positions were held by Catholics after the 1870s. There were only two ministerial directors in the Interior who were Catholic in the prewar period. Very few of the *Oberpräsidenten* of the Prussian provinces were Catholic, all non-Centrist, and these few were named only to the heavily Catholic provinces. *Landräte* in "overwhelmingly" Catholic districts were usually Catholic, but if the districts had only a slight majority of Catholics, were more likely to be Protestant, and if 50 percent or more Protestant, were certain to be Protestant.[19] Protestant officials were almost invariably sent to the Polish provinces and to Alsace-Lorraine. For offices higher than that of *Landrat*, the percentage of Catholics was greater in 1850 than in 1905. There seems to have been a deliberate effort made in the 1850s to eliminate radicals, Jews, and Catholics from the Prussian civil service. In the judiciary,

18. John R. Gillis, *The Prussian Bureaucracy in Crisis, 1840–1860* (Stanford, Calif., 1971), p. 206.
19. Muncy, p. 321.

however, there was a gradual rise in the percentage of Catholics, from 10 percent to 18 percent.[20]

The government's reasoning seems to have been that on the one hand, it was patently unfair to appoint a Catholic to office in a Protestant district, but on the other hand, it was risky to appoint one in a Catholic district, because he might be seduced by Center party influence or (in the Polish and Alsatian districts) identify too closely with the local inhabitants. There were a few cases, however, of Catholic officials serving in Protestant areas, especially in the judiciary. In 1905, Bülow named the Centrist leader Peter Spahn to be *Oberlandgerichtspräsident* for Kiel, in Holstein, which was hailed by the party as a breakthrough, but it set little precedent for the future.

For the most part, the imperial and Prussian governments made only evasive and deprecating replies to the Center's insistent demands for parity, until the middle of the war. In the year 1917 there was a decided change of heart, and a number of Catholic appointments to high office were made, including Center party members. With the deteriorating war situation and threat of social revolution, the Center suddenly appeared far less subversive to the regime than it had before.

Closely related to the problem of obtaining parity in government offices was a similar problem in the universities and the army, twin pillars of the establishment of the Second Reich. The Center was concerned about the small percentage of university professors who were practicing Catholics, even at Bavarian universities like the University of Munich. Figures for the 1890s reveal that only 43 percent of Bavarian professors, including professors of theology, were Catholic. In Prussia, only 11.75 percent of university lecturers (*Dozenten*) in nontheological faculties and only 8.75 percent of *Privatdozenten* were Catholic. Some universities tried to keep their faculties exclusively Protestant, notably Rostock, Halle, and Königsberg by statute; Berlin, Greifswald, Göttingen, and Marburg by tradition. To some it appeared that there existed "a single large clique of National Liberal professors who didn't want to let go of their monopoly."[21]

20. Gillis, p. 253.
21. Figures from David Blackbourn, "The Problem of Democratisation: German Catholics and the Role of the Centre Party," in Richard J. Evans, ed., *Society and Politics in Wilhelmine Germany* (London, 1978), p. 165. Universities listed and quotation cited in Christoph Weber, "Der 'Fall Spahn,' die 'Weltgeschichte in Karakterbildern'

Hertling had founded the Görres Society to help to correct this special kind of imparity, but it was a slow and difficult task, since it clearly required the upgrading of Catholic education at all levels. Hertling's speech in Constance in 1896 on "the causes of the backwardness [*Zurückbleibens*] of German Catholics in the area of scholarship" had begun the great "inferiority" debate which enlivened educated Catholic circles for some years. Many did not agree with his efforts to integrate Catholics into what they regarded as the sacrifice of church teaching to Godless science; among them was Bishop Korum of Trier who in a pastoral letter of 1902 strongly opposed "seductive" attempts to modernize Catholic scholarship. Similar views were expressed that same year in an article in *Historische Politische Blätter*. The situation was more complex than Hertling supposed.[22] Nevertheless, it was true that there was substantial prejudice against Catholics in university posts, as is shown by the excitement generated by the Spahn case.

Martin Spahn was the son of Peter Spahn, but he was more conservative politically and less orthodox in religious practice than his father. He had personally experienced prejudice early in his career when his professors at the University of Berlin had been reluctant to appoint him as a *Privatdozent* because they wished to keep the faculty there *katholikenrein*.[23] He was appointed, however, and in 1901, in response to pressure from the Center, the Reich government called the twenty-six year old Spahn to the post of professor of history at the University of Strassburg, recently founded to serve the needs of the (largely Catholic) population of the *Reichsland*. His appointment was in anticipation of the establishment of a complete Catholic theological faculty, a project still being negotiated in Rome.

The appointment aroused a great deal of protest from other members of the faculty at Strassburg and from well-known historians at other universities, who criticized Spahn's youth and Center connections and charged that it was obviously an act of political patronage. Theodor Mommsen wrote an article in the *Münchner Neuesten Nachrichten* in which he implied that a Catholic world-outlook disqualified a man for a university history position, and Friedrich Meinecke is

---

und die Görres-Gesellschaft I," *Römische Quartalschrift für christliche Altertum und Kirchegeschichte* 73 (1978): 87–89.
22. Weber, p. 94–104.
23. Ibid., p. 83.

quoted as having said that "Catholic history professors are and remain a monstrosity."[24] Liberals in the Reichstag opposed the grant of money for the new theological faculty because the bishop was allowed to help select the faculty, although similar concessions were usual at the universities of Bonn and Breslau.

The agitation over the Spahn appointment coincided with a movement among nationalist-*Völkisch* students to exclude the rapidly growing Catholic student corporations from recognition by the universities. The attacks were of less significance than the anti-Semitic campaigns waged by these student groups, but they can be seen as a paler manifestation of the same atmosphere of hatred and intolerance. In this case, Chancellor Bülow and the Prussian *Kultus* ministry halted any practical plans to expel the Catholic corporations.

One reason for the growth of exclusively Catholic student corporations and clubs in the German universities was the persistent survival of the "duel principle" in the fraternities and in the army officer corps. Before the 1850s, the prohibition of dueling by the Catholic church was not usually assumed to apply to the students' *Mensur,* and in fact it was rumored that Bishop von Ketteler and the Reichensperger brothers had all fought duels in their student days. But in this as in so many other respects, the church tightened its strictures in the 1850s, and it became impossible for a conscientious practicing Catholic to enter the fraternities and the university corps. This injured his chances for a later career in government or in the army, since the Catholic clubs were poor substitutes and regarded by other students as second-class at best.

In the Prussian army, dueling among officers had been officially condemned by the reigning kings on several occasions in the nineteenth century, but affairs of honor nevertheless continued and the punishment meted out to duelists was very light. Above all, it was the willingness to defend one's honor that counted. Refusal of a challenge was a disgrace and constituted grounds for dismissal from the service. Special "courts of honor" set up in the 1890s to reduce the occasion for challenges did not eradicate the principle, although actual duels fought, and the number of deaths resulting from them, diminished steadily.

24. Ross, pp. 26–28; Bachem, 6:236.

For the conscientious Catholic officer it was possible to advance in the army so long as the question of "defense of honor" did not arise; but once a challenge was made and refused, dismissal was the result, and no amount of protest or appeal to the army regulation against dueling was of use. Professional advancement in the army, then, was difficult for a practicing Catholic, at least until the attainment of cooler-headed middle age. The prewar German officer corps was 83 percent Protestant, 16 percent Catholic.[25]

Candidates for reserve officer status, so much coveted in Germany as a mark of prestige, were sometimes quizzed on their willingness to defend their honor, and known membership in a Catholic university corporation was likely to bring about such an examination. The Center party had won a slight victory in 1895 when a cabinet order was issued forbidding such questioning of reserve officer candidates. A further cabinet order in 1897 condemned dueling, and after that date most duels fought were between reserve officers rather than professionals, but refusal of a challenge was still grounds for dismissal.[26]

A Centrist interpellation made early in 1906 on the subject of dueling was referred by Bülow to a committee consisting of the Prussian minister of war, Karl von Einem, and the Reich secretaries for justice and the interior, Arnold Nieberding and Posadowsky. Their report concluded with the statement: "As long as duelling is recognized by wide circles of society as a means of rehabilitating one's honour, the officer corps will be unable to tolerate in its ranks anyone who is not prepared to defend his honour with weapon in hand." After an indignant protest from the Center, Bülow apologized to the Reichstag for the phrasing of the statement, but he did not seek to alter it.[27] Later that year the Center succeeded in inserting clauses in an army pension

25. Bachem cites the melodramatic case in 1864 of three Catholic brothers: one refused a challenge and all three were dismissed from the service after an examination forced them to admit that they would all refuse to fight a duel (9:171–74). Figures from Klaus Epstein, *Matthias Erzberger and the Dilemma of German Democracy* (Princeton, 1959), p. 67.
26. Martin Kitchen, *The German Officer Corps, 1890–1914* (Oxford, 1968), p. 52; also, Karl Demeter, *The German Officer Corps in Society and State, 1650–1945* (New York, 1965), pp. 144–45.
27. Terry Cole, "Kaiser versus Chancellor: The Crisis of Bülow's Chancellorship, 1905–6," in Evans, pp. 40–67.

bill saying that any injury to health incurred as the result of a duel was not to be covered by insurance provisions, and that refusal of a challenge was not to be considered one of the grounds for a man's being declared "unfit for duty."

The Reichstag voted on several occasions to urge the army to end dueling, with majorities obtained from the Social Democrats, the Radical-Progressives, and the Center with its allies. Antidueling leagues were formed in both Germany and Austria and attracted wide membership among Protestants as well as Catholics. But the government and the army continued to issue evasive statements which on the one hand deplored dueling but on the other hand persisted in recognizing refusal to defend one's honor as grounds for dismissal from the officer corps. In a memorandum of the spring of 1914, Minister of War von Falkenhayn wrote: "I consider it my duty to stand up to all attempts by parliament directly or indirectly to exert pressure on the ideas and the spirit of the officer corps."[28]

The "duel principle" was ended in the German army after World War I, but the *Mensur* in the universities continued. To forestall complaints that this custom created a barrier to career advancement for Catholics, dueling fraternities in the 1920s began to recruit Catholic students, using the argument (very welcome to many young Catholic men) that the *Mensur* was not a true duel and hence not condemned by the church. However, the argument was not accepted by the German bishops.[29]

The concessions to the Center made during Bülow's chancellorship: the piecemeal social legislation, the repeal of Article 2 of the Jesuit law, the Spahn appointments, were seen by the Center as merely the opening rounds in the continuing effort to raise the Catholic population of Germany from its second-class citizenship. Full parity in the civil service, legal recognition of labor unions, and total repeal of the Jesuit law still remained to be obtained from the favorable bargaining position the party now occupied. But these same halfhearted concessions were seen by the kaiser and his ministers, including Bülow, as very substantial payments for votes and as evidence of an intolerable

28. Kitchen, pp. 49–50.
29. Bachem, 9:169.

dependence upon the Center party, a dependence, moreover, which might lead at any time to an alteration in the constitutional role of the Reichstag.

It was unquestionably the Center's leadership, working against elements in its own ranks, which enabled the government to win a narrow victory for the tariff law of 1902 and the financial reforms of 1905–6. In the case of the tariff bill, great skill was needed to reconcile the representatives of the Christian Trade Unions who feared, with good reason, that the proposed tariff levels would raise the cost of food for consumers even higher than it already was. Karl Trimborn, a young deputy from the Rhineland, swung labor votes over to the measure by including in its complicated provisions a clause reserving some of its anticipated revenues for benefits for the widows and orphans of industrial workers. (This "Trimborn clause" was passed and was eventually incorporated in the general consolidation of the social insurance program in 1911, but Trimborn's original intentions were modified considerably in its execution, and the large revenue surpluses were never forthcoming.) Although the Center's labor wing was appeased and brought into line for the bill by the Trimborn clause, the Social Democratic party remained vehemently opposed to it and used unprecedented obstructionist tactics to prevent its passage. Count Ballestrem exercised all the powers of his office as Reichstag president to combat the Socialists and the law was finally passed at 4:30 A.M. on 14 December 1902 after a nineteen-hour session.[30]

The Center's leaders, always anxious to maintain respectability and dignity, were angry at the Social Democrats' obstructionism and in the next Reichstag elections, in June 1903, conducted a strongly anti-Socialist campaign, although the party refused to join the Conservatives and National Liberals in an election alliance.[31] The Social Democrats profited from the unpopularity of the tariff law with the German voters, and they returned a greatly increased delegation of eighty-one to the new Reichstag. The parties supporting the government lost correspondingly, but the Center lost only five seats and actually gained in the popular vote. Its value to the government was thus proportionately even greater than before.

30. Bachem, 6:151–69; Zeender, p. 93; August Bebel, *Abrechnung mit dem Zentrum* (Cologne, 1974), pp. 27–28.
31. Blackbourn, in Evans, pp. 175–76.

Immediately after the elections, Bülow dismissed his Reich treasury secretary and replaced him with Heinrich, Freiherr von Stengel, with the clear intention of winning Centrist support for a reform of the tax structure. Stengel had been finance minister of Bavaria and one of that state's delegates to the Federal Council; he was a Catholic, friendly with Centrists, and had already served Bülow as a liaison with the party.[32] Not only the Center's votes but also the ability of its financial experts such as Richard Müller-Fulda were needed to solve the Reich's chronic and worsening financial problems. Revenues from existing sources could not cover the mounting expenditures for arms and for Tirpitz's new fleet, especially since the country was experiencing an economic depression. New sources were essential, yet any move to introduce direct income or property taxes for the Reich would be sure to be opposed in the Federal Council and would also affect the federalist sensibilities of the Center, while additional indirect taxes would meet fierce resistance from the Left and from Centrists who did not want to put further burdens upon consumers. Stengel planned to work with the Center to find new revenue from some form of Reich inheritance tax and from indirect taxes on luxury goods.[33]

Committee work proceeded through the year 1905 into the spring of 1906. In return for its cooperation and assistance on a tax law the Center was rewarded with the granting of its long-standing wish for daily stipends for parliamentary deputies, which were finally approved by Bülow and the Federal Council in March 1906. This was a great boon to Centrists from the south and from outlying districts in Prussia, who had previously not been able to afford regular attendance at Reichstag sessions.

The tax reforms were duly passed in May, with some defections from Bavarian Centrists on the proposed tax on beer and from rural delegates on the inheritance tax. It was obvious even then, however, that this law was only a stopgap measure and that a more comprehensive reform would be necessary very soon. The rebellion in the German colony of Southwest Africa and the consequent military expenditures there made the need more urgent. Stengel, Posadowsky, and Tirpitz assumed that the present policy of conciliating the Center

32. Peter-Christian Witt, *Die Finanzpolitik des Deutschen Reiches von 1903 bis 1913* (Lübeck and Hamburg, 1970), pp. 77–80.
33. Ibid., pp. 80–81.

would continue, in order to secure the financial base for government operations, but Bülow had become increasingly restive with the relationship. In his memoirs he describes his uneasiness at having incurred the disapproval of the kaiser and his rigidly Protestant wife, and he cites "warnings" he received against continued concessions to the Catholic party.[34] Centrist support appeared to be indispensable for the passage of legislation in the Reichstag, but the kaiser's approval was indispensable for the chancellor's remaining in office. So long as he could only obtain majorities in the legislatures with the help of the party for which William reserved his "especial dislike,"[35] Bülow's position was precarious. If the colonial issue had not developed as it did in 1906, it is likely that he would have found some other opportunity to break with the Center.

It could not have been predicted that a rupture between the Center and the government would occur over colonial policy, since the party had never really had a colonial policy, any more than it had any foreign policy other than a commitment to smaller expenditure on armaments. From the beginning, some German Catholics had been interested in the colonies as bases for missionary work, and a German Catholic African Association had been founded in 1888 in Cologne. However, Windthorst, like his adversary Bismarck, initially showed a good deal of skepticism about the value of colonies. His Guelphish instincts led him to believe that colonial expansion would be of use mostly to "Hanseatic business interests" and he felt that Germany should not become officially drawn into African affairs because of agitation from them and from the missionary orders.[36]

The party paid little attention to the overseas empire from the days of its first establishment until 1905, except to ensure that all of the Catholic orders would be permitted to operate freely in all territories. This freedom had been guaranteed in the Congo Act of 1885 for some parts of Africa, but at first the Jesuit order had been forbidden in those German possessions not covered by the act. In 1889 the party succeeded in obtaining government permission for the society and all

34. Bülow, 2:13–16; 112–13. See *Zentrums-Album*, p. 241, for a cartoon illustrating Stengel's dependence upon the Center party.
35. Bülow, 2:109.
36. Bachem, 5:52.

other orders to work in all the colonies, and this was reconfirmed in a general colonial statute in 1900.

The colonies became the focus of attention in Germany when serious native revolts began in Southwest Africa. Colonies which ran themselves quietly and cheaply were unlikely to disturb national politics, but unexpectedly large expenditures on army forces and equipment were bound to excite notice, especially from the economy-loving and antimilitarist Centrists. It was a handicap that no member of the Reichstag fraction had any detailed knowledge of the colonies. The need was filled by the youngest man in the fraction, Matthias Erzberger, first elected to the Reichstag in 1903 at the age of twenty-eight.

Erzberger was from a small village in Württemberg. He had begun his career as a schoolteacher and then worked as an organizer for the Catholic workers' associations in the state. He had entered politics as a protégé of Adolf Gröber, who had once been just such an energetic young iconoclast as Erzberger became. But the similarities and the close relationship between the two men were short-lived. Gröber lost his youthful radicalism and he never became fully acclimated to Berlin, keeping many ties with Württemberg and remaining active in Stuttgart politics. Erzberger on the other hand left his Suabian origins behind him and became a full-time resident in Berlin, making a living by political journalism, writing articles and pamphlets on innumerable subjects to send to the Centrist press all over the country. He was not content to serve an apprenticeship on the national political scene but immediately began speaking out on major issues, often without permission or even previous consultation with older politicians. Gröber secured him a seat on the parliamentary Budget Committee (a favor he later regretted), and Erzberger quickly showed great aptitude for all matters financial, attracting his first public notice with his work on a military pensions bill. He was coached and encouraged in his parliamentary education by Richard Müller-Fulda, a man who shunned the limelight himself but who well understood how the Reichstag operated.[37]

If Erzberger found himself unqualified to speak or write on any

37. See Abbé Wetterlé, *Behind the Scenes in the Reichstag* (New York, 1918), pp. 83–90; 147, a highly prejudiced account.

subject, he did not for that reason forego the opportunity, but simply persevered until he had made himself master of the subject. In 1905 he threw himself into an investigation of the colonial administration. He found in all the African colonies evidence of waste, mismanagement, corruption, and callous treatment of the native African population. He began a series of anonymous articles for the *Kölnische Volkszeitung* which exposed these conditions and made abundantly clear the reasons for the revolts in South Africa. The Reichstag took notice.

The colonial administration had been a neglected department in the Foreign Office and had never been really competently led. In 1905 the office was scheduled to be upgraded with a separate title and a new director. Little improvement could be expected, however, since the kaiser exercised his prerogative to appoint one of his cousins, "Erni," Hereditary Prince zu Hohenlohe-Langenburg, a man who was unqualified for the post at any time, and certainly not during a crisis period of armed uprising in Southwest Africa.

The Center was especially wary of Prince Erni because he was an active member of the Evangelical League. Erzberger criticized his appointment and persuaded most of the Center fraction, though not the older leaders, to vote against the government's proposal for the creation of a new state secretary of the colonies, thus defeating the plan to give the prince a higher status.[38]

The Center party was at this time suffering from a lack of strong leadership because of the centrifugal effect of the regional interests of the older leaders. Lieber had died in 1902; Peter Spahn had just taken up a judicial post in Kiel, in Holstein; Bachem, resident in the Rhineland, was in poor health; and Hertling was preoccupied with his university work in Munich. Erzberger was in Berlin, acquiring a large and admiring following among the younger men in the fraction. He was especially popular with his fellow southerners. Repeated reprimands from the older men and requests at least to moderate his tone had no effect on his determination to continue the attack on the colonial administration, and "the majority of the fraction left Spahn and Bachem in the lurch in this struggle against Erzberger."[39]

Working on his own, but seen by the country as a representative

38. See Cole, in Evans, pp. 46-51.
39. Bachem, 5:348.

of the Center, Erzberger publicized the colonial scandals, and the government had little defense to offer. It was revealed that the wife of Prussian Minister of Agriculture von Podbielski owned shares in the controversial Tippelskirch Company which had received a monopoly contract to supply the colonies. Cruel treatment meted out to natives by colonial officials and settlers was described in lurid detail. Erzberger's defense of native Africans was widely derided and gave him the reputation of being a "nigger-lover."[40]

The new colonial director made no serious attempt to correct conditions. His assistant, Karl Helfferich, engaged Erzberger in debate but was beaten handily in the face of Erzberger's detailed evidence. Helfferich acquired at this time a dislike for the Centrist leader which later intensified and led to their fateful conflict in the postwar years.

In April 1906, Erzberger brought out a brochure called *The Colonial Balance Sheet*, summing up his findings. In the next few months the Centrist and Social Democratic members of the Reichstag Budget Committee refused to meet the government's request for additional funds to cover money already spent in quelling the revolt in Southwest Africa. Overspending without authorization from the Parliament, followed by requests for supplemental funds, had come to be the usual method of conducting business for the colonial administration, and even conservative Centrists like Gröber were beginning to balk at it. The committee also refused funds to build a railway in Southwest Africa, since this had been presented to them as a military necessity for the campaign, yet obviously could not be completed until long after the revolt was extinguished. Similarly, a request for a large indemnity to German settlers was refused on the grounds that the revolt was not yet ended; that the settlers might be encouraged by such rewards to continue the behavior toward the African tribes which had precipitated the revolt in the first place; and that the indemnity would set an awkward precedent for civilian disasters in Germany.[41]

In the face of this defeat, Hohenlohe-Langenburg resigned in Sep-

40. Epstein, "Erzberger and the German Colonial Scandals 1905–1910," *English Historical Review* 74 (1959): 637–63.
41. George Dunlap Crothers, *The German Elections of 1907* (New York, 1941), p. 33; Bachem, 6:359. The most complete description of the Center's role in the colonial crisis is to be found in Hans Pehl, *Die deutsche Kolonialpolitik und das Zentrum* (Limburg, 1934).

tember 1906. Bülow secured as his replacement an outsider to government circles, a Jewish liberal financier, director of the *Darmstädter Bank*, Bernhard Dernburg. Apart from the obvious need to find a man who was familiar with the business world and competent enough to correct the corrupt and inefficient practices of the colonial office, the appointment was probably made with the idea of pleasing the liberals in the Reichstag and enticing them into the government camp. Bülow had watched the Center party becoming even more disliked by the kaiser than it had been before the colonial exposé, and had begun to engineer a parliamentary coalition that would enable him to govern without Centrist support. The longtime Radical leader Eugen Richter had recently died, and his successors were inclined to abandon permanent opposition. In the tense international situation, support of the government's diplomatic, naval, and colonial policies seemed more desirable to the Radicals than it had in an earlier period. Bülow reasoned that the appointment of Dernburg would satisfy the Radicals' demand for practical reforms in the colonial office and free them to play a more positive role in a progovernment party alignment.

The choice of Dernburg was not in itself unwelcome to the Center, and it was a decided improvement on Prince Erni, but Erzberger and his friends did not hesitate to saddle the new director with all of the blame for past iniquities of the colonial administration.

A close friend and collaborator of Erzberger in the exposure of colonial scandals was another young deputy, Hermann Roeren. Roeren was an outspoken Catholic integralist, and it was he who had made the interpellation on dueling which had embarrassed Bülow and further convinced him to decrease his dependence upon the Center.[42] Roeren had become interested in colonial policy not, like Erzberger, from the financial angle but from his close personal contacts with the Catholic missions in Togoland. For several years he had been seeking to right a miscarriage of justice brought to his attention by the missionaries, involving an official in Togoland who had been imprisoned without trial for defending the rights of the natives too zealously. Roeren had found it impossible to make the slightest headway in the case through private petitioning and so decided to introduce it into the Reichstag debates. Roeren and Erzberger had both been willing to ob-

42. Cole, in Evans, pp. 42–43.

tain evidence for their cause wherever they could find it and had made use of documents received from, among others, civil servants who had been dismissed from their jobs in the colonial service. When this became known, it greatly damaged their case, because, however true the documented material was, it had been obtained by dubious and dishonorable methods. Their opponents could now defend the great colonial scandal by pointing to a kind of mini-scandal within the Center party, the "Pöplau-Wistuba Affair," so called from the names of the two informants of Roeren and Erzberger.

Years later, his unscrupulous methods were brought up again to Erzberger's discredit. It was also claimed that his investigations were a direct cause of Germany's losing her colonial empire, since his detailed and voluminous evidence was used by the Allies after the war to justify taking away Germany's colonies, in spite of the fact that the conditions described in his report were completely reformed after 1907.

The colonial crisis came to a head in December 1906, when once again the government asked the Reichstag to authorize supplementary sums to cover overspending in Southwest Africa. By this time the tribes had been almost completely subdued, some to the point of extinction, and, according to the government's own figures, only about four hundred bedraggled Hottentots were still holding out. Even the most conservative Centrists were disinclined to grant the government its request. But they were unprepared for the hot-tempered outburst which Roeren delivered on December 3, disclosing the details of the Togoland affair and accusing Colonial Director Dernburg of personal responsibility. Roeren called Dernburg a "stock-market rigger and juggler" among other rude and unjustified remarks, and Dernburg responded in kind, calling the Center's increasing interference in government policies an "unlanced boil."[43] The violent argument became a scandal in itself and brought about a complete rupture between the Center and the government.

According to Bülow, he tried to discuss the incident with Spahn and Gröber, indicating that he recognized that Erzberger and Roeren (that "thick-headed Westphalian") spoke only for themselves, and trying to work out a compromise on the budget. If appropriations were

43. *Verhandlungen des Reichstags* 222 (3 Dec. 1906): 4085–118.

not granted, he had decided to dissolve the Reichstag. Bachem, the party historian who was a close colleague of Spahn and Gröber at this time, says that they were not contacted. Certainly none of the leaders of any party expected that a dissolution of the Reichstag might result from the actions of the Budget Committee; Bülow might well have got his appropriations if it had been known.[44]

The Centrists on the committee were united in their decision to reduce the sum requested by the relatively small amount of eight million marks, the money to be saved by replacing combat troops with police troops for the final showdown with the four hundred Hottentots. They prepared a motion incorporating this change. The Centrists were supported by the Social Democrats, whose party had opposed the government's colonial policies throughout the crisis. The Radicals on the committee prepared their own motion, offering an even more moderate change in the government's bill. When the government bill and the Radical compromise were both defeated in the house, by the Center and the Social Democratic party, the chancellor, without permitting action on the Center's motion, ordered the dissolution of the Reichstag and called for elections.

44. Bülow, pp. 294–97; Bachem, 6:366–72; Erich Eyck, *Das Persönliche Regiment Wilhelms II* (Zurich, 1948), p. 457.

9
PREWAR POLITICS IN THE REICH AND IN THE *LÄNDER*, 1907–1914

The chancellor's election slogan was "For the honor and welfare of the nation, against Social Democrats, Poles, Guelphs, and Centrists." The government's campaign went far beyond the Pöplau-Wistuba affair and other immediate grievances to resurrect the old charges that the Catholic party represented a subversive and alien element in German society. The Radicals joined with Conservatives and National Liberals in the new "Bülow-Bloc," forgetting their own participation in exposing the colonial scandal and their traditional stand against extreme nationalism and militarism. The liberal parties were united as at no time since the debate on the school bill of 1892: "They were excited about fighting at the government's side against the Center, and they came to regard the expulsion of the Catholic party as an end in itself and the chief reason for the dissolution of the Reichstag."[1]

Election propaganda reverted to the anti-Catholic diatribes of the *Kulturkampf*. This was received with astonishment and bitterness by Centrists who had supported the government almost uninterruptedly for twelve years. Not only did the Evangelical League and the Pan-Germans participate in the anti-Catholic campaign but also the supposedly nonpartisan Navy League. Bülow's personal role in the election was especially disillusioning because of his earlier understanding and friendly attitude toward Catholic interests. His actions could not be ascribed to prejudice or ignorance but simply to cynical political calculation.

In self-defense, the party closed ranks. It would have been useless

---

1. Crothers, p. 122. See *Zentrums-Album*, p. 253, for a cartoon which shows the Bloc storming the Center Tower, labeled "*Vaterlandsfeindlich* Policy."

for the conservative leadership to continue to ostracize Roeren and Erzberger, since government propaganda identified them not only with the entire Center party but with the German Catholic population in general. Instead, the party's own campaign endeavored to present its past and present activities in as patriotic a light as possible. Nevertheless, there was a defection of "national Catholics" from the party, as there had been in the "patriotic elections" of 1887 and 1893, and fifteen "national" candidates competed with Centrists in the election. None of these was able to win a seat, in spite of support from Cardinal Kopp, who wrote to Bülow deploring the "disloyal and ungrateful" behavior of the Center.[2]

The close cooperation of the Bülow Bloc, uniting all the parties from Conservatives and Anti-Semites to the two Radical parties, made cooperation with the Social Democrats a necessity for the Center in the runoff elections and thus confirmed the government's linking of Catholics and Socialists as partners in an antinational "Red-Black Bloc."

In a multi-party system like Germany's, relatively few candidates were able to win absolute majorities on the first ballot, making runoff elections necessary in a large number of cases. When a candidate was eliminated on the first ballot, his party had to instruct its voters how to vote, or refrain from voting, in the runoff. This might be a local decision based upon local conditions, or it might be determined by a national pairing-agreement where two fairly congenial parties reciprocally supported each other. In the past, the Center in its unique position in the middle of the political spectrum had cooperated at one time or another with every single party. Its favorite partners were the two conservative parties and the Radicals, but none was wholly excluded from consideration and there were instances as far back as the 1870s of reciprocal agreements with the Social Democrats in the runoffs in large urban districts in the Rhineland. Never before, however, had the Center itself been shunned as a partner by so many parties, and this made Red-Black cooperation in many parts of Germany an unwelcome necessity.

Center voters in the runoff were not instructed explicitly to vote Social Democratic, but were told only to support those candidates who

2. Bülow, 2:299–300.

were in favor of "the extension of social reform, unaltered maintenance of the Reichstag fraction, against exceptional laws and in favor
of the Tolerance Motion [for full religious freedom in all states]."[3] The
formula fit the Social Democratic party and conveniently ignored the
Socialists' anticlericalism, which was indeed far less exploited by the
Social Democrats than by the liberal parties. Socialist candidates were
most actively supported by the Center in Dortmund, Duisberg, Biele-
feld, and in the South, especially Bavaria.[4]

The results of the election proved to be interesting and instructive
to the party. The Center did not suffer at all from the anti-Catholic
propaganda of the Bülow Bloc, as might be expected, since its voters
were nearly all of them Catholic and rallied instinctively to the defense; the fraction gained 5 seats, rising from 100 to 105 and continuing as the largest party in the Reichstag. Government propaganda did
prove effective against the Social Democrats, however, especially in
the east and north of Germany where no Red-Black cooperation was
possible. As in the patriotic elections of the past, large numbers of
"nonpolitical" nonvoters rallied to the government and swelled the
totals for the Bülow Bloc parties, every one of which gained seats. Socialist representation in the the Reichstag dropped from 81 to 43 seats.

On the one hand the results showed that the Center did not need
to fear loss of mass support from alliance with Social Democrats in
opposition to the government. On the other hand they showed that in
the future a return to support of the government on national issues
might be the way to defeat or postpone the triumph of socialism,
which was an important goal of the party. It was the second lesson
which was taken to heart by the Center's conservative leadership in
the next national elections.

More urgent than preparing election strategy for the future was
combating the victorious Bülow Bloc in 1907. For the next two years
the party remained grimly determined to "break the bloc" and break
Bülow with it. Colonial issues were forgotten by both sides. The
Southwest African revolt was ended; Dernburg was raised to ministerial rank in May 1907 and worked quietly to correct most of the abuses
in the colonial administration which had been exposed the previous

3. Bachem, 6:411.
4. Ibid.

year. Roeren kept silent in the Reichstag and was more and more isolated in the party because of the integralist conflict. Erzberger spoke
mostly on financial matters.

The chancellor on his part had no intention of readmitting the
Center to the government camp and persisted, against the advice of
several members of his cabinet, in isolating the party. Posadowsky and
Konrad von Studt, Prussian minister of religion and education, both
left office in June because of feeling in the liberal parties that their
friendly relationship with the Center was not compatible with the
new Bloc policies, and Treasury Secretary von Stengel left the following year for similar reasons. Tirpitz remained in office but expressed
concern that his naval program would be far more difficult to finance
without the help of the Center.

The chancellor's later justification for his action was that a party
like the Center "must not arrogate to itself a predominant position in
politics" and that the "government lived uninterruptedly under the
shadow of a threat of union between the Center and the Social Democrats." He wanted "not a majority against the Center, nor a majority
from which the Center was to be excluded, but a majority powerful
and strong enough in itself to do justice to national exigencies, if need
be without the help of the Center."[5] The "threat of union between the
Center and the Social Democrats" had actually been created by Bülow
himself, with his election slogans, and would only continue to exist
so long as he denied to the Center the role of government participant
which was so much more congenial to its leadership than uncomfortable partnership with the Socialists.

Until the end of 1908 the Bülow Bloc held together fairly well.
The Center tried several times without much success to split off one
or another of the coalition partners. When a stock exchange bill was
under consideration, the Center persuaded Conservatives in committee to support its motion to restrict commodity speculation, and this
angered the liberals. During consideration of the Reich Associations
Law, the Radicals were persuaded to join the Center in opposing the
speech paragraph (which forbade the use of languages other than German in public meetings) and this angered the Conservatives. Neither

5. Bülow, *Imperial Germany*, (New York, 1917), pp. 206–8.

of these frictions was sufficient to break the bloc, held together by the efforts of the National Liberal leader Ernst Bassermann.

The Associations Law of 1908 was a long overdue attempt to replace former restrictive and punitive measures against public meetings with a more lenient regulation setting forth conditions under which associations could be formed and public meetings could be held. The Center's labor leaders hoped that it would include a formal legal recognition of the rights of labor unions, but they were disappointed. The new law was not intended to be repressive and was certainly more liberal than the earlier Prussian state laws, though not as generous as those of the southwestern states. Its provisions were injurious to the rights of labor unions and national minorities, however, because they set a minimum age of sixteen for participants in associations and public meetings and prohibited the use of languages other than German in public gatherings, and for this reason the Center opposed the bill. The party was successful in putting through an amendment making an exception to the language restriction for districts where 60 percent or more of the inhabitants normally spoke a language other than German. The exception was to last for a transition period of twenty years; a similar exception was already made for the use of French in parts of Alsace-Lorraine. The amended version of the bill was passed by the majority of the House but was rejected by the Center as falling short of its goals for the union movement.

At the end of 1908 occurred the *Daily Telegraph* affair, the *Novembersturm*, in which the kaiser's indiscretions at first seemed likely to cause a revolt of the Reichstag in favor of constitutional reform. Indignation over the affair was universal, but of all the major parties, the Center was the only one which did not make a formal interpellation in the House, and Hertling as party spokesman let the kaiser off very lightly, shouldering Bülow with the entire blame for the publication of the unfortunate interview and refusing to follow the Social Democrats in their demands for constitutional change.[6] Erzberger even expressed his opinion to William that the chancellor had deliberately allowed the publication of the article in order to embarrass him.[7] The Center's

---

6. *Verhandlungen des Reichstags* 233 (10 Nov. 1908): 5397–401.
7. Epstein, *Matthias Erzberger*, pp. 84–85; Bülow, *Memoirs*, 2:554–55.

leaders saw the affair as an opportunity to discredit their immediate enemy, Bülow, rather than to weaken the ultimate source of their difficulties, William, even though Bülow's break with the Catholic party was undoubtedly motivated by his desire to conform to the prejudices of the kaiser. There seems to have been no interest in party ranks in the introduction of parliamentary government or ministerial responsibility at this time, and no desire to use the affair either to revive the election alliance with the Social Democrats or to forge a new alliance with the Radicals.

In the same month in which his reputation with the kaiser and the Reichstag was so damaged, Bülow submitted to the House a complicated bill for the reorganization of the country's finances, designed to increase revenues sufficiently to cover the ever-growing costs of military and naval preparedness. Incredibly, he expected to carry this through without the help of the Center party, the mainstay of government finance for the past twelve years. It was at this point that Treasury Secretary von Stengel resigned, feeling himself unable to steer the bill through without his customary assistants. Conservative party spokesmen also warned the chancellor that it would not be possible to achieve his goals without Centrist cooperation, but Bülow ignored their advice.

Finances were a perennial problem in the Second Reich, for constitutional, social, and political reasons. First, the Reich constitution made the national government dependent upon indirect taxes and matricular contributions from the states, and each year that passed brought new proof that these sources were inadequate. Second, the state and national governments were reluctant to tax personal wealth and sought always to put the burden of providing revenue upon the population at large. Third, the foreign policy of the Reich, with its peculiar combination of aggressive-expansionist and paranoid-defensive postures, made it necessary substantially to increase expenditures for the military and naval programs nearly every year.

Not only had the Center party no means of altering these three circumstances, it also reflected them faithfully in its own party program. First, the Center as a staunch defender of the federal principle had always insisted that the states should have a monopoly on direct taxation, even though its own financial experts were well aware of the difficulties of the existing arrangements. Second, although the party was vociferous in protesting increases in regressive taxes on sales and services, its conservative agrarian wing opposed any attempt to tax the inheritance of land or family property. Third, the Center party had traditionally opposed militarism and expansionism but, like the other parties, was responsive to the real and imagined pressures of "encirclement" and had become willing to agree to increased spending for military purposes.

Thus in 1909 there was in Center party ranks neither an interest in refusing the government its request for increased revenue nor an interest in restructuring either the constitution or the usual sources of revenue. There was simply a strong desire to discredit the chancellor by killing the government's particular proposal and replacing it with another bill accomplishing the same ends by more acceptable means.

The government's bill proposed a whole range of indirect taxes, some new, some existing but increased in rate, not only on luxury goods like tobacco and wine but also on gas, electricity, and even on advertisements. An increase in the amount of matricular contributions from the states was also included. The most controversial feature of the bill was its proposal for an inheritance tax, an extension of a very limited inheritance tax introduced in 1906, which had not applied to direct descendants.

When the bill was first read in the Reichstag there was scarcely a single item in it that met with the approval of all parties. The Center leadership decided immediately that this was the opportunity it had been waiting for. Center members of the Budget Committee were Peter Spahn, Karl Herold, and Richard Müller, a financial expert of many years experience. The new state secretary for the treasury, Reinhold Sydow, was without special skill or experience. The Centrists opposed the steep rise in matricular contributions and especially objected to the inheritance tax, which they claimed would penalize landowners and damage family relationships. These feelings were shared by the Conservatives, and negotiations were opened between the two parties to scrap the inheritance tax and find sources for the needed revenue elsewhere, preferably at the expense of industry. The new "Blue-Black" collaboration was unsuccessfully combated by the National Liberals and the Radicals, who finally stopped attending the committee meetings altogether. By June 1909, the Center and the Conservatives had written what amounted to an entirely new bill, providing all the money requested in the original, but without the inheritance tax and with a smaller increase in matricular contributions.

Bülow refused to accept the changes and insisted on retaining the inheritance tax, hoping to make up for the defection of the Conservatives by winning votes from the Social Democrats. He threatened resignation if the government's bill were rejected, and when it was rejected on June 24, he submitted his resignation to the kaiser, who accepted it. A few days later the new Reichstag majority of Center and Conservatives voted for the committee's altered bill, and it was accepted by the Federal Council. The Bülow Bloc was broken.

Bülow's resignation was of course not constitutionally required by the situation and it had more to do with his loss of the kaiser's support than with the finance bill, but if the chancellor had ever been inclined to use the confidence of the Reichstag as a counterweight to William's favor, he had lost that option irretrievably by his stubborn refusal to conciliate the party which still held the balance of power in the Parliament.

Bethmann-Hollweg, Bülow's successor, formerly Prussian minister of the interior, did not make that mistake, but neither did he have a close relationship with the Center. He was not sympathetic to nor familiar with Catholic interests. His contacts with the Center fraction were cold and formal. The party returned to its anomalous position of the years before 1906, of being in support of the government without being a government party. The alliance between the Conservatives and Centrists did not develop into a lasting coalition, although the Blue-Black Bloc did cooperate in the elections of 1912.

In this election there was no revival of anti-Catholic propaganda, and the Center directed its own slogans mainly against the Social Democrats. Its campaign platform was conservative, cautious, anti-Socialist, and antiliberal; even Erzberger was subdued and fully supported the alliance with the Conservatives. Runoff agreements were made with Conservatives and occasionally with National Liberals, while the Radicals and the Social Democrats cooperated with each other, in complete contrast to the election strategy of 1907. But whereas the Center benefited from the 1907 policy, it was noticeably hurt by the Blue-Black Bloc in 1912. The party lost sixteen seats, including those for Cologne, Düsseldorf, and Dortmund. Many votes were lost to Social Democrats in the large industrial cities because of resentment against the runoff agreements with conservative parties, and the prolonged labor union controversy probably also helped to weaken the Center's hold on Catholic workingmen and turned them to the Social Democrats. The Center helped parties of the Right in ninety-eight districts and received help from them in only thirty-three; in many districts Conservatives actively opposed Centrists.[8] All the parties of the Right lost seats in the election, the Center was pulled down with them, and the Social Democrats emerged the victors, with 110 seats in the new Reichstag.

A comparison of the two elections of 1907 and 1912 shows that the Center could win far more votes by allying with Social Democracy than by allying with the Right. But the winning of mass support was not regarded in the party as its sole or even its most important goal. There was a strong feeling in the prewar party leadership that the maintenance of a conservative, anti-Socialist platform was worth the sacrifice of votes; that although manhood suffrage had benefited the party in the past and had provided the party with numerical strength, this did not mean that the party would or should work for further democratization or for constitutional change. This is well illustrated by the Center's increasing ambivalence toward electoral reform in Prussia.

In 1873, Windthorst had announced the Center's support for the extension of the Reichstag franchise to Prussia. It was not remotely conceivable at that time that the Prussian government would agree to abandon the complicated three-class system, with its indirect vote and open balloting, for the secret ballot and direct manhood suffrage. Windthorst's statement had been made for its effect as political propaganda. But there is no reason to suppose that he was insincere, because in 1873 the Center had much to gain and nothing to lose by a change in the Prussian franchise. By the time the goal seemed possible of attainment, after William II had promised at least some degree of change in his speech from the throne in 1908, the situation had altered considerably. The chief beneficiaries of the introduction of the Reich franchise in 1908 would obviously be the Social Democrats. Moreover, if the change were to be accompanied by a much-needed reapportionment of seats, the party's rural constituencies would be reduced in

8. Bertram, p. 46.

importance, and even though this loss would be counterbalanced by a gain of seats for urban districts, this would have incalculable effects on the delicately weighed relationships within the party membership. For these reasons, although Windthorst's 1873 statement was frequently and reverently quoted in public meetings, few living Centrists were willing to adopt it as their own.

The Christian trade unions, with their strength in the large cities of the Rhineland, vigorously supported extension of the vote, but the Prussian *Landtag* fraction, who were the ones actually presented with the practical problem, were evasive and procrastinating on the question of franchise reform, from its first mention as a possibility in 1908, right up to the moment of General Ludendorff's urgent intervention in the matter in October 1918.

In 1910, after a great deal of public pressure, the Prussian government produced a bill for franchise reform. The bill hardly fulfilled the hopes of the Socialists and Radicals, since it retained the three-class system and the open ballot, but it did propose the introduction of direct voting in place of indirect and also created a new category of voter, the highly educated person or *Kulturträger*, to be added to the voting class hitherto reserved for the most wealthy. The House of Deputies committee chosen to consider the bill reflected the nervousness and uncertainty of the representatives of the middle parties, who realized that their interests were bound to suffer in the event of change, the Center's in rural areas, the National Liberals' in large cities, but who did not want to appear to their constituents to be obstructionist or reneging on their frequently reiterated commitment to reform. The Center's representatives first supported a recommendation for universal manhood suffrage, which was defeated in the committee, and then proposed the secret ballot, which was accepted. The new category of "culture-bearer" was rejected by the committee. The Center then refused to accept the change to direct voting and swung the committee to the retention of the indirect electoral system. In altering the bill, the party worked closely with the Conservatives, and in answer to critics who accused the party of betraying its longstanding commitment to the Reichstag suffrage, the Prussian fraction leaders Porsch and Herold defended themselves by stressing the fact of the party's dependence upon the Conservatives' backing in vital educational and religious questions, which were of so much more importance in the state legislature than in the Reichstag.[9]

The Center voted for the altered bill, inadequate though it clearly was, and it passed the lower house, but the cabinet was unhappy with the changes and withdrew the bill from consideration. In spite of renewed public demonstrations in the large cities, nothing further was done to alter the franchise in Prussia until 1917.

In the southern states, the party's attitude toward constitutional or electoral reform was determined in all cases by the benefits or disadvantages that change would bring. The four southern states had all introduced a democratic suffrage and the secret ballot in an earlier period, but had retained indirect voting and were in need of reapportionment of the seats in the legislatures. In the immediate prewar period there were reform moves in all of the south.

In Württemberg, Adolf Gröber had kept the Center since its formation in 1895 in close alliance with the radical-democratic *Volkspartei*, but this harmony was increasingly disturbed after the founding of a new agrarian-conservative party, the *Bauernbund*, which appealed to the same electorate of small farmers as the Center and forced that party to adopt a more conservative program in order to retain rural support. The move for constitutional reform sponsored by the *Volkspartei* further estranged the Center from the democrats and pushed it to the right in the Württemberg political spectrum.

In 1906, a constitutional reform was proposed which would alter the composition of the upper house of the legislature. As long as it had been in existence the upper house had had a permanent majority of Catholics, because of the mediatization of Catholic princes early in the nineteenth century, who had been given hereditary seats in compensation for the loss of their independence. The membership of the chamber was small and was growing steadily smaller because of the dying-out of families. The proposed reform would enlarge the upper house by adding to it a number of "privileged" seats in the lower house, which would make the upper house a more viable size and more representative of the state's notables and would also make the lower house completely elective and hence more representative of

9. Bachem, 7:125.

the people. New seats were to be added to the lower house, increasing the representation of cities, and the direct vote was to replace the indirect.

The Center voted solidly against the reform of the upper house, because the party feared that the enlarged house, now Protestant in majority, would be willing to sanction liberal education measures (which in fact proved to be the case when the reform was carried out.) On the other hand, Gröber supported the lower house reforms and succeeded in introducing proportional representation for the new urban seats. Because the Catholic population was widely scattered in Württemberg, proportional representation was advantageous to the Center.

In Baden, conversely, the population distribution was such that the Center saw no benefits to be derived from proportional representation, and so the party opposed its introduction into that state, but did support the direct vote, when these two changes were proposed in the constitutional reforms of 1904. The Center was the largest single party in the Baden *Landtag* after 1904, but it allied only with the small Conservative party, while the liberals continued to make up the majority. Baden was the first state in which the Social Democratic party joined a government coalition, the "Great Bloc," with the Radicals and the National Liberals. The Great Bloc broke up in 1913, partly because of a disagreement over religious instruction in the schools, in which the National Liberals temporarily deserted their usual anticlerical stand to side with the Center.[10] The Center remained in the rightist opposition in Baden as long as the grand dukes maintained a liberal "establishment" in the state, but after the war, in the republican years, the state Center governed in permanent partnership with the Left.

In both Württemberg and Baden, a great deal of time was spent in the legislatures discussing the probable eventuality of the succession of Catholic heirs in the reigning families. The prospect naturally interested the Center keenly, but all contingency planning proved to be, in the event, quite unnecessary.

The direct vote and proportional representation were introduced

10. Beverly Heckart, *From Bassermann to Bebel: The Grand Bloc's Quest for Reform in the Kaiserreich* (New Haven, 1974), pp. 263–64; see also Carl H. E. Zangerl, "Courting the Catholic Vote: The Center Party in Baden, 1903–13," *Central European History* 10 (1977): 220–40.

in Hesse-Darmstadt in 1911 in a constitutional reform which slightly improved the Center's position in that state. Hesse was the only state where the Center regularly cooperated with the local branch of the National Liberal party, even in the hotly contested election of 1907. No Great Bloc was contemplated for Hesse.[11]

Bavaria, like Baden, had a liberal government establishment, but here the Center, rather than the liberals, was the group willing to ally with the Social Democrats. Centrists and Socialists worked together to carry through the constitutional reforms of 1906 which reapportioned the seats in the lower house and introduced the direct vote, changes opposed by the liberal parties because their representation would be adversely affected. Not all of the reforms, which were drafted by the Center, were of a nature to increase popular representation, however. The minimum age for voting was raised from twenty-one to twenty-five, and the Center successfully defeated attempts to enlarge the upper house and make it representative of commerce and industry as well as of aristocracy and clergy, seeing the attempt as designed to liberalize the upper house. Self-interest rather than dedication to democracy characterized both sides in this contest.

The Bavarian Center represented agrarian interest in the state and campaigned on a platform of vigilant defense of states' rights. The party was confronted with an effective rival in the 1890s with the founding of the Bavarian *Bauernbund* (unrelated to the Württemberg party of that name). The *Bauernbund* originated as a break-off from the Center and outdid that party in its profarmer and anti-Prussian rhetoric, offering a more radical, populist approach.[12] It won seven seats from the Center in the national elections of 1893, and its competition encouraged a similarly strident approach from the Bavarian Center. Dr. Georg Heim, the organizer of the Bavarian Farmers' Association, emerged as a leader in this new style. He helped to engineer an alliance with the Social Democrats in the state elections of 1905, which boosted the Center's seats in the *Landtag* to 102 and the Socialists' to 12, giving the two parties the two-thirds majority needed to pass the constitutional reforms, and he led the Bavarian Reichstag

11. Dan S. White, *The Splintered Party: National Liberalism in Hessen and the Reich, 1867–1918* (Cambridge, Mass., 1976), p. 173.
12. See Ian Farr, "Populism in the Countryside: The Peasant League in Bavaria in the 1890s," in Evans, pp. 146–55.

fraction in wholehearted support of Erzberger in the colonial crisis of 1906.

This strategy won votes, but as in the case of the national party, was uncongenial to the conservative leadership. In 1911, when the national party was again safely in the conservative camp, the Bavarian Center permanently dropped its partnership with the Social Democrats, who were by then forging new ties with the liberals. The Center's leaders, Hertling, Dr. Pichler, Count Max Emanuel von Preysing, and other noblemen, had been carrying on a press campaign against Heim's radicals and had managed to elbow him out of key parliamentary committees. They were determined to make the Bavarian Center *"hoffähig"*: respectable and worthy of participation in the Regent's government.[13] The party broke with the Social Democrats by claiming that the Socialist South German Railway Workers' Union was being favored over the Christian trade unions in the state. The government responded to this quarrel by dissolving the *Landtag* for new elections.[14]

The Center lost seats in the election but kept its absolute majority in the lower house. Apparently, it was the need to reconcile this persistent majority, coupled with the increasing radicalization of the liberal party leaders in Bavaria and their approach to the Social Democrats, that led Prince Regent Luitpold in February 1912 very suddenly to dismiss his cabinet and appoint as minister-president the Centrist Hertling. There was also internecine conflict within the ministerial bureaucracy which controlled the Regent's policies.[15] The event which had been so dreaded in imperial circles from the 1870s through the 1890s had finally occurred: a Catholic-Centrist ministry governed in Bavaria.

The tranquility of the state and the nation was not in the least shaken by the event. Hertling was far from being either a separatist or a populist demagogue; he was not even a Bavarian by birth but only by virtue of his long tenure as professor at the University of Munich.[16] He immediately resigned his post as chairman of the Center Reichstag

---

13. Karl Möckl, "Gesellschaft und Politik während der Aera des Prinzregenten Luitpold," in Karl Bosl, ed., *Bayern im Umbruch*, (Munich, 1969), pp. 27–28.

14. Heckart, pp. 195–96.

15. Möckl, in Bosl, pp. 20–24.

16. Hertling's family had its origins in the Bavarian Palatinate but had moved to Darm-

fraction, gave up his Reichstag seat, and even maintained a reserved distance from the state party fraction after his appointment. His cabinet was moderate and none of the other ministers were from the lower house or closely connected with the Center party. Two of them were Protestants. His government cooperated with the Center majority but cannot be described as a transition to parliamentary rule in the state, because his position ultimately depended not upon the *Landtag* but upon the prince regent. In 1914, Hertling won the new Regent Ludwig's special favor by his successful efforts to crown him King Ludwig III in the place of the incurably insane Otto, and he received the title of count for this achievement.

Hertling's appointment brought both advantages and disadvantages to the national Center party. It was an event which lent prestige to the whole party and might prove to be a precedent for admission to the governing circles in Prussia and the Reich. It gave the party its first influence on the Federal Council, the powerful opponent of so many Centrist goals. On the other hand, Hertling had been one of the few Centrist leaders to familiarize himself with foreign policy questions, and his departure from the Reichstag fraction left the party without even his modest talents in that important field. Also, his successor as fraction head, Peter Spahn, was much less adept than Hertling at smoothing over disagreements within the party, and he never achieved a good relationship with Erzberger. Hertling had once considered Erzberger an "inflated simpleton"[17] but had come to recognize his worth and to arrive at a rapport with his following as well as with the older men of the party. Upon leaving for Munich to take up his new post, he had written to his wife:

> I had succeeded in winning the confidence of pretty nearly the whole fraction. I had a very good relationship with Erzberger, and the complaints raised earlier about his intractable nature [unverträglisches Wesen] were beginning to die down; his really invaluable energy was being recognized more and more. Müller-Fulda, who, as you know, is inclined to play the role of outsider, was attached to me and did nothing contrary to my intentions. I got

---

stadt in Hesse before his birth in 1843. His seat in the Reichstag was for Bavaria from 1896 to 1903, but after 1903 was for Münster (Ernst Deuerlein, ed., *Briefwechsel Hertling-Lerchenfeld, 1912–1917*, 2 vols. [Boppard-am-Rhein, 1973], 1:5–6).

17. Ibid., p. 33.

along in friendly fashion with the sensitive Gröber and talked over everything with him beforehand. The Bavarians with few exceptions have lost their original misgivings about me. Of the influential people in the fraction, probably only Spahn stayed aloof from me, but he, unfortunately, lost any influence and especially any sympathy in the fraction.[18]

Although he kept in touch with national party affairs through his correspondence with Count von Lerchenfeld, the Bavarian ambassabor in Berlin, Hertling never regained the position of confidence in the Center Reichstag fraction which he gave up in 1912.

Hertling as minister-president of Bavaria had become a member of the Federal Council, and he promptly used his position to try to repeal or to mitigate the effects of the remaining section of the law against the Jesuit Society. He proposed a modification of the police regulations concerning the "activities of the order," but only succeeded in eliciting a very broad and unfavorable definition of the phrase, which was of little value.[19] After this failure the party brought a bill for total repeal of the law to the Reichstag floor for the fifth time, in February of 1913, and again obtained a majority for it. It is interesting that on this occasion the bill received no votes at all on the Right and only three from the Radical-Progressives; that is, there was less, and not more, support in conservative and liberal circles for repeal than there had been in the 1890s. The majority would not have been possible without the unanimous vote of the Social Democrats, those atheist Marxists so regularly attacked in Centrist pamphlets and speeches.

Since the Federal Council as usual did not act on the vote, the status quo was unchanged at the time the First World War began. Because Germany's war was fought almost entirely beyond the frontiers of the Reich, the letter of the law permitted the Jesuit order to work freely among the troops, and many of its members distinguished themselves in this service. Government officials assured the Center's leaders that "after the war" the order would be reinstated in Germany, but the party persisted in urging legal action before that uncertain date. Finally, in April 1917, the Federal Council took up the Reichstag's

18. Ibid., p. 37.
19. Bachem, 9:349–56; 359–61.

1913 decision and seconded it, not without some rearguard threats from some Protestant states to nullify the act in state legislatures.

The campaign to repeal the Jesuit law had lasted for twenty-seven years. In all that time, in spite of the perennial agitation from extremist Protestant circles and the periodic demonstrations and newspaper crusades against the international Jesuit conspiracy and the machinations of Rome (familiar to many countries besides Germany) the really effective opposition to the order seems to have come from the princely courts and the upper echelons of the bureaucracies in the German states. These circles were by no means immune to popular prejudice, and the Vatican did not help matters by issuing the Canisius Encyclical of 1897 and the Borromeus Encyclical of 1906, both of which singled out the German princes of the sixteenth century for special denunciation. But it seems likely that the stubborn resistance of the German princes to granting full freedom of action to the church was political: a desire to maintain the existing social and political structure, in which the church and its defenders were to continue in inferior status.

The Center's fight to reestablish the Jesuit Society in the Reich had been paralleled by efforts in the individual states to improve the position of the church. Few of these efforts were successful. In Bavaria, the party hoped to eliminate the *placet* (claimed by that government not only in appointments but upon publications and even interpretation of doctrine); in Baden and Württemberg, to permit the establishment of male orders; in Prussia, to abolish the remaining restrictions on the orders. None of these goals was attained. The Bavarian government used its prerogatives less and less, but insisted upon the retention of the principle. In the southwest, the situation in regard to the male orders was particularly frustrating because no change in the law was necessary: in Baden and Württemberg any order could legally be established with the permission of the state government, but such permission was not once given for the establishment of a male order before 1918.

Although neither the Polish representatives nor those of Alsace-Lorraine fully identified themselves with the Center party, the Center was active in defending the interests of these national minorities throughout the prewar period. This does not at all imply that the Center favored the return of Alsace and Lorraine to France or the creation of a Polish national state. On the contrary, the party believed that it could act as a bridge for the national minorities, enabling them more easily to become permanent members of the German national community. Even after the war, the party leadership continued to believe that Alsace-Lorraine could have become fully Germanized if only the Reich government had followed a policy of greater conciliation and had taken advantage of the bond of Catholicism (since five-sixths of the population of Alsace-Lorraine was Catholic) rather than considering it additional evidence of subversive tendencies. Instead, anticlerical legislation incorporating both Prussian and Reich laws was introduced into the *Reichsland*, many church-affiliated schools were closed, and a kind of "permanent *Kulturkampf*" existed there.[20]

Not all of the political representatives of Alsace-Lorraine were allied with the Center, but those who supported the National Liberals and, in later years, the Social Democrats, did not identify themselves as separatists or "protesters," while those who sat with the Center Reichstag fraction after 1875 definitely did. Many of them, including the ardent French nationalist Father Emile Wetterlé, were openly republican as well. Such intransigence became increasingly embarrassing to the German Center, but the party hoped that the separatists could be reconciled with autonomy and fair treatment of linguistic and religious grievances: "Center apologists argued that the clericals really did not believe in their own particularist propaganda—Circumstances beyond their control, so they maintained, forced the Alsace-Lorraine Center candidates to adopt nationalism as an electoral tactic, without accepting it in principle. The anti-Catholic attitude of many German immigrants [into Alsace-Lorraine] obliged the Center to insure its standing with the native voters by espousing nationalist slogans . . . even . . . French clichés."[21]

The German party worked actively to introduce a greater degree of self-government for the *Reichsland* and hoped that the Alsatian politicians would formally enter the national Center party when it was achieved. But when the new constitution was introduced in 1911, giving the provinces self-government, though not the full status of a

20. Silverman, pp. 93–103.
21. Ibid., p. 155.

Land, a completely separate Alsace-Lorraine Center party was created instead, and as a consequence, a coolness developed between the two parties. This may explain the relative silence of the national Center at the time of the Zabern Affair in 1913, when the party did not make a separate interpellation in the Reichstag, as the Socialists and Progressive did, though it did vote for the motion of lack of confidence in the government. When war came, Father Wetterlé fled to France, but most Alsace-Lorraine Centrists remained loyal and continued to work for *Land* status within the Reich.

The Center's Alsatian policy of Germanization was in contrast to its Polish policy. In the east, the party fervently believed that Germanization was equivalent to Protestantization, and defense of Catholic interests in these provinces was intimately bound up with the defense of the use of the Polish language, in the schools and in daily life. The defense continued even into the immediate prewar period when Polish nationalism was becoming more militant and less under the direction of the clergy. It has a parallel in the sympathy shown by the Austrian (German) Catholic People's party and even on occasion by Lueger's Christian Social party, to the Slavic nationalities in Austria-Hungary. No policy could have been more calculated to irritate German nationalists and prevent the Center from ever being admitted into the German imperial establishment.

Part of the battle was lost in the years of the *Kulturkampf*, when the German language was introduced into all statesupported elementary schools, but an exception was made in religious instruction classes, where Polish was to be permitted on a temporary basis, presumably until the children had become familiar with German in their other classes. In 1887 the Prussian minister of education and religion, Gossler, ordered the use of German in all classes, including religious instruction, but pressure from the Center and from Archbishop Dinder of Posen-Gnesen persuaded him to rescind the ordinance. (Ironically, Dinder had originally been instated as archbishop because of his own German nationality.)

Gossler resigned in 1890 after the failure of his school bill and Caprivi began an era of conciliation of the Poles. But in 1900, permission was again withdrawn for the use of Polish in the middle and upper grades in the schools in Posen, perhaps as a result of persistent lobbying by the recently formed Association for the Advancement of the

German Nationality in the Eastern Marches, or *Hakatisten* Society. This provoked a lengthy and widely publicized, but ultimately unsuccessful, strike by school children in Posen, reluctantly sanctioned by Archbishop Stablewsky. The strike lasted until 1907 and eventually spread into parts of West Prussia and Silesia. By that year there had been "280 removals of Poles from local offices; 80 students expelled from gymnasiums; 35 clergymen sentenced to a total of 20 months in jail and fined 6,350 marks"; and numerous other fines and imprisonments.[22]

The Center press was loud in support of the school strike, and the party not only protested in the Prussian *Landtag* but introduced an interpellation in the Reichstag denouncing the excessive punitive action. The chancellor refused to respond, saying that the matter was of concern only to the state of Prussia and not to the Reich.

The Prussian government's policy of suppressing the Polish language was supplemented by attempts throughout the period of the Second Reich to alter the demographic composition of the eastern provinces. The Center consistently fought these attempts, vigorously objecting in 1886 to Bismarck's expulsion of thirty thousand aliens from Germany (immigrants from Russian and Austrian Polish districts, two-thirds of them Catholics, one-third Jews). In this it was seconded by many Protestant landowners who depended upon the immigrants as a floating labor pool. The party also opposed the Settlement Act of 1886 which set up a fund to buy out Polish landowners and to colonize German farmers in the Polish provinces. Windthorst defended the Polish interest "monomaniacally,"[23] and as usual the party claimed that the entire scheme was aimed at eradicating the Catholic faith from these areas. This was an exaggerated reaction to a move which clearly had other motives. Yet it is true that the commission which carried out the (largely futile) colonization scheme sent very few German Catholic settlers to the east because they became too easily "polonized." Nor did the *Hakatisten* Society recruit many German Catholic members.[24]

22. Figures from Richard Wonser Tims, *Germanizing Prussian Poland* (New York, 1941), p. 99; Trzeciakowski, p. 633.
23. Wahl, 2:275; see also Richard Blanke, "Bismarck and the Prussian Polish Policies of 1886," *Journal of Modern History* 45 (1973): 211–39.
24. Wahl, 3:664. Tims, p. 215.

The Expropriation Law introduced in 1908 after the obvious failure of the colonization scheme was also fought by the Center in the Prussian House of Deputies and by Cardinal Kopp in the House of Lords. The party succeeded in restricting the geographical area to be subject to land confiscation to Posen and West Prussia, but the rest of the bill passed over its protests, because on this issue the National Liberals always supported the government. The Expropriation Act was seldom implemented, and in general the Polish population in Prussia was not adversely affected by any of these efforts. By the end of the period, migrants seeking work in the west had established Polish-speaking communities in the industrial Rhineland. Polish workers often joined the Christian trade unions, and union representatives in the Center had been especially anxious to eliminate or modify the restrictive language clauses in the Associations Law of 1908.

The Polish party in the Reichstag and *Landtag* had always been separate from the Center party and, as was the case with the Alsace-Lorraine delegation, the passage of time strengthened rather than weakened its nationalist character. For its part, the Center did not welcome Polish members into its own organization; there was no party paper published in Polish, and Polish candidates were not entered for Center seats, except for a few assimilated individuals like Paul Letocha, who had given up their distinctively Polish identity.[25] In the last ten years before the war, Polish party candidates were entered against Centrists in some districts, often with success.

Throughout the prewar years and during the war itself, no Centrists anticipated the actual separation of the Polish provinces from Germany. The party's policies were designed to achieve the probably hopeless goal of making the Poles content to remain in Germany. During the war, exactly the same attitude can be observed in regard to the occupied areas of Russian Poland and the Baltic Coast: concern over the proper treatment of the Polish and Lithuanian Catholic populations and dismay at the assignment of Protestant military commanders to the areas, but little aversion to the occupation as such, until defeat was imminent. The Center's brand of chauvinism was hardly that of the typical German nationalist, but it was real.

25. Ross, pp. 70–72.

10

DIVISIVE ISSUES ON THE EVE OF WAR: UNION CONTROVERSY AND *ZENTRUMSSTREIT*

In the last decade before the war, the Christian trade unions grew rapidly in size and influence and came to form a significant part of the Center's left wing, although they remained underrepresented in the party organization. Their existence was a fact, but it was not a fact altogether accepted and approved by German Catholic leadership or by the church hierarchy. Even within the ranks of the Center party there were those who rejected the idea of interdenominational labor unions and favored instead the organization of labor in exclusively Catholic and less activist associations, or even advocated the return to guildlike corporations as an alternative to unions. Sharply differing views resulted in a prolonged controversy over the Christian trade unions, the *Gewerkschaftsstreit*, which was ended only in 1914.

The division of the German labor movement into three separate branches (the Socialist Free unions and the liberal Hirsch-Duncker unions being the other two) was undeniably a great handicap for its successful development. But by the 1890s, when Catholic workers were first encouraged by the publication of the papal encyclical *Rerum Novarum* to organize in an effective way, the Socialist Free unions were too staunchly partisan and too belligerently anticlerical to accommodate them, and the growth of separate organizations was almost inevitable.

Catholic attempts to organize workers and protect them from the atomizing effects of modern industrial society began much earlier in the century, with the formation of the journeymen's associations by Adolf Kolping, a Rhenish priest who was concerned about the rootless existence of young industrial workers. These associations were in many ways a revival of medieval guilds, providing security, companionship, and instruction for young workers under the paternalistic guidance of clergy and laymen, many of whom were large landowners. Moral and cultural uplift was a goal of the associations, as well as the less easily defined goal of creating a self-consciousness among industrial workers of being a *Stand*, or integrated, organic part of their society rather than a class engaged in a struggle with another class, as described in Marxist writings. At the time of Kolping's death in 1865, there were 328 of these associations in Germany, with 19,914 members.[1]

As the associations grew in number they expanded their functions to include practical assistance such as the establishment of savings banks and negotiations with employers about wages and working conditions, but in no instance did they advocate the strike or collective bargaining. The growth of Marxian socialism and the advent of the *Kulturkampf* encouraged the associations to move into the political arena, but the effects of the law against the Social Democrats and the government's suspicion of Catholic activities both helped to put an abrupt end to this, and those associations which survived the 1870s became purely confessional and educational in the 1880s.

In 1880, Franz Brandts, a successful Catholic textile manufacturer of München-Gladbach, and Franz Christoph Moufang, a priest who had worked with Ketteler in Mainz, founded an association of this type called *Arbeiterwohl* ("Workers' Welfare"). The Centrist politician, priest, and university professor Franz Hitze became general secretary of the organization and the editor of its newspaper. Brandts, Hitze, and Windthorst then collaborated in the formation of the *Volksverein* in 1891. Hitze's membership in the Reichstag and Prussian *Landtag* provided the liaison between the educational and propagandistic activities of the *Volksverein* and Center party leadership.

The signal for the further evolution of the workers' associations into true labor unions was the publication of the papal encyclical *Rerum Novarum*, "On the Rights and Duties of Capital and Labor." Leo XIII's famous message began with a detailed argument against social-

---

1. Marshall Dill, Jr., "The Christian Trades Union Movement in Germany before World War I," *Review of Social Economy* 11 (1953), n.p. The German word *Arbeiterverein* will be translated in the following discussion as "workers' association," in order to distinguish the term from *Gewerkschaft*, "labor union."

ism, but then proceeded to recommend numerous measures of state intervention to protect labor, and, most significantly for those Catholic social organizers just waiting for a hint of encouragement, specifically approved the organization of labor for self-help:

> Employers and workmen may of themselves effect much, in the matter We are treating, by means of such associations and organizations as afford opportune aid to those who are in distress. . . . Among these may be enumerated societies for mutual help; various benevolent foundations. . . . The most important of all are workingmen's unions, for these virtually include all the rest. . . . Such unions should be suited to the requirements of this our age—an age of wider education, of different habits, and of far more numerous requirements in daily life.[2]

The pope then warned against unions organized "on principles ill-according with Christianity" and advocated associations by "Christian workingmen"; he went on to lay down principles for their management. Neither collective bargaining nor the strike were mentioned in the encyclical, and the words "union" and "association" are not clearly differentiated. But the message, in all its ambiguous language, provided more than sufficient encouragement for Catholic social reformers to begin to supplement the educational work of the labor associations with more directly economic activities.

Hitze and other directors of the *Volksverein* moved quickly in this direction and helped to set up in 1892 the first "technical divisions" (*Fachabteilungen*) in some of the associations, to deal explicitly with economic and political concerns. The technical divisions were intended primarily 1) to promote professional training by means of lectures, libraries, and discussion groups; 2) to instruct workers about existing social legislation; 3) to explain specific abuses and their possible correction; and 4) to establish sickness-benefit funds, employment bureaus, and savings accounts.[3] They were not intended to stimulate or encourage direct action by workers nor to agitate for higher wages nor to perform any of the more aggressive functions of true unions. They were further weakened by the fact that any given association would usually include workers from several different in-

2. Etienne Gilson, ed., *The Church Speaks to the Modern World: The Social Teachings of Leo XIII* (New York, 1954), pp. 231–32.

3. Theodor Böhme, *Die christlich-nationale Gewerkschaft* (Stuttgart, 1930), p. 45.

dustries, so that the local technical division for a single industry might be so small as to be totally ineffective. Nevertheless Hitze in the beginning saw the divisions as a step toward genuine worker self-help. He urged the election of division leaders by the workers themselves rather than their appointment by the paternalist heads of the associations, the president, who was always a priest, and the lay vice-president, usually a local landowner or manufacturer. He expected the technical divisions to act as "preparatory schools" for true labor unions.[4]

In the meantime, Catholic workers themselves were beginning to take action, alarmed by the steady increase in size and power of the Socialist unions and envious of their success. The growth of the Free unions in the Rhineland was clearly caused by the attraction to them of thousands of Catholic workers. In 1894 a Catholic miner, August Brust, organized the Christian Miners' Union in Dortmund. It was a true union in that it was vocational, that is, only for miners, and interdenominational, sponsored by a Protestant pastor as well as a Catholic priest. Collective bargaining was its goal, and the use of the strike was not ruled out, though sanctioned only in extreme cases. Brust, who was strongly supported and assisted by Hitze and the *Volksverein* in his venture, also published a union paper, *Der Bergknappe*, which was influential in urging the formation of similar unions elsewhere.

Christian unions were quickly organized in the textile and metal industries, as well as in the mines, and they proved far more effective than the technical divisions in meeting the competition from the Socialist unions. They held their first national congress in 1899 in Mainz, Bishop von Ketteler's city. At this meeting the two principles of interdenominationalism and political neutrality were agreed upon and were maintained insofar as possible throughout the history of the unions. "Political neutrality" applied only to the actions of the unions as organizations, however; individual workers who were Catholic (and these were always a large majority in the industrial unions) consistently supported the Center party. The principle of political neutrality also did not permit the union members to forget the major reason for the existence of Christian unions: in all but one major union (the tex-

4. Ibid., p. 46.

tile union in München-Gladbach) the members were required to declare themselves opposed to Social Democracy.[5] In 1900 the membership was 78,664; by 1905, it was 188,106, still only about 14 percent of the membership in the Socialist Free unions.

In 1901 the annual Congress of Christian Unions established a general secretariat over the national organization and elected as its head a young cabinetmaker from Bavaria, Adam Stegerwald, at that time president of the Christian woodworkers' unions. He served as president of the national organization from 1903 to 1929. This centralization took place under the direction of the *Volksverein* and the school for workers which it maintained in München-Gladbach. The school provided "ten-week courses in popular economics for trade union members and their secretaries and newspaper editors, and after 1907 extended its offerings to other vocations: artisans, retail salespersons, farmers, civil servants, technicians, teachers, and clergy." The *Volksverein* also distributed thirty million educational leaflets and "exerted direct influence over five journals."[6]

In the Cologne area, the three organizations worked amicably together, the unions for economic goals, the *Volksverein* and the older associations for educational and spiritual goals. Many of the association leaders urged their members to join a union also. The first union representative in the Reichstag, Johannes Giesberts, was a leader in both the unions and the associations. His newspaper, the *Westdeutsche Arbeiterzeitung*, was the chief organ for the associations in western Germany, and it strongly supported the unions. Its next editor, Joseph Joos, became head of the Catholic associations and a well-known Centrist politician but never joined a union.

The political influence of the Christian trade unions in the prewar period was not great, but they were represented in the Reichstag after 1905, and in the state legislatures even earlier (in Bavaria, after 1899, and in Prussia, after 1903). All of the *Landtag* representatives from the unions were Center party members and the principle of political neutrality decided upon at the national congresses of 1899 and 1901 caused no difficulties in practice. In the Reichstag, however, the unions sent one man in 1907 to sit with the Economic Union, a bloc

5. Ludwig Frey, *Die Stellung der christlichen Gewerkschaften Deutschlands zu den politischen Parteien* (Berlin, 1931), p. 15.
6. Mittman, pp. 177–79; see also Ross, p. 59.

of splinter parties of much more rightist views than the Center, and another union man was elected as a National Liberal in 1912. An awkward incident arose in 1908 over the Associations Bill which severely tested the principle of political neutrality. Franz Behrens, the Protestant union man sitting with the Economic Union, voted with the rest of his party in support of the bill, although he did move that the clauses forbidding attendance at public meetings by persons under eighteen, and forbidding the use of foreign languages at public meetings, not be applied to labor unions. His motion failed, but the bill became law.

Behrens's behavior was strongly condemned by the union leadership. Political neutrality of unions implied that the members would ordinarily be free to support any political party, but in this case, where union interests were clearly involved, Behrens's loyalty to his party was interpreted as a betrayal of the unions and the working class (and also as an anti-Catholic gesture, since the language clause in the bill was aimed at the Catholic Poles). Behrens was eventually forgiven, but the incident foreshadowed a number of future difficulties which arose in the 1920s when the industrial unions, largely Catholic in spite of their interdenominational structure, joined a national organization in a merger with predominately Protestant, nationalist civil servants' and white-collar workers' unions.[7]

Even though only a handful of members of the Christian trade unions sat in the parliamentary fractions before 1919, there is no doubt of the close ties between the unions and the party. The *Volksverein* provided the link and delivered the votes of hundreds of thousands of Catholic workingmen to the Center every election. But the actual legislative results of this social consciousness were meager. It has been suggested that the unions and the *Volksverein* were used as tactical weapons by the party's leadership, and that it had no real commitment to serious social reform but simply sought to prevent the workers' vote from being won by the Social Democrats. Such an interpretation "explains the lack of future of its specific social-political work and its failure under changed political constellations after 1918."[8] Certainly the politicians were not unhappy with the con-

7. Behrens's case is described in Frey, pp. 81–82. Behrens joined the German Nationalist party after World War I but left it in 1929.
8. Mittman, pp. 174–75.

straints upon action provided by the Wilhelmine administrations in Prussia and the Reich, and they were content after the war to allow the initiative in social and economic policy to be seized by the Social Democrats. But on the other hand, they were possessed of sufficient practicality and goodwill toward labor to avoid becoming committed to the corporative theories favored by right-wing Catholics outside the party and the unions.

The approach of the Center's social reformers was pragmatic, based upon the use of existing parliamentary procedures and upon the adversary relationship of labor to capital, which existed in all modern industrial nations of the time whether or not identified with the "class struggle" described by the Marxists. There was considerable dissatisfaction among some Catholic intellectuals about this tacit acceptance of contemporary realities. To them, industrial capitalism and parliamentary liberalism were twin evils in society and should be confronted rather than accommodated. These theorists formulated an alternative Catholic ideology, corporativism, and from time to time attempted to win support for it from Centrist leadership.

Corporativism dealt with both the economic and the political fields, attempting, in the former, to avoid the evils of both socialism and capitalism and, in the latter, to avoid a liberal Parliament while retaining the concept of representation, or even democracy, in some sense of the words. Its origins lay in the early nineteenth century in the works of Adam Müller (1779–1829) and Franz von Baader (1765–1841). Müller, a member of the romantic school and a convert to Catholicism, first formulated his political ideas in deliberate opposition to the ideals of the French Revolution. His answer to egalitarianism was a defense of fundamental, God-given inequality and natural hierarchy; he denounced the theory of government by contract and assumed instead the organic nature of the state, a concept already developed in German philosophy.

Müller's ideal state was based on the "natural inequality" of occupational and personal status; in effect, he proposed a retention and expansion of the medieval system of "estates," keeping the clergy and nobility in the highest ranks. The active political role would be played by a monarch, limited and assisted by the two highest estates, while the two other estates of industry and commerce would regulate the economic life of the nation in their separate corporations, or guilds.

The peasantry, characteristically, was not considered to be a separate estate but rather an appendage of the nobility.[9]

The originality in Müller's writings lay not in the ideas he discussed, which were centuries old, but in the fact that he formed them into a coherent system. It was only after being faced with competition from the liberal ideas of the French Revolution that the supporters of the old regime began to analyze the earlier bases of government and social harmony. When conservatives became self-conscious, they were often deceived into admiring an artificial and inaccurate picture of political and economic life in the Middle Ages.

Müller was an employee of the Austrian imperial government in the last years of his life, a paid apologist for the Metternich regime. He was a man who refused to come to terms with any aspect of modern society. But his works interested and influenced later writers who tried to use them as a basis for a workable modern system. One line of his followers began the "Social Catholic" movement, while another can be traced forward to twentieth-century fascist writers, among them Othmar Spann, the Austrian economist who used Müller's philosophy to justify a form of totalitarianism and who was a favorite of one faction in the National Socialist movement. It was the former rather than the latter school of thought which appealed to German Catholics in the Second Reich and the Weimar republic, although some had hopes that National Socialism might develop an acceptable form of corporative society.

The doctrines of Müller reappeared, but significantly altered, in the works of the South German Franz von Baader, who was Catholic by birth rather than a romantically motivated convert like Müller. He lived to witness the early stages of the Industrial Revolution in Germany, a phenomenon which had not affected Müller. Baader was a theologian and a mystic and his thoughts on economics represent only a part of his writings, but these proved to be more enduring and influential than his devotional works. Baader, like Müller, rejected rationalism, individualism, and liberalism entirely, but his milder and more amiable temperament softened the conclusions he drew from the rejection. He proposed an "organic state" in which the hierarchy of

9. Ralph H. Bowen, *German Theories of the Corporative State* (New York, 1947), pp. 31–38.

estates, or *Stände*, would remain and would mediate between the individual and state authority. But the *Stände* would be active in protecting the rights of their members whatever the occupational group they represented. By retaining the old guild system, Baader hoped to avoid the terrible consequences of industrialization which he had observed in England and France. Thus his corporations would perform some of the functions of trade unions, with the vital difference that they would be composed of the entire vocational group rather than simply the labor class within the group. This is the distinctive feature in all corporative schemes. The state government would itself attempt to correct injustice in the working of the economy (a rejection of the liberal doctrine of nonintervention) but would deal with the estates, not with individual citizens.[10]

Baader's ideas received renewed attention in the years following the unification of Germany, when industrialization was proceeding rapidly. Corporativism seemed to be favored in the writings of Bishop von Ketteler, although he was more concerned with the practical aspects of social reform and the formation of specific groups or corporations than with any overall plan for revising the system of government. Franz Hitze's work, *Kapital und Arbeit und die Reorganization der Gesellschaft*, published in 1880, contained a detailed description of a corporative order for Germany. It envisaged the organization of vocational groups on the local level and also proposed a separate Chamber of Estates to supplement (not replace) the territorial Parliament. His plan gave the state more of a role than Baader's had done and also recognized the continued need for a parallel political legislature.[11]

Corporativism achieved international recognition with the publications of Karl Joseph von Vogelsang (1818–90), a Protestant from Mecklenburg who was converted to Catholicism in 1850 under the influence of Ketteler and Görres and later settled in Austria. In 1879 he founded the *Monatsschrift für christliche Sozialreform*, which served as a vehicle for his social ideas. In Vogelsang's scheme, the participation of the state was essential and membership in vocational cor-

---

10. Ibid., pp. 46–53; Gottfried Salomon, "Franz-Xaver von Baader," *Encyclopedia of the Social Sciences* (New York, 1930), pp. 373–74.
11. Bowen, p. 101.

porations would be compulsory, not only in handicrafts and industry but also for agriculture. The *ständisch* order would "substitute for the horizontal membership in classes a vertical membership in vocational groups.[12]

Corporativists and anticorporativist social reformers both claimed to find support and encouragement of their views in the encyclical *Rerum Novarum* issued by Leo XIII in 1891. The encyclical gave great impetus to Catholic social reform movements by its recommendation of associations to help the workers and of state intervention when necessary to protect the welfare of the poor. Leo XIII also sanctioned Catholic participation in parliamentary government, thus encouraging both the means and the ends of the reformists, but he explicitly rejected the spirit of liberalism and socialism at the same time that he appeared to acknowledge many of their claims. The encyclical denounced the principles of liberalism and socialism and proposed as alternatives to them principles which were entirely compatible with those of the Catholic corporativists.

The encyclical brought out two concepts which were of especial interest to corporativists: that of the organic state and that of the union of capital and labor in the same associations rather than unions exclusively for labor engaged in a sort of struggle against capital. Of the former point, the encyclical said:

> The great mistake made in regard to the matter now under consideration is to take up with the notion that class is naturally hostile to class, and that the wealthy and the working men are intended by nature to live in mutual conflict. So irrational and so false is this view that the direct contrary is the truth. Just as the symmetry of the human frame is the result of the suitable arrangement of the different parts of the body, so in a State is it ordained by nature that these two classes should dwell in harmony and agreement, so as to maintain the balance of the body politic. Each needs the other: capital cannot do without labor, nor labor without capital.[13]

Nothing specific was said in *Rerum Novarum* about vocational groups, and the papacy did not fully commit itself to corporativism until 1931, with the publication of *Quadrigesimo Anno*. After 1891,

12. Gerhard Stavenhagen, "Karl von Vogelsang," *Staatslexikon*, 8:278–82.
13. Gilson, p. 214.

however, corporativism came to be recognized as the preferred theoretical ideal of the church for social and economic organization.

The economic functioning of the future corporative state was described in some detail by the Jesuit scholar Heinrich Pesch, whose *Lehrbuch der Nationalökonomie*, published in five volumes between 1905 and 1923, was an exposition of "solidarity" (*Solidarismus*), his alternative to capitalism and socialism. Pesch rejected, or rather, ignored, the formal laws of economics and its interpretation as a science. He conceded that what he called "private" economics had profit as its goal but felt that national economics was a man-made method of attaining the goal of the "temporal material welfare of the nation as a whole." He denied the immutability of the "laws" of supply and demand and claimed that they did not always determine value. In his solidarist economy, the wage market was to be eliminate by the establishment of vocational groups, or corporations, for which the existing trade associations, cartels, and labor unions would form the nuclei. These corporations would themselves bargain to fix wages and prices, with the state setting a minimum wage and acting as arbiter in case of dispute.[14] Private ownership, even of a capitalistic kind, would remain, but the power of decision-making would be in the hands of the vocational groups and the state rather than with the ownership exclusively.

The vocational groups themselves would exist on three levels: on the local level, where employers and employees of any industry or occupation would meet separately, like existing unions and management-associations; on the district level, where they would meet together in true corporations; and on the national level, where there would be a supreme national council of the different vocational groups in the country. Compulsory membership would be justified in order to "incorporate" all persons in the country. Members of the district and national councils would not represent their class, that is, would not sit as "employer" or "employee," but would represent the vocation as a whole.[15]

By the time of the publication of Pesch's final volumes, the German empire had fallen, and the establishment of a republic was presenting new problems for Catholic theorists. Corporativism experi-

14. Abram L. Harris, "The Scholastic Revival: The Economics of Heinrich Pesch," *Journal of Political Economy* 54 (1946): 38–58.
15. Richard E. Mulcahy, *The Economics of Heinrich Pesch* (New York, 1952), pp. 180–87.

enced a considerable revival in the early twenties, as it seemed to offer an alternative to unpleasant realities.

How much practical effect did corporative theory have upon Catholic politicians and social reformers in the prewar era? On every occasion when the Center party leadership was confronted with the possibility of accepting corporativism as part of its program it decisively rejected it. In 1882, a committee set up by the Catholic Congress of that year, headed by Prince Karl zu Löwenstein, with Hitze and Karl von Vogelsang both participating, drew up the Haid Theses, so-named for Löwenstein's castle in Bohemia where the committee met. The Haid program recommended corporative organization in industry, and a national representation of *Stände* "in place of the present ideological and plutocratic constitutional electoral system."[16] The program was roundly denounced by Windthorst, who considered it old-fashioned in its suggestion of a return to guild-monopolies, and who naturally deplored its condemnation of the parliamentary system in which he had so conspicuously distinguished himself. The Center party refused to consider the program seriously or to make it part of the party platform.

Twelve years later, in 1894, a similar corporative program, based on Vogelsang's writings, was drawn up by a theologian, Dr. Peter Oberdörffer, which was again rejected by the entire Center Party leadership. Only a few agrarians supported the Oberdörffer program, in pursuit of their goal of divorcing the Center from any practical economic policy and thus winning their independence on the tariff question. Even Franz Hitze by now had given up his interest in corporativism and was devoting himself fully to working within the existing parliamentary and capitalistic systems.

As for the creation of actual corporations, very few of the organizations sponsored or supported by Catholic politicians resembled them. The unions were of course exclusively for workers, and the workers' associations were directed by clergy, not industrialists. The associations' vice-presidents, originally landowners or paternalistic manufacturers, were, by the end of the imperial era, more and more likely to be workingmen themselves.

The Chamber of Commerce set up in Prussia in 1897 was from

16. Bachem, 4:130.

the beginning dominated by major industries, and the handicraft chambers also represented single interest groups, not entire "vocations." Only in the vocation of agriculture were corporations of the sort envisaged by Catholic theorists actually created. The *Bauernvereine* which came to play such an important role in German politics did claim to represent large landowners, small farmers, and peasant tenants alike. Catholic landowners were as active as Protestant in forming these organizations. The Centrist political leader Schorlemer-Alst organized the first local Catholic *Bauernverein* in 1862 and it was expanded by 1871 into the Westphalian *Bauernverein*. Associations for Silesia, the Rhineland, Bavaria, the Palatinate, and Baden followed, with a total of twenty-six units by the year 1921, when they united in a national organization.

The Center party, which was strongly influenced in the prewar years by the landowners, supported the *Bauernvereine* and worked closely with them. The party leaders retained a sentimental belief that paternalism was preferable on the land to the materialist democracy of urban industrial unions. But in just such degree as the agrarian societies were corporate, representing all members of the vocation, they were authoritarian and antidemocratic, favoring the interests of the great landowners. Their defenders in the Center argued that the relationship between large landowners and small farmers in the west and south of Germany, where most of the Catholic organizations were formed, was more egalitarian and less reminiscent of the days of serfdom than the servility prevailing in the Protestant northern and eastern regions. But the *Bauernvereine* did not offer a really attractive model for idealistic corporativists who hoped to eliminate class conflict from society.

When the Prussian government established a Chamber of Agriculture in 1894, the Center party voted against the plan. Again in 1908, when the Reich government attempted to set up a Chamber of Labor which would represent both workers and employers, the Center, without rejecting the idea out of hand, worked in cooperation with the Social Democrats and the Radicals to make the proposed chamber more representative of workers and to make union officials eligible to serve in the chamber. These modifications were unacceptable to the government, which retracted the bill.

Corporativism, then, continued to be the theoretical ideal among

German Catholics, but in practice was ignored or rejected at every point by their political representatives in the Center party and the union movement. The revival of interest in the theory after the war had very little more practical consequence.

A much more practical issue in the prewar period was the controversy over the legitimacy of the Christian trade unions. The unions were generally well thought of in the industrial cities of the Rhineland, but in other parts of Germany they were looked on with great suspicion, chiefly because of their extension of membership to Protestants; but also because of their willingness to use the strike weapon, which the technical-divisions of the associations did not condone. Cardinal-Archbishop Anton Fischer of Cologne supported the unions, but the majority of the hierarchy did not, and in 1900 the Bishops' Conference issued a pastoral letter denouncing the unions and intimating that their eventual goal was to join with the Socialist Free unions. (Such a merger had actually been considered by the union leadership, but only on the unlikely condition that the Free unions abandoned their Marxist affiliations.)[17] Hitze replied to the pastoral letter by announcing in the Reichstag that the Center party favored the new unions. The controversy was well launched, and was not to be ended until 1914.

The leadership of the opposition to the unions was Franz von Savigny, nephew of the Savigny who had helped to found the Center. He was an integralist Catholic who headed the workers' associations in Berlin, and he was able to enlist the formidable support of Cardinal-Archbishop Kopp of Breslau and Bishop Korum of Trier for his "Berlin camp." Savigny and his followers worked assiduously to create more associations and more technical divisions within them, in order to compete with the growing number of unions. The great Silesian land-owner and industrialist Count Ballestrem, who employed fifty-five hundred workers himself, contributed funds to the Berlin faction; there was a special hostility in the east toward the unionization of Polish workers.[18] Although the vast majority of the lay Catholic political and social leadership in Germany favored Cologne-München-

17. Frey, pp. 26–27; Emil Ritter, *Die katholisch-soziale Bewegung Deutschlands im neunzehnten Jahrhundert und der Volksverein* (Cologne, 1954), p. 316.
18. Ross, pp. 55, 71, 159.

Gladbach, Berlin had the backing not only of influential German bishops but of the integralist party in Rome. Cardinal Kopp sought repeatedly to elicit official preference for the associations from the Vatican. Pope Pius X disliked the Cologne faction and made numerous informal remarks favoring the associations, but he refused for many years to issue a definitive statement on the subject.

The position of the unions was made even more precarious by the fact that Protestant social reformers were also divided on the question of the desirability of interdenominational organizations. Some officials of the Reich and Prussian governments, however, looked with favor from the beginning on the Christian trade unions, seeing them as a distinctly preferable alternative to the Socialist unions. State Secretary of the Interior Posadowsky based much of his social policy on the support of the Christian and liberal Hirsch-Duncker unions, hoping that they would eventually draw more workers to them and that the German labor movement would in this way become loyal to the monarchy and "cleansed of the scum of socialism."[19] As a matter of fact, the Christian unions were more outspokenly monarchist and patriotic than the exclusively Catholic associations, and this was part of their appeal to Protestant members. Posadowsky's plans were interrupted by the colonial crisis of 1906–7 and he was obliged to resign because of his close relationship with the Center, but his successor as secretary for the interior, Bethmann-Hollweg, continued to favor the Christian unions.[20]

In September 1912, after personal efforts by Hertling, then minister-president of Bavaria, Pope Pius X finally agreed to intervene in the union controversy, and issued the encyclical *Singulari Quadam*. The encyclical, as expected, indicated a clear preference for the exclusively Catholic associations and their technical divisions, but it did permit the toleration of interdenominational unions in those dioceses where the bishops considered them necessary and agreed to supervise them, "because on the one hand they include a significantly larger number of workers than the exclusively Catholic organizations and because on the other hand gravely damaging consequences would ensue if this

19. Born, p. 174.
20. Ibid., pp. 207–8.

does not happen."[21] The pope had obviously been impressed by reports of the gains of Socialist unions in areas of heavy Catholic population density.

The unions were only too happy to receive this measure of toleration from the Vatican: as in the case of the encyclical *Rerum Novarum*, a mere hint of approval was sufficient to encourage a movement which had already shown such signs of success. A majority of German bishops acceded to the request for toleration and an end to controversy and put it into effect after a special meeting in Essen in November 1912, presided over by Bishop Karl Joseph Schulte of Paderborn. But Cardinal Kopp, after temporary acquiescence, soon renewed the campaign against the unions, and the long *Gewerkschaftsstreit* continued.

The Christian unions then suffered attack from a completely different source. The Social Democratic press accused union leaders, specifically Stegerwald and Giesberts, of "selling out" and "betraying" German workers in order to win Vatican approval, opposing a miners' strike that year for the same reason, and conspiring to elect National Liberal candidates in the election of 1912. The Protestant newspaper *Wartburg* and other Protestant polemicists echoed the Socialists' charges. The governing board of the united organization of the Christian trade unions took the matter to court and sued the editors of eleven Social Democratic and Protestant newspapers for libel, winning the case easily since no evidence for any of the charges was presented.[22]

As the union controversy showed no sign of abating and the Berlin-Trier Orientation continued influential in Rome, the Reich and Prussian governments became increasingly apprehensive about the possibility that the pope would order outright suppression of the interdenominational unions. In 1913, Bethmann-Hollweg, now Reich chancellor, appealed through the Prussian ambassador to the Vatican urging an end to the conflict and recommending official sanctioning of the unions, saying that "there can exist no doubt that the Christian trade unions form the most effective weapon against the Social Demo-

21. Deuerlein, "Der Gewerkschaftsstreit," *Theologische Quartalschrift* 139 (1969): 77–79.
22. Ibid., pp. 65–66.

cratic organizations." The chancellor's appeal and a similar message from Hertling as minister-president of Bavaria succeeded in preventing condemnation of the unions and moderated the intensity of the quarrel.[23]

The end of the union controversy, like that of the related *Zentrumsstreit*, came with the death of Cardinal Kopp in March 1914 and the simultaneous outbreak of war and death of Pius X in August 1914. The Berlin Orientation ceased to be of any influence or importance. Membership figures for the two rival workers' movements show clearly that the practical advantages of true unionism had weighed more heavily with Catholic workers than the ideological purity of the technical divisions. In 1913, membership in the technical divisions was not much more than 10,000, while that of the Christian trade unions stood at 342,785. On the other hand, the Catholic workers' associations themselves, with their educational and cultural emphasis, were flourishing, with a total membership of 462,707 in 1914.[24] There was relatively little overlap between the two organizations. It has been estimated that only about 29 percent of association members were also members of a union.[25] In 1920, at the unions' National Congress in Essen, it was agreed that the remaining technical divisions would fully merge with the unions, while the associations would continue to exist as noncompetitive, parallel organizations.

Ironically, in spite of years of championing the principle of interdenominationalism, the Christian industrial unions never attracted more than a small minority of Protestant members. In part, this can be attributed to the fact that the unions were established in those parts of the country where the working-class population was in great majority Catholic, and in part to the fact that most Protestant industrial workers in these years had very tenuous connections with the churches, if indeed they had any ties at all, and hence had no compelling reason for not joining the larger and more militant Free unions.

The question of Protestant membership in the Christian trade unions was a practical one; the question of Protestant membership in the Center party was for most of its history a purely theoretical one,

23. Ross, pp. 112–13.
24. Figures cited in Deuerlein, p. 62; Jeanette Cassau, *Die Arbeitergewerkschaften* (Halberstadt, 1927), app. p. 1.
25. Oswald Wachtling, *Joseph Joos* (Mainz, 1974), p. 19.

since the invitation of 1870 to Protestants to join the party had been accepted only by a handful of individuals. For a few years just before the war, however, it was a key issue in an internal party quarrel known as the *Zentrumsstreit*.

The controversy coincided with the pontificate of Pius X and originated from his personal pronouncements. It was related to the union controversy but distinct from it. Pius X was concerned primarily with theological questions, not with political and social relationships. He was disturbed by the spread of theological "modernism," which was more important in France than in Germany. Yet his pronouncements, and the sometimes misguided zeal of his staff in the Vatican, led to much confusion in Catholic political circles in Germany, where modernism was virtually unknown.

The papal encyclical *Pascendi dominici gregis* of 1907 condemned modernism and called for the promotion of "integralism," a wholehearted Catholic consciousness in all aspects of intellectual endeavor and, presumably, of life in general. The encyclical was followed in 1909 by the imposition of an antimodernist oath upon all Catholic clergy (concerned, of course, solely with theological orthodoxy.)

Following the lead of the encyclical, a number of Catholic clergy carried integralism, or integrism, to the extent of applying it to matters of practical politics as well as to theology. As a French Catholic historian has written:

> The integrists refused to accept the modernist standpoint in much the same way as the intransigent and authoritarian Catholics had opposed Catholic liberals and Catholic democrats. . . . They restricted themselves to the traditional elements in the faith and held that these were not open to any further development. They appealed to authority to guard them vigilantly and this led them to put their trust exclusively in scholasticism and frequently to call the attention of the hierarchy to those bishops and members of the faithful who appeared to be deviating from that philosophy.
> . . . The tactical difficulty arose from the fact that integrism tended to group the faithful in a circle closed to the world and keep them in the blind alley out of which the intellectual members of the clergy, the professors, and the more learned laymen were striving to lead the Church.[26]

26. Adrien Dansette, *Religious History of Modern France*, 2 vols. (Freiburg, 1961), 2:310.

To German Catholics identifying with integralism, the pope's messages had relevance to the developments within the Center party and its affiliated organizations. These men were dissatisfied with the continued emphasis the Center placed upon being a political party rather than a confessional pressure group; with the theoretical inclusion of Protestants in the party; and with the actual inclusion of Protestants in the recently formed Christian trade unions. Even before the encyclical *Pascendi dominici*, there had been discontent. In 1896, for example, when Hertling, Centrist politician, university professor and founder of the Görres Society, recommended in a public speech that Catholic scholars associate more with their Protestant colleagues and overcome their inferior position (i.e., in numbers and influence) in German universities and the professions, his speech was considered by some to be an insult to Catholic scholarship.[27] Particular excitement was aroused in integralist circles by the publication in 1906 of an article by Dr. Julius Bachem in the *Historische-politische Blätter* entitled "Wir müssen aus dem Turm heraus!" ("We must come down from the tower!") The "tower" referred to in the article was the Center party as a stronghold, and a defender, of Catholicism. It recommended no more than the original goal of the party founders, the inclusion of Protestants, and especially, the candidacy of Protestants sympathetic to the Center in electoral districts where they might have a good chance of winning. In no sense did Bachem actually suggest that the party should abandon its support of Catholic interests or become a completely interdenominational "Christian" party, but he was accused of both these things.

During the *Zentrumsstreit*, the integralists steadily condemned the use of the word "Christian," so popular with Center publicists in propaganda and organizational appeals, as if it implied a merger of Catholic and Protestant doctrine into some kind of universal religion. This they identified with the modernist heresy denounced by Rome. In fact, nothing of the sort was ever contemplated by any Centrists, but it is true that the word "Christian" was used to attract like-minded Protestants into some socially or politically oriented organizations, such as the Christian trade unions and the Windthorst League, which opened its ranks to Protestants in 1907.

27. Bachem, 6:168–69.

Catholic integralism was a force operating largely outside the Center party, but there were a few deupties in legislatures who defended its viewpoint. The most active were Hermann Roeren, a jurist from the Rhineland representing the Trier district in the Reichstag and the Prussian *Landtag*; Dr. Franz Bitter, a lawyer from the north of Germany, in the area of the Catholic "diaspora"; Count Hans von Oppersdorff of Silesia, editor of a Berlin weekly *Klarheit und Wahrheit*; and Franz von Savigny, sponsor of the "technical divisions" of the workers' associations which rivaled the Christian unions. Because Berlin and Trier were the focal points of this faction, as in the related union controversy, its supporters were collectively known as the Berlin-Trier Orientation. Cardinal Kopp of Breslau and Bishop Korum of Trier were powerful backers of Berlin-Trier.

Most of the Center party leadership, however, and many of the German bishops, actively or passively, were ranged on the other side of the conflict, known as the Cologne, or Cologne-München-Gladbach Orientation, from the location of the *Kölnische Volkszeitung* and the *Volksverein*, or sometimes as the Bachemite faction, after the publishing concern and Dr. Bachem whose article had stirred up so much excitement. The Cologne Orientation wanted the Center to continue as a political party with a program on political, economic, and social issues, as well as religious, and defended interdenominationalism in those party-affiliated organizations whose activities were primarily economic or social.

On Easter Tuesday in 1909, Roeren, Bitter, and a mixed gathering of integralist clergy and laymen met in Cologne (in the enemies' camp) and agreed upon two basic guidelines: the first, that although the Center party was a political party and as such represented the interests of all the people in all areas of public life, it must do so "in harmony with the basic principles of the Catholic world-outlook." The second was that "the great influence which the *Volksverein* exerts on Catholic life demands [that it have] closer ties to the episcopacy." A proposed third statement to deal with the question of the Trade Unions could not be agreed upon.[28]

To nearly all of the Center's leaders (at this time, Hertling, Spahn, Gröber, C. Bachem) these were formulas for political disaster. Ob-

28. Ibid., p. 207.

viously the party faced questions every day concerning economic and social matters on which there *was* no specific "Catholic world-out-look." The effect of becoming such an exclusively confessional party would be to leave all delegates free to vote on these issues as they pleased, with no party discipline or unity possible (the position taken by some landowning aristocrats in the 1890s over the grain tariffs.) Closer ties for the *Volksverein* with the episcopacy were equally im-practicable, since on the social questions with which the *Volksverein* dealt, the episcopacy itself was divided and had no clear line of instruc-tion; in fact, Archbishop Fischer of Cologne, the home diocese of the *Volksverein*, was a firm adherent of the Cologne-München-Gladbach Orientation, while Cardinal Kopp opposed it, and Pius X is said to have "abominated Bachemism . . . and the entire Cologne faction." [29]

There was agreement in the party that the Roeren move must be combated, but the lack of a national, or even a Prussian state organi-zational structure was a great handicap in resolving the controversy. In November 1909, a joint session of the executive committees of the national and Prussian fractions met to try to persuade Roeren to sign a definition of party responsibility which was more in line with ma-jority opinion. Roeren signed the definition but continued pamphle-teering and propagandizing against what he saw as the dangerous in-terdenominationalism and non-Catholic activities of the Center party.

In 1910 the controversy was exacerbated by further moves by Pope Pius X: the administration of the antimodernist oath to the clergy and the issuance of the Borromeus Encyclical, commemorating the three hundredth anniversary of St. Charles Borromeo, sixteenth-century bishop of Milan and a hero of the Counter-Reformation. The encycli-cal enraged many German Protestants because of its tactless refer-ences to the German princes in the Reformation. The Catholic press was alarmed at the language in the document, and some papers refused to reprint it, but the full text did appear in *Germania*.[30] It seemed un-necessarily to reopen the wounds of the *Kulturkampf*. The Evangelical League was given ammunition against Catholics, and the Catholic in-tegralists felt bolstered in their attacks on interdenominational ten-dencies. (Pope Pius's office actually issued an apology, regretting any

29. Ross, p. 55.
30. Bachem, 6:331.

misunderstandings and stressing that the encyclical's remarks referred only to sixteenth-century events.) At the same time, a liberal speaker in the Reichstag revived memories of the 1870s, when he suggested that clergy taking the antimodernist oath should not be considered employable as state officials.[31] Protestant Guelphs were alienated from the Center and refused cooperation with the party in the next elections.

Party officials again attempted to discipline Roeren in 1910, but with little effect. Early in 1912 he was forced to resign from his position in the party and he did not run for reelection in 1912. Count Oppersdorff was also expelled but won a seat in the Reichstag that year from a Polish district.

It would seem at first glance surprising that the controversy aroused such anxiety and excitement in party circles when obviously the great majority of the Center's supporters were solidly behind the Cologne Orientation. But the party was sensitive to accusations of lack of religious orthodoxy and felt insecure when its opponents appeared to include not only prominent members of the hierarchy like Cardinal Kopp but also the pope himself. The decision of Pius X in 1912 on the union controversy did not entirely condemn the Cologne Orientation, it was true, but it strongly favored Berlin-Trier.

In the spring of 1914, a particularly disturbing incident occurred when the printed version of a speech concerning the controversy by Theodor Wacker, the combative priest who headed the Baden Center, was actually put on the Index of banned writings by the Vatican. No indication of the specifically condemned passage was given, but the ban was presumably imposed because of Wacker's description of the "impossibility" of party political activity being in practice directly or closely influenced by the church hierarchy. His speech had cited as an example of this the intervention in the drawing up of the Civil Code in 1896, when the party had succeeded in persuading the Vatican that its political strategy was correct, thus overruling instructions from Rome received earlier.[32]

The Center was dismayed and confounded by the condemnation. Wacker submitted to the ban, but he continued as head of the Baden

---

31. *Verhandlungen des Reichstags* 162 (14 Dec. 1910): 3720–21. The speaker was Karl Schrader of the *Freisinnige Volkspartei*.
32. Bachem, 7:266; see also Deuerlein, pp. 77–79.

party with the full support of his colleagues. Naturally, the Roeren integralist faction was elated at such confirmation of its views. Much effort was put into trying to reestablish Wacker and into determining just what had offended the Vatican offices, but the whole incident was forgotten and left unresolved in August 1914, when the death of Pius X and the outbreak of war changed the entire situation.

The new Pope Benedict XV had much more weighty matters to consider and he regarded such internecine quarrels as divisive and destructive. Integralism was specifically condemned in his encyclical *Ad Beatissimi* of 1 November 1914 and lost all momentum in Germany. Roeren retired from public life and died in 1920; Cardinal Kopp had died in March 1914; and Savigny died in 1917.

The *Zentrumsstreit* was over, but some of the questions raised during its course were questions which continued to affect the later history of political Catholicism, in the Weimar republic and also after World War II. The question of the admission of Protestants into the party was one which reemerged in the first years of the republic; there was even a well-publicized but totally unproductive effort to form a new "Christian" party in 1920, using the interdenominational Christian trade unions as its nucleus. Until 1945, however, any such effort, or even the modest inclusion of a few Protestant candidates as recommended in the Bachem "tower" article of 1906, was futile because of the complete lack of response from Protestant circles in Germany. Practicing Protestants in Germany tended either to be "nonpolitical" or associated with conservative movements, some of which were explicitly anti-Catholic. Only after twelve years of National Socialism was the need for concerted political action by both branches of the Christian faith felt by Protestants in any significant measure, resulting in the negotiations which created the Christian Democratic Union and Christian Social Union of contemporary times.

It would be a serious mistake to equate the two sides in the prewar *Zentrumsstreit* and in later debates about interdenominationalism with a left-wing or a right-wing political orientation. Berlin-Trier was *not* in all respects more conservative than Cologne, and the Cologne-München-Gladbach philosophy was *not* in all respects more democratic or social-minded than Berlin. If this had been so, the persistent linking of the young Centrist democrat Matthias Erzberger with the Berlin faction would be mysterious indeed. But in fact the more conservative position on religious doctrine was not always synonymous with the more conservative political position. When the Cologne Orientation advocated affiliation with Protestants in the party and its related organizations, it was recognized by everyone that these Protestants (real or hypothetical) would have to be, in the nature of things, politically conservative. The Christian partners the Bachemites were seeking were hardly to be found in the ranks of the supporters of the professionally atheist Social Democrats or the anticlerical liberal parties. An exclusively Catholic Center party could cooperate with Social Democrats and liberals on a pragmatic basis. True interdenominationalism would have meant a permanent right-wing orientation in the party, and this was deplored by left-wing democrats like Erzberger.

Erzberger was a pious Catholic who was personally friendly with Roeren and Oppersdorff, and the rumors that he belonged to the Berlin Orientation probably stem from these associations.[33] He never supported the entire integralist program and he certainly was in favor of interdenominational trade unions. But he opposed Adam Stegerwald's efforts to found an interdenominational "Christian" party in 1920 because he felt that this would be a conservative party which would make continued cooperation with Social Democracy impossible. His friend Roeren was a fanatical integralist, but he had also been a stormy anti-Establishment fighter in the colonial debates of 1906. He and his friend Oppersdorff were champions of Polish national interests, a cause scorned by Protestant conservatives in Germany.[34]

On the other hand, a leading advocate of the Cologne Orientation and personal antagonist to Erzberger, was Professor Martin Spahn, who was not only not noted for piety or even orthodoxy in his religious views but was also an extreme right-wing conservative. In 1910, he was challenged by members of the Berlin Orientation, when he attempted to take his seat in the Center Reichstag fraction, and accused of being anti-Catholic ("Martin Luther Spahn"). He was accepted into the fraction by a vote of 49 to 21, with 4 abstentions; he later left the Center to join the German Nationalist party in 1920 and became a National Socialist in 1933.[35] Such examples demonstrate that the *Zen-*

33. Epstein, "Erzberger's Position in the *Zentrumsstreit* before World War I," *Catholic Historical Review* 44 (1958): 1–16; Ross, p. 130.
34. Ross, p. 124.
35. Ibid., p. 129.

trumsstreit was more than an argument about correct religious policy. It coincided with, and perhaps helped to conceal or camouflage, a much more fundamental controversy over the political and social program that the party should follow.

The coming of the war found the Center weakened by the battles of the union conflict and the *Zentrumsstreit* and without direction in its leadership. The party's lack of real commitment to constitutional reform in the Reich and franchise reform in Prussia is evident. Even the left-wing of the party under Erzberger feared the growth of Social Democracy too much to make decisive moves in the direction of parliamentary responsibility.[36] Yet if the alliance with the Conservatives in support of the government continued, it was likely to bring about the loss of a substantial part of the Center's diverse electorate.

36. Epstein, *Matthias Erzberger*, pp. 85–95.

11
THE WAR YEARS

The coming of the war was as much a surprise to the leaders of the Center party as it was to the German public, and they accepted the government's explanations of its causes and its progress without question.[1] They shared in the national upsurge of patriotic feeling and, as the war continued, came to believe that its requirements would bring opportunities for the full integration of Catholics into Germany society.[2] In the last two wars fought by German troops, in 1866 and 1870, the Catholic population in the former had been largely situated on the losing side of a civil conflict and in the latter had been accused by many, though without justification, of being sympathetic to the French enemy. Now in the First World War, Catholic and Protestant Germans were united and fighting on the side of Catholic Austria for the liberation of Catholic Poles and Lithuanians from despotic Russian rule. War offered a chance for Catholic soldiers to reveal courage equal to that of Protestants, and for civilians, increased opportunity to advance in government service. Parity seemed within reach at last, and by 1917, government officials of Prussia and the Reich had explicitly promised a change in appointment policies.[3] Karl Trimborn served in the German administration of Belgium. Adam Stegerwald the labor leader served in the Treasury Office, then in the Reich Nutrition Office, and in 1917 was named to the Prussian House of Lords. Peter Spahn was appointed Prussian minister of the interior in 1917, and a former Centrist parliamentarian attained the highest rank of all at the

1. *Die Ursachen des Deutschen Zusammenbruch im Jahre 1918: Das Werk des Untersuchungsausschusses der Verfassunggebenden Deutschen Nationalversammlung und des Reichstages, 1919–1926*, 12 vols. (Berlin, 1925–29), 7:218–21, testimony of Johannes Bell.
2. Zeender, "The German Center Party during World War I: An Internal Study," *Catholic Historical Review* 42 (1957): 442–44.
3. Bachem, 8:19.

end of that year when Count Hertling accepted the chancellorship of the Reich. In 1917, also, the Federal Council finally agreed to the Reichstag's decision of 1915 to "end all exceptional laws" and totally repealed the law banning the Jesuit Society.

All of these attainments were highly gratifying to the party. The postwar world, as far as could be foreseen from the ill-informed perspective of the first war years, would see a continuation of this trend. The party's war aims were as grandiose and expansionist as those of other German organizations. German occupation and protection of the western border areas being detached from Russia was not seen as a hardship for the inhabitants of those areas but as an opportunity for economic and cultural enrichment. A "special relationship" with Belgium, if not complete annexation, was expected, and Centrists supported the German government's encouragement of the Flemish movement: just as the annexation of Alsace-Lorraine in 1871 had added to the proportion of Catholics within the new Reich, so might the annexation of Belgium and Luxemburg. Bavarian Centrists as well as the Bavarian government hoped that Alsace could be annexed to Bavaria, thus increasing the state's holdings on the left bank of the Rhine.[4] Ludwig III led the governments of several states in 1916 in opposing Bethmann-Hollweg's policies on the grounds that they were too moderate, and urged the annexation of Belgium and the resumption of unlimited submarine warfare.[5] In the Reichstag, Adolf Gröber and Peter Spahn not only supported the government's annexation plans but helped to formulate them.[6]

The Center press was united in approving the conduct of the war, but the papers varied considerably in the degree of chauvinism and aggressiveness. The editor of the *Kölnische Volkszeitung*, Julius Bachem, was forced to resign in 1915 by the publishers because of his moderate views, and he was replaced by his cousin Carl Bachem who directed the paper in a patriotic line "which almost tried to surpass the Pan-German League." The *Düsseldorfer Tageblatt* was equally vehement, but *Germania* and the *Westdeutsche Arbeiterzeitung*, the organ of the workers' associations, were more cautious on the subject of

4. Deuerlein, *Briefwechsel*, 2:855–56.
5. Willy Albrecht, "Das Ende des monarchisch-konstitutionellen Regierungssystems in Bayern," in Bosl, p. 283.
6. Zeender, p. 447.

war aims and annexations.[7] The *Volksverein*, the Christian trade unions, and the workers' associations all welcomed the chance to differentiate themselves from the Marxists in their devotion to the national cause.

The members of the Reichstag had little opportunity to help the war effort, since parliamentary initiative was not encouraged by the government. This fact made it possible for increased influence to be wielded by one Center fraction member who was able to play an active and important role in the war effort, Matthias Erzberger. His multiple ventures, delegated or self-imposed, brought him a position in the fraction rivaling and isolating the chairman, Peter Spahn.[8] Just as, in 1905 and 1906, Erzberger had seen the party's need for colonial expertise and speedily acquired it, now he had turned propagandist and diplomat and entered the international scene as no Catholic party politician had done before. He operated a propaganda bureau for the dissemination of information to neutral countries and served on missions to friendly and neutral countries, in the course of 1915 visiting Italy, Austria, Hungary, Turkey, Rumania, and Bulgaria. He became the confidant of Chancellor Bethmann-Hollweg and in Rome became the friend and admirer of his former antagonist Prince Bülow, then serving as special ambassador from Germany. His valiant efforts to keep Italy and Rumania neutral were failures because of the refusal of the Austro-Hungarian governments to make territorial concessions on the scale which the Allies were prepared to offer.

While in Rome on these occasions, Erzberger was also concerned to ensure the independence of Pope Benedict XV, because the war had revealed the lack of legal guarantees in the anomalous papal status since 1870. Conservative Catholic factions in Roman politics favored Italian neutrality as the best means of preserving papal neutrality and independence, but they were overruled by the annexationists in the regime.

Erzberger's contacts with the papacy in Rome, although they failed to obtain either Italian neutrality or a change in the pope's sta-

7. Hugo Stehkämper, "Julius Bachem," in Morsey, *Zeitgeschichte*, p. 40; Wolfgang Stump, *Geschichte und Organization der Zentrumspartei in Düsseldorf 1917–1933* (Düsseldorf, 1971), pp. 17–18; Zeender, p. 447; Morsey, *Die deutsche Zentrumspartei, 1917–1923* (Düsseldorf, 1966), p. 56.
8. Morsey, *Zentrumspartei*, pp. 54–55.

tus, were of value to him later in convincing him of the crucial importance of Belgian independence for a negotiated peace settlement. His
dramatic conversion to the need for a peace without annexations was
not brought about by any reassessment of the morality of Germany's
war aims, but solely by the discovery of Germany's real military situation, specifically, by information about the effectiveness of the submarine campaign. By his own account, he had had an illuminating
conversation with an admiralty officer as early as February 1916 about
the naval war and the chances of success with the unrestricted use of
submarines (not yet limited in response to United States' protests).
Erzberger produced figures from one of his numerous contacts which
seemed to show that even if German submarines sank the largest possible number of ships, the Allies would still be able to replace them at
a faster rate. The officer not only agreed with the figures but said that
the capacity of the German fleet had been overestimated and that submarine warfare would not be sufficient to defeat England.[9]

Erzberger became convinced that the entry of the United States
into the war would be disastrous for Germany and not nearly compensated for by the effects of the resumption of unlimited submarine warfare. This was also the reasoning of the chancellor. But the Center's
fraction leaders Spahn and Gröber were not convinced by these arguments and considered Bethmann-Hollweg's stand to be the result of
weakness. They wanted to urge the government to resume unrestricted submarine warfare. The final wording of a resolution introduced by Gröber on 16 October 1916 was a compromise reached between Erzberger and the more belligerent party leadership: "The
Imperial Chancellor is solely responsible to the Reichstag for all his
political decisions in connexion with the war. In taking his decisions
the Imperial Chancellor must rely upon the views of the Supreme
Command. If it is decided to initiate a ruthless submarine campaign,
the Imperial Chancellor can be certain of the agreement of the Reichstag." It has been suggested that the resolution meant that the Center
would support Bethmann-Hollweg even if he decided *against* resumption of the submarine campaign, but the implication that the chancellor should defer to the supreme command was clear; "the Center

9. Matthias Erzberger, *Erlebnisse im Weltkrieg* (Stuttgart, 1920), p. 215.

party's defection to the ranks of the U-boat enthusiasts drastically undercut Bethmann-Hollweg's parliamentary position."[10]

Resumption of unrestricted submarine warfare and the consequent entry of the United States into the war were important reasons for Erzberger's decision to present the Peace Resolution in July 1917. Other factors were: the failure of his own private conversations in Stockholm in March to effect a peace settlement with Russia; a message from Count Czernin, the Austro-Hungarian foreign minister, doubting whether his country could survive another winter of war; and his knowledge of an imminent peace-mediation move from Benedict XV. Eugenio Pacelli, the papal nuncio to Bavaria, had arrived in Munich that spring and had presented a first, tentative peace offer to German headquarters at the end of June. Although this was not well received, the Vatican planned a formal public announcement of the peace offer for August, and Erzberger's move was timed to anticipate and to harmonize with the papal initiative.[11] He was well aware that the restoration of Belgian independence was an absolute condition of peace in Benedict's proposal.

Characteristically, Erzberger did not discuss the peace resolution with his fraction or its executive council, or with Spahn; he did consult with several individual friends (Gröber, Johannes Giesberts, Dr. Maximilien Pfeiffer, and Count Praschma) whose reactions differed widely. The resolution was first proposed in a speech in the Reichstag Committee on Naval Affairs on July 6. The sudden and dramatic presentation of the gravity of the war situation had the effect of convincing the Reichstag majority of the necessity for a formal resolution on Germany's war aims, which was officially presented by Fehrenbach on July 19 and passed with a majority of 212 to 126 votes. The majority did not include the National Liberal party, however, which disturbed the more conservative Centrist deputies, and five Centrists voted against the resolution (including Count Praschma and Heinrich Held

---

10. Gröber resolution from Arthur Rosenberg, *Imperial Germany: The Birth of the German Republic, 1871–1918* (Boston, 1964), p. 146; final quotation from Konrad H. Jarausch, *The Enigmatic Chancellor: Bethmann-Hollweg and the Hubris of Imperial Germany* (New Haven, 1973), p. 297; see also Zeender, pp. 456–57.

11. Eberhard von Veitsch, *Bethmann-Hollweg* (Boppard-am-Rhein, 1969), p. 269; Epstein, *Matthias Erzberger*, p. 191.

of Bavaria) while Spahn and Gröber, whose approval of the wisdom of the resolution was known to be halfhearted at best, were absent because of illness.[12]

The Peace Resolution, phrased in general terms, called for a "peace of understanding" and renounced "forced" cessions of territory. The Inter-Party Committee, established by the three majority parties which had supported the resolution (Center, Progressives, and Social Democrats), sought to implement its recommendations by working out terms for a peace settlement and also to decrease the role of the high command in policy-making and to work toward Prussian suffrage reform and perhaps even eventual constitutional reform in the Reich. The Center's representation on the committee varied between four and eight members, with Erzberger holding an obviously dominant position among them. Spahn attended only for the first few days, after which his illness, and then his appointment as Prussian minister of the interior, removed him from parliamentary party life. Gröber, his successor as fraction chairman, was also absent for some time because of illness but took an active part on the committee after February, 1918. Other Centrists who attended regularly were Müller-Fulda, Trimborn, Fehrenbach (until June 1918, when he was chosen to be president of the Reichstag), and Wilhelm Mayer-Kaufbeuren of the Bavarian Center, all of whom were to continue in influential roles during the first months of the republic and to support the Weimar Coalition formed then by the three majority parties. But their claim to speak for the party and the electorate, and Erzberger's claim to lead them, were derived only from the emergencies of war, defeat, and revolution. Agreement between the Center fraction and the men on the Inter-Party Committee, and between the fraction and the electorate, was limited and difficult to achieve. Communication was particularly poor between the chauvinistic party press and the better-informed Centrist committee members.

Between 6 and 13 July 1917, the chancellor lost the last vestiges of support both among Erzberger and his followers and with the high command. In a meeting of the Center fraction on July 12, the majority agreed to back Erzberger in his determination to get rid of Bethmann-

12. Epstein, p. 191; Mittmann, p. 321; *Verhandlungen des Reichstags* 310 (19 Jan. 1918): 3598.

Hollweg, though the motives of the members were divided; many conservatives in the fraction, including Spahn (who suffered a fainting spell during the heated discussion) were critical of the chancellor because of his support for Prussian suffrage reform and his apparent wish for the eventual parliamentarization of the Reich government.[13] In any case, the Center played little or no role in the resignation of Bethmann-Hollweg, which was dictated by the high command,[14] and none at all in the choice of his successor.

The new Chancellor Michaelis was unknown to everyone in the party. His agreement to accept the Peace Resolution "as I understand it" was ominous for its future, since its wording was already so ambiguous as to admit of a wide range of interpretations.

At the end of July 1917, there was a joint meeting of the Center's National Committee with the Augustine League, the organization of the Center-affiliated press. At this meeting, Gröber and Spahn were both absent and Erzberger was leader by default, but after the initial shock of the Peace Resolution had worn off, the party showed itself unwilling to accept his advice or his leadership. He read aloud to the sixty-four persons at the meeting the memo he had received from Count Czernin, to try to convince the dissidents of the urgent necessity for a negotiated peace. (This indiscretion later became the basis for one of the many charges of treason leveled against Erzberger by his enemies, who implied that the note was more recent and more secret than it was, and that he had read it to a huge assembly of hundreds of Center voters rather than to a small group of the leadership.) Erzberger brought up the question of Alsace-Lorraine and urged that it be made into an autonomous grand duchy headed by the son of Ludwig III of Bavaria. Earlier in the war he had seriously considered the annexation of part of Alsace-Lorraine to Bavaria; this was a retreat, leaving the way open for Bavarian acceptance of a moderate peace.

He was also far more explicit at this meeting than he had been earlier about the need for constitutional change, and this was coolly received by his audience. The Bavarians especially feared that any constitutional change would be in the direction of centralization. Erzberger himself rejected complete parliamentarization, saying that the

13. *Die Ursachen des Deutschen Zusammenbruch*, 7:227–43, testimony of Martin
     Spahn.
14. Ibid., p. 221; Vietsch, p. 274; Jarausch, p. 377.

choice of chancellor should remain in the hands of the kaiser but require the consent of the governments of the larger states. He was evidently hoping to clear himself of the charge that he favored a nonannexationist peace in order to promote left-wing policies at home[15] and to emphasize his continued support of the federal structure of the Reich.

The backlash against the Peace Resolution intensified in the following months. The *Vaterlandspartei* was founded in September explicitly to combat its program, and many Centrists supported it, especially in the west of Germany. When the Düsseldorf branch of the *Vaterland* party was formed, many older Centrists joined it and the *Düsseldorfer Tageblatt* expressed its approval; however, the future Chancellor Wilhelm Marx, at that time chairman of the local Center and prominent in the Rhineland provincial party, refused to join, and the National Committee of the Center advised its voters against joining and repudiated the actions of the *Düsseldorfer Tageblatt*.[16] The *Kölnische Volkszeitung* went so far as to say, in August, that it would be a departure from Center party tradition to support the papal peace proposal—a reference to Windthorst's defiance of Pope Leo XIII thirty years earlier.[17] Allied governments soon became aware that support of the Peace Resolution and the papal peace note was considered cowardice and treason by wide circles of German opinion, and they ceased to consider them seriously as a basis for negotiations.[18]

The rapid German successes on the eastern front at the end of 1917 and the conclusion of the Treaty of Brest-Litovsk with Russia finally overruled the Peace Resolution altogether, or at least stretched its meaning to strange dimensions. It was the expressed opinion of the Center fraction leaders that the treaty was fully compatible with the resolution. Old Centrist sympathies for the oppressed Catholic subjects of the czar revived with the attractive prospect of setting up "independent" border states. Gröber in his speech to the Reichstag defending the treaty cited the right of self-determination as justification

---

15. Deuerlein, pp. 885–86; Morsey, *Zentrumspartei*, pp. 64–65; Bachem 9:9. Bachem is too favorable to Erzberger here, saying that the committee "nearly all" supported him, contrary to the reports in other sources.
16. Stump, p. 18; Zeender, p. 464.
17. Zeender, p. 461.
18. Bell, in *Die Ursachen des Deutschen Zusammenbruch*, 7:313.

for the new states and said that if they wished to align themselves with Germany that was their business and did not constitute "annexation."[19] Peter Spahn is said to have favored the attachment of "the whole Baltic area to Prussia . . . under a real and not a personal union, in order that the area might later be turned into a Prussian province."[20] Other Centrists, including Erzberger, objected to the plan of a personal union between Germany and the Baltic states if this were to mean their rule by William II, but hoped to see a Catholic German prince there; Erzberger was pleased when in the summer of 1918 the Lithuanian National Council voted to choose the duke of Urach, of the Catholic branch of the Württemberg dynasty, to be the ruler of that country.

As the weeks passed and the "independent" eastern states were not evacuated and looked more and more like fiefdoms of the German army, doubts began to be expressed by Center members of the Inter-Party Committee, particularly concerning exceptional legislation introduced by the army, which hindered the development of local self-government and the free exercise of religion and religious education. Gröber said in the committee on June 26: "The occupation is nothing but a military dictatorship." Above all they began to be uneasy that no definitive statement had been issued, even by the summer of 1918, promising the independence of Belgium, which Erzberger, Trimborn, and Gröber all agreed was essential to a peace settlement.[21] But in spite of such doubts, and dismay at the generous interpretation of what constituted "border adjustments" by the army, the Center's leaders were impressed with Germany's eastern victories and less willing to be bound even by the vague phrasing of the Peace Resolution than they had been the previous summer.

By the time of Brest-Litovsk, the incompetent Michaelis had been replaced by Hertling, then minister-president of Bavaria. Hertling had been offered the post at the time of Bethmann-Hollweg's resignation but had declined it because of his advanced age (he was seventy-four). In November 1917 he was prevailed upon to accept the post of chan-

19. *Verhandlungen des Reichstags.* 311 (20 Feb. 1918): 4004–7.
20. Fritz Fischer, *Germany's Aims in the First World War* (New York, 1961), p. 601.
21. Ralph Haswell Lutz, *The Fall of the German Empire, 1914–1918*, 2 vols. (Stanford, Calif., 1932), 1:791; Erich Matthias and Rudolf Morsey, eds., *Der Interfraktionelle Ausschuss, 1917–1918*, 2 vols. (Düsseldorf, 1959), 2:388–89; 418, 454–55.

cellor and, after a brief attempt to divide the two positions, of Prussian minister-president as well, in spite of criticism that it was not appropriate for a Bavarian to preside in Prussia. He thus became the first Centrist, and the first leader of a political party, to head the government. The choice did not signify a step toward true parliamentary government, however, since it had not been made by the parties (Hertling in fact resigned his party membership) or by the Reichstag. The appointments of the Progressive Friedrich von Payer as vice-chancellor and of the National Liberal Dr. Robert Friedberg for vice-president of the Prussian cabinet provide better evidence of response to the Reichstag majority and a transitional stage toward parliamentary rule than does the choice of Hertling, which was suggested by the army. The supreme command seems to have thought that the appointment of a conservative Centrist was the best way to "paralyze" Erzberger, and it certainly had that effect.[22] Erzberger could not work openly in defiance of Hertling (who had not favored the Peace Resolution), and the party's pride in seeing one of its own as chancellor was so great that it overrode all the mounting evidence of his incapacity to handle the job or to stand up to General Ludendorff. It was prophetic that Erzberger was told by State Secretary Wilhelm Solf that Hertling's appointment was conceived in Protestant circles as a "unique gift to the Reformation Jubilee" (the anniversary of Luther's publication of the 95 Theses) and that "German Catholics would be made responsible for a bad peace."[23]

When Hertling agreed to become minister-president of Prussia it was with the understanding that he would proceed with the government's program to reform the suffrage in that state, a move considered by Bethmann-Hollweg and the Prussian cabinet to be essential for the war effort. The government's motive was not so much to appease Allied opinion as to appease the increasingly militant Prussian workers, Socialist and non-Socialist, who threatened to disturb the *Burgfried* if the inequitable three-class system and outdated apportionment of seats were not altered.

Hertling was willing to attempt the task, even though he had not supported electoral reform in Bavaria and remained opposed to any genuine parliamentarization. His cabinet in Bavaria had not differed

22. Zeender, p. 462.
23. Matthias and Morsey, 1:333.

markedly from those of the earlier bureaucratic regimes and in fact contained only one other party man, Minister of the Interior Max Freiherr von Soden-Fraunhofen, who had served at one time as a Centrist deputy in the *Landtag* lower house but had been in recent years, like Hertling himself, a member of the upper house. In the war years, even this tenuous tie to Bavarian public opinion was broken when Soden resigned in a quarrel about the great domestic issue of the war in Bavaria, the production and distribution of food. Soden had supported the agitation of the Centrist populist demagogue and organizer of the farmers, Georg Heim. Heim claimed, apparently with justification, that Bavarian farmers were being exploited by Prussian influence in the Reich Nutrition Office. Bavarian Minister of War Kress von Kressenstein countered his attack with strict censorship of the news of Heim's activities. Eventually both Soden and the war minister resigned and were replaced by professional bureaucrats.

From that time, in 1915, Hertling's government did not favor Bavarian farmers or the Center party, but neither did it court the Socialists and liberals in the *Landtag*, who championed the cause of consumers in the food crisis and sought for electoral reforms to increase their influence. In the fall of 1917, the Social Democrats and the liberal parties both brought reform proposals before the house, but they were both rejected by the Bavarian Center, which sought only to maintain its existing advantages. Only in October 1918 did the Bavarian lower house unite to establish parliamentary government and proportional representation.[24]

Hertling's lack of interest in reform in Bavaria made it unlikely that he would put much effort into obtaining a more representative suffrage in Prussia. In fact, in spite of many months of activity, the Prussian reforms had not yet been carried through by the time of the November revolution in Germany.

The question of suffrage reform was returned to public attention inadvertently by the Conservatives in the House of Deputies, who attempted in January 1917 to push through a highly unpopular measure to increase the number of entailed landed estates. Progressive and National Liberal deputies thereupon protested, reviving the public de-

---

24. Friedrich Münch, "Die agitorische Tätigkeit des Bauernführers Heim," in Bosl, p. 342; Horst Gies, "Die Regierung Hertling und die Parlamentarisierung in Deutschland, 1917–1918," *Der Staat* 13 (1974): 474–76.

mand for reform which had been heard in 1910. A retaliatory Conservative attack on all aspects of parliamentary government made in the *Herrenhaus* provoked even the Free Conservative press to join the agitation for reform.[25] Bethmann-Hollweg was sympathetic and drew up a far-reaching program, including equal suffrage and direct, secret balloting. Interior Minister Loebell refused to accept this, and William II could not be persuaded to equal suffrage, but he did issue the Easter Message that spring promising extensive changes of some sort.

The revival of this subject was highly embarrassing to the Prussian Center party, much more so in some ways than the Peace Resolution had been. The same factors leading the Center to reject equal voting applied in 1917 as in 1910; not only was a reduction in the Center's representation likely but, more important, the expected decrease in Conservative seats and increase in Social Democratic seats would seriously jeopardize Centrist clerical educational policies. Carl Bachem called it "suicide" for the party, and Cardinal-Archbishop Felix Hartmann of Cologne vigorously opposed any change. On the other hand, the *Volksverein*, the Christian trade unions and the Catholic workers' associations were enthusiastically in favor of equal voting and in fact were demanding the Reichstag suffrage for Prussia. Stegerwald, head of the union organization, spoke out for manhood suffrage at the union congress in May (at the same time continuing to advocate a *Machtfried*, a "peace of the sword").[26] The issue threatened to cause a deep split in the ranks of the Center.

In April 1917 the Prussian government, itself divided and not wishing totally to enrage the Conservatives, had offered a compromise involving a system of plural voting which won the approval of the Free Conservatives, the National Liberals, and the two Centrist papers *Germania* and the *Kölnische Volkszeitung*. Loebell presented the bill in June, proposing plural votes for older men, men with families, and men possessing specified amounts of property and education. Plural voting was promptly denounced by the Christian trade unions as well as by the Progressives and Social Democrats. When a *Landtag* committee was formed in July, its members were unable to agree. The Center fraction in the Reichstag was by now willing to support manhood

25. Richard Patemann, *Der Kampf um die preussische Wahlreform im Ersten Weltkrieg* (Düsseldorf, 1964), pp. 50–51.
26. Wachtling, p. 32; Zeender, p. 458.

suffrage for Prussia but did not attempt to influence or to answer for the *Landtag* fraction.[27] Meanwhile, that same month, Bethmann-Hollweg had persuaded the kaiser of the necessity for the equal vote, but at the cost of the support of half the Prussian cabinet.

Although Bethmann-Hollweg fell in August, his opponents in the Prussian cabinet fell with him, and the survivors, led by Bill Arnold Drews, the new interior minister, were determined to carry through electoral reform. Shortly after Hertling became minister-president, a draft bill was completed. This December bill provided for the equal vote, reapportionment of seats, an end to hereditary seats in the House of Lords, and a limitation of the king's powers of appointments to that house. It was completed none too soon, as a major strike in Berlin in January 1918 showed that public opinion was becoming aroused. The strikers demanded not only suffrage reform but a total democratization of government.[28]

The strongly negative reaction to the strike on the part of the Center Reichstag fraction had the effect of disrupting cooperation between the party and the Social Democrats in the Inter-Party Committee.[29] Reaction from the Prussian *Landtag* deputies of the Center and the National Liberal Party was equally negative, but since reform was now not only inevitable but supported by Minister-President Hertling and Minister of Justice Peter Spahn, the Centrists in the *Landtag* committee sought to soften the bill's effect by drawing up "safeguards" to ensure the continuation of existing religious and educational policies. The safeguards were to require additions to the Prussian constitution and a provision that any constitutional amendment would henceforth need a two-thirds majority of the legislature.[30] However, a resolution proposing the safeguards was rejected by the other committee members of both Left and Right, embittering the Center's representatives.

When the House of Deputies considered the government's bill in May 1918, most of the Center's deputies supported it but it was defeated by a combination of Conservatives, Free Conservatives, nearly half of the National Liberals, and sixteen Centrists. After the third reading also resulted in rejection, the Centrists and Conservatives

27. Patemann, p. 87.
28. Lutz, 2:232–33.
29. Matthias and Morsey, 2:206–8.
30. Patemann, p. 179.

worked out their own compromise in which the Conservatives now accepted the safeguards and both parties agreed to plural voting: this passed the *Landtag* but again split the votes of the Center and National Liberal delegations, with only thirty-three votes of approval from the Center's ninety-three seats, and it did not satisfy the government or, of course, the Christian trade unions. The cabinet considered a dissolution of the *Landtag*, but this was not acceptable to the high command in this stage of the war. The Center *Landtag* fraction was pulled one way by increasingly militant union leaders who threatened secession from the party, and the other way by Cardinal Hartmann and his supporters, who were still as late as September 1918 denouncing equal suffrage even if the safeguards were obtained.[31]

By the end of September 1918, the question of Prussian suffrage reform had become less urgent than the need for parliamentarization at the national level. When General Ludendorff suddenly requested instant introduction of parliamentary responsibility, Hertling was unwilling to accept it and resigned. Incredibly, throughout the momentous events of October and into the first week of November, committees in the Prussian legislature continued to wrangle about the suffrage issue, proposing this or that qualification. When the revolution came, no consensus had been reached on suffrage reform, either in the *Landtag* or in the Prussian Center party.

In late September of 1918 the Center Reichstag fraction was still in ignorance of the imminence of defeat. Hertling not only did not communicate with his former colleagues but was himself unable to grasp the full significance of the military situation. Erzberger and the Social Democrats were anxious for Hertling's resignation, but Gröber and Trimborn were not willing to "sacrifice" a man of their own party "in order to exchange him for an unknown quantity," and even the Inter-Party Committee had no alternative candidate for chancellor. In the end, Hertling was never asked to resign by the Reichstag but chose to leave voluntarily when the high command's insistence upon parliamentary reform made it clear that he would have to accept Social Democrats into his government.[32]

The Inter-Party Committee drew up a program for the new chan-

---

31. Ibid., pp. 176, 196, 214.
32. Morsey, *Zentrumspartei*, p. 73; Gies, pp. 490–91.

cellor and intended to exercise a veto over his actions, but its members did not take the logical course of naming one of themselves as chancellor; instead they recommended Prince Max of Baden, a man with the reputation of a liberal yet, so the committee hoped, able as a prince and convinced monarchist to stand up to the kaiser and the high command.[33] The choice of Prince Max was not a particularly congenial one to the Center. Erzberger, if not the rest of the fraction, was aware of the poor impression the naming of a member of a ruling dynasty, with the title of prince, would create upon Allied opinion; and the whole party had reason to feel wary of a member of the liberal Baden ruling family which had so consistently worked to keep the Catholic population in that state in a second-class status.[34]

One reason for the party's hesitancy to move to full parliamentary government was a concern for the restrictions imposed by the Reich constitution. The constitution of 1871 made no provision for a Reich government as such. The chancellor and the state secretaries who in the later years of the Second Reich formed a de facto government legally derived their executive powers from their membership on the Federal Council as part of the Prussian state delegation. Article 9, sentence 2 of the constitution stated that "No one can be a member of the Federal Council and the Reichstag at the same time."[35] This "incompatibility clause" made it impossible for a parliamentary government of the French or British type, in which the ministers were themselves members of Parliament, to be introduced in Germany. But any alteration of the constitution to make it possible would have the effect of destroying the intended executive role of the Federal Council and hence would modify the federal nature of the Reich. "Parliamentarization and federalism were mutually exclusive."[36]

The Center party's dedication to federalism made its leaders reluctant to sanction constitutional change and made Centrist members on the committee particularly vulnerable to Conservative arguments against it. If a parliamentarization of the Prussian government had

33. Matthias and Morsey, eds., *Die Regierung des Prinzen Max von Baden* (Düsseldorf, 1962), p. xxviii.

34. Theodor Eschenburg, *Matthias Erzberger* (Munich, 1973), pp. 100–101.

35. Huber, *Dokumente*, 2:293.

36. Udo Bernbach, "Aspekte der Parlamentarismus-Diskussion im Kaiserlichen Reichstag," *Politisches Vierteljahresschrift* 8 (1967): 63.

been carried out at the same time as that of the Reich, in conjunction with electoral reform, a reasonable coordination of state government and the Federal Council with the leadership of the Reich could have been obtained without a change in the federal structure, but the Prussian ministry remained responsible solely to the king until the outbreak of revolution.[37]

Even if membership on the Federal Council were disregarded as no longer essential for the state secretaries, parliamentary government would still be precluded by Article 21, paragraph 2, of the constitution, which stated that "If a member of the Reichstag takes a salaried Reich office or a salaried state office in a federal state, or enters into an office in Reich or state service with which a higher rank or higher salary is connected, he thereby loses seat and voice in the Reichstag and can only regain his position there through reelection."[38] In the naming of Prince Max's cabinet it was decided that, rather than to stir up federalist feelings in the Center and in the Federal Council itself, Reichstag deputies could be appointed state secretaries on an informal, *ad hoc* basis, without being formally "named to office."

In the constitutional revisions made on October 28, prompted by messages from President Wilson demanding a fully representative government, Article 21, paragraph 2 was eliminated, allowing deputies to be formally named to office in the Reich government without losing their seats. Article 9, however, was never changed. None of the Reichstag deputies who took office with Prince Max, nor the single liberal deputy who became a Prussian minister, could sit on the Federal Council.

The Inter-Party Committee, and especially its Centrist members, were unwilling to transform the Reich government wholly into a parliamentary body. It named party representatives only to those positions deemed "political" and to the position of state secretary without portfolio. These men were to act as confidential liaisons (*Vertrauensmänner*) between the Reichstag on the one hand and the chancellor and the "nonpolitical" ministers (a category which included the state secretary for foreign affairs) on the other. The political secretaries were to be recallable by their parties, while the nonpolitical professional

37. Ibid.
38. Huber, 2:295.

ministers were not. This peculiar arrangement was christened "German parliamentarianism" by the Centrist Trimborn.[39] Most members of the Center's Reichstag fraction saw parliamentarization as primarily a means of saving the monarchy, an essential goal in their minds; even Erzberger rejected any thought of the kaiser's abdication as late as October 31.[40] On November 7, ten days after constitutional reform in the Reich, the Center fraction refused to support a proposal for parliamentarization of the state government of Prussia.[41]

Although the Center's leaders did not welcome constitutional change, they took care to be well represented in the new regime. Trimborn became state secretary for the interior, and Gröber and Erzberger were named state secretaries without portfolio. The kaiser was very reluctant to appoint Erzberger, and Gröber was apparently included in order to ensure that the entire Center party, and not just Erzberger's following, would be behind the cabinet.[42] In addition to receiving these positions, the party leadership hurriedly found or created lower-level posts for as many Centrists as possible, showing a zeal which is understandable in view of the former exclusion of party men from higher administration, but was unseemly under the circumstances.[43] There was little of the feeling of pride and elation in these appointments that there had been earlier in Spahn's and Hertling's advancement, however. This was not simply because of the realization of defeat and the desperate difficulties of the task before them. The Center had seen the earlier appointments as evidence that at last the party, and German Catholics in general, were accepted as worthy of inclusion in the royal and imperial ruling circles; now it had become clear that they had merely been evidence of the imminent collapse of those circles.

The most urgent work of the new government was to appoint a representative to serve on the armistice commission, since the supreme command had recommended to Prince Max that a civilian be included in its membership. One of the numerous accusations leveled against Erzberger in the republican years was that he volunteered him-

39. Bernbach, pp. 65–69; Huber, *Deutsche Verfassungsgeschichte seit 1789*, 5 vols. (Stuttgart, 1978), 5:536–37.
40. Bachem, 8:247; Epstein, p. 267.
41. Huber, 5:596–97.
42. Matthias and Morsey, pp. 43–44; 60–77; 124–26.
43. Ibid., pp. 124–26.

self for this thankless mission, or that at any rate he accepted nomination with alacrity. Neither the evidence nor common sense is in accord with this version of events. Witnesses are agreed that Erzberger did not seek the job and that he was persuaded by his colleagues, Gröber and Trimborn among them, to go; he was not originally named as head of the commission but was asked to head it later by the military members of the commission.[44] What really seem, as much as anything else, to have damned him in the eyes of his enemies were his unquenchable good spirits and the optimism with which he set off to negotiate with the Allies. Victory was lost, all hope of annexations and satellites had faded, but a "peace of understanding" must surely be attainable.

Unfortunately, Erzberger was unable to achieve any significant modification of the Allies' conditions, and by accepting the thankless task of heading the commission he unwittingly made it possible for rightist extremists to transfer all blame for the unfavorable terms of the armistice and the subsequent peace to himself and other "pacifist civilians" and away from the army officers who had originally demanded an armistice. The image of "Erzberger the traitor" became an integral part of the stab-in-the-back legend and irreparably damaged his reputation and that of his party.

44. Ibid., pp. lviii–lxii; Epstein, pp. 272–73.

12

REVOLUTION AND THE MAKING OF A CONSTITUTION, 1918–1919

The cabinet of Prince Max had barely adjusted to the shock of being told by the army command of the need for an immediate armistice when the new shock wave of mutiny and street revolution occurred. The Center party as an organization had no response to make to the totally unexpected events, and it virtually ceased to exist. Its new and seldom-convened National Committee was not called into session, and Erzberger, the only man in the leadership who might have been able to rally party members to some sort of united action, was still away on the armistice mission. Gröber and Trimborn stayed in their posts just long enough to agree to the armistice terms and then resigned from the government. Trimborn traveled home to Cologne, in the Rhineland; Fehrenbach, president of the Reichstag and former head of the Inter-Party Committee, home to Karlsruhe in Baden; Porsch, chairman of the Prussian *Landtag* fraction, home to Breslau in Silesia. The Center had begun its existence as a loose federation of state and provincial organizations, and it now appeared to be dissolving into its component parts. Just as its leaders took themselves away from Berlin, so its largest units, in the Rhineland and Bavaria, were tempted to separate themselves from the troubled capital and even from the Reich.

For the older men the revolution was a catastrophe. Hertling, ill and in retirement in Bavaria, wrote to a friend "God help us, that is the only thing one can say," and died soon after, on 4 January 1919. Porsch refused to admit that his fraction members' mandates were no longer valid and expressed doubt that a new Parliament would be legitimate. Fehrenbach, upon his arrival in Baden, is described as being "in a state of complete physical and mental dissolution . . . he groaned and wept incessantly into a large handkerchief. His speech [to his Centrist colleagues] ended with the hopeless utterance *'Finis Germaniae!'"*[1]

But while the national organization was in disarray, local groups were forming as early as the first week of revolution, often under the leadership of younger men who had been serving in the Reichstag or state parliaments. Even before Erzberger returned to Berlin on November 13, meetings had been held and committees formed in the capital. By the fifteenth, with Erzberger's help a party general secretariat had been set up to handle communications and propaganda, with Maximilien Pfeiffer serving as the party's first paid national secretary. On the twelfth, a new Bavarian organization had been founded, the Bavarian People's party [*Bayrische Volkspartei*, or BVP], under the direction not of the wartime Center head Heinrich Held, who had been hoping to enter the royal cabinet in the fall of 1918 and who repudiated the revolution, but by Sebastian Schlittenbauer and Georg Heim, the leader of the Christian Farmers' Association whose demagoguery had ostracized him from the prewar Bavarian Center party. During the course of the war, Bavarian farmers had lost faith in the monarchy, blaming Ludwig III for his apparent complete subservience to Reich food policy. Heim and Schlittenbauer were both members of Kurt Eisner's revolutionary assembly.

The new name of "Bavarian People's party" did not at first mean a breach with the national Center organization, but it did symbolize the particularist and separatist resurgence in that state, where the population had feared Allied invasion from the south after the collapse of Austria-Hungary and continued for some time to hope for a separate and more favorable peace settlement with the enemy. The BVP and Eisner's regime were in most matters of policy diametrically opposed to one another, but both for different reasons temporarily joined in a separatist pulling-away from Berlin. The BVP welcomed all "German brothers in Bohemia and in the German Austrian *Länder*," and an important plank in its platform was the inclusion of German Austria in Germany, either as a separate new *Land* or, as suggested by Heim in an

1. Morsey, "Georg Graf von Hertling," and Helmut Neubach, "Felix Porsch," in Morsey, *Zeitgeschichte*, pp. 51, 120; Heinrich Köhler, *Lebenserinnerungen des Politikers und Staatsmannes, 1878–1949* (Stuttgart, 1964), p. 93, for Fehrenbach.

article in the *Bayrische Kurier* December 1, in a union with Bavaria.[2]

By the end of November, the Center had reorganized in Württemberg, Baden, and Hesse and was represented in the new governments in these three states. The young schoolteacher Joseph Wirth began his Weimar career by accepting the post of finance minister in the new Baden cabinet. None of the governments of the three southwestern states was willing to join Bavaria in Eisner's attempt to establish autonomy of the south.

It is unlikely that the Center party would have reemerged in Germany so quickly, if not intact, as least as living state and local units, if it had not been for the actions of the new *Kultus* minister in the revolutionary Prussian government, Adolf Hoffmann. (The Center was not represented in this government at all.) Hoffmann, an Independent Socialist and the author of a book entitled *The Ten Commandments and the Property-Owning Class*, made it clear that the revolution in Prussia would not be simply social and economic but would affect religion and education as well. His radical program, announced on November 13 and made an official government decree by the twenty-ninth, included not only the abolition of confessional schools and religious instruction in all schools but plans to "stop all subsidies to the church, to confiscate church property and buildings, to convert church holidays into nature festivals, to abolish theological faculties, and to deprive the clergy of their status as officials and of their eligibility for public office." Similar moves seemed likely to be carried out in Bavaria, Saxony, Württemberg, Brunswick, and Hamburg,[3] This had the effect of galvanizing into action many Centrists, like Porsch in Silesia, whose initial reaction had been to retire from public life. The Hoffmann decrees may almost be said to have called the Center party into new life. Protest demonstrations were held throughout Prussia, and the clergy in particular were impressed with the need for Catholic participation in politics. The prospect of a new *Kulturkampf* rallied the Catholic population much as had the old one.

Hoffmann's decrees also alarmed and aroused Protestant churches in Prussia and were responsible for attracting a number of Protestants,

---

2. Karl Schwend, *Bayern zwischen Monarchie und Diktatur* (Munich, 1954), p. 60; Buchheim, p. 355.

3. Karl-Wilhelm Dahm, "German Protestantism and Politics, 1918–1939," *Journal of Contemporary History* 3 (1968): 34; Morsey, *Zentrumspartei*, p. 113.

including some clergymen, to the ranks of the Center during the first months following the revolution. Protestant aid was welcomed in the fight against the decrees, and the historically interdenominational nature of the Center was recalled frequently in public statements.

The wish to attract Protestants to the party was the occasion for long debates on a possible change of name: the names of "Free German People's party," "Christian Democratic People's party," and "Christian People's party" were all considered in November and December of 1918. The party in Silesia, on the other hand, used the name "Catholic People's party" in the elections of 1919, explicitly denying any welcome to Protestants, just as in 1871 the Silesian party had insisted that its candidates declare themselves "convinced and loyal Catholics."[4]

Labor leaders Heinrich Brauns and Adam Stegerwald were hopeful that a name change would mean a substantive change, the creation of a large interconfessional party which could confront Social Democracy effectively; others merely wanted a change of name for cosmetic purposes and did not expect or desire any basic change in electorate or in platform. There was some apprehension also that if the old name were given up that former integralists or others would make use of the name "Center" to form a rival, exclusively Catholic party.[5] In the end, the decision was made to retain the old name which, after all, had never had the literal meaning of "Catholic." Many branches of the party used "Christian People's party" as a subhead in the election campaign of 1919 but subsequently dropped it.

By December 20, a new set of party guidelines had been drawn up which served as a platform in the January elections. These guidelines were based principally upon an earlier list prepared by the Berlin organization and were more conservative than a Cologne manifesto of November 19, which had had a distinctly socialist slant, advocating the expropriation of hereditary landed estates and denouncing unearned incomes and excessive war profits.[6] The December guidelines were more circumspect, continuing to denounce "class rule, materialism, mammonism, and anarchy" but urging an end only to "uneconomically expanded large landed estates." The platform looked for the

4. Günter Grünthal, *Reichsschulgesetz und Zentrumspartei in der Weimarer Republik* (Düsseldorf, 1968), pp. 24–25.
5. Morsey, p. 101.
6. Ibid., p. 102.

uniting of "German stock" with Germany but did not mention Austria by name. A federal state structure for the Reich was to be maintained; Upper Silesia and the colonial empire were to remain German. The platform recommended universal suffrage with proportional representation, equality of opportunity for women, and "the development of the economy in the cause of social justice."[7]

The program managed not only to gloss over the question of capitalism versus socialism but also the vital question of separatist movements, now observable not only in Bavaria but in Silesia and the Rhineland. A great demonstration held in Cologne on December 4 advocated the secession of the Rhineland from Prussia and the possible division of the Reich into four republics, of which two would be Rhineland-Westphalia and Bavaria-Austria. Motives behind the movements were ostensibly the reaction to the Hoffmann decrees and the fear that Catholic interests would be hurt by "Red Berlin," but there was at the same time the underlying hope for a better peace and more lenient occupation terms from the French. The Rhenish movement emphasized in December 1918 and throughout the next four years that it aspired to autonomy *within* the Reich and not separation from Germany, as sponsored by the French, but accusations of pro-French sympathies and even of treason were nevertheless leveled against it. Although Rhineland separatism was never officially sanctioned by the Center party, most of its adherents were Center supporters and very few from other parties were involved with it.

In spite of the proclaimed goal of a "Rhineland-Westphalia" state, many districts in the area were never seriously caught up in the separatist movement. The Center party in Düsseldorf explicitly repudiated it, as did the Westphalian provincial organization under Karl Herold.[8] The most active Rhineland separatists were those connected with the local Cologne branch of the party. Karl Trimborn was the only Centrist of national prominence to be closely identified with the movement in the early months, but Ludwig Kaas and Wilhelm Marx were sympathetic. Konrad Adenauer, mayor of Cologne, was convinced that France would insist upon the breaking-up of Prussia and that a West German republic of some kind was the only alternative to a French

7. Eduard Heilbron, ed., *Die Deutsche Nationalversammlung im Jahre 1919*, 2 vols. (Berlin, 1919–20), 1:138–39.
8. Stump, pp. 28–29; Morsey, p. 125.

satellite state.[9] Archbishop Hartmann was strongly opposed to the movement. *Germania* reflected the feeling of most Centrist leaders outside the Rhineland when its editorial pages urged that the issue be referred to the National Assembly.

The Rhinelanders' appeal to be set *"Los von Berlin"* had one positive effect, which was the decision of the Socialist government in Berlin to dismiss *Kultus* Minister Hoffmann and to rescind all his November decrees concerning education and church-state relations. This was announced on December 28, and on the same day the official Rhenish Center party organization declared its support of the indivisibility of the Reich. The question of the divisibility of Prussia was postponed until the meeting of the National Assembly.

The party's election campaign in January was vigorous and explicitly anti-Socialist, in spite of cooperation with the Social Democratic party in the south, and the accommodations to the revolution made in the platform. It was also anti-Hoffmann in spite of the cancellation of the offensive decrees. Many Protestant and Catholic clergy fought side by side on this issue as they had never done in the original *Kulturkampf*.

Two pressure groups were of new importance in these elections, women and labor unions. Catholic women's organizations had not demanded the vote before the war, although Helga Dransfeld, organizer and head of the *Frauenbund*, had personally been won to the idea as early as 1906. However, they were now prepared to make use of the vote which had been given them, and the party platform had espoused the ideal of the equality of women, a notion never seriously contemplated by Catholic politicians before November 1918. Dransfeld had been quick to call meetings together of the representatives of women's organizations on November 22, to recruit them for election activity, and to help in framing the new constitution along lines favorable to women. Her efforts were partly successful, since women were very helpful in rallying votes for the Center in the campaign, but few ran for office or sought any more active role than that of propagandist or fund raiser. Dransfeld herself was elected to both the National Assembly and the Prussian Assembly.

9. Morsey, pp. 118–22; Epstein, "Adenauer, 1918–1924," *Geschichte in Wissenschaft und Unterricht* 19 (1968): 556.

The Christian trade unions also found themselves in an unexpect-edly important position, and their leader Adam Stegerwald found the hectic atmosphere of November and December an ideal climate for empire-building. On November 15, representatives of German indus-try, facing the threat, as it seemed then, of complete socialization, signed an agreement with union representatives which secured for them many of the demands they had been working for, including the eight-hour day, collective bargaining and mediation committees, and an end to company unions.[10] Although the Socialist Free unions were skeptical, the Christian unions were enthusiastic. A few days later, Stegerwald brought his unions into an amalgamation of all non-So-cialist unions in Germany. This merger, originally sponsored by the liberal Hirsch-Duncker unions, was called at that time the German Democratic Federation of Unions. Stegerwald was chosen head of the entire organization, which included not only industrial unions but white-collar workers and civil servants. The Christian unions found that their members were in great demand as candidates for the Na-tional Assembly. In just such measure as the Center party was anti-Socialist its leaders felt that they must demonstrate that they were in no way antilabor.

The election campaign was a success, for although proportional representation hurt the party, the women's vote favored it. The first elections held were in Baden, where the Center emerged as the strong-est party, with 39 out of 107 seats. The party also did well in Württemberg but declined in strength slightly in Bavaria, where the Bavarian People's party obtained only 66 out of 180 seats under the new electoral laws. Bavaria sent 18 delegates to the National Assem-bly who sat with the 68 Center delegates and 3 faithful Hanoverians, making a voting bloc of 89. Because of the border changes dictated by the armistice, the party's old allies from Alsace-Lorraine and the Pol-ish districts were no longer present, but Upper Silesia was still repre-sented at this time, and many votes in border districts which had for-merly been cast for the Polish party went directly to the Center. *Germania* estimated that the noticeable increase of Center support in

10. Dill, "The Christian Trade Unions during the Last Years of Imperial Germany and the First Months of the Weimar Republic," *Review of Social Economy* 12 (1954): 102.

Berlin was the effect of the women's vote and the support of Protestants alarmed about the anticlerical measures of the government. Very few women won seats, however, with five each in the Center delegations of the National and the Prussian assemblies, a smaller percentage than the average.[11]

The makeup of the Reichstag fraction was altered from prewar years. Noble landowners had not been desired as candidates, and industrial workers and union officials had been welcomed and favored. The clergy were also less prominent than before. There were over twenty Centrist labor delegates in the National Assembly, of whom seven represented the workers' associations, the rest the industrial and employees' unions. The state assemblies showed similar trends but less startling changes in social composition. The change in the social makeup of the parliamentary delegations was the result of campaign strategy in a revolutionary period and did not mean that there had been a corresponding change in the actual power structure of the party. Already by the next elections in 1920, the ratio of landowners and clergy to workers had shifted significantly in favor of the former.

Following the elections, a three-day debate took place in the Reichstag fraction on the question of whether or not to join a government coalition. There was much resistance among the party's supporters to cooperating with the Socialists so soon after fighting a strongly anti-Socialist election campaign. But the assembly fraction itself was keenly aware of the advantages to be gained by participation and the importance of being involved in constitution-making when so many vital interests of German Catholics were at stake, to say nothing of the need to prevent a radical socialization of the economy. Windthorst's words were recollected: "a policy of abstinence is laziness or stupidity."[12] Erzberger and Stegerwald both urged that the party enter the coalition, although Stegerwald refused to take a ministry himself and chose instead to enter the Prussian state government. In the end, the Center participated in Weimar coalitions in the Reich, Prussia, Württemberg, Baden, and Hesse.

The press attempted to answer the criticism leveled at the party by the voters; here again the specter of former minister Hoffmann per-

11. Morsey, pp. 144–46.
12. Bachem, 8:379.

formed an invaluable service in showing the probable effect of the party's refusal to enter the government. Although most of the criticism was of participation in the government, there was also some feeling that the party was underrepresented in the Reich cabinet, since it had obtained none of the key posts, with Erzberger sitting without portfolio, Giesberts for the Post Office, and Bell minister for the soon-to-be-lost colonies. The word "sacrifice" was frequently heard in 1919 and in later years from many who felt that the Center had taken on responsibility without any of the rewards of power and prestige.[13]

This feeling was understandably acute during the agonizing debate over the peace treaty. The parties of the Right bore no responsibility, the German Democratic party, heir to the Progressives, felt free to leave the government (June 19) rather than accept the unacceptable, but the Center's ministers were painfully aware of the consequences of not signing the treaty; the Rhineland, Silesia, perhaps Bavaria, were hostages to the Allies. A physical breakup of the Reich with "separate democratic states in the West and . . . military dictatorship in the East" was a possibility which Erzberger and others saw clearly.[14]

The Center fraction at first decided to recommend signing of all articles except those dealing with the "points of honor" (227 to 231, concerning war guilt and the foreign trial of German leaders), and this formula was accepted by the majority in the assembly. The Allies rejected it and insisted that the treaty be signed in its entirety. It was at this point that the Democratic party left the government and refused to enter a new one. The Center agreed to continue in a new cabinet with the same three ministers under the Social Democrat Otto Bauer, but when the day arrived for a reply to the Allies, June 23, all but fourteen of the Center fraction had decided against signing, the three cabinet ministers among them. Their determination had been strengthened by the testimony of General von Märker who had announced categorically to the fraction that acceptance of the treaty would mean mutiny in the army. Yet none of the opposition parties or individuals would consent to form a government committed to rejection of the treaty. At this moment came General Groener's famous telegram urging acceptance, and this proved to be decisive in deter-

13. Morsey, pp. 608–12.
14. Eschenburg, p. 137; Hugo Stehkämper, *Der Nachlass des Reichskanzler Wilhelm Marx*, 3 vols. (Cologne, 1968), 1:239–41.

THE GERMAN CENTER PARTY, 1870–1933

mining the Center's attitude. The party resolved to join the Socialists in accepting the treaty if they could, in effect, receive guarantees of immunity from reproach. The assembly agreed to vote to empower the government to sign, thus tacitly sanctioning acceptance; and on the insistence of Centrist Minister Johannes Bell and Wilhelm Mayer, of the Bavarian People's party, the opposition parties made declarations "that they acknowledged the patriotic motives of the parties which voted for the acceptance of the treaty in their fatherland's hour of direst need." [15]

When the time came for the actual signing of the treaty, Bell balked and would not sign for himself; he felt it was particularly humiliating for him, the colonial minister, to put his name to the total dissolution of the German colonial empire. President Ebert and the rest of the cabinet pleaded with him and arranged that his title be changed to the less embarrassing one of federal minister, whereupon, "under duress," he signed. It is hardly necessary to add that the declarations handed in by the opposition parties did not protect the men who signed the treaty from future vilification as traitors and cowards.

The Weimar Constitution was adopted by the assembly a little more than a month after the signing of the peace treaty. The republic was not popular with a large proportion of the Center's electorate, but the republican constitution was far more favorable to Catholic interests than the laws and institutions of the Second Reich had been. The success of the Center's committee members in achieving their goals in church-state relationships is astonishing considering that on this issue the Social Democrats and the two liberal parties were in essential agreement and easily outnumbered the Centrists and their rather unreliable allies in *Kulturpolitik*, the German Nationalists.

The party had six representatives on the twenty-eight member constitutional committee of the assembly; of these, four were permanent (Peter Spahn, Adolf Gröber, Karl Trimborn, and Konrad Beyerle, a legal historian from Bavaria) and the other two were changed according to the subject under discussion. There was no serious difficulty within the committee about the political and organizational clauses, although many conservative Catholics in Germany objected to the

15. Alma Luckau, "Unconditional Acceptance of the Treaty of Versailles by the German Government, June 22–28, 1919," *Journal of Modern History* 17 (1945): 219–20.

second sentence in the constitution: "the supreme power of the state is derived from the people" (*Das Staatsgewalt geht vom Volks aus*). This appeared to base sovereignty on human, rather than divine, sources and offended the monarchist feelings of many, including those who, like Martin Spahn, the son of Peter Spahn, left the Center to join the German Nationalist party at about this time. But Gröber summed up the opinion of most politically aware Centrists in his speech to the assembly in February 1919: "According to our convictions all authority is from God, the republican as well as the monarchical, and the obligation to obey of those who are under the authority is exactly the same, whether the authority is a monarchy or a republic." The example of Pope Leo XIII and his effort to rally the French clergy to the Third Republic was cited in his argument, and the offending phrase on sovereignty justified by comparison with a similar phrase in the 1831 constitution of Catholic Belgium.[16] In contrast to this accommodation, the older Centrists spoke at great length against the adoption of the red-gold-black flag.

The question of whether the republic should have a unitary or a federal structure was more controversial. The original draft of the constitution by Hugo Preuss had proposed a highly unitary state, virtually destroying the federal structure of imperial Germany. The Center and especially its partner the BVP were committed to the retention of states' rights. On the other hand, the party recognized that strong state governments were a danger to Catholic interests in those states where Catholics were in a minority. Anticlerical measures in Saxony and Brunswick and, for a time in Prussia, had shown that clearly. The party, therefore, supported a degree of federalism but attempted to provide overall ultimate jurisdiction of the national government in religious and educational matters, which in the empire had been left solely to the *Länder*.

The representatives of the Bavarian People's party insisted vainly that the reserved rights (*Reservatrechte*) of Bavaria, granted at the time the state joined the Reich in 1871, had the status of international treaties and hence could not be abrogated by a parliamentary vote. The rights were permanently lost, but the Bavarians were more successful

---

16. *Stenographische Berichte über die Verhandlungen der Deutschen Nationalversammlung* 326 (13 Feb. 1919): 52; Max H. Meyer, *Die Weltanschauung des Zentrums in ihren Grundlinien* (Munich, 1919), pp. 7–15.

in their attempt to strengthen the role of the second chamber, the Reichsrat. They were *not* able to ensure that votes in the Reichsrat would be by block (that is, that the delegates would be bound as a group to represent the wishes of their state governments), but they did succeed in having the sentence removed that said that the members were *not* to be bound by instructions. In articles 76, 77, and 88, the power of the Reichsrat was extended somewhat by granting it a suspensive veto on constitutional amendments which could be overridden only by a popular referendum and by requiring its consent to administrative regulations "for the execution of the Reich statutes" and to Reich regulations regarding communications.[17]

Some of the federalists hoped to break up the "unnatural" state of Prussia into "organic" and "historic" units. A separate statehood for the Rhineland, for Rhineland-Westphalia, or for Silesia could be obtained peacefully and legally if the constitution permitted the partition of Prussia into several federal states. Socialists and liberals and Prussian conservatives were united in opposition to such a plan, but in the end Article 18, the "anti-Prussian clause," was included as a kind of safety valve to relieve separatist feelings in the Rhineland.

Article 18 provided for the possible division of a state into smaller units, in most cases by the consent of the state government but also by simple national statute "if the territorial change or formation is demanded by the population and the paramount interest of the Reich requires it." In 1924, a referendum to separate Hanover from Prussia was initiated by the Center's Guelph allies in Parliament, but it failed to obtain the necessary support. The article actually contained several uncomfortable implications for the federalists themselves. If a state could be broken down into "organic," "historic," or geographically convenient units, then the separation of the Palatinate from Bavaria would be a natural step (accomplished in the years after World War II) and this the BVP consistently opposed. Also, if Prussia were to be broken up, Catholic minorities not included in a Rhenish, Westphalian, or Silesian state would have no political influence whatsoever, like those in Saxony and other overwhelmingly Protestant *Länder*, whereas in Prussia it was possible, as had already been shown in the months since the Center had been represented in the Weimar Coalition gov-

17. Konrad Beyerle, *Föderalistische Reichspolitik* (Munich, 1924), pp. 32–39.

ernment there, for Catholic interests to be defended over the whole of the state. The "anti-Prussian clause," then, was too problematical for actual implementation, but its supporters did succeed in breaking up that state for purposes of representation in the Reichsrat, where each of the thirteen Prussian provinces and the city of Berlin were given separate votes in addition to the thirteen votes cast by the state government as a whole. This proved to be of little benefit to the Catholic west, as it turned out, because its chief effect was to add the conservative votes of the northern and eastern provinces to those of conservative states in the Reichsrat against the votes of democratic Prussia and its western provinces.[18]

On social and economic matters the Centrist committee members did not care to challenge openly all efforts to nationalize industry because of the strong anti capitalist feelings in their trade union electorate. Their main efforts here were to slow down the impetus to socialism and make sure that nationalization, if it was to be carried out at all, would be considered "case by case" and under conditions of "urgent necessity," a phrase added to Article 153 by Franz Hitze.[19] The nationalization clauses turned out to be as much a safety valve for the Socialists as the anti-Prussian clause was for the Rhinelanders, and the shelving of the whole question after 1919 was a relief to the Center.

The clauses dealing with the factory councils (*Betriebsräte*) and the plan for a National Economic Council, sponsored by left-wing Independent Socialists who saw in them the equivalent of the Russian soviets, were of interest to the right wing of the Catholic labor movement, who saw in them the possible equivalents of the vocational groups favored by Catholic corporative theorists. They were less favored by the practical leadership of the Christian trade unions and the majority Social Democrats.[20] Like the plans for nationalization, the council system was allowed to die a natural death.

Altogether, the political, social, and economic portions of the constitution caused surprisingly little conflict between the Center and its liberal and Socialist associates. The clauses dealing with the relations

---

18. Arnold Brecht, *The Political Education of Arnold Brecht: An Autobiography, 1884–1970* (Princeton, 1970), p. 225.
19. Morsey, p. 226.
20. Dill, pp. 106–8.

between church and state were both more important to the Center and more difficult to work out, while those dealing with education caused more heated and prolonged controversies than any other in the entire document.[21] The original draft of the constitution was discouraging to the Catholics on the constitutional committee because it was based upon the old liberal concept of complete separation of church and state. The Social Democrats, the German People's party (formerly National Liberal party), and the Democratic party were in essential agreement on this question. "Separation" was acceptable to the Center insofar as it meant an end to government control over church administration and government vetos on appointments, but not when it was interpreted to mean an end to financial support. It was conceded even by the Center that the previous policy of most of the states, of insisting that every person be a member of a church (for purposes of taxation, census, and education) should not be retained, and the constitution explicitly ensured the right to abstain from worship as well as the freedom to worship. Much of Article 135 actually closely resembled the Center's Toleration Motion of 1900. About the religious organizations themselves, the original constitutional draft contained only a short paragraph: "Every religious organization shall arrange and administer its affairs independently but shall be subject to the general laws. No religious organization shall enjoy privileges over others from the state. Principles for the relation between state and church shall be laid down in a federal statute whose execution shall be left to the individual German states."[22]

The Center delegation felt that this was not enough to secure the Catholic church against the encroachments of the state, especially a state which might be Socialist. The party's aim was to expand and widen this clause. On this issue, the two opposing sides reversed their usual policies in a curious way: the Socialists insisted that the matter of religion came under the jurisdiction of the *Land* governments, while the Center wanted safeguards included in the national constitution. The reason for this was that in several of the states, notably in Saxony, Brunswick, Hamburg, and Bremen, the new Socialist govern-

21. Wilhelm Ziegler, *Die deutsche Nationalversammlung 1919–1920 und Ihr Verfassungswerk* (Berlin, 1932), p. 124.
22. Otis H. Fisk, ed., *Germany's Constitutions of 1871 and 1919* (Cincinnati, 1924), p. 269.

ments had already passed legislation secularizing education and otherwise limiting the activities of the churches. In the Second Reich, ironically, the Center had also striven to obtain Reich controls over these same states for their favoring of the Evangelical church over the Catholic minority.

The majority Social Democrats, supported by the Democrats, wanted the principle of separation of church and state written into the constitution, but the Center was able to block this. In the end, the matter of religion was treated at considerable length in the constitution and the wording of the clauses represented a compromise between the two sharply divergent points of view. In practice, the compromise proved to be a clear victory for the Center. Essentially, it curtailed the rights of the state to interfere in church affairs but did not change or limit the status and privilege of the Catholic church, while the right of the state governments to approve church appointments was withdrawn and the Protestant-Evangelical churches were disestablished in all the *Länder*.

In discussing the sources of income for religious bodies, the Social Democrats and the liberal parties at first refused to consider contributions by the republic toward the maintenance of church organizations, while the Center refused to consider the total financial independence of the churches. However, the German tradition of government responsibility for the upkeep of the churches, which was derived from the fact of wholesale expropriation of church property by the state in past centuries, was too ingrained for its opponents to put up much of a fight on the issue, and the Center received support here from Protestant interests in the Nationalist and People's parties. The result was another compromise permitting religious societies to become public corporations and to "raise taxes upon the basis of the civil tax lists." Even this concession to the churches was superfluous, because in Article 138 of the constitution it was stated that "Contributions by the state to religious organizations that are based upon statute, treaty, or special legal title, shall be commuted by *Land* legislation. The principles for this shall be laid down by the Reich government."[23] In this short clause the Socialists and liberals conceded more than would at

23. *Die Verfassung des deutschen Reichs vom 11 August 1919* (Berlin, 1929), p. 30, Art. 137, 138.

first appear. No federal law was ever passed in the Weimar years laying down principles for the commutation of financial agreements between the churches and the states, and state support of both Catholic and Protestant churches from designated tax lists continued to be the rule.

In the Second Reich the battles over education had been fought on the state level, because the Reichstag had had no jurisdiction over the subject. Now, as in the case of church administration, the Center wanted a national policy which would prevent anticlerical excesses in the states at present governed by Socialists, and the Socialists and liberals were also agreed that there should be a national public-school system. This was the extent of agreement about education. The Democratic party and the People's party, which represented the preponderant number of elementary schoolteachers in the country,[24] believed that the model for the basic elementary school (*Volksschule*) in the country should be the "community" or "simultaneous" school already existing in the southwestern states, and in Nassau and Frankfurt in Prussia, a school which would be nondenominational for both students and instructors, with religious instruction part of the curriculum like any other subject. The Social Democrats had always included in their program the demand for completely secular schools, with no religious instruction whatever, but a great many of their deputies were inclined to support the liberals in order to reach the desired goal of a national school system, so long as religious instruction was not to be compulsory in the community school. Neither plan suited the Center, of course, and its remarkable degree of success in the school question was the result not only of tenacious infighting and well-timed blackmail, but also of splitting the self-confident and experienced negotiators of the Democratic and People's parties (whose collective memories extended back to the defeat of the clerical school bill of 1892) from the less-united and less-experienced Socialists.

The earliest tactic used by the party in its hopelessly outnumbered position was to evade the issue of the type of school in the constitutional clauses altogether and to ensure instead the maintainance of religious education in the schools, and the retention of private schools. The party won the right to include in the educational clauses a paragraph about religious instruction. Although the Social Demo-

24. Grünthal, p. 63.

crats on the committee had previously insisted that they would make
their decision on the entire constitution dependent upon the rejection
of such an inclusion, they finally agreed to be satisfied with the addition of a provision for state supervision of religious instruction. The
paragraph in final form ran as follows: "Religious instruction shall be
a regular subject in school curricula, except in secular schools. . . . Religious instruction shall be taught in conformity with the principles of
the respective religious organization without prejudice to the state's
right of supervision. . . . Participation in religious classes is left to the
decision of the person who is responsible for the religious education of
the child." [25] This was a victory for the Center; however, a motion that
private schools be retained, introduced in the assembly by Gröber, was
rejected. ("Private" meant only that schools could be established outside the regular school systems; since the church itself received financial support from the states, the private church-run schools ultimately
were supported from public funds.) The assembly majority would accept the motion only if a clause were inserted that private schools
should not be inferior to state-run, which would have defeated the
whole intention of the motion, since most of the private schools
which the party wished to preserve were small one-room or two-room
"dwarf" schools set up in rural districts where the Catholic population
was not large enough to justify a public denominational school for
them. In the end, the assembly majority decided to phase out private
schools gradually over the next eight years, eliminating them entirely
by 1928, and the Center was forced to let the matter drop, although it
continued to be an important plank in the party's educational platform.

As the weeks of committee negotiation passed, between March
and June 1919, the Social Democrats and the liberals appeared to be
winning in their attempt to make the community schools the norm in
the constitution. Several states had already taken steps to eliminate
denominational schools (Saxony, Brunswick, Hamburg, and Bremen),
and the Prussian government had only been dissuaded by the constant
vigilance of the Centrist ministers in the cabinet and by fears that the
Polish-speaking inhabitants of Silesia and other border districts were
being pushed "into the arms of Poland" by that country's promise of

25. *Die Verfassung*, p. 33, Art. 149.

237

denominational schools.[26] In the committee draft, as it was being written, the school clauses were to recommend the community school, permit private schools only with case by case approval, and require that religious instruction be strictly voluntary and left to the discretion of the state governments.

Total defeat of the Center's program seemed imminent, when an unexpected event changed the entire picture. The Democratic party suddenly left the cabinet on June 19 because its ministers refused to sign the Versailles treaty. It was vital that a new government be formed immediately, and a coalition of the majority Social Democrats and the Center was the most feasible and desirable solution to the crisis. Firm evidence is lacking, but there seems reason to believe that Gröber informed President Ebert that Social Democratic accommodation on the school question was essential for Centrist participation in the new Bauer cabinet. In addition to this pressure, the use of the anti-Prussian clause was held as a threat over the Social Democrats in the event of an unsatisfactory outcome in the education negotiations.[27] Whatever maneuvering went on behind the scenes, it is certain that the committee draft was abruptly scrapped and the assembly was presented with a new draft, referred to as the First Weimar School Compromise. It was far more favorable to the clericals than the original draft, repeating many of the provisions of the 1892 Zedlitz bill, but at the same time containing provisions attractive to the Socialists.

In the First Weimar School Compromise, three kinds of schools were to be permitted throughout Germany: the denominational, the community or simultaneous, and the secular; the criterion for the establishment or retention of any of these schools was to be the "wish of those responsible for the education of the children."[28] In theory, of course, the completely secular schools were regarded by Catholics as the worst possible solution, but in practice, permitting them to be established in certain instances as a kind of "denominational" school for nonbelievers would allow Protestant and Catholic schools to be continued undisturbed without resentment from the Socialists and freethinkers and might actually remove potential troublemakers from the

26. Grünthal, p. 47.
27. Ibid., pp. 52–53.
28. Ziegler, p. 158; *Verhandlungen der Deutschen Nationalversammlung* 328 (18 July 1919): 1673–77.

denominational schools.[29] The First Weimar School Compromise would also have made it possible to introduce denominational schools into Baden and Hesse for the first time, a longtime goal of the Center.

Unfortunately for the Center, the National Assembly reacted with indignation to the compromise. Not only were the Democrats and the People's party furious, but many majority Socialists felt that the plan was divisive and that the creation of separate secular schools was less democratic and less favorable to their interests than community schools for all children. The party delegation as a whole could not be won for the compromise. The result, after much wrangling, was the Second Weimar School Compromise. Although Gröber's name was one of those associated with its drafting, it was a disappointment for the Center, but not so crushing a defeat as had seemed likely in the spring.

In the Second School Compromise, which was incorporated in Article 146 of the constitution, the community school was favored over the other two kinds and was specifically designated as the basis of a new "organically planned" national school system. No petition was to be necessary for the establishment of a community school, whereas a denominational or a secular school could only be set up when demanded by a sufficiently large number of parents. But the education clauses in the constitution did not automatically guarantee legislation for their enactment. In spite of the intensity and vehemence of the debates over these clauses, they were merely an expression of intention. A small and seemingly insignificant article, number 174, gave the final victory to the clericals after all: "Until the enactment of the Reich statute provided for in Article 146, paragraph 2 [which was to arrange for the establishment of community schools on a national scale] the existing legal status shall continue."

No such national statute was ever passed by any German government in the Weimar period (or indeed, since then) because the Center was almost continuously represented in the cabinet. In spite of the intentions in the constitution, the community school could not become the standard type of school so long as this was the case. Article 174 was tested almost immediately, when the Saxon government passed a law changing denominational schools in that state into com-

29. Grünthal, pp. 101–2.

munity schools. The Catholics took the case to court and won a decision forbidding the change.[30] Subsequent attempts on the part of Saxony to modify the religious character of its schools or even to limit religious influence to specific courses in religion, were fought by the Center and in many cases these were also defeated by judicial decision. The standard public elementary school in more than three-quarters of Germany remained denominational, differing from the imperial school system chiefly in the introduction, in some urban areas, of a number of secular schools. On the other hand, there was certainly the tacit understanding in Prussia that so long as the Catholic denominational schools continued unaltered, the Protestant schools could continue the "blurring" process begun even before the war and become, in effect, community schools which provided religious instruction only in certain set, noncompulsory courses.

The Center, then, failed to make denominational education an accepted principle in the republic but had to be content with its status as the result of a political bargain. The party also failed to introduce the denominational school into Baden and Hesse, because in this case Article 174 hindered rather than helped its cause. Many Catholic clergy and laymen bitterly reproached the party and the republic for these failures. A historian of the Center writing today has summed up the work of the party in the construction of the constitution: "Beyond a doubt, the most was accomplished that could possibly be done in the given political-parliamentary power relationships and on the basis of freedom of belief and conscience. Yet in spite of this, the Centrist parliamentarians by no means won the unanimous thanks of the Catholic population, to say nothing of those of practicing Christians in general."[31]

30. Georg Schreiber, *Zwischen Demokratie und Diktatur* (Regensburg-Münster, 1949), p. 60.
31. Morsey, p. 220.

13

THE ORGANIZATION AND COMPOSITION
OF THE CENTER IN THE WEIMAR REPUBLIC

By the end of the first postwar year the threat of a genuine Marxist revolution was past and the new constitution, however unappealing, provided for the Catholic church and the Catholic population in Germany a position not only secure but highly advantageous, superior to their legal and social status in the empire. There was no longer a possibility of a second *Kulturkampf*. Consequently, the tentative moves to change the nature of the Center party—to change its name, to widen its membership to include Protestants, to increase the importance of industrial laborers and reduce that of the clergy and aristocratic landowners—could safely be abandoned and, in large part, were abandoned. The "new" Center party of the Weimar republic was not substantially very different from the old Center party.

The postwar party had a smaller electoral base which continued to shrink slightly in every election until 1932. The Versailles treaty had reduced the Catholic population of Germany proportionately much more than the Protestant, excluding nearly 19 percent of Catholics and less than 5 percent of Protestants. Most of these were inhabitants of Alsace-Lorraine and the Polish districts, whose votes had gone to the Center's allies, but the loss of Upper Silesia after the plebiscite in 1921 hurt the party directly. A more significant factor in reducing the Center's representation in the legislatures was the change to proportional representation and the party list-system in the elections. It is estimated that these changes, including the reapportionment of seats, reduced the Center's delegation to the Reichstag by nearly a quarter. Between 1874 and 1912 the Center's percentage of seats in the Reichstag fluctuated between a low of 22.9 percent and a high of 26.7

percent (in 1890); in 1919 it was 21.6 percent and had dropped to 17.2 percent by 1924 (including BVP seats).[1]

Neither boundary changes nor changes in electoral procedure are reasons for concluding that the Center was receiving less support from the Catholic population still within the borders of the Reich, but there is evidence that such was the case, presented in a meticulous study of Catholic support for the party made in 1928 by Johannes Schauff, a young Catholic scholar who served briefly as a Centrist deputy in 1932 and 1933. The gains brought about by the women's vote and the votes of a few prewar supporters of the Polish party in the east were more than offset by the fact that far fewer Catholics voted for the Center in the republican years than in the early years of the empire. From over 80 percent support in the 1880s, the slow decline continued until the last prewar election showed only 54.6 percent support. If statistics are projected into the republic for male voters only, the 1919 figure would have been 53.9 percent declining by 1924 to 48.3 percent. Including the women's vote, there is an actual rise to 62.8 percent in the revolutionary year 1919, but this dropped back to 56.4 percent in 1924 and to 47 percent in the 1930 elections.[2] These percentages represent an average for all of Germany, including votes for the Bavarian People's party, but there was a great deal of variation in loyalty of Catholics to the Center, with the highest degree found in the west, Rhineland and Westphalia, and the least in Bavaria, where the Catholic vote for the BVP averaged about 10 percent less than Catholic votes for the Center in the rest of Germany.[3]

The women's vote was clearly vital for the survival of the Center, more so than for any other party. Schauff estimates that the Center's voters were 59 percent female, those of the Nationalist party 56 percent female, 51 percent and 47 percent female for the People's party and Democratic party, only 43 percent for the Social Democratic party, and 37 percent for the Communist party.[4] This was hardly a source of satisfaction to the Center's leadership, which was more inclined to deplore the fact that the Center was becoming a "woman's party."

1. Schauff, pp. 164, 20–22, and app.
2. Schauff's figures are extended beyond 1924 in Helga Grebing, "Zentrum und katholische Arbeiterschaft" (Ph.D. diss., Free University of Berlin, 1952), p. 18, and app.
3. Schauff, pp. 134–36.
4. Ibid., p. 66.

There were frequent expressions of dismay at meetings of the Reichstag delegation and the National Committee in October 1920.[5] The small number of Centrist women candidates in 1919 was reduced still more when several stepped down in the 1920 elections. Only three women sat in the Center's delegation in 1920. Women were represented on the national Executive Council and on the Executive Council of the fraction, however, in an extension of the old party policy of balancing regional and occupational elements.

Personal reactions to this modest entry of women onto the political stage varied, but for the most part seem to have been negative, at least among the older Centrists. Gröber was well known for his dislike of women in the Reichstag; Trimborn was more welcoming. Heinrich Köhler, active in Baden politics in the republic, reveals strong prejudices against women in politics in his memoirs, but very few of his male colleagues meet with his approval either. Joseph Wirth, also from Baden and at one time a close friend of Köhler's, defended the cause of equality for women in a speech at the Catholic Congress in 1921 but was severely criticized for doing so. Stegerwald and Heinrich Brauns, minister of labor for most of the republican period, both cited the preponderance of women in the Center as additional reasons for transforming the entire nature of the party.[6]

The activities of the few women who did sit in the legislatures were confined in the main to matters concerning the family, such as education, family subsidies, prohibition of pornographic literature and films, and so forth. Dransfeld, who had shown considerable talent for organization and public relations in her work outside the Reichstag, took almost no part in parliamentary life.[7] The Center's Catholic philosophy, which placed so much emphasis on the importance of the family was not compatible, at least in the 1920s, with the concept of a major role for women, even unmarried women, in the political world. The Center's female supporters do not seem to have wished this. It is characteristic that in 1931 at a time of great economic and

5. Morsey, p. 356.
6. Morsey, pp. 363, 402, 407, 568; Morsey, "Karl Trimborn," in Morsey, *Zeitgeschichte*, p. 92; Köhler, pp. 229–30.
7. Ferber, in Morsey, *Zeitgeschichte*, pp. 135–36; see also Claudia Koonz, "Conflicting Allegiances: Political Ideology and Women Legislators in Weimar Germany," *Signs* 1 (1976): 663–83.

political crisis, Helene Weber of the Center's Reichstag delegation called for and personally drew up a motion demanding the dismissal of married women from government service, as a contribution toward solving the unemployment problem.[8]

The addition of women to the electorate made the Center party even more a microcosm of Germany than it had been before the war. Every occupation found some representation in the party, and as a result of conscious policy in choosing candidates, in the Reichstag fraction as well. The leadership continued to come largely from the legal profession and upper ranks of the civil service, though in the 1920s the business of politics was much more likely to be the full-time occupation of a Center leader than in the earlier years. Fewer persons than before held double mandates in the national and state legislatures. Peter Spahn returned to the Reichstag fraction and was active there until his death in 1925, but he was no longer in a position of leadership. Gröber died at the end of 1919, never fully reconciled to the effects of the revolution. Their places were taken by Konstantin Fehrenbach of Baden, who also served as chancellor of Germany in 1920 and 1921, and the Rhinelander Karl Trimborn, leader of the Reichstag fraction after Gröber's death and elected party chairman at the first national party congress in 1920. Both of these men were noted for their ability to mediate among the factions, a necessity for leaders of such a diverse party. Before the war they had been considered democrats; after the war they appear conservative, unable to react rapidly to the changed circumstances or to do much more than, as a party historian has said, hand over the party as an inheritance to the younger generation.[9] Trimborn died in 1921; Fehrenbach returned to the Reichstag after his chancellorship and served as its head from December 1923 until his death in 1926, but his leadership was weak and uncertain.

Of the younger men who led the party in the middle 1920s, the most successful was Wilhelm Marx. Marx was a Rhinelander like Trimborn, a former judge, member of the Prussian House of Deputies from 1899 and of the Reichstag from 1910. He was only nine years younger than Gröber and Trimborn (both born in 1863) but possessed of a heartier physical constitution and lived on until 1946. Marx was

8. Morsey, ed., *Die Protokolle der Reichstagsfraktion und des Fraktionsvorstands der deutschen Zentrumspartei, 1926–1933*, 2 vols. (Mainz, 1969), 2:550–51.
9. Morsey, *Zentrumspartei*, p. 582.

an expert mediator and compromiser, respected by all, not associated with any faction or political wing, a "Man of the middle in the party of the middle" as he delighted to call himself.[10] He served as party chairman from 1921 until 1928, and as chairman of the Reichstag fraction from 1921 to December 1923 (leaving to become chancellor) and again for a time in 1926.

In personality Marx could not have been more different from Joseph Wirth, the former mathematics teacher from Baden who entered politics only after the war. Wirth enjoyed the power and the personal contacts he derived from his position in the Reichstag and as chancellor in 1922, but cared much less for the maintenance of good relations within his own party. As a consequence, although he had a circle of followers in the same way that Erzberger had had, he was never considered for the posts of party chairman or fraction head.

Heinrich Held, leader of the Bavarian People's party throughout the 1920s, and Felix Porsch of the Prussian party were both *Honoratioren* of the prewar party, conservative men who had temporarily retreated from the realities of the 1918 revolution. Held was a former journalist turned publisher, who had begun his political career as a member of the left wing in the Bavarian Center, a follower of Heim the *Bauerndoktor* and supporter of the Christian trade unions, but by the time of the outbreak of the war he had altered both his social standing and his political views, and in the republican years he led his party, the BVP, along the path of reaction and isolation until he was succeeded after 1929 by men or more dynamic, though equally parochial, opinions. Porsch was a lawyer and *Justizrat* whose first political experience had been in the municipal government of Breslau in his native Silesia. He first sat in the Reichstag in 1881 as its youngest member, but left in 1893 in the dispute over the army bill of that year, and from then on devoted his time exclusively to Prussian politics, serving as the head of the *Landtag* Center fraction continuously from 1904 until his death in 1930. Unlike Held, Porsch was able to adapt himself and the state party to changed circumstances and, with the help of his able lieutenant, Dr. Joseph Hess, created a stable coalition with the parties of Weimar in Prussia.

10. *Offizieller Bericht des Zweiten Reichsparteitages der deutschen Zentrumspartei* (Berlin, 1922), pp. 73–77.

Members of the clergy were less visible in the Center's national and state delegations than before the war, but were no less influential in the party. Franz Hitze and Heinrich Brauns of the *Volksverein*, Karl Ulitzka, head of the Silesian provincial party, and Johann Leicht of the Bavarian People's party sat in the National Assembly in 1919, joined by university professors Ludwig Kaas of the University of Trier and Georg Schreiber of the University of Münster. Schreiber, a papal House prelate and member of innumerable academic societies, became the parliamentary spokesman for his party on religious, educational and academic matters and published a yearly chronicle of the party's activities. Prelate Joseph Schofer headed the Baden Center party and Georg Wohlmuth led the *Landtag* fraction of the Bavarian People's party. As tensions increased among the various social and economic pressure groups in the party, the clergy served more and more as indispensable mediators, a trend which culminated in the election of Kaas as national party chairman in December 1928, breaking the Center's tradition that a layman should hold this position.

Although there were a great many Catholic priests active in the Center party, for the first time after 1918 a substantial number of clergy deserted the party, either to become "unpolitical" or to support the German Nationalist party. Repugnance to democracy and the republic, and to Centrist cooperation with Social Democracy, motivated these defectors as it did large numbers of intellectuals, "academics" whose departure from the party was troubling to the leadership. Peter Spahn's son Martin and his son-in-law Karl Görres both left the Center in 1919 and helped to form a Catholic Committee in the DNVP. Martin Spahn was the university professor whose appointment to the University of Strassburg in 1901 had been seen as a step toward parity for Catholics in academic life (he had since moved to the University of Cologne), and Görres was a descendant of the nineteenth-century writer Joseph Görres. It was especially bitter that these men and other professional persons should forsake the party which had worked for so long to increase their numbers and opportunities.

The Catholic Committee set up in the German Nationalist fraction was outspokenly anti-Center as well as antirepublican, and it carried on its own press operations in vigorous dissent to the Center. At every party meeting in the 1920s speeches stressed the need for reconciliation with these departed academics and, in particular, the need to win the university students who were described as being in great majority more sympathetic to the DNVP than to the Center. The union of Catholic student corporations proved increasingly susceptible to nationalist and *völkisch* ideology.[11]

It might seem upon examining the Center's delegation in the National Assembly that the landed aristocracy had deserted the party as decisively as the academics, and in February 1920 a Union of Catholic Nobility was formed for the purpose of promoting a restoration of the monarchy. Some did defect to the Nationalists, but the influence of great landowners in the Center was by no means at an end. Many returned to become candidates for the Reichstag in 1920 and 1924, and there were always representatives of landowners in the state legislatures. Most of the Catholic agrarian societies in the country were headed by aristocrats and they often continued to dominate local party organizations. Klemens, Freiherr von Löe, a prominent Centrist, was president of the Rhenish Agrarian Association, member of the Central Committee of the Board of Agriculture for the Rhineland, and member of the Reich Economic Council. Engelbert, Freiherr von Kerckerinck zur Borg, was president of the Westphalian Agrarian Association, president of the Federation of German Agrarian Associations, and member of the national Executive Council of the Center party. Franz von Papen was the leader of a small group of intransigent aristocrats in the Prussian *Landtag* whose disruptive activities were often backed by the leaders of the agrarian associations. Prince Ernst von Löwenstein, who served on the party's Executive Council, was one of the very few aristocrats who supported the democratic republic.

Small farmers continued to be important in the party and in the electorate. Johannes Blum was their spokesman in the Reichstag after 1924. The Center was also, by geographical accident, the chief defender of Germany's wine producers. For some years, Peter Kerp led a determined bloc of Reichstag deputies in their interest. Farmers, winegrowers, artisans, and white-collar employees formed a central core of the Center's supporters and the party leadership always expressed especial concern for these members of the *Mittelstand*. Craftsmen were led in the Reichstag by Thomas Esser, who served as vice-president of

---

11. Ibid., pp. 114–15; Wolfgang Zorn, "Student Politics in the Weimar Republic," *Journal of Contemporary History* 5 (1970): 128, 131, 143.

the Reichstag from 1926 until 1933. In 1924 Esser's followers, backed by the Center, presented a nine-point program to prop up the guild system. Very few of these anachronistic proposals were enacted into law but the party thought it important to make the gesture. Otto Gerig headed the Center's bloc of "employees," white collar workers, and often cooperated with Esser in matters of common interest. Through their membership in the League of Employees' Unions this group had contacts in both the Christian trade unions and the German Nationalist party, and in this way came to act as mediators between the Center and the political Right, and eventually with the National Socialists, in the years after 1930.

Civil servants were represented in all German parties; led by Joseph Allekotte after 1924, they maintained a large and influential pressure group in the Center. The party made great strides in the direction of parity in civil service positions by obtaining the hiring of Catholics sympathetic to the Center and by increasing the rate of promotion from the lower ranks.

The role of industrialists in the postwar Center was as inconspicuous as it had been before the war; official party statements and campaign oratory continued to emphasize that its principles were as much opposed to materialistic capitalism as to Marxism. The rapid promotion of labor representatives into the top ranks of the party in 1919 seemed to be evidence of this indifference, not to say coolness, toward the interests of business. Yet, in fact, there were major industrialists active in the Center, and their influence was not insignificant, especially after the creation of an Advisory Council on Commerce and Industry in 1920, a national extension of Rhenish and Westphalian Councils organized in 1914. Not only did the council offer much-needed advice on industrial questions to the Reichstag and government ministers, as for example during the 1923 crisis in the Rhineland, but it often came to the rescue of the party's finances,[12] so that of all the pressure groups within the Center, this smallest in membership often spoke with the greatest persuasiveness.

Industrialists prominent in the party included Clemens Lammers, member of the Boards of Directors of *I. G. Farbenindustrie* and the *Deutsche Bank und Discontogesellschaft*, industrial representative

12. Morsey, p. 602.

for Germany at the World Economic Conference of 1927, director of the Dawes Bank, member of the Executive Council of the Reich Federation of German Industry, and Centrist deputy to the Reichstag from 1924 until his abrupt resignation in 1929, precipitated, apparently, by his failure to receive a cabinet post; Florian Klöckner, member of the executive boards of numerous foundries, mines, and banks, alternate chairman of the Industrial and Commercial Council of the Center party, Reichstag deputy from 1920 to 1933, and member of the Center's National Committee; his brother Peter Klöckner, organizer of the syndicate of Georgs-Marien Mines and Foundries and other companies merged with the Klöckner firm, of which he was chairman; and Rudolf ten Hompel, general director of the *Wickingschen Portland Zement und Wasserkalkwerke*, director of many banks and industrial associations, presidial and board member of the Reich Federation of German Industry, cofounder of the Westphalian and national Industrial councils of the Center, and Centrist deputy to the Reichstag from 1920 to 1928.

In contrast to the representatives of commerce and industry, who wielded considerable power but were kept in the background, the trade unions were exploited to the utmost in campaign literature and public pronouncements but were less influential in directing party policy in spite of the hundreds of thousands of votes they delivered to the Center in every election. To a certain extent this lack of power stemmed from internal conflicts in the union movement, dating from the immediate postwar era.

In November 1918 in the first days of upheaval there had occurred an amalgamation of all of the non-Socialist unions, in an attempt to form a common front against what then appeared to be the serious threat of Marxist revolution. The union of unions, at first called the German Democratic Federation of Unions, later shortened to German Federation of Unions (*Deutsche Gewerksschaftsbund* or DGB) included the Christian industrial unions, the democratic-liberal Hirsch-Duncker unions, and associations of civil servants and employees. Adam Stegerwald, head of the Christian industrial unions, was named chairman of the DGB, whose original membership has been estimated at one and a quarter million.[13] As the danger of radicalism receded, the

13. Dill, "The Christian Trade Unions during the Last Years," p. 104.

Hirsch-Duncker units became restive because of the religious emphasis of the other branches of the federation. They finally withdrew altogether to form a separate organization in November 1919, after the top policy-making body of the federation had issued a statement declaring the goal of the DGB to be "to prevail over the materialism which disintegrates our people by the cultivation of universal, moral, Christian, and national ideas."[14] Significantly, the word "democratic" had by that date been deleted from the title of the federation.

The DGB then comprised three central organizations: the League of Industrial Unions, the League of Employees' Unions, and the League of Civil Servants' Unions. The civil servants' unions were led by the higher ranks of railroad and post office employees; (workers in the lower-ranking and manual jobs were organized with the industrial unions). The League of Employees' Unions was dominated by its largest unit, the German National Clerks' Union (*Deutschnationale Handelsgehilfen Verband*, or DHV). This organization had its origin not in western Germany, like the industrial unions, but in the Protestant north; from the time of its establishment in Hamburg in 1893, it had expanded to Berlin and Leipzig and then throughout the rest of the country. The ideology of the Clerks' Union was profoundly different from that of the major industrial unions in the DGB. It was not only simply anti-Socialist but extremely nationalistic, and "Christian" largely in the sense that it was explicitly anti-Semitic. Its activities were for the most part propagandistic rather than economic, and its avowed objective was "to train youth in the honor of their calling and to awaken and cultivate German racial consciousness."[15]

The Clerks' Union was not officially connected with any political party, and its members had ties with all the parties of the Right and middle including the Center, but it was closest to the DNVP (until 1929) and was monarchist and antiparliamentarian in orientation. As the predominantly Catholic industrial unions were either enthusiastically republican or at least tolerant of the new republican regime and loyal to its constitution, it was impossible for the DGB as a whole to

---

14. Böhme, p. 83.
15. Ibid., p. 73. See Larry Eugene Jones, "Between the Fronts: The German National Union of Commercial Employees from 1928 to 1933," *Journal of Modern History* 48 (1976): 462–82; and George L. Mosse, *The Crisis of German Ideology* (New York, 1964), pp. 258–62.

take any political stand. Although the Clerks' Union was much smaller in size than the League of Industrial Unions, it could wield a proportionately greater influence in the federation because the leaders of the industrial unions preferred to conciliate this one branch rather than endanger the unity of the federation. The relative strength of the Clerks' Union increased in the later years of the republic, because the industrial unions reached their peak of membership in the years 1920 to 1922, numbering some 1,049,000 in 1922, declining to 605,400 in 1924, and recovering only to 799,000 in 1929, while the DHV grew steadily during the decade, reaching 300,000 in 1927.[16] Although the leadership of the DGB was always recruited from its largest unit, the League of Industrial Unions, the head of the Clerks' Union (for most of these years, Hans Bechly) could virtually veto any policy pronouncement of the federation which did not suit his own organization.

To minimize friction between the two antagonistic groups, the Essen Congress of the DGB in 1920 decided that the unions should try to send representatives to the Reichstag from as many non-Marxist parties as possible in order to lessen the sharp distinction between Centrist and Nationalist union members and to establish a policy for these representatives only when union issues were directly involved. On other issues, it was decided that the deputies or candidates for office should decide their policies for themselves. As it turned out in practice, deputies from the employees' unions and in fact all of those deputies sitting with parties other than the Center, nearly always simply voted with their delegations. The deputies from the industrial unions sitting with the Center, in contrast, frequently abstained from voting when the fraction's stand was considered not in the unions' interests, and occasionally voted against the fraction, on both social and political questions. "Political neutrality" was a necessary fiction which smoothed relations among the different units of the DGB when they met together, while at other times each group went its own partisan way.

During the Weimar years, union delegates sitting with the Center averaged about fourteen in number, after the high representation of nineteen in 1919 and 1920. Union delegates sitting with the DNVP

16. Figures from Cassau, app.; Jones, p. 463; Böhme, pp. 82–83; Helga Timm, *Die Deutsche Sozialpolitik und der Bruch der grossen Koalition im März 1930* (Düsseldorf, 1952), p. 39.

numbered between four and seven, until the secession of 1929 in protest against Hugenberg's election as party chairman. One or two union men in each session were to be found sitting with the DVP, one with the Democratic party in 1919 (but none after that) and an average of three with the Bavarian People's party, after its break with the Center in 1920.[17]

As general secretary of the union federation, it was Stegerwald's task to prevent friction between the Catholic-democratic and Protestant-nationalist branches of the DGB. This task absorbed his attention so completely that he eventually alienated the members of the League of Industrial Unions, who came to feel that their interests were being slighted.

From the time that the federation was first formed, Stegerwald and Brauns, a cleric and *Sozialpolitiker* with the *Volksverein*, had hoped that it might form the nucleus of a new party, replacing the Center, and uniting Protestants and Catholics in a common political front against Marxism, as the federation had united them on the economic front. Their efforts to create such a party were unsuccessful in 1918 and again in 1920. Stegerwald and Brauns entered the Reichstag in 1919 and, together with Stegerwald's former secretary Heinrich Brüning, first elected in 1924, and Otto Gerig of the Clerks' Union, they represented the views of the top federation leadership. But there were also a number of union men in the fraction who had much closer connections with the rank and file of the industrial workers: Johannes Giesberts from the prewar union movement, Heinrich Imbusch of the Miners' Union, described by a colleague as "a Catholic Communist of the purest water,"[18] Josef Andre and Joseph Ersing were among these.

Although the rival "technical divisions" of the Catholic workers' associations had declined rapidly in importance during the war and were finally merged into the unions in 1920, the associations themselves continued to exist. They lost membership to the unions, especially younger men, and Stegerwald publicly gave up his own membership in 1921, saying that he felt the associations were "useless." Many workers resented the continued leadership of the associations

17. Frey, app.
18. Köhler, p. 223.

by clergy, and there was a move to introduce lay leadership after the war, which in its turn was resisted by the clergy.[19] In spite of these difficulties the associations continued active and sent several representatives to the Reichstag. Their leader in the 1920s was Joseph Joos, editor of the *Westdeutsche Arbeiterzeitung*, a gentle and conciliatory figure who contrasted strikingly with Stegerwald's abrasive personality.

Representatives of labor in the Center party thus by no means formed a single pressure group but included at least three distinct groups which could and often did take different stands on party policies.

The old Center party had been a federation of state and provincial parties which had acquired a national superstructure only on the eve of the war. After the war, the national organization was elaborated and made more effective, and the party for the first time developed a network of local branches and a system of subscription membership rolls. The local parish house could no longer double as the Center's meeting place, not least because so many priests in the Weimar years had dropped their ties to the party. Local and district units were established in 1922; these enrolled members over the age of seventeen, who paid a yearly fee of two marks (temporarily raised during the inflation years 1922 and 1923). The number of subscribed members never corresponded to the number of voters, and some donations were made by persons who did not become members. Branches were established wherever the prewar party had been active, and in addition, 195 branches were added in northeastern Germany where the party had scarcely been organized at all before the war. (East Prussia actually had the highest percentage in the country of Center voters enrolled as party members, with figures approaching two-thirds; this evidently represented a legacy from the prewar Polish party.)[20] In addition to the regular party units, each Reichstag electoral district had a special unit, elected by the local and district organizations and other state and provincial bodies, whose duty it was to choose the party's candidates: no longer was this a task for the *Honoratioren* alone.

19. Wachtling, pp. 57–63.
20. Morsey, pp. 591–92.

Immediately after the war, a party general secretariat had been established to serve as a center for publications, communication, and propaganda, and its director became the first paid official the party had ever had. The office was filled by Maximilien Pfeiffer from 1918 to 1920, Hermann Katzenberger from 1920 to 1922, and Heinrich Vockel from 1922 to 1933. The secretariat distributed pamphlets and election posters, arranged to coordinate speakers for party gatherings (a haphazard undertaking before the war), and published newssheets. Financing the secretariat and its staff was always a problem. New party members were asked to donate to it voluntarily and local organizations were supposed to contribute sums proportionate to the number of voters in their districts, but these sources were never sufficient, and private contributions made up the difference. Parliamentary deputies regularly gave a percentage of their salaries to the general secretariat or to the state organizations for election expenses.[21]

The National Executive Council and National Committee met frequently throughout the Weimar years and replaced the fraction as chief policy-making body (though in fact there was a great deal of overlapping membership in the three bodies). The National Committee, which originally had 55 members, grew steadily until it was an unwieldy 222 by 1928, because of continuing efforts to give representation to all socioeconomic groups within the party.

Just as the local Catholic parish house could no longer serve as a Center branch organization, so the Catholic congresses, revived after a hiatus in the war years, could no longer serve as party rallies. In fact, these meetings served as painful reminders that the party no longer represented all German Catholics. Instead, Center party congresses were inaugurated as yearly assemblies to help formulate policy, elect party chairmen, and fill vacancies in the Executive Council and National Committee. These congresses actually met only five times during the republican years, in 1920, 1922, 1924, 1925, and 1928. The congresses were attended by some 400 to 500 delegates; a breakdown of the delegates to the Congress of 1922 shows that these included 24 members of the Executive Council, 120 members of the National Committee, members of the Reichstag fraction (many of them in-

21. Ibid., p. 601.

cluded in one or the other of the first two bodies), nine members of local parliamentary fractions (mostly from Hamburg and Bremen), and 200 regional delegates chosen especially for the congress.[22]

The congresses proved to be political rallies rather than real policy-making bodies, and in the elections for offices the nominations of the National Committee were usually endorsed by acclamation. Thus Karl Trimborn was chosen as party chairman by a harmonious show of hands in 1920, and Wilhelm Marx was elected in this way in 1922, 1924, and 1925. Only at the 1928 Congress did the conflicting factions reject the nomination of the committee and insist upon nomination from the floor and secret written ballots. Whether or not this signified a step in the direction of greater democracy within the party cannot be determined, since there were no further congresses after 1928, but at the time the unprecedented events were seen as a deplorable lack of harmony.

Although in all of its organizations the party continued the prewar practice of representing every region and occupation, many in the party believed that balance was not truly achieved, that the civil servants and substantial *Bürger* of the prewar party still dominated the Weimar councils, to the detriment of the interests of young people and of labor. The labor unions felt chronically underrepresented, although there was always at least one representative of labor on the Executive Council. An editorial in the *Westdeutsche Arbeiterzeitung* in 1927 declared: "It is intolerable that an electoral district in which 90 percent of the industrial workers of the Center live is represented at the national congresses or in party affairs by a director in a large industry."[23] Similar complaints were heard from the *Windthorstbund* and other youth groups about the proportion of older men in the Center's top ranks.

Perhaps in an extension of traditional party aims of balance, occupational advisory boards (*Beiräte*) were established in the 1920s which in effect formed powerful lobbies for particular interests. The oldest and most effective of these was the Council for Commerce and Industry, which was officially sanctioned by the party congress of

22. *Offizieller Bericht*, p. 16.
23. Grebing, p. 217.

1920. By 1922 there were also advisory boards for agriculture, *Mittelstand* interests, civil servants, and white-collar workers, many of them organized only at the provincial level in the Rhineland and Westphalia. In 1922 councils were also established for religious and educational affairs and for the women's organizations. In 1928 the founding of a national Workers' Advisory Council signified an attempt to redress the lack of power felt by this occupation group.[24] Party leadership did not really welcome these pressure groups but believed them to be inevitable and hoped that they would prove more manageable within the party than outside it.[25]

The Center's close association with the *Windthorstbund* continued, and it was reconfirmed in the postwar years as the official youth organization of the party. It was open to persons under the age of twenty-five; the estimated membership rose from about 20,000 in 1914 to about 30,000 in 1933, and after 1922, members of its board of directors were represented on the party National Committee. For most of the Weimar period the league was under the direction of Heinrich Krone. It was strongly republican in the early postwar years but showed a marked preference for the "leadership principle" in the years after 1930.

Catholic university student organizations were generally more conservative and critical of the republic than the *Windthorstbund* and less closely allied with the Center. The *Görresring* and others were closer to the DNVP and were increasingly attracted to *völkisch* ideology, though probably less so than the Protestant student corporations.[26] Catholic students in secondary schools had not been organized in special clubs or leagues before the war, partly because so many German schools at that level were still exclusively of one denomination or the other, and partly because the administration in Prussia had actively sought to prevent the formation of Catholic clubs. The postwar Catholic school organization *Neudeutschland*, which was founded in 1918 and had seventy-six branches by the end of 1919, was definitely antirepublican in orientation, supported *völkisch* views, and opposed

24. Morsey, "Die deutsche Zentrumspartei," in Matthias and Morsey, eds., *Das Ende der Parteien 1933* (Düsseldorf, 1960), p. 288.
25. Morsey, *Zentrumspartei*, p. 596.
26. Morsey, pp. 593–95; Zorn, pp. 128, 131, 143.

the München-Gladbach school of social Catholicism, but was divided on the question of affiliation with the Center party.[27]

The *Volksverein*, that phenomenally successful popular social organization of the prewar period, declined steadily in the republican years. Its membership fell from a high of 805,000 in 1914 to 695,000 in 1921 and 380,000 in 1932, and the society eventually found itself in serious financial difficulty.[28] It went into liquidation in 1930 and its records, revealing confusion and mismanagement of funds, were later exploited by the National Socialist regime in an attempt to prove corruption.

The *Volksverein* was in competition with too many other organizations, many of whose functions and membership overlapped. In districts with a large Catholic population, in addition to the *Volksverein* and the Center party there might be as many as three other kinds of society: one based upon the member's economic or professional affiliations, one based upon his class or *Stand* (for example, unions, associations for Catholic laborers, white-collar workers, and so forth), and one organized for purely religious and congregational activities. If the prospective joiner was under twenty-five, moreover, there would probably be one or several youth groups to which he might belong. Since most of these organizations had grown up independently of each other and of the party, there was no obvious way to solve the problem of these too numerous, overlapping societies. This undoubtedly contributed to the demise of the *Volksverein*, because as a rule, the professional or economic-based societies and the avowedly congregational were more popular in the postwar period than the *Volksverein*, which was associated in people's minds with the older Catholic philosophy of a stratified society and a strong paternalist church influence on social and economic matters.[29] The dissolution of the *Volksverein* can be seen as a symptom of the increasing separation of political Catholicism from German Catholic society as a whole.

27. Ronald Warloski, "Catholic Students and Revolutionary Germany: The Establishment of *Neudeutschland* in 1918–1919," *Catholic Historical Review* 53 (1968): 600–620.
28. Stehkämper, *Nachlass*, 4:123–67; *Kölnische Volkszeitung*, 10 Dec. 1928; *Frankfurter Zeitung*, 10 Dec. 1928.
29. Constantin Noppel, S. J., "Gärung im katholische Vereinswesen," *Stimmen der Zeit* 104 (1923): 346–57.

The Catholic press continued to be as diverse and as provincial-minded in the Weimar years as in the empire. No paper supporting the Center attracted a national readership or maintained foreign correspondents. The *Kölnische Volkszeitung* ceased to belong to the Bachem family in 1920, and its coverage became more local and concerned with Rhenish affairs than it had been. *Germania* continued to be the official Centrist organ but never attained a circulation of more than ten thousand. The problem of defining official Centrist policy was a difficult one in the republican years, and the editorial pages of *Germania* reflected conflict within the party. The paper became the object of a continuing struggle between right-wing and left-wing Centrists to determine its policies.

In the closing years of the war, Erzberger and some of his supporters in the party had been disturbed by *Germania*'s provincial, conservative tone and its aristocratic ownership and had determined, even before the establishment of the republic, to alter the paper's slant and make it more representative of the Reichstag fraction and the Berlin metropolitan area. Their plan was to persuade the board of directors to a recapitalization of the paper, greatly increasing the number of corporate shares so as to outnumber the Rhenish, Westphalian, and Silesian aristocrats who had been in control. The plan was initially successful, and a countermove in 1920 by a group of noblemen seeking to reverse the trend failed because of a lack of wealthy buyers.

Until 1924, *Germania*'s editorial policies were strongly republican, under the direction of Karl Spiecker and Heinrich Teipel. The high point of the paper's left-wing orientation was probably reached in 1923, when the editors went far beyond official Center party policy in criticizing the Cuno government of that year. Unfortunately for the republicans, the largest block of shares in the company was held not by one of them but by a "nonpolitical" banker, Franz Semer. Semer's feelings toward Erzberger underwent a change at the time of the latter's trial in 1921, and in 1924 he sold his shares to the Westphalian nobleman Franz von Papen, apparently breaking an agreement with Erzberger to keep them in the hands of republicans. Papen immediately began an attempt to change the paper's orientation, but although he forced Teipel off the editorial staff in 1925, he did not succeed in remaking it into an organ of the extreme Right; after 1924, *Germania* returned to a colorless middle position editorially, echoing official party pronouncements but no longer providing leadership in policy-making.[30]

The Executive Council of the Center party would occasionally issue mild statements of censure when a newspaper or an affiliated organization expressed opinions sharply opposed to party policy (as in 1923 when Marx resigned from the board of directors of *Germania* after the editors' attack on Cuno), but the party seldom undertook to expel a paper or an organization from its amorphous family. To have done so would have been to shatter completely the illusion that the Center represented all German Catholics. Thus the Catholic press, the youth groups, the congregational societies, and the vocational associations were all free to sympathize with or to criticize the Center as they pleased, and the crises of the Weimar years made it certain that the party could expect far less loyalty in the ranks than in Windthorst's day.

A detailed study has been made of the local Center party organization in Düsseldorf, which can be taken as descriptive of the party in much of western Germany.[31] The Düsseldorf party's membership figures fluctuated widely from one year to the next but never exceeded 50 percent of the Center's votes from that city. Fewer than half of the members were women, about 27.8 percent were industrial workers, 17 percent civil servants, and 27.5 percent were engaged in business. A great many members ceased to pay dues in the later years of the republic, but in spite of this the local organization was solvent at the time of its dissolution in 1933. The Christian trade unions were strong in Düsseldorf, and there were more white-collar employees organized in the Christian unions than in the Socialist unions. The workers' associations, on the other hand, declined steadily. Local economic advisory councils were formed and were active, with the least active being the Women's Council which "always had to be revived again before each election." Most of Düsseldorf's Catholic clergy were no longer active in the Center, and many of the younger ones were antidemocratic and supported the Catholic Committee of the DNVP. The *Windthorstbund* was very active in Düsseldorf and much more leftist on the is-

30. All information on *Germania* from Jürgen A. Bach, *Franz von Papen in der Weimarer Republik* (Düsseldorf, 1977), pp. 194–275.
31. All information on Düsseldorf from Stump, *Geschichte und Organization der Zentrumspartei in Düsseldorf, 1917–1933*.

sues than the rest of the party, especially the inner-city branch. The local Christian industrial unions did not support the republican *Reichsbanner* organization, but the *Windthorstbund* did. The local Catholic newspaper, the *Düsseldorfer Tageblatt*, was so far to the Right of official party policy that its editor was forced to resign through party pressure in 1920. A rival "social weekly for hand and head workers," *Aufwärts*, was started that year, under the influence of Stegerwald and the union leadership. In 1926 the two papers merged.

Local party congresses in Düsseldorf were rallies, not forums for the discussion of issues or even of municipal affairs. The Executive Council decided everything of importance ahead of time. Any democratization of the Center party in the Weimar republic evidently did not penetrate its local branches.

The Bavarian People's party as organized in its permanent form after September 1920 was similar to the Center but retained more of the paternalist-authoritarian character of the prewar years. Its small Executive Council made most of the party's important decisions; its larger State Committee met infrequently, and not at all after 1930 (ostensibly to save party members the cost of travel and expenses). The heart of the party's strength lay with Heim's Christian farmers' associations, and at the time of its founding the associations' preponderance was ensured by an ingenious arrangement devised by Heim and his colleague Sebastian Schlittenbauer whereby one-half of the members of the party's Executive Council and State Committee had to be representatives of occupational organizations. Since the farmers' associations had a membership far larger than any other occupation group, their representatives exercised a commanding influence until the system was changed to individual party membership in September 1920.[32]

When in 1924 there was still protest about the narrow base of the leadership (the Executive Council included only one representative from the party's Reichstag fraction, for example), the council was more than doubled in size, but since this change made it very unwieldy, a new subcouncil was created which soon had the effect of restoring the former exclusivity.

32. Klaus Schönhoven, *Die Bayerische Volkspartei, 1924–1932*, (Düsseldorf, 1972), pp. 53–59.

Like the Center, the BVP established vocational advisory councils, of which the Economic was the most important. On this council the interests of the farmers' associations (headed after Heim's retirement in 1924 by Franz Xaver Long) were supposed to be balanced by those of commerce and industry, with Joseph Dorn the spokesman for business and Johannes Imlet for the Christian trade unions. The Economic Advisory Council often supplemented the funds the party received from membership dues. The BVP did not have its own youth group until 1925, and its function was intended to be purely educational: to learn and to serve. The Bavarian party leadership felt that the Windthorstbund had had an "injurious" effect on the Center and did not want an independent-minded youth organization in the state.[33]

Of the more than 500 newspapers circulating in Bavaria, approximately 120 were friendly to the BVP, but as was the case in the rest of Germany, the distinction between Catholic papers and party papers was not always evident. Most of these papers had very limited circulations. The Bayrische Kurier came the closest to expressing the official BVP philosophy. The party also had its own correspondence service, whose editor Karl Schwend later became the party's historian.

The Bavarian People's party was not so much a microcosm of Bavarian society as the Center was of the nation. It had the smallest percentage of support from Catholics than any branch of the Center but on the other hand, attracted a slightly larger percentage of Protestant voters. Its Reichstag and Landtag delegations reflected the temporary prominence of industrial workers in 1919, but by 1920 this was substantially altered. Farmers and civil servants formed much the largest contingent in both fractions. The two fractions were headed during most of the republican years by clergy: Prelate Leicht in the Reichstag from 1920 to 1933 and Prelate Wohlmuth in the Landtag from 1924 to 1933. Both fractions were characterized by an unusually high rate of turnover, which naturally had the effect of strengthening the small permanent leadership. Only ten of sixty-six representatives in the Landtag held office continually from 1919 to 1933, in great contrast to the Center's stability in this regard. Only half of the 1919 Reichstag delegates returned in 1920. The 1920 exodus was due in part to disagreement with the break with the Center which occurred that year,

33. Ibid., pp. 67–73.

but there seems no clear explanation of the high turnover in 1924 and 1928. It may have been a result of the consistently suspicious, antagonistic attitude toward the Reichstag fraction shown by the state party leadership in Munich, which expected to advise, but would not be advised by, the Berlin delegation.

The Center party in the Weimar republic was a more highly structured organization than the prewar confederation of state and provincial parties, and it had a large and loyal electorate, but this surface vigor concealed a declining state of health which was all too evident to the party leadership. The postwar Center lacked the integrating forces which had bound the old party together in spite of its loose formal structure. The prewar party had had just as heterogeneous a composition as the postwar, but it had possessed a much more clearly defined platform and a much more strongly felt sense of mission. Of that platform, little remained. The Center had been the champion of federalism, the defender of the rights of regional and ethnic as well as denominational minorities. Now, the Poles, Alsatians, Danes, were no longer in the Reich to be defended, while the separatist impulses of Rhinelanders and Bavarians were seen by the national party as dangerous to German unity. The new Prussian government had eliminated most of the grievances of the Catholic minority which had generated much of the Center's program in that state, and in the south, Catholic influence was now reasonably proportionate to its share of the population. On crucial issues such as finance, the majority of the postwar Center had abandoned the idea of effective federalism altogether in favor of centralization.

Another old plank in the party platform, antimilitarism and anti-"Prussianism," had also become largely irrelevant in Weimar Germany. In the economic and social sphere the party had always been flexible, but two consistent prewar positions were now challenged: the Center could no longer call itself the chief sponsor of social welfare legislation in the republic because the Social Democratic party was now actively engaged in influencing government policy. But at the same time, the Center's devotion to agrarian interests was now challenged at every turn by the strong labor and consumer elements among its own supporters. Social and economic policy thus became wholly a matter of pragmatic bargaining on every individual issue, with no clear line of consistency.

But what of the defense of Catholic interests, the original basis of the Center-tower's strength? Here the party had been altogether too successful. The Weimar Constitution gave the Catholic church nearly everything for which it had been striving in the previous thirty years. Ties of all the *Länder* with the Protestant churches were broken, state participation in church appointments was ended, but financial support was retained. All religious orders could function in complete freedom in all parts of Germany. With the threat of Red revolution gone by 1920, the Center had literally written itself out of a job in this respect. The one exception was the question of the public schools, and it is therefore not surprising that the party leadership came more and more to base its public relations efforts on the school issue, until by 1927 and 1928 it became the one subject upon which the diverse factions in the party could unite.

The obtaining of parity for Catholics in government positions was an old goal which could not be achieved instantly through legislation or constitutional provisions. The civil service at the national and state levels could not be dismissed wholesale to make room for aspiring Catholic Centrist candidates. Both the Center and the Social Democratic party worked steadily in the Weimar years to introduce as many of their supporters as possible into government positions but this was necessarily a slow process. In Prussia, Socialist Minister of the Interior Carl Severing and the Centrist leader Joseph Hess openly defended their efforts to widen the civil service from its former narrow base, and Hess accused the Nationalists in the *Landtag* of opposing the state government because they could no longer expect to see their sons automatically advanced in the service.[34] The Social Democrats wanted to carry out a general reform of local government and the civil service, but the Center, on the contrary, desired only to see its candidates admitted to the same professional corps of officials which had previously shunned them. Change was effected earliest in the higher ranks of the service, where the incumbents could legitimately be dismissed for political reasons: *Landräte*, *Regierungs-* and *Oberpräsidenten*, ministerial directors and state secretaries. Middle and lower ranks were less easy to transform, but steps were taken to increase the rate of promotions from lower to higher positions, and in 1920 a law was passed

34. Carl Severing, *Mein Lebensweg*, 2 vols. (Cologne, 1950), 2:72–73.

modifying the educational qualifications for some posts.[35]

At the end of ten years of such efforts the percentage of Catholics in the higher ranks of the Prussian service averaged between 20 percent and 29 percent, still less than the approximately 33 percent of Catholics in the population. The middle ranks were much less representative. In Württemberg, where the percentage of Catholics in the population had risen to 30.8 percent, the proportion of Catholics in the civil service was far lower than in Prussia.[36] In spite of this slow rate of progress, however, it was clear that the deliberately discriminatory policies of the Wilhelmine era were being overcome and that consequently the issue of parity, like so many others, was no longer a vital one in the Center's platform.

Above all, whatever specific interest was in question, in the Second Reich the Center party had been the political voice of German Catholicism. The Weimar party was no longer representative of all German Catholics, and its leaders were acutely conscious of this. The defection of the "academics," a large proportion of the clergy, the Bavarians, the lack of any common program or outlook with the Austrian Christian Social party—all this meant much more to the men who led the Center than the fact that hundreds of thousands of Catholic workers and millions of Catholic women were still loyal to the party. The problem of how to win back the defectors and how to win future generations of educated Catholics from the universities preoccupied every party gathering in the early 1920s.

The split in the ranks of political Catholicism was largely caused by differing attitudes toward the republic and toward cooperation with Social Democracy, and so all party pronouncements were worded with utmost care to express support of the Weimar Constitution and existing governments without showing undue devotion to republican principles. Close alliance with the Social Democrats in Constitution Day ceremonies, or in demonstrations for the black, red, and gold flag, or in the *Reichsbanner* organization was avoided.[37] Parliamentarianism

35. Eberhard Pikart, "Preussische Beamtenpolitik 1918–1933," *Vierteljahrshefte für Zeitgeschichte* 6 (1958): 122–26.
36. Stehkämper, 3:367–82; Bachem, 8:393–94, 430–31.
37. *Frankfurter Zeitung*, 8 Aug. 1924; Thomas Knapp, "The German Center Party and the Reichsbanner," *International Review of Social History* 14 (1969): 167–69.

was criticized as divisive and antithetical to "true" democracy and "organic" groups and communities. When at the 1925 party congress the delegates of the Left tried to obtain a resolution in support of the republic, the final wording arrived at was simply that "the Center party acknowledges the German republic established in the Weimar Constitution and consideres its defense, and its penetration by the Center spirit, to be the duty and obligation of the party."[38] The party chairman Wilhelm Marx was accustomed to declare on public and formal occasions that the Center was not and had never been either a monarchist or a republican party; that it was and had always been a constitutional party which supported and cooperated with the constitutional government, whatever that happened to be.[39] This explanation, known in the party as the "Marx formula," did not satisfy the enthusiastic republicans, although they occasionally found it useful for their own purposes. Monarchism was still the preferred ideal for conservative Catholics. Most aristocratic landowners, a group which had played such an important role in the prewar Center party, accepted the temporary necessity for the party to be "constitutional" but hoped to steer it toward monarchist goals in the future. The issue was a critical one in the presidential elections of 1925, when Marx as the candidate of the People's Bloc was accused of going beyond "constitutionalism" to outright republicanism.

It was partly in an attempt to win back antirepublicans and antiparliamentarians that the ideas of Catholic corporativism experienced a revival, especially after the issuing of the encyclical *Quadrigesimo Anno* in 1931 by Pope Pius XI and the establishment of a kind of corporative system by the Austrian regime. Corporativism was no more seriously considered a part of Center party platform than was monarchism, but like monarchism, corporativism was a convenient device for criticizing Weimar parliamentary democracy and provided a unifying factor for quite diverse opinion-groups. A "monarchist" might be an admirer of the Wilhelmine variety of monarchism or the British; a "corporativist" might emphasize the hierarchical or state-control aspects of that system or might expect the system to provide more truly

38. *Frankfurter Zeitung*, 18 Nov. 1925.
39. *Offizieller Bericht*, pp. 73–77.

democratic representation of the working classes, artisans, and farmers. Republican and parliamentary ideals, however suited to the practical situation in Germany, could never serve the purpose of uniting German Catholics as they had been united in the past.

14
THE CRISIS YEARS, 1920–1924

In the first five years of the republic the Center was continuously represented in the national government and therefore bore responsibility for meeting the almost insoluble problems of the period: the unanticipated burden of reparations, the loss of Upper Silesia, mounting inflation and the French occupation of the Ruhr in the terrible year of 1923. It would have strained the capacity of any political organization to be obliged to act on these matters and to justify its actions to the voters. The Center was also plagued with a series of internal crises in these years which threatened to break up the party. The secession of the Bavarians, the Erzberger case, Stegerwald's attempt to form a power base for himself outside the party, and the recurrent threat of Rhineland separatism were all tests of party unity, tests which the Center managed to pass, with some degree of success, by the beginning of 1924.

The Bavarian People's party formed in November 1918 by Georg Heim was a genuinely new party, but at first a close partnership was maintained with the Center Reichstag fraction. The nominal chairman of the new party was Karl Friedrich Speck, but he had little power: the real leaders were Heim and Heinrich Held, who preferred to operate behind the scenes, a decision which proved to have unfortunate consequences in 1923. The party has been described as separatist and monarchist, and this was true to the extent that its leaders disliked the republic and gave only grudging recognition to the Weimar Constitution; Heim was a member of the monarchist *Heimat und Königsbund*. The actual restoration of the Wittelsbach dynasty to Bavaria was not seriously contemplated, however, until the last months of the republic, when it was conceived as a desperate countermeasure against the possibility of National Socialist rule.[1] As in conservative circles in the rest of Germany, monarchist slogans were used in Bavaria chiefly as a means of criticizing the republic.

Separation from the Reich was probably more seriously considered, in the first weeks of revolution, and Heim is on record as having favored the union of Bavaria with German-Austria in some sort of Danubian state to be loosely affiliated with the rest of Germany, a dream corresponding to the plan of the Rhenish separatists for a Rhenish-Westphalian republic in the west but compromised in the same way by French interest.[2] The Bavarian party as a whole took no steps toward separation, and sent a delegation to the National Assembly which sat, as expected, with the Center. In the course of the year 1919, however, the national and local leaders of the Bavarian People's party went through a fateful divergence of experience. While the Reichstag fraction was participating fairly amicably in parliamentary government and the writing of the constitution, the party in Munich was reacting with shock and revulsion to the establishment of a soviet republic there and blaming not only local Socialists but "Red Berlin and the Jewish press" for Bavaria's troubles. Whereas the Reichstag delegation realized that the Center and BVP between them had achieved much in the constitution, the Munich party accused them of losing the *Reservatrechte* of the empire and of compromising with Social Democracy. The break with the national party was thus in part also a break between the Munich leadership and the BVP Berlin delegation. It occurred over the financial measures carried out by the Reich minister of finance, Matthias Erzberger.

Erzberger, with his usual ebullience, had drawn up the government's tax proposals without consideration for what he thought of as outdated federalist principles. His new measures of June 1919, which have been described as the most brilliant and lasting work which he did for Germany,[3] deprived the *Länder* of most of their powers of tax collection. It was this, rather than the nature of the taxes themselves, that outraged the BVP, which was "painfully disillusioned" and humiliated by the laughter which its protests met with on the floor of

1. Schwend, pp. 514–25; see also Werner Gabriel Zimmermann, *Bayern und das Reich, 1918–1923* (Munich, 1953).
2. Zimmermann, pp. 126–32; Schwend, pp. 63–66.
3. Epstein, *Matthias Erzberger*, p. 331.

the Reichstag.[4] The Center delegation, on the other hand, supported its minister fully. Erzberger went on to compound his offense by admitting in several speeches during 1919 that he favored the abolition of the *Länder* altogether and hoped that Germany would become a closely unified nation, with provinces ("I use the expression again— Reich provinces") as purely administrative units. A particularly emphatic unitarist speech by Erzberger in Stuttgart on 6 January 1920 was answered three days later with the decision of the Bavarian People's Party Congress to withdraw the party officially from the government and from any sort of partnership with the Center party, in the Reichstag or elsewhere.

Before the war, the Bavarians had been among Erzberger's warmest friends, and they had followed his lead enthusiastically in the colonial crisis, but the intensity of the personal attacks upon him at this time make it clear that he had become the symbol of all those policies of the Center which offended them: not simply the sponsor of a centralist financial program but a near-Socialist who had led the Center into all manner of things offensive to Bavaria. As early as September 1917, Schlittenbauer had said that the Bavarian party "won't let itself be Erzbergered [*lasse sich nicht vererzbergern*]."

The secession was far from unanimous. Every single member of the Reichstag delegation voted in the minority against the break at the congress, as did the labor union delegates.[5] The Reich minister of the treasury, Wilhelm Mayer-Kaufbeuren, resigned from the cabinet and simultaneously from the party. Others succumbed to Held's urging but believed the split was a temporary tactical maneuver and hoped for a quick reconciliation. In spite of several attempts at reunion, however, the two parties remained separate from this time until the end of the republic. The situation was further embittered by the decision of the Center organization in the Bavarian Palatinate to remain with the national party; the following year a split within the Palatinate party occurred, producing active election competition in that province. Elsewhere, the two parties did not compete, because although the Bavarians often threatened to run candidates in the other *Länder*, they never had the financial resources to do so.

4. Beyerle, pp. 32–39, 49.
5. Quotation from Schönhoven, p. 19; Schwend, pp. 130–31.

The BVP in succeeding months worked out an elaborate federalist program in anticipation of constitutional revision, which was known in its final form as the Bamberger Program of 1922. It purported to speak for federalists from all parts of Germany but was accepted only in Bavaria and only by the Bavarian People's party in that state, being rejected by all other parties in the *Landtag*.[6]

The first national Center Party Congress, which opened in January 1920, was considerably dampened by the absence of the Bavarians, and much discussion was devoted to the possibility of a reunion in the near future. Erzberger, who had provided the occasion if not the reason for the Bavarian secession, took very little part in the congress because he was by this time engaged in the libel suit he had brought against Karl Helfferich. It is significant that the congress did not give him a vote of confidence in connection with the case but merely passed a resolution that there was no reason to impugn his personal honor.[7] For the next year and a half, the Erzberger case was to prove an embarrassment and a source of disunity in the Center.

Karl Helfferich had been an antagonist of Erzberger's since their confrontation in 1906 when Erzberger had accused Helfferich, at that time a councillor in the Colonial Division of the Foreign Office, of encouraging monopolies in the colonial trade and of bearing part of the responsibility for the African rebellion of that year. Already at that time, "for Helfferich, Erzberger was a particularly unscrupulous example of the demogogic democratic politico."[8] Helfferich had left the Colonial Office then to go into private business but had reentered government service in the war, becoming treasury secretary in 1915 and then deputy chancellor in the spring of 1916. Ironically, Helfferich and Erzberger took the same position on unlimited submarine warfare in 1916, both supporting Bethmann-Hollweg in his efforts to convince the Reichstag of its dangers, but Helfferich was opposed to the Peace Resolution and to Erzberger's role in the resignation of Bethmann-Hollweg. His government career was cut short when he was not retained in Hertling's cabinet, and when he joined the German Nationalist party after the war, he found it unexpectedly difficult to make a new career in politics. He did not win a seat in the National Assembly

6. Schwend, pp. 34–38, 135–42.
7. Morsey, p. 294.
8. John G. Williamson, *Karl Helfferich, 1872–1924* (Princeton, 1971), p. 75.

but had to stand by and listen to Erzberger denounce his wartime financial policies as disastrous. He began writing articles and making speeches with the deliberate goal of destroying Erzberger as a symbol of Germany's defeat and the hated new republic.[9] A number of these defamatory articles were collected and published in a pamphlet entitled *Away with Erzberger!* in August 1919. The Reich cabinet agreed that Erzberger must sue for libel, not only to defend his own reputation but also that of the government of which he was a member.

The trial lasted from January to March 1920. It was conducted under circumstances overwhelmingly favorable to Helfferich's defense, at a time when Erzberger was working as minister of finance as well as trying to prepare his case.[10] Naturally, the trial attracted wide attention and gave national publicity to the accusations made by Helfferich, who thus appeared more like a prosecutor than a defendant; the publicity resulted in Erzberger's being attacked and wounded by a would-be assassin, weakening him in stamina if not in spirits. The charges made against Erzberger at the trial did not directly concern his role in sponsoring the Peace Resolution or negotiating the armistice (although this was constantly in the minds of his critics) but instead, accused him of conflict of interest in his business dealings during the war, "untruthfulness," and "offenses against the proprieties," charges much more petty than that of treason, yet at the same time much more difficult to combat with dignity. He was accused, among other things, of evading his own tax laws, which incensed property owners all over Germany.

Most of the allegations were proven to be false, and Helfferich was declared guilty of libel, but a hostile judge decided that Erzberger was indeed guilty of three cases of impropriety, seven of mixing business and politics, and six of perjury (out of a total of sixty allegations made by Helfferich.) His mixing of business with politics had been shown to have profited him not at all, but "finance ministers are supposed to be hardheaded, calculating men, and to be made a laughing-stock in these questions hurt Erzberger almost as much as the revelation of huge, ill-gotten gains would have done."[11]

Erzberger resigned as finance minister immediately and set about

9. Ibid., pp. 288–91.
10. See Epstein, pp. 350–67 for a full account of the trial.
11. Williamson, p. 319.

preparing for his perjury trial and personal rehabilitation. He was completely cleared of the perjury charges in the spring of 1921, and an investigation into alleged income tax irregularities also brought a favorable decision in August 1921, a few days before his assassination. But these belated vindications could do little to counteract the effect that the trial had had upon the country and upon the Center party.

The Center delegates in the Reichstag and the National Assembly had followed Erzberger, though often reluctantly, in his exposure of the colonial scandal, his attempts to end the war, and his actions in the armistice negotiations, and they had also supported his policies as finance minister, but they wavered now. For the older political leaders, especially, who had little knowledge of or respect for modern business operations, it was far more distasteful to have to justify one of their colleagues in this kind of matter than to defend him against charges of lack of patriotism or of treason.

It was troubling, too, that in much of the scurrilous Erzberger propaganda that circulated in 1920 and 1921 his Catholicism was emphasized. The same old linking of the Catholic faith with antinational and anti-German activities, which had been dormant since the *Kulturkampf* except for a brief revival in the 1907 elections, seemed to have reappeared. Many members of the Catholic minority fixed their resentment of renewed anti-Catholic sentiment on Erzberger himself, just as members of a Jewish minority may sometimes blame individual Jewish wrongdoers for inviting anti-Semitic outbursts. Throughout his political career, Erzberger had been a threat to those Catholics who hoped to become fully accepted as respectable, patriotic, conforming Germans. His well-known personal piety and devotion to the church merely made matters worse, from this point of view. Furthermore, those Catholics who felt threatened by Erzberger were likely to be those who felt uncomfortable about the Center party's new alignment with the republic and the Social Democratic party. It was vital to the Center's leadership that they be conciliated, and a hearty support of Erzberger would not accomplish that.

On the other hand, he could not be totally repudiated by his party, partly for the very reason that he was a good Catholic, one of their own, strongly defended by some sections of the party membership. The Center in his home state of Württemberg stood by him, and the youth organizations and the rank and file of the labor unions (not the leadership) made him a hero. His defenders on the Left described the attacks on him as a vendetta carried on by property owners against his unpopular tax laws.[12]

Faced with the dilemma of what to do about Erzberger, the top organizations of the national party responded with endless procrastination and postponement of a decision. At the end of his trial, the National Committee voted 49 to 10, and the Executive Council voted 7 to 3, that he resign his seat in the Reichstag. (His three supporters on the council were Richard Müller-Fulda, his old friend the financial expert and businessman, now retired from Parliament, and Joseph Wirth and Prelate Schofer of the Baden party, both fellow-southwesterners.) However, the Württemberg Center Party Executive Council and its state committee put his name at the head of the state list of candidates for the elections of June 1920. He accepted election but agreed not to appear in the Reichstag until his appeal on the decision and his perjury trial were both concluded. (After some months, his appeal was denied.)

Later in June, the party's National Committee voted to accept a motion made by the new Reich Chancellor Fehrenbach that Erzberger should refrain from political activities, but any further judgment was again postponed. When the "case" was brought up again in October in the Reichstag fraction, the same split between conservative northern and western condemnation and leftist-labor, southwestern support was still present. Trimborn and Dr. Kaas from the Rhineland argued against Erzberger's return to politics, on the grounds that he was alienating the intellectuals from the party. Stegerwald was particularly antagonistic to the idea of his return, but other union representatives defended Erzberger vigorously. On October 30, the National Committee heatedly discussed the case and urged Erzberger not to attend Reichstag sessions or fraction meetings; but it stopped short of a move to expel him.[13]

In the spring of 1921, after perjury charges against him had been dropped, Erzberger made himself more visible and undertook a lecture tour through the country, enthusiastically expounding on the "solidarity" theories of Heinrich Pesch, his latest answer to Germany's eco-

---

12. Eschenburg, p. 168; Morsey, p. 301.
13. Morsey, pp. 301, 360–63; Epstein, pp. 370–72.

nomic problems. This new stand increased his popularity with the workers' associations, but not with the Christian trade unionists, who regarded "solidarity" as a political trick and not in the real interests of labor.

The fraction and the party National Committee were still unwilling to readmit him to a decision-making role. Erzberger spoke in his own behalf at a committee meeting June 29 and was answered by a score of speakers urging him to continue sacrificing himself for the good of the party.[14] Even Joseph Joos of the workers' associations, a consistent supporter, sided with the majority against him. It was agreed that he should continue to postpone a comeback until some propitious moment in the future. Erzberger personally intended that this should be at the opening of the autumn session of Parliament.[15] What the reaction of his opponents in the party would have been to that, cannot be determined. His murder by nationalist extremists on August 26 solved the "Erzberger problem" for the Center. Genuine feelings of horror and grief were surely mingled with a certain relief in the minds of many. The party stood united behind their Chancellor Wirth when he condemned the outrage and prepared emergency legislation against the terrorist organizations. The Center could accept Erzberger the dead martyr more comfortably than Erzberger the living politician. For some years his contributions to the party and to Germany were buried with him. It is interesting to note, however, that ten years after his death, one of Erzberger's severest critics during his lifetime, Carl Bachem, wrote an eloquent defense of him at the conclusion of his lengthy history of the Center party.[16]

Although Erzberger was admired by many labor voters and their representatives, one of his bitterest opponents was the leader of the Christian trade unions, Adam Stegerwald. Stegerwald's political outlook and personality formed a complete contrast to Erzberger's, but his activities in 1920 and 1921 were equally threatening to the unity of the party. Whereas Erzberger was a democrat and a republican, Stegerwald was an authoritarian and an admirer of the Wilhelmine system which had elevated him briefly to the Prussian House of Lords. Erzberger was a devout Catholic and maintained close contacts with the

14. Morsey, pp. 393–99.
15. Epstein, p. 312.
16. Bachem, 9:400–501.

clergy. Stegerwald was of course a Catholic too, but he believed that the clergy should not take an active part in politics. Erzberger was jovial, easygoing, exercising leadership through persuasion and expert knowledge; Stegerwald was, by all accounts, abrasive, harsh, lacking in higher education and culture, but able to lead because of organizational ability and a domineering personality.[17] Both men were born in the south, Erzberger in Württemberg, Stegerwald in Bavaria, but both made their permanent home in Berlin. Both men began their careers in the Catholic labor movement, but Erzberger became a professional politician and journalist at an early date, while Stegerwald rose to be the head of both the industrial unions and the German Federation of (Christian) Unions before he decided to enter politics directly. Now in 1920 he proposed to use the DGB as the basis for a new political party in which he would presumably rise even higher on the national scene.

In the immediate postwar period, Stegerwald's position was an enviable one, because he was a man in whom both the Right and the Left had confidence. He was a Reichstag delegate and had been chosen to be a member of the Center's Executive Council. The Social Democrats trusted him because he had been a proven friend to labor; the conservatives trusted him because he was a proven enemy of the Social Democrats. Thus in 1919 he was named minister of public welfare in the Prussian cabinet headed by the Social Democrat Paul Hirsch. He continued as general secretary of the DGB and tried to minimize the inevitable friction between the largely Catholic and democratic industrial unions and the largely Protestant and nationalist employees' unions.

In 1920 Stegerwald, his secretary, the young former army officer Heinrich Brüning, and Heinrich Brauns, the *Volksverein* director who had accepted the post of Reich minister of labor after Stegerwald had rejected it, worked together on a plan to found a new political party. Both Stegerwald and Brüning had been influenced by Martin Spahn, the son of the former Center chairman who had left the Center and moved to the extreme Right of the political spectrum, soon to join the Nationalist party. The plan for the new party was dramatically made public in a speech written by Brauns and Brüning and delivered by Stegerwald at the Trade Union Congress in Essen on November 21.

17. Joseph Joos, *Am Räderwerk der Zeit* (Augsburg, 1948), p. 60; Köhler, p. 223.

The proposed new party would "unite the two Christian denominations in common opposition to Marxism, materialism, and doctrinaire liberalism." It would have room for people of all classes, "especially the intellectual," rejecting the Marxist notion of the class struggle in favor of a real *Volksgemeinschaft*. It would obviously *not* have room for Erzberger or for the Catholic clergy so prominent in the old Center party.[18]

Stegerwald was concerned that the Erzberger scandal and the Center's willingness to take part in coalitions with the Social Democrats had threatened to break up the diverse elements in the DGB. The Clerks' Union (DHV), the most intransigent branch of the organization, had expressed approval of his plan; he also expected support from Bavarians, perhaps even hoping to include the BVP in the new party.[19]

The Center Reichstag fraction, which had been informed of the speech before it was delivered, was very cool to the plan, and was uncertain whether it presented merely a new tactic to attract Protestant voters to the Center, since the influx of Protestants in the 1919 elections had proven to be temporary, or if it was an invitation to the Center to destroy itself. Brauns pointed out the regrettable dependence of the Center on the women's vote; Erzberger retorted that instead of trying to win new Protestant voters the party should win back the estimated four million Catholic workers who had defected to the Social Democrats in the last election. In a National Committee meeting in October, Wirth called the plan "grotesque" and Schofer deplored the diminished role of Catholicism in such a party.[20]

While many union members were at least briefly attracted to the idea of a new party (for example, Jakob Kaiser), the workers' associations and their spokesman Joos were totally opposed. His editorial in the *Westdeutsche Arbeiterzeitung* called the plan "unthinkable."[21]

18. Morsey, pp. 370–71; Heinrich Brüning, *Memoiren, 1918–1934*, 2 vols. (Munich, 1972), 1:75. Morsey believed Brauns to have been the author. Brüning says that he wrote the draft with Brauns's approval and advice. Spahn's role is discussed in Jones, "Adam Stegerwald und die Krise des deutschen Parteisystems," *Vierteljahrshefte für Zeitgeschichte* 27 (1979): 13–14. See also Zeender, "German Catholics and the Concept of an Interconfessional Party, 1900–1922," *Journal of Central European Affairs* 23 (1964): 424–39.

19. Jones, pp. 14, 21.

20. Morsey, pp. 363–69.

21. Wachtling, pp. 81–84.

Public reaction to the speech among Center supporters was at least interested, and some one hundred thousand printed copies of it were sold, but from Protestant circles there was no response at all outside the union organization.[22] A daily newspaper, *Der Deutsche*, was founded which became the voice of Stegerwald and the union directorship, but no actual steps toward the formation of a new party were taken. The Centrist press was critical, and the party's left wing felt that the Essen Program was designed to pull the Center away from its coalition with the Social Democrats and into a rightist coalition. One of Stegerwald's closest associates, Hermann Ullmann, the editor of *Der Deutsche*, later described his *Volksgemeinschaft* as a catchword and a "quarry" from which the National Socialists mined much propaganda material.[23]

Conservatives, on the other hand, came rather quickly to believe that the Center already embodied the "German, Christian, Democratic, and Social" ideals of the Essen Program; it had, after all, been interdenominational in principle since its foundation in 1870. In the words of a party historian, the Essen Program was given a "first-class funeral."[24]

Soon after this public discussion of his Essen proposal, in February 1921, Stegerwald had an opportunity to test himself as a political leader when he replaced Hirsch as minister-president of Prussia, after state elections showed a shift to the Right in voters' opinions. He was elected in a preliminary vote by the *Landtag* by a majority of 332 out of 388, including the votes of the majority Social Democrats. It was assumed that he would form a government of the Weimar Coalition, which still controlled a comfortable majority. Instead, Stegerwald began negotiations to conciliate the Right by bringing at least the People's party into the coalition. His secretary Brüning records that this was intended as a step toward creating a base for his new party, and to "teach the Mosse and Ullstein [liberal] press not to tell the Center party what to do."[25] Offers to the Right included promises to save the Prussian civil service from an influx of Socialists who, accord-

---

22. Morsey, p. 375.
23. Hermann Ullmann, "Das Essener Program, November, 1920," *Deutsche Rundschau*, 11 (1950): 900.
24. Morsey, p. 378.
25. Brüning, p. 79.

ing to Stegerwald, were "untrained and did not understand how to run the machinery of government."[26] This was a strange maneuver from a Centrist whose party was striving equally as hard as the Social Democratic party for parity in the civil service.

The Prussian Social Democrats, annoyed by the implications of the Essen speech and by these unnecessary negotiations, saw no reason to accommodate themselves to the demands of the People's party, and in the second vote of confidence taken by the *Landtag*, Stegerwald was confirmed by a narrow majority which included both DVP and DNVP support but none from the Socialists. His new cabinet was eventually composed only of Centrist and Democratic ministers, with two ministers without party affiliations. He had proved, as he said in an angry speech to the *Landtag*, that he was not the "toy of the parties,"[27] but he had also shown little talent as a statesman or as the potential leader of a new party. His weak government lasted only a few months and after his resignation in November 1921 (when he was replaced by Otto Braun) he never again held office in Prussia , nor did he ever regain the confidence of the Social Democrats. From that point on, his future career as a politician had to be restricted to the Center party as it was, and not as he hoped it would be.

The same trend to the Right which put a Centrist in the place of a Social Democrat in Prussia had resulted in the party's assuming the Chancellorship in the Reich. The elections of June, 1920 showed the beginning of that polarization which was eventually to destroy the Weimar republic, with majority Social Democrats losing to the Independent Socialists and Communists, and the parties of the Right increasing in strength at the expense of the German Democratic party. The Center's representation declined only slightly, taking into account the secession of the BVP, though because of an increase in the total number of seats in the house, its proportionate strength was less. There was also a significant shift in the socioeconomic makeup of the new Center fraction. Landowners recovered much of their prewar status, particularly in the state legislatures, while the number of women and labor delegates declined.

Formation of a government after the elections proved difficult.

26. Helmut J. Schorr, *Adam Stegerwald* (Recklinghausen, 1966), p. 66.
27. Severing, 1:332.

The Bavarian People's party refused to work with the Social Democratic party, the Independent Socialists refused to join any government
at all, and after protracted negotiation a minority cabinet was formed
of Center, DDP, and DVP, with toleration by the majority Socialists.
Fehrenbach reluctantly agreed to serve as chancellor and Wirth continued in the post of finance minister which he had occupied since Erzberger's resignation. Stegerwald refused the Labor Ministry, which was
then accepted by Brauns, who thus became the first Catholic priest to
serve as a cabinet minister, holding the position until 1928 under
many different chancellors.

The chancellorship was regarded by Fehrenbach and the party as
a burden and a sacrifice rather than an honor. The practical consequences of the peace treaty were being brought home in these months,
with the working-out of payments for reparation and the efforts of Poland to detach Upper Silesia from Germany. The refusal of the Bavarian government to disarm the home guards there not only created difficulties between the Reich government and the state but exacerbated
Germany's relations with the Allies, who threatened an invasion of
the Ruhr Valley. Fehrenbach was unable and unwilling to provide leadership under these trying circumstances. When the Reparations Commission presented the final sum of the German debt early in May 1921
and the DVP refused to be a partner to accepting it, Fehrenbach and
the rest of the cabinet resigned.

A chancellor was needed who could get the backing of the Reichstag for the fulfillment of the unpleasant obligations of the treaty.
Fehrenbach and other fraction members were opposed to the Center's
making yet another "sacrifice" in taking on the job. With attacks still
raging against Erzberger, the party remembered too well the Center's
onerous share in arranging the armistice and in signing the peace
treaty. For chancellor, several members of the fraction recommended
Konrad Adenauer, the mayor of Cologne, as a man with a special interest in the vulnerable position of the Rhineland. But on this occasion
as on several others in the republican years, personality factors seem
to have determined the decision against him as well as his lack of
experience in national affairs.[28]

The Social Democrats, who were essential members of a majority

28. Morsey, p. 382.

coalition, favored the choice of Joseph Wirth, the finance minister, and the fraction therefore persuaded him to accept the post, although his lack of expereince in national affairs was nearly as total as Adenauer's. Wirth was reluctant to take the post, but once in office he showed a greater enthusiasm for power and responsibility than any Centrist had previously done, with the exception of Erzberger (of whom Wirth was a staunch supporter). Wirth was one of the youngest members of the Reichstag fraction, a former mathematics teacher who had come to Berlin from Baden as the protégé of the older men in the state party, as Erzberger had come north from Württemberg as Gröber's protégé. His youth, optimism, and ardent republicanism set him apart from the older men in the party. They had pushed him into that position of national leadership which they themselves were unwilling to fill in such times, but they were never prepared to grant him a role of equal significance within the Center party. Wirth is probably the best-known Centrist of the Weimar years, but his popularity was greatest with Social Democrats and Democrats; he never held the office of fraction head or party chairman and it seems to have been more the accident of his Catholic origins and upbringing that determined his career as a Center man than any deep identification with its principles or its constituency. One of his brothers actually became a Social Democrat and another was a member of the Democratic party.[29]

Wirth's talents were considerable but were coupled with an inability either to win the rest of his party to his own ideas or to accommodate himself to theirs. He remained a loner, identified with no particular social group or class (labor admired him, but he never directed the decisions of union representatives in the party), and by 1927 he had even managed to alienate himself from his former sponsors in the Baden party.

After some difficulty, Wirth formed a government of the Weimar Coalition. The Center was represented in the cabinet by three other men, Brauns for Labor, Giesberts for the Post Office, Andreas Hermes for Nutrition (and later Finance), with most of the other posts filled by Social Democrats. A new position of "minister for reconstruction" was created for Walter Rathenau, Wirth's friend and adviser, who pro-

29. Köhler, p. 170.

vided the technical skills needed to make the "policy of fulfillment" a reality. Rathenau, a talented writer, an industrialist, and a Jew, became for the *völkisch* and nationalist extremists a symbol of all the humiliation of defeat, and probably deflected their rage from the person of the chancellor himself, who was regarded by many as simply "Rathenau's tool"; for otherwise, Wirth might well have shared Erzberger's fate.

Although the Center Reichstag fraction fully supported Wirth's actions as chancellor, there was an undercurrent of dissatisfaction with the "Red-Black" coalition. When Wirth spoke at the first Catholic Congress in eight years, held in August, 1921 in Frankfurt, immediately after Erzberger's murder, his defense of the republic and condemnation of right-wing extremism were considered "too political" by many of those present. In October, Wirth resigned suddenly in protest against the loss of most of Upper Silesia to Poland; in the ensuing negotiations for his second cabinet, the Center fraction was insistent that he try to include representatives of the People's party and the BVP. This proved to be impossible to do, and when Social Democrats entered governments in both Prussia and Württemberg that fall, uneasiness in the party increased.[30]

The party congress in January 1922 revealed these feelings clearly, because much of the discussion was concerned with ways to regain support of the Bavarians and of those "academic" Catholics like Martin Spahn who had joined the DNVP Catholic Committee. The new party program drawn up by the congress was carefully worded to avoid any reference to republicanism: "constitutional party" and "people's party" were the preferred expressions. The program's positions on foreign affairs, finance, and economic and social matters were innocuous and vague. The chief business of the congress was to elect a party chairman to replace Trimborn, who had died in July. Wilhelm Marx, head of the Executive Council of the Reichstag fraction, was nominated by the National Committee and elected by acclamation.

Marx was the quintessential "man of the middle." A former jurist from the Rhineland, of similar background to the older generation of leaders like Trimborn and Peter Spahn, he belonged to no particular

30. Morsey, pp. 411–13, 420, 427.

group or faction and he was above all a conciliator who was far more likely to achieve the desired harmony within the party than Wirth or Stegerwald would have been.

The election of a man of the middle at a time when the Center had been allied with the Left for most of the past four years must be interpreted as a move to the Right and, by implication, as a rejection of the policy of Erzberger and Wirth. Marx's speech at the congress is a fair sample of his style and shows his success in balancing and reconciling the factions within the party: the Center supported the constitution, just as it had supported the constitution of 1871. The Center respected the authority of the state, because any violent move against authority was unchristian. On the one hand, the Center should be happy to support the present state "wholeheartedly" because "the state is the people" and because the constitution embodied many Centrist demands. On the other hand, the party opposed many parts of the constitution and would seek changes if the circumstances were favorable. On the one hand, the Center should continue to cooperate with the Social Democrats. On the other hand, the Social Democratic party was certainly the "notorious enemy of Christianity and religion."[31]

Marx found material for a little heavy-handed humor in published rumors of factional strife within the party, remarking that the *Berliner Morgenpost* had described him as a right-wing Centrist who did not agree with the chancellor's foreign policy. On the contrary, he said, he was in full support of Chancellor Wirth, and certain other persons had even called him a *left-wing* politician. If he was both Right and Left then surely he must be a real Center man.[32]

The choice of Marx was of special significance for future Center policy because his personal interest was the attainment of Catholic goals in the sphere of *Kulturpolitik*, and he was active as the chairman of the Catholic School Organization. Religious and educational issues had united German Catholics in the past and might be able to unite them in the future.

In the spring of 1922, Marx expressed the party's confidence in its chancellor and the party backed him in the emergency legislation

31. *Offizieller Bericht*, pp. 73–81.
32. Ibid., p. 81.

pushed through the Reichstag after the murder of Rathenau. There was some discontent, however, that the intent of that legislation was one-sidedly against the Right, and neither the party nor the Christian trade unions endorsed the protest strike and demonstration in July. Instead, the events after the murder had more the effect of intensifying the party's demands that the coalition be enlarged to include at least the DVP and BVP.

This shift in feeling toward the Right was very evident at the Catholic Congress of August 1922. It was held in Munich, a concession to the Bavarians, which emphasized the continuing divergence of these congresses from the Center party; and Wirth was not invited to attend. It was the stated intention of the organizing committee to make this congress less "political" than the last, by which they meant, less identified with the Center. In fact the congress turned out to be exceedingly political, resembling, according to witnesses, a demonstration for the Wittelsbach dynasty and a planned "prelude to a great monarchist, antirepublican action."[33] Bavarian monarchists played a prominent role and members of the royal family received highest honors. Non-Catholics Ludendorff and Gustav von Kahr were conspicuously in attendance at the beer parties of the student fraternities. The highlight of the congress was a speech by Michael, Cardinal von Faulhaber, archbishop of Munich, in which he called the 1919 revolution "perjury and high treason . . . eternally burdened and stigmatized with the mark of Cain."

The Cardinal's strongly antirepublican sentiments were loudly applauded by his audience but did not go entirely unchallenged, because the organizing committee had unwittingly selected a loyal republican and democrat to be the president of the congress. Konrad Adenauer, the mayor of Cologne, had been chosen, after much indecision, as the most acceptable non-Bavarian candidate (since by tradition the president was never a native of the host city) because he was not associated with the Center's Berlin leadership and because he was a representative of the occupied Rhineland and had been linked to the move to detach the Rhineland from Prussia at the end of 1918. But Adenauer surprised and dismayed his sponsors by making pointed re-

---

33. Information on the Catholic Congress of 1922 from Stehkämper, *Konrad Adenauer als Katholikentagspräsident 1922* (Mainz, 1977), pp. 1–85.

marks condemning Bavarian separatism and by insisting that at least one flag of the German republic be displayed in the meeting hall along with the ubiquitous blue and white Bavarian flags. At the close of the congress he created a sensation by publicly rebuking the cardinal for his inflammatory antirepublican speeches.

The incident touched off a debate in the press, with Catholic newspapers in Bavaria and Silesia siding with Faulhaber and the Rhineland papers defending Adenauer. Both Adenauer and Faulhaber sent reports to the Vatican justifying their stands, and Chancellor Wirth informed Rome that the cardinal was endangering the unity of the Reich and the reputation of German Catholics. It is not known how these reports were received, but the cardinal's later public pronouncements were more subdued and less provocative. Nevertheless, the outcome of the congress was certainly detrimental to the interests of the Center party and was greeted with satisfaction by the Catholic Committee of the DNVP.[34]

In the following month, September 1922, the merger of the Social Democratic party with the Independent Social Democratic party had the effect of increasing pressures on Wirth from his own fraction to try to include the People's party in his government, but at the same time made the Social Democrats themselves less willing to compromise with the DVP in spite of prompting from President Ebert. A breakdown of negotiations in November resulted in Wirth's resignation. It has been suggested that Wirth was forced out of office by his own party's desire to form a new government of the Right, but most sources agree that the fraction was willing for Wirth to continue as chancellor and that he himself felt unable to preside over a cabinet in which the Social Democrats were not represented.[35] It was seven years before he held office again in the Reich. With the fall of Wirth the Center's commitment to the democratic republic became measurably weaker.

Dr. Wilhelm Cuno, who became chancellor after Wirth's resignation, was the director of the Hamburg-Amerika Line and was chosen for his business knowledge. He was a Catholic who had been a member of the DVP until the Kapp *Putsch*; since then he had associated himself with the Center but was not close to the party leadership. Two

---

34. Morsey, pp. 475–78.
35. Grebing, *Geschichte der deutschen Parteien* (Wiesbaden, 1962), p. 99; Knapp, "Joseph Wirth," in Morsey, *Zeitgeschichte*, p. 166.

of the Centrists in Wirth's second cabinet, Brauns and Hermes, had not got on very well with Wirth and did not resign with him but remained in Cuno's government. The Bavarian People's party also consented to be represented, now that the Social Democrats were not.

The Center expressed confidence in the new minority government, and in the first days following the French invasion of the Ruhr Valley in January 1923, Marx spoke strongly in favor of the policy of passive resistance advocated by the chancellor. As the months passed, however, and Cuno's reputation as a man of expertise and international contacts began to fade, the Center started to exhibit the same signs of uneasiness about this minority cabinet of the middle as it had about Wirth's government and to urge a widening of the coalition to include the Social Democrats. The French occupation affected those areas of the west where the party had its largest electorate, and the Center was constantly made aware of the distress and dislocation there. The Rhenish Center party clearly transmitted the message that the inhabitants of the region believed that the government had abandoned them. Other members of the party were unhappy at the failure of the government to tax business profits sufficiently. In August, an editorial outburst against Cuno in *Germania* was a decisive factor in bringing about the chancellor's abrupt resignation.[36]

A new government of the Great Coalition was formed by the leader of the People's party, Gustav Stresemann, with representatives from all the parties from the Social Democrats to the People's party, with the exception of the Bavarian People's party, which refused to work with the Social Democrats. Brauns continued in the Labor Ministry, the Post Office was given to Anton Höfle (soon to be embarrassingly implicated in the Barmat financial scandal), and a third Centrist, Johannes Fuchs, former *Oberpräsident* of the Rhine Province, took the newly created Ministry for Occupied Territory. In addition, Marx saw to it that Centrist state secretaries were placed in ministries not held by the party.

The Center was probably the least troublesome to Stresemann of the coalition parties in these extremely critical months, but the Christian trade unions were dissatisfied with his labor policies, and Brauns had to be dissuaded by Marx and Fehrenbach from leaving the

36. Stehkämper, *Nachlass*, 1:286, 301–2; Bach, pp. 231–37.

cabinet on this issue. There were also some doubts and uncertainties in the Center Reichstag fraction concerning the Enabling Act presented by the government and the daring currency reform it proposed to put into effect, but the party's industrialists Lammers and ten Hompel were enthusiastic backers of the *Rentenmark* and played an important role in explaining it to the Center delegation.[37]

In the autumn of 1923, the chronic problem of Rhineland separatism flared up again to embarrass national and local Center party leaders with whom many of the separatists had been associated in the past. In October, a series of abortive *Putsche* occurred in Düsseldorf, Bonn, Trier, Koblenz, and other cities, in some places encouraged by the French. Although all of these coups were vehemently condemned by the party, a few Centrists, including Adenauer, were wondering once again, as in 1918, if some kind of separation might not be the best way to help the Rhinelanders and the Reich to obtain the evacuation of French troops and a better reparations settlement.[38]

Adenauer's pessimistic conclusion that his province had been abandoned by the central government was all too well confirmed in November when the cabinet seriously considered ending all government payments of salaries and other expenses in the Rhineland and refusing to allow the new currency to circulate there. Hans Luther, finance minister since October, spoke in favor of this drastic step, fearing that the new currency would lose its effectiveness if it was allowed to "slip through the gap in the West." He was upheld by Karl Jarres, the People's party mayor of Duisburg, and by Brauns but opposed by Fuchs, Centrist minister of occupied territory. Conferences were held on several occasions at which Adenauer and other Rhinelanders were present. Monsignor Ludwig Kaas was among those who insisted that "we are staying with Prussia and the Reich," and Adenauer accused the cabinet of wanting to sell out the Rhineland in order to avoid reparations payments.[39] No final decision was ever made to cut the ties with the Rhineland, and the government did not, after all, stop payments there. Rapidly improving economic conditions in 1924 allowed the matter to be quietly forgotten. Many years later, in 1953, Adenauer

37. Stehkämper, 1:302; Morsey, pp. 524–26.
38. Paul Weymar, *Adenauer, His Authorized Biography* (New York, 1957), pp. 50–55; Terence Prittie, *Konrad Adenauer, 1876–1967* (Chicago, 1971), pp. 56–57.
39. Morsey, pp. 530–35.

remarked bitterly: "the slanderous lie that, in 1919, I worked for the detachment of the Rhineland from Germany has been refuted and disproved a hundred times over . . . but the fact that the Reich government themselves tried to detach the Rhineland and parts of Westphalia is never mentioned by anyone!"[40]

At the same time that the Rhinelanders believed that the Reich government was failing to take responsibility for them, the Bavarian government was openly defying the Reich. The Bavarian People's party had steadily supported Rhineland separatism and had permitted the single Reichstag delegate for the "Rhenish People's party," elected in 1920, to sit as a *Hospitant* with its fraction.[41] Stresemann's abandonment of the passive resistance policy in the Rhineland in September proved to be the signal for renewed intransigence in Bavaria, which culminated in the Hitler *Putsch* of November.

The Bavarian People's party had been able to expel the Social Democrats from the Munich government on the day following the Kapp *Putsch* in 1920, but neither Heim nor Held had been willing to assume the responsibility of becoming minister-president, in spite of their party's control of the *Landtag*. Instead, the party put its trust in a succession of monarchist bureaucrats from the old regime: Gustav von Kahr, the leader of the home guard, who was minister-president from March 1920 to September 1921; the more moderate Count Lerchenfeld, minister-president from September 1921 to November 1922; and Eugen von Knilling, minister-president from November 1922 to May 1924. None of these men were familiar with the workings of Parliament, although the latter two had been members of the Bavarian cabinet in the war years, and none had close party ties to the BVP. Kahr, a Protestant, is described as being "not certain himself if he were a member."[42] Kahr's cabinet included, beside members of the Bavarian People's party, one representative of the Bavarian *Bauernbund* (an agrarian party somewhat to the Left of the BVP) and a minister of justice from the German Nationalist party, Franz Gürtner, who continued to hold this office throughout the republican years. The Social Democratic party never held a ministry in Bavaria from the time it was ousted in March 1920 to the end of the republic.

40. Weymar, p. 50; see also Stehkämper, 2:116–21.
41. Schwend, p. 153.
42. Schönhoven, p. 39.

Kahr, whose stubborn defense of the home guard and refusal to obey the disarmament regulations and emergency legislation passed by the Reich government was a constant embarrassment, was finally forced by the *Landtag* to resign in September 1921, and for the next year, Lerchenfeld kept the state on a more compliant course; however, his government loudly protested Wirth's Law for the Protection of the Republic and issued a counterordinance denying the applicability of much of the law to Bavaria. In the spring of 1922 the BVP reissued the Bamberger federalist program which included a demand for the right of the *Länder* to carry out Reich orders themselves. President Ebert wrote personally to Lerchenfeld and succeeded in persuading him to withdraw the counterordinance, but a few months later he was forced out of office by Bavarian nationalists in the coalition parties and replaced by Knilling.

Knilling has been described as "vain, weak and vacillating."[43] He allowed the nationalists full opportunity to organize and his attitude encouraged the growth of Hitler's National Socialist movement. In September 1923, when the attention of the Reich government was centered upon the Rhineland crisis, Knilling yielded to extremist pressure and restored Kahr to power, naming him state commissioner general. Prelate Wohlmuth of the BVP *Landtag* delegation was dubious about the wisdom of this move, but Heinrich Held, after consultation with ex-Crown Prince Rupprecht, approved it.[44]

Kahr immediately placed the state under martial law, demanding the allegiance of the Bavarian army units to himself rather than to the national command and thus provoking confrontation with Berlin. General von Lossow of the Bavarian *Reichswehr* supported Kahr and defied orders from the central command. Stresemann's government was unable to move quickly or decisively enough to forestall these events. Whatever Kahr's plans may have been, whether to restore the Bavarian monarchy, as he had spoken of doing, or to protect his state from the Communist revolution he claimed to expect momentarily in the Reich,[45] they were brought to an abrupt end by the Hitler *Putsch* of November 8 and 9.

43. John W. Wheeler-Bennett, *The Nemesis of Power: The German Army in Politics, 1918–1945* (New York, 1956), p. 165.
44. Schwend, pp. 215–16.
45. Ibid., p. 231.

This finished Kahr's career, because he was repudiated both by the radicals for failing at the crucial moment to support Hitler and by the leaders of the Bavarian People's party for becoming involved with forces whose goals were far different from their own dreams of an orderly restoration of prewar conditions. An apologist for the party has argued that the state government disregarded the Reich decrees in 1921 and 1922 for constitutional reasons alone, solely as a matter of principle. "It is possible," he wrote in 1924, "that radical circles have mistaken this defensive struggle for a support of their illegal plans. The Bavarian People's party . . . has nothing to do with them." He drew a distinction between the "legal defiance of the laws" in August 1922 and the "dictatorial action" of September 1923, which the party "and Herr von Kahr himself most of all" regretted exceedingly.[46]

The argument is unconvincing, but there is no doubt that the BVP was dismayed and chastened by the November events. Catholic conservatives in Bavaria were further estranged from the radicals during the trials of the National Socialists, when Ludendorff made pointedly anti-Catholic remarks and blamed Cardinal Faulhaber (wrongly) for stopping the *Putsch*. Cardinal Faulhaber did publicly condemn the *völkisch* agitation by drawing a sharp distinction between its goals and the authoritarian-monarchist views which he himself had expressed a year earlier.[47] A tactful handling of the matter by Chancellor Stresemann enabled the BVP to extricate itself from an untenable position without humiliation, and in February 1924, in Marx's first administration, an agreement was concluded between the national and state governments in which the Bavarians recognized the supremacy of the Reich army command. Kahr resigned at that time, Knilling resigned a few months later, and Heinrich Held finally stepped out from behind the scenes to take over the minister-presidency himself. From then on, the Bamberger federalist program was pursued only by constitutional means, which is to say, it was relegated to the realm of rhetoric.

46. Beyerle, p. 66.
47. Eyck, *A History of the Weimar Republic*, 2 vols. (New York, 1967), 1:271–72.

15
THE CENTER IN COALITION, 1924–1926

Stresemann was forced to resign the chancellorship late in November 1923 because the Social Democrats resented the restraint shown toward Bavaria in contrast to the rough treatment meted out to leftist radicals in Saxony. The Center's leadership had backed Stresemann all the way and was grateful for the lenience toward the Bavarians and unconcerned about the suppression of the Communists in Saxony. The Centrist press condemned the Socialists' move, and mutual recriminations made it unlikely that the two parties could work closely together in the near future. The German Nationalist party made overtures to enter the cabinet, but expected to be included in the Prussian government as well, which was refused by all of the parties in the Prussian coalition. After various solutions to the problem had been considered, Marx was asked to head a minority cabinet of the middle (including the BVP).

In spite of the events in Saxony, the SPD was willing to tolerate Marx's government and to grant it another Enabling Act to carry out the currency stabilization. There was little to indicate, in the spring of 1924, that the Center had come to "the end of the republican era" in its own history,[1] but in retrospect the years 1924 to 1926 can be seen as a time of disengagement from republicanism and the policies of the first postwar years.

For three years, coalition policy was the subject of an internal conflict in the Center, with those holding real authority in the party favoring the inclusion of the DNVP in the Reich cabinet, against a hard-fought struggle by Wirth, the youth groups, and the labor representatives to prevent this. Since two prominent labor leaders, Stegerwald and Brauns, ranged themselves on the side of Marx and those

1. Morsey, p. 533.

who wanted a right-wing orientation, Catholic labor was seriously divided against itself, resulting in internal revolt against the union leadership and the defection of labor voters to new splinter parties and to the established parties of the Left.

The decision of conservatives in the party councils to woo the DNVP is not really surprising when it is recalled that the prewar Center was always most comfortable in alliance with the Conservative party and that the party was anxious to win back Catholics who had joined the Nationalists and equally anxious to reunite with the Bavarian People's party. The two liberal parties of the middle, the DDP and DVP were, after all, the descendants of the anticlerical bloc of the *Kulturkampf* and stood in the way of much-desired legislation for confessional schools; moreover their parliamentary representation, particularly that of the Democrats', was shrinking, and incapable of providing a majority for a government without one or the other of the two large "wing" parties. Although of these two the Social Democratic party had proved unexpectedly cooperative in Prussia on religious and educational policy, the natural partner for achieving the Center's goals in *Kulturpolitik* was still seen to be the DNVP, in spite of anti-Catholic and even anti-Christian, *völkisch* elements within that party.

In the same month when the party press was deploring the recent events in Bavaria and citing the continued hostility of the BVP toward the Center as proof of the Center's rejection of particularism and its devotion to national interest,[2] Marx was opening negotiations with the Bavarians in the hopes of joining forces in the national elections scheduled for May. Marx and Stegerwald discussed a rapprochement with Prelate Leicht, chairman of the BVP Reichstag delegation, and suggested that they agree to eliminate competition in the Bavarian Palatinate by presenting a combined list of candidates in that district. Since the Center had previously run its own successful candidate there, this was a sacrifice for that party, but Leicht rejected the offer. The Bavarian party wanted to keep open the possibility of putting up candidates for the federalist cause in other parts of the country. The Center responded to this with a threat to run its own candidates in all four electoral districts in Bavaria. Neither party had any serious intention of carrying out these threats, however, because of the expense

2. Article in *Germania*, cited in *Frankfurter Zeitung*, 1 Mar., 1924.

which would have been entailed. The failure of Marx's overtures, and the subsequent withdrawal by the BVP of its single representative in the cabinet, Justice Minister Erich Emminger, vindicated the Center's left wing which had opposed a reconciliation from the beginning. (Later in the year, the Center offered a further concession by agreeing to stop publication of its weekly newsletter in the Palatinate and instead to send reports only to registered Center party members, which reduced rivalry in the December elections.)

In the Rhineland, meanwhile, a break-off from the Center had occurred with the founding of a new party for Catholic workers in the Ruhr by Fritz Hüske, an ironworker. The new party's headquarters were in Essen, and it used the catchwords of the Essen Program in its title, the Christian-Social People's Community, but it was organized in opposition to Stegerwald and the official union leadership, and particularly opposed the refusal of Marx's government to restore the eight-hour day (suspended in the crisis of 1923). In the May election, the Christian-Social People's Community received over 124,000 votes, mostly in districts previously considered safe for the Center.[3]

A similar workers' protest party had been formed in Bavaria in 1920 as a result of the split of the BVP from the Center. Vitus Heller had founded the Christian Social party of Bavaria after he had discovered that the Bavarian People's party had no use for radical-social Catholics. The Christian Social party had originally had ties with the national Center party and even received financial aid from Erzberger and Brauns, but it was never officially recognized. In 1924, when the Center's leadership was anxious to conciliate the BVP, these ties were dropped; in 1925 Heller broke entirely with the Center and in the following year he agreed to merge with Hüske's Rhenish Christian-Social People's Community to form what then became known as the Christian Social Reich party, or CSRP.[4] None of these new splinter groups received support from the official Christian trade unions or from the workers' associations, but their appearance was a sign of increasing discontent with Centrist policies among Catholic workers.

The elections of May 1924 reveal a continuing polarization of votes, with the German Nationalist party becoming the largest in the

3. Knapp, "The Red and the Black: Catholic Socialists in the Weimar Republic," *Catholic Historical Review* 61 (1975): 400.
4. Ibid., p. 401; Wachtling, pp. 89–92.

Reichstag with 106 seats, the new Communist party receiving 62 seats, and the DVP, DDP, and Social Democrats all showing steep declines. Only the Center held steady, dropping from 69 to 65 seats not because of the vote but because of the loss of the delegation from Upper Silesia, now in Poland. The BVP lost a quarter of its seats, obviously because of its share in the November fiasco, and the quarrel between the two Catholic parties in the Palatinate resulted in a splitting of the vote and the loss of one of the two seats there, the remaining seat being won by the BVP.

The Nationalists demanded entry into the government as a consequence of their victory in the election, suggesting Admiral von Tirpitz as chancellor and Marx as vice-chancellor. The immediate reaction in the Center press and party was one of indignation: an editorial in *Germania* said on May 8, "We must refuse to serve as a fig leaf for German Nationalist policy," and Joos published an open letter calling for a Great Coalition and protesting the exclusion of the Social Democrats from the cabinet.[5]

Nevertheless, a few days later Marx began conferences with the Nationalists, even talking personally with Tirpitz about his terms for consenting to become chancellor. The Rhenish Center organization objected to these conferences but did not succeed in putting an end to them. When Tirpitz and then Bülow proved impossible to agree upon, the Nationalists proposed Stegerwald as chancellor, but this the Center leaders rejected. The Nationalists refused to serve in a cabinet headed by Marx.[6] Since the German People's party vetoed a Great Coalition, and a Weimar Coalition had no majority in the Reichstag, Marx's minority cabinet of the middle stayed in office on a temporary basis.

The most vital item for consideration that summer was the Dawes Plan for the implementation of reparations payments and the evacuation of the Ruhr by Allied troops, which could not be passed without the votes of a large number of DNVP deputies. The fact that forty-eight of them did accept the plan, including Martin Spahn and other Catholic emigrés from the Center, encouraged Centrist conservatives, Stegerwald and Theodor von Guerard in particular, to try

---

5. *Frankfurter Zeitung*, 8 May, 1924; *Kölnische Volkszeitung*, 22 May 1924.
6. *Kölnische Volkszeitung*, 31 May 1924.

again to cooperate with the seemingly tamed Nationalist party. The People's party reopened negotiations for a widening of the cabinet. Again, the press, local Center organizations, and workers' associations petitioned against a *Bürgerblock* of the Right. Marx stated on October 5 that he personally favored a government of *Volksgemeinschaft*, one that would include representatives of all parties from the Social Democrats to the Nationalists. He was seconded in this improbable proposal by the Center's Reichstag fraction which agreed to cooperate with "any party or any party members" who would support the constitution and the present foreign policy, an obvious bid to moderate Nationalists.[7] Negotiations were broken off when the Democratic party refused to participate in any kind of rightist cabinet, and the Reichstag was dissolved for new elections.

Coalition policy naturally dominated the Center's Third Party Congress, held in late October 1924. Marx promoted *Volksgemeinschaft* and the "middle way," implying now that the middle way required a balance of Left and Right but not, as in 1923, a balance of Social Democracy with the People's party, but with the DNVP. Wirth and Joos on their part took up the theme of the "middle way" to urge avoidance of a rightist cabinet; both criticized Guerard for overstepping his authority in engaging in friendly discussions with Nationalist leaders. The party congress closed with the reelection by acclamation of Marx to the party chairmanship, and the choosing of a slogan for the forthcoming elections in December: "Strengthen the Middle! Strengthen, above all, the heart of any healthy Middle, the German Center party!"

The voters seem to have heeded the exhortation, because the Center won four additional seats, the middle parties of DVP, BVP, and SPD all regained some strength, and the Communists and National Socialists lost substantially. The German Nationalists, however, returned with a gain of six seats, after having conducted a strongly antirepublican and anti-Stresemann campaign.

After these elections, the People's party insisted upon the immediate formation of a rightist cabinet. The Center exhibited the same split personality as earlier in the year: the Reichstag fraction made a "final" refusal of a Right coalition on December 12, while Marx and

7. *Frankfurter Zeitung*, 9 Oct. 1924.

Brauns took part in secret talks at Brauns's house on December 19, at which a "cabinet of personalities" was planned in order to introduce some Nationalists into the cabinet as individuals, with guarantees of allegiance to the republic, the flag, and Stresemann's foreign policy.[8]

In January a government was finally formed, not by Marx but by his finance minister, Dr. Hans Luther, who was not affiliated with any party. The Nationalists held no fewer than four ministries, including the important Interior Ministry. The Center kept Brauns in the Labor Ministry as its only representative, and a member of the BVP took the Post Office.

Fehrenbach, who had been among those opposed to a rightist cabinet in October, now justified the party's participation in this one in a speech to the Reichstag in which he called it a "great sacrifice" and warned that any deviation by the cabinet or by individual ministers from the constitution or from domestic or foreign policy approved by the Center would cause the party to withdraw from the government.

Others in the fraction proved less flexible than Fehrenbach. In the vote of confidence for the Luther government, three abstained from voting, two (Wirth and Heinrich Imbusch) voted against the government, and fourteen were absent. Of the dissidents, thirteen were delegates from the trade unions or workers' associations. Only four labor representatives in the fraction voted for the government, among them Brauns, Stegerwald, and Brüning.[9]

This was evidence of a serious rift between Stegerwald and the membership of the industrial unions brought about by his active effort to bring Nationalists into the government and his claim to speak for all the Christian unions in his newspaper *Der Deutsche*. The revolt was launched by Imbusch, head of the Christian Miners' Union, who had wanted to see the Center cooperate in a coalition with the Social Democrats. At the Congress of the Miners' Union in August 1924, he had attacked Stegerwald and accused him of far exceeding his mandate from the unions. Stegerwald, he declared, had directly violated the principles of political neutrality that he, of all men, ought to have been most careful to uphold. He had spoken too often about the "community of the people" and the "welfare of all" and too seldom about the

8. Stürmer, *Koalition und Opposition in der Weimar Republik, 1924–1928* (Düsseldorf, 1967), pp. 78–79.
9. *Verhandlungen des Reichstags* 384 (20 Jan. 1925): 121, 231–34.

welfare and interests of the trade unions whose leader he was supposed to be. His paper *Der Deutsche* had a "poisonous" effect on the unions' interests and was "edited in an undemocratic, unsocial spirit, directly inimical to miners." In short, Imbusch concluded, Stegerwald was behaving in a way which could not be tolerated any longer by the Christian Miners' Union.

Stegerwald took no public notice of this outburst and, six weeks later, at the October Congress of the Christian industrial unions, he again appealed for the inclusion of the Nationalists in the cabinet. "To whom are the Christian unions closer," he asked, "the international stockjobbers, the international Freemason lodges, the mechanistic philosophy of bourgeois democracy and Social Democracy, or the Catholic and Protestant German people?" The speech was received coldly by its audience, and the only applause Stegerwald was given was when he assured the congress that he had not become a reactionary and was still in favor of shorter working hours and higher wages for labor.[10]

Imbusch's reply to Stegerwald's speech was a reiteration of his August attack, frequently interrupted by applause. He was supported by representatives of the metalworkers' and textile workers' unions as well as his own miners. Stegerwald then felt obliged to retract part of his speech and admitted that his opinions were personal and not intended to represent the sentiment of the unions, which he agreed should avoid taking political positions. The congress ended with unanimous approval of a resolution stating that the Christian unions should remain politically neutral. Two weeks later the resignation of the editor in chief of *Der Deutsche* was announced. The unity of the DGB had been maintained and the industrial unions appeared to have won a victory over Stegerwald. The victory was a limited one, however, because it did not mean the triumph of the political opinions of Imbusch's views over Stegerwald's but only the restoration of "neutrality," a principle which could never operate effectively and which permitted the administration of the DGB to continue publicly expressing opinions very much at variance with the opinions of the majority of its "followers." The refusal to vote confidence in Luther's government was the first, but not the last, open resistance of the leftwing

10. *Frankfurter Zeitung*, 26 Aug. 1924, 14 Oct. 1924, 25 Oct. 1924.

union representatives to the decisions of the Center leadership.

Soon after the controversial Luther government was formed, the sudden death of President Ebert made further elections necessary. The parties of the Right formed the Loebell Committee in order to choose a common candidate for the presidency, and the Bavarian People's party took part in its discussions from the beginning, but the Center at first did not. When the Social Democrats chose to run Otto Braun, the minister-president of Prussia, without consultation with the Center, the party joined in the Loebell Committee's negotiations for a short time, but neither of the two Catholic parties would accept the candidature of Dr. Karl Jarres, former mayor of Duisberg and interior minister in 1924, because he was associated with the anti-Catholic Evangelical League and had made difficulties, when minister of the interior, about the terms of the Bavarian Concordat. Both parties withdrew from the discussions and briefly considered a common candidate, but the BVP would not approve the choice of Marx, whom its leaders felt to be too leftist and too ready to cooperate with Socialists; they were willing to consider Stegerwald, but as might be expected, his name was decisively rejected by the Center's left wing.[11] Consequently, in the first election, the Center ran Marx and the BVP ran Heinrich Held. Held did not even campaign outside Bavaria and received fewer votes in that state than usually went to the BVP in parliamentary elections. After this poor showing the Bavarians showed renewed interest in a common candidate on the Right, so long as it was not Jarres. Prelate Leicht of the BVP Reichstag fraction tried to mediate between his party and the Center to find a compromise candidate who would please both parties, and he personally supported Marx in the second election, but the more right-wing Munich leadership, particularly Heim and the young Fritz Schäffer, swayed the party to the support of Hindenburg.

This fateful decision—which may very well have determined the future of the Weimar republic, because the votes cast by the party's usual supporters were enough to make the difference between victory and defeat for Hindenburg—seems to have been motivated by nothing more than a desire to show the Center that the Bavarian party was truly independent and to register protest at the Center's association

11. Schönhoven, pp. 120–21; Wachtling, p. 103.

with Social Democrats in the People's Bloc formed for Marx. Support for Hindenburg was simply an extension of the fraternal quarrel between Bavarian People's party and Center.[12]

The Center's decision to join in the People's Bloc with its former partners in the Weimar Coalition was probably motivated by the need to conciliate those elements in the party which had been disturbed by the Luther government, and it was also a response to pressure from the Prussian Center party which was engaged in trying to achieve a stable government in that state against the determined opposition of a few monarchist Centrist aristocrats.[13] Since the Social Democrats believed that a candidate from a middle party would have a better chance of victory, and since the DDP had no nationally known figure to present except Defense Minister Gessler, who was considered too controversial, Marx was chosen as the People's Bloc candidate.

It should not have been a problem for the Center to support its own man; the "sacrifice" was on the part of the other two parties in the bloc. Yet the Center received sharp criticism from conservative Catholics for even consenting to join a common front with the despised Socialists, not just in Bavaria but in Prussia from Catholics like Clemens, Freiherr von Loë, and Franz von Papen, who boasted of his support for Hindenburg and sent him a telegram of congratulation after his victory. High officials at the Vatican and many members of the German clergy disapproved of Marx's candidacy and favored Hindenburg. In addition to genuine defections, distortions and out-of-context quotations from papal and episcopal pronouncements were circulated in order to discredit Marx. At all times during the republic the Vatican received information from German sources which were strongly biassed against the Center party. It was reported to Rome, for example, that Center voters were sometimes told to vote for Social Democratic candidates, although this was not only untrue but was virtually impossible under the list system used in the republican elections and had occurred only under the previous system of runoff elections in the prewar years. Marx himself was particularly disturbed at hearing that Abbot Ildefons Herwegen of the highly respected and in-

12. Karl Holl, "Konfessionalität, Konfessionalismus und demokratische Republik," *Vierteljahrshefte für Zeitgeschichte* 17 (1969): 257; Schönhoven, p. 131.
13. Holl, p. 258.

fluential Maria-Laach monastery had ordered his monks and lay brothers, who usually voted Centrist as a matter of course, to abstain from casting votes in the presidential election because it was so controversial.[14]

If Marx's association with Socialists and republicans made him unacceptable to many Catholics, his Catholicism just as certainly made him unacceptable to many Protestant or freethinking Democrats and Social Democrats. Many DDP supporters were greatly disturbed at the idea of putting in office as president not only a Catholic but a decidedly clerical Catholic who was head of the Catholic School Organization. Willy Hellpach, the Democratic candidate in the first election, was "astounded" at the choice, and many Democratic voters did not see the contest as one of the republic against its enemies but rather as concerned with the older ideological quarrel between tradition and progress. Although conservative Protestants and the Evangelical churches themselves would almost certainly have been in Hindenburg's camp no matter who the republican candidate was, many liberal or nonpracticing Protestants were persuaded to join it by the choice of a clerical candidate by the People's Bloc.[15] The revival of anti-Catholic sentiment and the widespread distribution of anti-Catholic propaganda, especially evident in Saxony, was highly disconcerting to Catholics of all political persuasions. In a final irony, many of them blamed Marx's candidacy, and Marx himself, for reviving the spirit of the *Kulturkampf* in Germany.[16]

A further factor in the defeat of the People's Bloc was the reluctance of Marx to attack his opponent. In his campaign speeches Marx "never touched on Hindenburg's lack of political experience, his age, or his monarchism. Nor did he dwell on the marshal's errors of judgment during the war, which might have some bearing on his qualifications as president."[17] Hindenburg was allowed to present himself as the preserver of the eastern provinces in wartime, while the parties of Weimar had been unable to save Upper Silesia in time of peace. The politeness of Centrist campaigners to Hindenburg was in contrast to

14. Stehkämper, 1:404–11, 2:369–75.
15. Holl, pp. 263–67; see also Robert Pois, *The Bourgeois Democrats of Weimar Germany* (Philadelphia, 1976), pp. 50, 52.
16. Stehkämper, 1:402–6.
17. Andreas Dorpalen, *Hindenburg and the Weimar Republic* (Princeton, 1964), p. 80.

Nationalist propaganda, which did not hesitate to accuse the Center of having "sold out to the Socialists" and having compromised its religious principles by cooperating with Marxists.[18]

Undoubtedly, many Catholics voted for Hindenburg against Marx, but the supposition that these were voters who normally supported the Center does not seem to be borne out by election statistics.[19] Marx won a majority in election districts of the Rhineland and Westphalia, and in the Silesian districts of Breslau and Oppeln. In Württemberg and Baden, in spite of the rightist coalition in office in Württemberg, Marx received more votes in the second election than the three Weimar parties together received in the first election. He received an absolute majority in the Palatinate and at least a quarter of the votes which usually went to the BVP in that part of Bavaria. Every one of the districts which returned a majority for the People's Bloc, with the single exception of Berlin, was an area of heavy concentration of Catholic voters, and there was no heavily Catholic district in Germany which failed to return a majority for Marx, except the three eastern districts in Bavaria.[20] A non-Catholic candidate running in the name of the democratic republic could never have done so well as this. It was the decision of the BVP to back Hindenburg that ensured Marx's defeat. The national Center leadership, however, was surprisingly quick to forgive the Bavarians, and soon renewed its efforts to reconcile the two parties.

Joseph Wirth had hoped that the People's Bloc could be preserved after the presidential elections and form a loose confederation of the Weimar parties for future cooperation, but this plan met with no response even from the left wing of the Center.[21] Instead, the party's Reichstag fraction aligned itself closely with the German Nationalist party by backing a bill for protective tariffs on agricultural products and even agreeing to a forcible limitation of debate on the bill, a move described by the Social Democratic opposition as an "assault" on their rights. There was widespread criticism of this move in the press, including in some Centrist papers, and it seemed to many that the frac-

18. Schreiber, Politisches Jahrbuch, 1925 (München-Gladbach, 1925), pp. 52–54.
19. Zeender, "The German Catholics and the Presidential Election of 1925," Journal of Modern History 35 (1963) :377–78.
20. Frankfurter Zeitung, 27 Apr. 1925.
21. Ibid., 31 May 1925.

tion had wholly identified itself with Luther's government, whereas in January, the party had endorsed it only provisionally, and with reluctance.

A few days after the tariff bill was pushed through, on August 24, Wirth announced that he was leaving the fraction, though he still intended to remain a member of the party. His defection created consternation in party ranks and inspired others to take a firmer stand. The *Windthorstbund* of Berlin-Brandenburg "left" the party on August 25, and a number of league branches in the southwest followed its lead. The *Westdeutsche Arbeiterzeitung*, organ of the workers' associations, approved Wirth's action; its editor Joos sympathized, while not sharing Wirth's "passionate combative nature" and following suit.[22] At a meeting of the Baden state Center party Wirth spoke to "continuous applause." As chairman of the Reichstag fraction Fehrenbach felt obliged to publish a letter justifying the Center's actions on the tariff bill and defending the party against Wirth's allegations. The letter tacitly acknowledged the criticism of the limitation of debate and explained that a third of the fraction was absent when the vote on debate was taken. Marx also wrote privately to Wirth to explain the reasoning behind the party's moves, expressing his opinion that the Left was actually relieved not to have responsibility for financial measures and that, in any case, the alternative to Luther's government would only be another rightist cabinet.[23]

As it happened, the party was not required to reach a decision about continuing in the coalition because in October the Nationalist ministers were forced by their party to resign after the signing of the Treaty of Locarno. The following month, the Center held its national party congress in Kassel, at which those delegates who had opposed participation in the Luther cabinet reminded everyone that they had always warned it would end in failure. The meetings of the congress were unusually well attended and the delegates chose sides in a kind of oratorical duel which took place between the supporters of Wirth and the upholders of the official party fraction policy. Wirth was backed by a number of labor leaders from Düsseldorf and Koblenz and by the influential Dr. Karl Spiecker, managing editor of *Germania*, a

22. Wachtling, pp. 107–8.
23. *Kölnische Volkszeitung*, 26 Aug. 1925; *Frankfurter Zeitung*, 7 Sept. 1925; Stürmer, pp. 104–5.

democrat and intellectual who represented three voting districts of Greater Berlin at the congress. Defending the fraction were Marx, Brauns, Schreiber, and Stegerwald.

Wirth took the offensive, speaking of his republican movement as a "crusade" and constantly heckling the other speakers. He found an ideal target in Stegerwald, whose general unpopularity made him a better scapegoat than the amiable Marx. Stegerwald had alienated himself further from his labor constituents by his defense of the coalition and of the protective tariff law. His speech at the congress was interrupted so often by Wirth that it became a debate. The interchange is revealing of the ideological conflict within the party.

> STEGERWALD Wirth pays more attention to the forces in parliament. I pay more attention to the forces in the German people.
> WIRTH But those are not political forces!
> STEGERWALD They certainly *are* political forces. I'm aiming my attack at those sham-democratic forces which are not rooted in the German people, and which have nothing to say about the country's troubles but want to decide how the people should educate their children.
> WIRTH Now say something for once about the destructiveness of nationalism!
> STEGERWALD It shouldn't even have to be debated that the kind of nationalism which disrupts the nation is in the highest degree unchristian. I'm against those ideas that have no traditions behind them. The most important thing is to develop as organic a democracy as possible, and I'll be glad to help to do that with Wirth . . . and Joos. On the question of the republic, I take the standpoint that Dr. Brauns took yesterday.
> WIRTH Brauns took no standpoint at all yesterday!
> STEGERWALD (ignoring him) In the same way, when I was Prussian minister-president I declared that any action against the form of government must be prevented at all costs.
> WIRTH That's not enough!
> STEGERWALD I'm not only a political figure, I am also a trade union leader and I have hundreds of thousands of followers who are not enthusiastic republicans.[24]

Wirth's own speech, uninterrupted by heckling, made a strong impression on his audience. He ended it with a rousing exhortation to the congress to encourage Centrists to join the *Reichsbanner*, (the na-

24. *Frankfurter Zeitung*, 18 Nov. 1925.

tional militia founded in 1924, largely with Social Democratic back-ing) and to defend the republic, in order to prevent "driving millions to radicalism or lethargy."[25]

Wirth's concentration on Stegerwald and his implication that he, and not Marx, was the most responsible for the Center's entering the coalition and approving the tariff bill, may have been well meant but left the impression that Marx was at best weak and at worst a dupe or a fool. It was not Stegerwald alone, but Marx himself and others in leadership positions such as Brauns, Schreiber, and Fehrenbach, who had led the party in the past two years and kept it from too warmly embracing the *Reichsbanner* and the republic. Marx in his closing speech at the congress pointedly "regretted" that Wirth in the last year had been ill or traveling in America and so had been "out of touch" with the fraction, the Executive Council, and the National Commit-tee. Brauns criticized Wirth for discussing internal problems in the open at such a large gathering, and said that Wirth's fall as chancellor had been brought about by the unwillingness of the Social Democratic party to compete and to take full responsibility in government.[26]

The Wirth faction did achieve one victory at the congress. A reso-lution drawn up by Dr. Spiecker was unanimously passed, saying that "the Center party acknowledges the German republic established in the Weimer Constitution and considers its defense and its penetration by the Center spirit to be the duty and obligation of the party." The congress also issued the statement that "the party is united on all im-portant points. Unfortunately, complete agreement has not yet been reached."[27] Conflict within the party in fact continued until the end of 1928.

Luther's cabinet remained in office for three months without re-placement being made for the four departed Nationalist ministers. Fehrenbach had refused a presidential request to form a new govern-ment of the Great Coalition and the efforts of the Democrat Erich Koch foundered over differences between the DVP and the SPD, prin-cipally concerning the restoration of the eight-hour day. Luther finally

25. Ibid.
26. Heinrich Brauns, "Zentrum—Partei der Mitte," in Hubert Mockenhaupt, ed., *Hein-rich Brauns: Katholische Sozialpolitik im 20. Jahrhundert* (Mainz, 1976), pp. 114–17.
27. *Frankfurter Zeitung*, 18 Nov. 1925.

formed a minority cabinet in which the Center was represented by Brauns, Marx, and Haslinde.

The chancellor fell from office in May 1926 because of indignation over his decision (actually, President Hindenburg's decision) to allow German legations and consulates outside Europe, and in European seaports, to fly the red, white, and black flag of the Wilhelmine Reich. Center speakers denounced the flag order on the floor of the Reichstag and the fraction was prepared to offer a motion condemning Luther's action, but it was not willing to force his resignation on the issue, and consequently voted against the no-confidence motions of the Social Democrats and Democrats. Wirth and his friend Dr. Friedrich Dessauer were absent when the votes were taken.[28] As the no-confidence motion was successful even without the Center, another unwelcome government crisis resulted.

On this occasion, Adenauer, mayor of Cologne, was once more considered as chancellor, but his efforts to form a cabinet failed, evidently because of personal objections from Stresemann. The Center fraction was informed through a Socialist contact that Stresemann considered Adenauer "too strong" a personality and wanted a chancellor "through whom he can really exercise the office of chancellor himself." The foreign minister also seems to have believed Adenauer to be overfriendly to France.[29] In the end the more malleable Marx took office with the rest of Luther's minority cabinet intact (with the Centrist Bell taking over the ministries of Justice and Occupied Territory from Marx).

No real solution had been found to the continuing crisis, and the Center's internal conflict over political orientation had simply been muted temporarily by the continuation of a minority government of the middle. Wirth had rejoined the Reichstag fraction after Luther's resignation, but a new rebellion by leftists broke out in June 1926 over the issue of the referendum on the expropriation of the property of the former ruling princes.

The referendum, as initiated by the Communists and now seconded by the Social Democrats, proposed to expropriate the former

28. Morsey, *Protokolle*, 1:36–37; *Verhandlungen des Reichstags* 390 (11 May 1926): 7220–25.
29. Morsey, *Protokolle*, 1:38–40; Weymar, pp. 78–86; Fritz Stern, "Adenauer and a Crisis in Weimar Democracy," *Political Science Quarterly* 73 (1958): 14–27.

princes and their families without compensation. It attracted tremendous public interest and tempted large numbers of Catholic workers to support it. Nationalist propaganda hurt the efforts of the middle parties to persuade their voters to vote against the proposal by claiming that every vote of no was a vote for monarchism and a swing to the Right; Hindenburg's partisan intervention was also unwise and provocative. Because of this kind of agitation the Democratic party, which had originally called for compensation to be paid the princes, changed its position and released its voters to vote as conscience directed or for the lesser evil. *Germania* advised its readers either to vote no or to cast an invalid empty ballot, but the advice was defied by many thousands of Center voters. A Catholic committee was formed in the Reichstag to support the expropriation and several local party organizations and branches of the *Windthorstbund* declared for a yes vote. Wilhelm Elfes, of the *Westdeutsche Arbeiterzeitung*, advised against a yes vote but acknowledged that most of his readers would be for the expropriation. Vitus Heller, head of the new merger, the Christian Social Reich party, advised his followers to vote yes. The decision of the *Reichsbanner* organization to recommend a favorable vote caused dissension among those in the Center who were affiliated with it.[30]

When the referendum was completed, the total number of "yes" votes, though not enough to permit the expropriation, was far larger than the normal combined votes for the Communist and Social Democratic parties; moreover, the additional votes came from precisely those areas which were the strongholds of the Christian industrial unions: Cologne, Aachen, Düsseldorf, Westphalia. A Communist speaker in the Reichstag exulted: "The tower of the Center is tottering. It is tottering now as never before."[31] In Bavaria, on the other hand, where an amicable settlement with the Wittelsbachs had already been worked out, the proportion of favorable votes was the smallest in the country.

The question of the princes' property was referred back to the state governments to settle by compromise and soon ceased to be an

30. Wachtling, p. 112; Knapp, "The German Center Party and the *Reichsbanner*," pp. 169–70.
31. *Frankfurter Zeitung*, 29 June 1926; *Verhandlungen des Reichstags* 390 (29 June 1926): 7692.

inflammatory issue. It had revealed a serious rift between the Center and large numbers of its electorate.

Meanwhile, Wirth continued his personal struggle to turn party policy back to that of the immediate postwar years. When he had rejoined the Reichstag fraction he had seemed to accept a recent decision of the party's National Committee that the Center should be a mediating party of the middle rather than side with either Right or Left. Only two weeks after that decision, however, Wirth published an article in the *Berliner Tageblatt* (a Democratic paper) which appeared to call for the founding of a large new republican party, a revival of the People's Bloc plan he had promoted after the presidential elections of 1925. In a second article in the same paper he revealed his intention of founding a republican magazine. The magazine was issued for the first time in October 1926: the *Deutsche Republik*, a weekly which he published in cooperation with a Social Democrat, Paul Löbe, president of the Reichstag, and a Democrat, Ludwig Haas. A source highly critical of Wirth, Heinrich Köhler, claims that the purpose of the new magazine was to make money and to serve as a "pedestal" for Wirth and his ambitions, and that Löbe and Haas had little to do with it. He also reports that Wirth was a close friend of the editor of the *Berliner Tageblatt* and transmitted information about Center party affairs to the liberal newspaper.[32] The editor of the *Deutsche Republik*, Heinrich Teipel, had previously been an editor of Stegerwald's *Der Deutsche*, another "pedestal" for another ambitious would-be party-founder, and had then served as an editor of *Germania*, until obliged to leave because of his pronounced leftist stand.

Wirth's articles and the proposals in them were received coldly by the conservative leadership in the Center, who found it especially irritating that they appeared so soon after the decision of the National Committee. Wirth seemed to be recommending the establishment of a two-party system in Germany, a move which was considered by Professor Schreiber to be desired only by "naïve, completely unhistorical and impractical minds."[33] Editorials in *Germania* gently but firmly rejected the proposals. The atmosphere was far less favorable to Wirth than it had been the previous summer.

32. Köhler, pp. 181–83.
33. Schreiber, *Politisches Jahrbuch, 1926* (München-Gladbach, 1926), p. 81.

In August 1926, the Catholic Congress convened in Breslau. The separation of this institution from the Center party organization was now complete, and the political overtones were distinctly right wing, although no Nationalist party leaders actually spoke. The featured speakers were Count Lerchenfeld, former minister-president of Bavaria and a monarchist member of the Bavarian People's party, and Princess Starhemberg of the Austrian Christian Social party. The themes of the congress were the fear of widespread defection from the church and the need for unity among German Catholics. If unity of German Catholics meant, in the long run, political unity, and if the Catholics in the BVP, the DNVP, and the Austrian Christian Social party were not willing to change their antirepublican orientation, then the Center would have to accommodate itself to them. Yet by doing so the party would continue to alienate its labor wing, as had already been clearly shown in 1925 and 1926.

There was little sign in the fall of 1926 that the Nationalist party was anxious to establish closer connections with the Center and other middle parties, since its leaders were deliberately pursuing a policy of obstructionism in Marx's government. They abandoned their intransigence briefly in November, however, in order to support the Center's bill "for the protection of youth from trashy and filthy writings" (*Schund-und Schmutzgesetz*), which consequently was passed in the Reichstag against most of the votes of the Democratic and Social Democratic fractions (although it was sponsored by the Democratic Minister of the Interior Wilhelm Külz). The debates on this bill were reminiscent of those at the time of the Lex Heinze in 1899 and recalled the common interest of the Center and the prewar Conservatives in matters of *Kulturpolitik*. The lineup of votes on this otherwise unimportant bill started rumors that a reorganization of the cabinet was imminent, and that *Kulturpolitik* would prove to be the issue on which the Center and DNVP could work together. The Center press insisted that the vote was only an "incident," while the Nationalist paper *Kreuzzeitung* said that the vote had been a tactical error on the part of the Nationalist fraction.[34] These denials did not stop the rumors in the liberal press that some sort of a bargain was in the making between the two parties concerning religion and education.

34. Schreiber, *Politisches Jahrbuch, 1927/28* (München-Gladbach, 1928), p. 66.

While the national Center party was experimenting with a move to the Right, the Prussian party was holding steady to the Left and resisting efforts to break up the Weimar Coalition in that state. The party was proportionally stronger in the *Landtag* than in the Reichstag because although the percentage of Catholic voters was the same in Prussia as in the Reich, in the Reich their votes were divided between the Center and the Bavarian People's party, and the two parties were seldom in agreement. The Prussian party had a very diverse membership, with a strong agrarian wing inherited from the prewar era, led by Karl Herold, described as "frankly the prototype of a property fanatic," and a strong industrial labor wing led by Rudolf Hirtsiefer.[35] Nominal chairman of the *Landtag* fraction was still Felix Porsch, who held the post from 1904 until his death in 1930, but in the later 1920s his role was largely an honorary one and the actual leadership was in the hands of Joseph Hess, chairman from 1930 until his death in 1932. Hess was a master at holding the party together and in keeping it allied with the Social Democrats against the wishes of a number of influential Centrists.

Stegerwald in his brief term as minister-president had managed to antagonize both Social Democrats and Democrats. He had resigned in November 1921, and the new minister-president, Otto Braun, had eventually succeeded in forming a stable government of the Weimar Coalition. Braun and Hess between them were able to deal successfully with the practical issues dividing the Center from the Socialists and the liberals, most especially the problem of the public-school system, which was solved by permitting the Socialists and liberals to proceed with the transformation of formerly Protestant schools into community or secular schools while leaving Catholic denominational schools unchanged.

After the elections of December 1924 when the Luther government was formed in the Reich, the People's party demanded that Braun's Prussian cabinet be "adjusted" in the same way that the national cabinet had been. The Weimar Coalition was not strong enough to survive without the support of the DVP, having only 222 seats, 4 short of an absolute majority, but there was no majority on the Right either, because the opposition was split between the parties of the

---

35. Otto Braun, *Von Weimar zu Hitler* (New York, 1940), pp. 56, 112.

Right and the Communists on the Left. The Prussian Center fraction held that a balance between Reich and Prussian governments was desirable and that a right coalition in the Reich necessitated a left coalition in Prussia, whereas the position of the People's party was that the two should be coordinated. The result was deadlock from January to May 1925.

In February, the *Landtag* elected Marx as minister-president and it seemed possible that he could effect a compromise. He put together a cabinet of Centrists and Democrats with the Social Democrat Carl Severing serving as minister of the interior "without party affiliation," secured Socialist toleration, and hoped to be confirmed with the help of tiny splinter parties which wanted to avoid new elections. Instead, he was brought down in a vote of confidence because of the deliberate absence of four members of the Center fraction, agrarian aristocrats who were determined to block a left coalition in Prussia. Two of them pleaded illness, but Franz von Papen and Friedrich Loenartz made no excuse. This created a furor in the Prussian party, and the rest of the fraction asked the state Executive Council to force Papen and Loenartz to give up their mandates. Papen replied that his mandate was not from the fraction but from his constituents of Westphalia-north, and his action was promptly approved by the agrarian leagues of both Westphalia and the Rhineland, headed by Freiherr von Loë and Freiherr von Kerckerinck zur Borg respectively, and by the Agricultural Advisory Council of the Westphalian Center party. Papen recalled in his memoirs that "it was not so easy to get rid of such an uncomfortable frondeur."[36]

The majority of the provincial party organizations in Prussia were furious with Papen and his friends who were numerically so few but socially so prominent. At the heavily attended Rhenish Center Party Congress held in April, Loë attacked not only the Prussian coalition but the entire postwar policy of the Center party. He admitted the numerical minority of the aristocrats but implied that more than ordinary weight should be given to agriculture in the party councils because it was "the most important class." His speech aroused loud protests, and Hess declared that he should not be permitted to injure the party's interests in such a way. Loë then left the hall, and the remain-

36. Franz von Papen, *Memoirs* (London, 1952), p. 106; Bach, pp. 65–71.

ing delegates voted unanimously to support Marx as minister-president.[37]

None of the "frondeurs" was expelled from the party, and they continued to hold the balance of power in the *Landtag* until the elections of 1928 gave the parties of Weimar a less precarious backing. Marx's candidacy for the national presidency obliged him to give up state office, and the 1925 cabinet crisis was finally ended in May with the formation of a new Braun government of the Weimar Coalition. The agrarian dissidents modified their demands after Hindenburg's election (which a number of them openly supported), and only two, including Papen, were absent when a vote of censure by the Nationalist party was proposed, so that Braun was sustained by a bare majority. The Center fraction continued to consider the widening of the coalition throughout 1925 but without conviction. From then until 1932, as the national party oriented itself more to the Right, its leaders could pacify the left wing by pointing to the balancing effect of the Left coalition in Prussia, which demonstrated that the Center was truly of the middle.

A look at Center policy in the southwest reveals the flexibility of the party and its regional diversity, as well as the paramount importance of educational issues at the state level. In Hesse, the Weimar Coalition organized after the revolution in 1919 remained in office harmoniously until 1930. In Baden, the revolution brought the defeat of the liberal establishment of the prewar era and gave power to the Center more in proportion to the numbers of Catholics in the state.[38] Baden was 58 percent Catholic in the postwar years, one of the highest percentages of any region in Germany. Loyalty to the Center among Catholic voters was not so high as in Württemberg or the Rhineland, however, probably because of its strong liberal tradition. Nevertheless, the Center fraction was much the largest in the *Landtag*, with over one-third of the seats. From the first days of the revolution, the Center was represented in the government. Transition to the republic was smoothed by the quick acceptance of the situation by Archbishop Nörber of Freiburg, who had close ties to the party dating from the

37. *Kölnische Volkszeitung*, 16 Apr. 1925.
38. Information on Baden from Karl Dees, "Die Krisis der Weimar Koalition in Baden," *Die Hilfe* 32(15 Sept. 1926): 382–84, and *Frankfurter Zeitung*, Nov. 1925–Nov. 1926, passim.

prewar years when church and party worked together to combat the liberal government. These close ties with the church were loosened after Nörber's death in 1920, and many clergy gave up political interests or turned to the Right, as they did in other parts of Germany.[39] There were always a large number of clergy in the *Landtag* fraction, however, and the party was headed by Prelate Joseph Schofer after Theodor Wacker's death.

Until 1925, the Center governed in a Weimar Coalition, which controlled two-thirds of the seats in the legislature. The first state president was a Social Democrat; later a Centrist, Heinrich Köhler, served for a year in 1923–24 and was then replaced by a Democrat, Willy Hellpach (candidate of his party for the Reich presidency in the first presidential election). Hellpach had also served as minister of education for Baden and was an enthusiastic defender of the state's "simultaneous," or community, schools. The Center in Baden (as in Hesse) had seemed to be content to retain the community schools, because although they were interdenominational they guaranteed separate religious instruction and separate training for teachers of religious instruction classes. But in 1925, when the national Center began agitating for a school bill which would ensure the extension of denominational schools into Baden and Hesse, the state party turned against the Baden system and against Hellpach. The *Landtag* fraction demanded that the Education Ministry be given to a Centrist. The Democrats refused and withdrew from the cabinet. The Center then arranged a temporary cabinet with the Social Democrats, since the two parties between them commanded a majority of forty-four out of seventy-two seats. Discussions were then held about the possible inclusion of the People's party in the government, with or without the Democrats. The numerical strength of the DVP in Baden was negligible, but the Center hoped to be able to leaven the two-party cabinet, while the Democrats wanted to strengthen the anticlerical forces. The People's party refused to join if the Education Ministry were given to a Centrist. In this crisis there was a deep rift between the liberals, with their long-standing anticlerical tradition, and the Center, whose policy of the "middle" ceased to exist when clerical issues were at stake. In these quarrels, the Socialists usually showed themselves less adamant

39. Köhler, pp. 150–58.

than the liberals, which proved to be the case in this instance.

During the Baden crisis the rump cabinet continued in office, with the Education Ministry being jointly occupied by the ministerial director, a Centrist, and the Socialist minister of the interior. For the time being, the Center wielded the decisive influence. The liberals accused the Socialists of allowing themselves to be pushed around by the Centrists, which they vigorously denied. As the year wore on and no reconciliation took place between the Center and the Democratic party, more areas of conflict between the two former allies were noticed for the first time. The Center accused the Democrats of being hostile to farmers. Prelate Schofer tried to appeal to the almost nonexistent particularism of Baden Catholics against the "secularism and centralism" of the Democrats. Finally, as continued and exclusive proximity to the Social Democrats was making the Center uncomfortable, negotiations for a readjustment of the cabinet were begun again in November 1926, a full year after the conflict began.

The final settlement was a compromise: the Democrats reentered the government and received the controversial Education Ministry, but another, less well known party member held it in place of Hellpach. The Center kept the ministries of Finance and Justice as before, and in addition received the office of minister-president, filled by Köhler who was also serving as finance minister for the Reich at that time. The Socialists kept their man in the Ministry of the Interior. The People's party was not represented after all, because of the technical difficulty that there were only four seats in the cabinet and there was no ministry left.

The break in the bloc of "middle" parties which occurred in Baden in 1925 was a preview of events in the national government in 1927. It was to become evident that the Center's alliance with the liberal parties was not much more stable than its temporary partnerships with Socialists or Nationalists.

In the neighboring state of Württemberg, a completely different coalition policy was being followed by the state Center party. While in Baden the Center governed in tandem with the Social Democrats, excluding the liberals because of differences over *Kulturpolitik*, in Württemberg after 1924 the Center governed with the Nationalists, excluding both Socialists and liberals, because of differences over social and economic policy. Würtemberg's percentage of Catholics in the population was only about 31 percent, but loyalty to the Center was higher here than anywhere in Germany except the "diaspora" regions where Catholics formed a tiny and defensive minority.[40]

The prewar state party had been led by agrarians, reflecting economic interests in the state. After the revolution, the party had governed amicably in a Weimar Coalition, under a Social Democratic minister-president until 1920 and then under Democratic leadership.[41] With these parties the Center had legislated on such crucial matters as the new state constitution and new church and school regulations. In 1920, there were five deputies in the *Landtag* from the Christian trade unions, among them Josef Andre, a prominent member of the Reichstag fraction as well. Their number declined in later elections until in 1928 there were only two representatives of labor in the fraction, and the agrarians regained their prewar importance. The state party had stood by Erzberger steadily in his difficulties, but after his death, conservatives began to steer the state party to the Right in order to prevent Catholic farmers from transferring their allegiance to the Nationalist party.

The Nationalist party in Württemberg was organized as the *Bürgerpartei und Bauernbund* (not connected in any way with the independent Bavarian *Bauernbund*) of which the agrarian half, the Farmers' and Winegrowers' League, was by far the most powerful. The *Bauernbund* had been trying for years to lure Catholic farmers and winegrowers away from the Center with promises of reduction of property taxes on farms and other incentives to agriculture. The Center leadership believed the party's position would be safeguarded if it joined rather than opposed the *Bauernbund*, because it, too, relied much more on farmers than on urban dwellers for its votes. The two parties could then work together to promote a clerical education policy, which had been impossible when cooperation with the Democrats had been necessary. The Democratic party's defeat in the elec-

---

40. Schauff, p. 15; Brecht, *Federalism and Regionalism in Germany* (New York, 1945), p. 42.
41. Information on Württemberg from Wilhelm Keil, "Der Fall Württemberg," *Deutsche Republik* 2 (1928): 1214–17; Johannes Fischer, "Die Rechtsregierung in Württemberg," *Die Hilfe* 34(15 Jan. 1928): 28–29, and "Das politische Gesicht Württembergs," *Die Hilfe* 34(1 Aug. 1928): 349–51; *Frankfurter Zeitung*, 15 July 1925.

tions of May 1924 left the way clear for realignment of the coalition parties.

In the new *Landtag,* out of a total of eighty seats, the Nationalists held twenty-five and the Center seventeen. Since the fractions of the Democratic and People's parties refused to support any government formed by these two parties because of their clericalism and frank hostility to industry, the Nationalists and Centrists governed alone. Stuttgart was the only capital outside Bavaria where the Center ever took part in such a coalition.

In the new government the Center controlled the ministries of Justice and the Interior; the positions of minister-president and minister of education were held by the Nationalist Wilhelm Bazille, a man detested by both Left and liberal parties but defended and praised by the Center. The opposition in the *Landtag* was astonished that the Center agreed to Bazille as minister-president, for he had been almost boorishly critical of the previous governments and of the republic. He was credited with having said that "everything the leaders of democracy had done was either stupid, unnecessary, laughable or dangerous," and he had been openly admiring of Kahr's actions in Bavaria. Curiously enough, he was criticized by the Left for being a foreigner (his father had been French and had never become a German citizen, even during the war) but was not thought the less of by the Right for that fact. The policy of the Württemberg Center in approving of this man was deplored by a great many Centrists in the national party, but because of the loose organizational ties of the Center, it was not possible for the Reich party councils to dictate the policy of any state party. In any case, the party leadership would not have cared to interfere and risk another secession like that of the Bavarians.

Like the Center in Württemberg, the Bavarian People's party became dependent upon a partnership with the Nationalist party, but whereas in Württemberg the Center was a minority party, the BVP always controlled the largest bloc of seats in the *Landtag.* Its dependence upon the much smaller Nationalist party and upon even smaller splinter groups was caused not by numerical weakness but by a stubborn refusal to cooperate with Social Democracy. In the immediate aftermath of the Hitler *Putsch,* the party was anxious to cut its ties with the radical Right, wanted nothing to do with the *völkisch* parties, and urged that Franz Gürtner, Nationalist minister of justice, be removed from office because he had shown Hitler and his followers such lenience at their trial. But the election of May 1924 brought in a solid *völkisch* bloc of twenty-three seats in the legislature, and the Nationalists insisted not only upon keeping Gürtner in office but on inviting the *völkisch* parties to participate in negotiations for a new government. Since the BVP rejected even the possibility of a Left coalition, it lacked all bargaining power in the negotiations. Fortunately for the BVP leadership, the *völkisch* bloc was not seriously interested in the responsibilities of government, but the Nationalists persisted in retaining Gürtner, and after a prolonged crisis of fifty-three days they achieved their wish.[42] Gürtner stayed on as minister of justice in Bavaria until he left to take office as minister of justice in Papen's national government in 1932 and Hitler's in 1933.

Held agreed at this time to govern openly, now that the bureaucratic old guard had been thoroughly discredited by the actions of Kahr and Knilling, and accepted the office of minister-president. He kept the party firmly against reconciliation with the Center through 1924 and against any participation in a Reich cabinet in which Social Democrats were included. When Luther's right-wing cabinet was formed in the Reich in January 1925, the BVP was willing to join it, but significantly, its representative, Karl Stingl, the post office minister, was not a member of the BVP Reichstag fraction, which was always distrusted by Munich as too liable to be corrupted by contact with Berlin and the national Center party.

---

42. Richard Kessler, *Heinrich Held als Parlamentarier: Eine Teilbiographie, 1868–1924* (Berlin, 1971), p. 517; Schönhoven, pp. 96–106.

16
RETURN TO *KULTURPOLITIK*: THE MARX
GOVERNMENT OF 1927

The internal debate over political orientation and coalition policy which raged in the Center during the three years of 1924 through 1926 was temporarily ended or at least muted in 1927 when the party united in an effort to obtain several long-sought goals in the field of religion and education. Although the Weimar Constitution had given the Catholic church a position of great security and even privilege in Germany, it had not ensured the continuation of Catholic schools, and it had not established a legal relationship with the Vatican. A school law acceptable to Catholics and a national concordat with the papacy were important demands in the Center party program. Success in satisfying these demands was seriously jeopardized, however, by events in 1925 in Bavaria.

By 1925 the Bavarian People's party had given up hope of interesting the rest of the country in its federalist program, but in the spring of that year national attention was focused on a particular federalist issue which proved to be highly controversial: the question of the constitutionality of a Bavarian Concordat with the Vatican. Before the establishment of the republic, several of the *Länder* including Bavaria had had treaties with the Vatican concerning the organization of dioceses, the financing of the church, and education in the denominational schools. There was some doubt that these treaties were still binding for the republic; in any case, there was need for revision. A national concordat had not been possible under the empire because the kingdom of Prussia and most of the other states had been bound to the established Evangelical churches. When the Weimar Constitution disestablished the Evangelical churches the way seemed clear for the conclusion of some sort of national agreement. In that event, there would be no need for separate state treaties.

Centrist members of the new republican government opened negotiations with representatives of the Vatican and in 1921, during Wirth's chancellorship, a draft for a concordat was actually approved by President Ebert. The draft was little more than a restatement of the clauses in the constitution concerning religion. There was some feeling in official circles that a concordat might help Germany's diplomatic position and counteract the supposed partiality of the Vatican toward France. Negotiations were discontinued, however, partly because of more pressing issues and partly because of strenuous opposition from the Bavarians, who claimed that a national treaty would infringe upon the rights of the individual states.[1]

As soon as plans for a *Reichskonkordat* had definitely been abandoned, Papal Nuncio Eugenio Pacelli transferred his headquarters to Munich, where he began conferring with members of the Bavarian government about the preparation of a draft for a Bavarian concordat. The final version of this treaty was ratified and promulgated in January 1925. Constitutional justification for such a treaty was found in Article 78, which stated: "In matters whose regulation is under state jurisdiction, the states can conclude treaties with foreign states; the treaties must be approved by the Reich government." It is likely that this clause was inserted for the express purpose of making possible a Bavarian Concordat.[2] It is worth noting, however, that an official Reich approval was given neither to the Bavarian nor to the Prussian Concordat (concluded in 1929), although in both cases the government in office sent informal assurances to the respective state governments that the treaties did not violate the constitution.[3]

The Bavarian treaty of 1925 was extremely favorable to the interests of the Catholic church. Its ratification by the *Landtag* was possible only because of the numerical strength of the BVP and its political prudence, the former ensuring nearly enough votes to pass the treaty unaided and the latter providing simultaneously with the Catholic treaty a generous agreement with the Bavarian Protestant churches. With the support of the Nationalists, who were appeased by

1. Schreiber, *Zwischen Demokratie und Diktatur*, pp. 75–80.
2. Heinrich Oppenheimer, *The Constitution of the German Republic* (London, 1922), pp. 27–28.
3. Information on the Bavarian Concordat from Nikolaus Hilling, "Das bayrische Konkordat," *Hochland* 12 (1925): 675–79.

the equal privileges accorded to the Protestant churches, the concordat was put through over the clamorous opposition of all the other parties in the legislature.

Most of the provisions of the treaty were offensive to the opposition merely in principle, for they were the same formal statements found in previous agreements between state and church: the basic framework of this treaty was the same as that used later in the Prussian Concordat and in the *Reichskonkordat* of 1933. The state agreed to continue specified financial aid to the church, to respect the freedom and independence of its organization, and to permit a church veto on undesirable appointments to the faculty of state theological schools. The church, in return, agreed to allow the state a veto on high church appointments (a veto which the national constitution forbade a state to "impose" but which could presumably be "permitted") and to allow as bishops, heads of orders, priests, or teachers only German citizens educated in Germany. There was little in these clauses to account for the storm of protest which arose from all over Germany, except insofar as anticlericals might resent the consolidation of church power and centralists begrudge the states the right to conclude such agreements. The clauses which aroused protest were those which conceded almost complete freedom to the Catholic church in its direction of Bavaria's denominational schools. Whereas previously the fact that all teachers in the Catholic elementary schools were Catholic ensured in practice that the instruction would be likely to be orthodox, the concordat now explicitly gave to the church the right to exclude anything from the curriculum that was in any way hostile to Catholic teaching: "The instruction and education of the children in Catholic *Volksschulen* will be entrusted only to such teachers as are suitable and are prepared to instruct in Catholic doctrine in a dependable fashion, and to educate in the spirit of the Catholic faith." Similar provisions were included for secondary schools, and the Bavarian government agreed that at least one professor of history and one of philosophy at the universities of Munich and Würzburg were to be acceptable to the bishops of Bavaria.

No doubt the actual conditions in Bavarian schools were changed very little by these provisions, but liberals and Socialists saw in them the destruction, the very negation of the principle of state public education. Moreover, they felt that the fact that the Bavarian government had taken upon itself the right to make such an agreement was an insolent denial of national supremacy in educational policy, a supremacy that was guaranteed in the constitution. Indignation of the non-Catholic population over the Bavarian Concordat made any immediate plans for a national treaty impossible to realize, although that had been an important plank in the Center's platform for 1924 and 1925.

The Luther government of 1925 was embarrassed by a Social Democratic interpellation in the Reichstag protesting the concordat. The motion read: "The Bavarian government has presented to the Bavarian *Landtag* the draft of a blanket law containing a *concordat* with the Catholic church and treaties with the Protestant churches. These . . . treaties violate the Reich constitution in many respects. Does the Reich government know this fact? What does it intend to do in defense of the Reich constitution?"[4] It is interesting to note, in the light of later events, that Deputy Wilhelm Frick speaking for the National Socialists was vehemently opposed to the idea of a future *Reichskonkordat.*

The Luther government did nothing to challenge the Bavarian Concordat but was sufficiently impressed by the debate to postpone indefinitely the negotiations which had been started for a Reich treaty with the Vatican.[5]

The Center's delegation in the Reichstag was of course sympathetic to the Bavarians in the debate over the concordat, but many of them felt that the unfavorable public reaction hurt the chances for a national treaty. Relations between the two parties were further strained during the presidential election campaign of that year when the BVP's endorsement of Hindenburg lost Marx the election. Foreign policy disagreements also kept the breach from healing; the Bavarian People's party denounced the Treaty of Locarno and opposed Germany's entry into the League of Nations. In the final Reichstag vote, the Bavarian fraction did accept the Locarno treaty, but several of its members abstained in the vote on league entry, and Held made a number of speeches on foreign policy in 1925 and 1926 which seriously embarrassed the Reich government and the Center party. The conflict between Wirth and the Center's conservatives also did nothing to pro-

---

4. *Verhandlungen des Reichstags* 386 (17 June 1925): 2368, 2400–2402.
5. Schreiber, p. 92.

mote unity between the two Catholic parties. However, by the end of 1925, opposition to reunion was growing weaker in the Bavarian party. Its party congress in December modified its monarchist stand and left the question of the form of government to the individual conscience, with change to be effected only by constitutional means.[6] A year later, Held and the party chairman Speck asked the party congress to approve a reconciliation, if the Center could be brought to make some federalist concessions. The formation of Marx's rightist coalition in January, 1927 provided the opportunity for such an agreement.

Marx's minority government was overthrown in December 1926 as a result of an attack by the Socialist Philipp Scheidemann on its army policy. The Social Democratic motion of no-confidence was seconded by the DNVP, not because that party in any way agreed with Scheidemann's opinions, but because it had been seeking an opportunity to bring down the government and form a new right-wing coalition. This was also President Hindenburg's intention.[7] But the key to the formation of a rightist coalition lay with the Center, which was hopelessly divided on the question of cooperation with the Nationalists in a government. The usual lengthy negotiations began, which as in earlier government crises had the effect of giving more and more initiative into the hands of the President.[8]

The Center fraction appeared to be immovable in its insistence upon a cabinet of the middle, but the liberal press had been reporting for months that *Kulturpolitik* was to be the basis of an agreement between the Center and the DNVP, and that the Nationalists' cooperation over the *Schund- und Schmutz* bill had been an invitation to join forces on this basis, in order to achieve a favorable school law and a national concordat. The Center fraction denied any such collusion, and concrete evidence is lacking, but the course of events is suggestive that a bargain was indeed struck.

At the same time that Marx, Stegerwald, and Wirth were assuring the press that the Center could not possibly join a right-wing government, and Stresemann was trying to effect a compromise (perhaps that the Nationalists should have a single liaison man in the cabinet, or that the Center should tolerate a rightist cabinet without actually en-

6. Schönhoven, pp. 176–78.
7. Stürmer, pp. 172–80.
8. Eyck, 2:102–3.

tering it), Prelate Kaas, Guerard, Brüning, and Brauns were considering offering the DNVP "three or four seats" in a cabinet to be headed by Marx; and Prelate Leicht of the BVP, acting as intermediary, was negotiating with Westarp, the Nationalist fraction head. The decisive event was the dispatching of a letter to Marx by President Hindenburg virtually ordering him to form a rightist (*bürgerlich*) cabinet. The letter, which may have been suggested by Brauns and Guerard, permitted the Center's leaders to claim to be acting under a "state of compulsion" (*Zwangslage*), but this was not convincing to the party's left wing. Wirth's friend Teipel wrote that "the independence of the fraction was sold with behind-the-scenes work and sham maneuvers."[9]

The new government included three Nationalists, one of whom, Minister of the Interior Walter von Keudell, had been closely identified with the Kapp *Putsch*. His special interest was in religious and educational affairs. There were two Centrists in addition to Marx, Brauns for Labor and Köhler for Finance. Stresemann kept the Foreign Ministry, and there was one other man from the People's party and one from the Bavarian People's party. The Democratic party, suspicious of clerical intrigues, had refused to join the coalition, and Gessler, who remained as minister of defense, was obliged to resign his membership in that party. The composition of the cabinet provoked considerable indignation within Center ranks, but the Reichstag fraction was finally persuaded to endorse it after the drawing up of a long list of conditions which the DNVP must accept, a so-called manifesto similar to the guidelines written in 1925 for the Luther government. Wirth, however, after helping to compose the manifesto, again withdrew from the fraction and joined the opposition for the duration of the government, a move which was "regretted" by the fraction's executive committee.

Whatever the motives for the formation of the coalition may have been, it is certain that the *Kultur* experts in both concerned parties wasted no time in preparing the way for a national concordat and a school bill. Keudell, a devout Protestant himself, made two crucial changes in the Ministry of the Interior as a preliminary step: Heinrich

9. Becker, "Brüning, Prälat Kaas und das Problem einer Regierungsbeteiligung der N.S.D.A.P. 1930–1932," *Historische Zeitschrift* 196 (1963) :76; Eric Sutton, ed., *Gustav Stresemann: His Diaries, Letters, and Papers*, 3 vols. (London, 1935–40), 3:107–9; Morsey, *Protokolle*, 1:80–90; Grünthal, pp. 201–4; *Frankfurter Zeitung*, 21 Jan. 1927, 29 July 1927, 23 Aug. 1927 for Teipel.

Schulz, a Social Democrat who had written three books on the necessity for a national school system, was replaced as state secretary for educational questions by a Centrist, Ludwig Pellenpahr; and Arnold Brecht, a democrat and a liberal, was replaced as head of the constitutional division by a man of much more conservative views.[10] These changes ensured agreement within the ministry for the legislation which Keudell and Marx intended to draft.

As it turned out, no amount of bargaining or secret agreement between the Center and the Nationalist party could provide them with enough votes to override the opposition of every other party in the Reichstag. The DNVP itself was split on religious and educational issues and had a vocal anticlerical wing. It was a constant disappointment to the Center that Nationalist support of Protestant interests was never as enthusiastic as Centrist support of Catholic interests, since the only hope for the preservation of church rights and privileges in a country with the population distribution of Germany lay in enlisting the support of both denominations. In the Weimar period the DNVP proved a very weak reed in defense of "Christian" policies.

Shortly after the new government took office, Nuncio Pacelli again began meeting with Centrist representatives in order to prepare a draft for a national concordat. The proposed treaty contained no references to education like those in the Bavarian Concordat, but with memories of that controversy still fresh, it was unlikely that the Center would succeed in getting approval for it, whatever the wording; as a matter of fact, the Vatican had repeatedly indicated that it placed little value on a treaty that did not mention education. Not only could the opposition parties be expected to object to a treaty but the German People's party, in spite of its eagerness to join a rightist coalition, was by no means reconciled to clerical legislation as a condition of its existence. Stresemann did his best to mediate between the Center and his party on this issue, but he found himself accused by his colleagues of supporting the "machinations of the Vatican" and of "lapsing" on the concordat question. It was true that he had formerly been a member of an avowedly anticlerical organization, the Liberal Union, founded in the spring of 1926 by representatives of the two liberal parties. One of the union's goals was the combatting of a national concordat, and

10. Grünthal, p. 209; Stürmer, p. 233; Braun, p. 225.

when the Marx-Keudell cabinet was formed it was denounced by the union as a conspiracy which was intended to impose confessional schools and a concordat upon the country.

In March 1927 Stresemann tried to assure his party that the DVP leadership would never tolerate a reactionary policy in religious and educational matters. This had in turn alarmed the Center, and Kaas and Guerard had been deputized to convince the foreign minister to change his stand and to assure him that the proposed *Reichskonkordat* would not resemble the Bavarian treaty and would not even mention education. Stresemann, anxious to hold the cabinet together for the sake of his foreign policy, thereupon dissociated himself from the Liberal Union. In April he spoke out in favor of the concordat at a meeting of the People's party and was sharply opposed by his listeners.[11] The next week he repeated his views in the Reichstag: "There is no divergence between the foreign minister and the party leader. . . . If you want to know my personal opinion, I won't try to hide the fact that, since a concordat has been concluded in Bavaria, and we are ultimately to be confronted with the conclusion of a concordat between Prussia and the Vatican, I believe that it is desirable that there should be a *Reichskonkordat.*" He added that he had been assured by Kaas and other Centrists that there would be no concessions in education like those made for Bavaria.[12]

Stresemann's sole success was in persuading his party, in May, not to join a projected Democratic motion against a concordat. If the DVP had participated in such a motion, the coalition might well have broken up then. It seemed by the summer of 1927 that the possibility of concluding a *Reichskonkordat* was as remote as it had been in 1921 and 1925. This did not convince the Center to abandon the matter, and Dr. Kaas in particular made it clear that so far as he was concerned it was one of the most important planks in the party platform. In September, at the Catholic Congress in Dortmund, Kaas spoke of his conviction in very strong terms:

> It is difficult, actually impossible, to go further with the question of a concordat at this moment and in this position. . . . But this much can and must be said with . . . all clarity: German Ca-

11. Sutton, 3:286–89.
12. *Verhandlungen des Reichstags* 393 (5 Apr. 1927): 10506–8; Stürmer, p. 232.

tholicism sees in the concordat problem no question of secondary or subordinate importance. . . . We German Catholics see in the concluding of an agreement between the new German people's state and the Catholic church the *test* of whether or not the new democracy and the organization which serves its purposes is prepared to help build for the . . . Catholic a structure on German soil in which he can live and work according to the teachings and precepts of his faith.[13]

Six years later, Kaas was able to negotiate the Concordat of 1933 after the "new democracy and the organization which serves its purposes" had been replaced by the National Socialist regime.

The Center had greater hopes, at first, for the passage of a favorable school bill. The draft prepared by Keudell was actually the latest in a series of drafts which had been drawn up but never brought before the Reichstag. The intent of all of them was to ensure the preservation and if possible the extension of the denominational school system.

The official Center interpretation of the school clauses in the constitution had come to be that they provided equality among the three kinds of schools, confessional, community, and secular, although this interpretation contradicted Article 146 which explicitly stated that the community school "is the rule" and was to be preferred over the other two forms in a national school system. In 1919 and 1920, with the memory of anticlerical acts by the Prussian and other state governments still fresh, Centrist speakers and newspapers had acknowledged this. Marx himself wrote in private letters on several occasions that according to the constitution, new schools would have to be community schools and parents would have to petition for separate denominational schools.[14] But by 1921, pressure from the episcopacy and the Catholic School Organization (headed by Marx) had led many of the party's *Kulturpolitiker* to adopt the interpretation of the equality of the three kinds of schools. The Catholic School Organization was nonpartisan, which is to say that it had many supporters from the Catholic Committee of the DNVP, who were not overly concerned with fidelity to the Weimar Constitution.

The first Reich school law draft was prepared during Fehrenbach's chancellorship. The Center hoped to have Social Democratic coopera-

13. Schreiber, p. 133.
14. Stehkämper, 2:409; Grünthal, pp. 88–92.

tion in committee because of the draft's recognition of the equality of secular schools with the other forms of schools. Discussions broke down, however, over the question of the number of students to be required for the establishment of an elementary school. The Center insisted that this be as low as forty children, a one-class "dwarf" school, like so many of the existing Catholic schools in areas of mixed denominations, while the Socialists wanted the size to be large enough for at least four classes. The Catholic School Organization blamed the breakdown of discussions on the Center's attempt to cooperate with the Socialists, and Cardinal Faulhaber singled out this failure and the constitutional school clauses for special attack in his speech at the Catholic Congress of August 1922.[15] At the beginning of 1924 this school law draft was scrapped completely because of the impossibility of agreement and also because of the precarious financial situation of the country.

By the terms of Article 174 of the constitution, until a Reich law should be passed, former school systems were to be maintained in the states, and this meant that legally, no completely secular schools at all could be established, since none had existed before the war. This was a grievance to the Social Democrats who tried, after the failure of the 1922 draft, to arrange for emergency legislation to permit the establishment of secular schools in Prussia. Their plan would also have permitted construction of new denominational schools, but the Center rejected it because of unwillingness to give secular schools any legal advantage. In practice, however, the Prussian state government was quietly proceeding to secularize a high proportion of formerly Protestant denominational schools after obtaining the consent of the parents involved, and this was done with the tacit approval of Hess and the Prussian *Landtag* Center fraction. "The Center in all these questions allowed a certain latitude when Protestant areas were being dealt with, but resisted any departure from the legal state of affairs' favorable to its *Weltanschauung* in those areas where Catholicism predominated."[16] Secular schools were privately regarded as useful by many Centrists; they prevented the Socialists from making common cause with the liberals to demand implementation of community schools as

15. Morsey, *Zentrumspartei*, p. 477.
16. Braun, p. 230.

"the rule" and they prevented "unsuitable" children from attending denominational schools and undermining them with atheist propaganda.[17] Publicly, however, it was unadvisable to express these sentiments.

By the end of 1925 the Center's chances of obtaining a favorable school law had worsened because it no longer had much support from the Bavarian People's party. The Bavarians were afraid that a Reich law might overrule the terms of the Bavarian Concordat. Nuncio Pacelli had obtained a statement from the Reich government in 1920 that the concordat, as yet unwritten, "will not be disturbed by later Reich laws" but it was by no means certain that this was binding upon future governments.

A second factor hurting the Center's position was that in Luther's government of 1925 the Nationalist party had prepared a draft for a school law which not only favored confessional schools but made the establishment of secular schools almost impossible. The Center Party and the Catholic School Organization were at first attracted by this draft but finally rejected it because it left most of the implementation to the states and did not sufficiently protect private schools in areas where one confession was in a small minority. The Nationalist draft received a great deal of adverse publicity and hurt the chances of the Center's own program by its alienation of the Social Democrats.

Marx was clearly aware of how little real support the Center could expect from the DNVP on religious issues. He wrote in July 1925 to Pope Pius XI that "the parties of the Right are *no more* the conservative parties of earlier years. . . . A large element in them is animated by a growing hostility to everything Catholic," and he concluded sadly in a private letter, at the end of the year, not only that it would be very difficult to conclude a suitable school law with the Left but that "with the Right it is not much different. . . . It is more and more evident that in these questions of *Kultur* we stand entirely alone!"[18]

In 1926 the liberal Interior Minister Külz, of the Democratic party, drew up a draft for a school law which strongly favored community schools, and there was a serious possibility that if the liberal parties could make up their differences with the Social Democrats that that

17. Stehkämper, 2:403; Grünthal, p. 290.
18. Stehkämper, 2:378; Grünthal, pp. 184–85.

party would accept such a law. The draft was violently denounced by Martin Spahn of the Catholic Committee of the DNVP, who called it, among other things, a "brutal attack by world Jewry" and condemned the Center for participating in a cabinet that would even consider it.[19] This put the Center on the spot and made it vulnerable to the Nationalists' overtures in December and January. Abandonment of the alarming Külz draft and preparation of a new bill in which the Center could take the initiative—these were to be the justifications for joining a rightist government.

The 1927 draft was prepared in strict secrecy with no liaison with the state governments, which was to create problems with the Reichsrat later in the year. To minimize controversy, it was timed to be made public in July, when the Reichstag was not in session, but this hope was in vain. In an ominous prelude, a Centrist bill for the prolongation of the existence of private schools, intended by the constitution to be phased out by 1928, was decisively defeated in February.

The school bill, sponsored by Keudell and Marx, declared the equality of the three kinds of schools but actually favored denominational schools over the other two since it required a petition by parents to establish a new type of school, and the vast majority of existing German schools were at least nominally of the denominational type.[20] The number of children needed to justify a new school was set at the very low figure of forty, which would permit the replacement of the old one- or two-class Catholic private schools with similar public schools in areas where Catholics formed a small minority.

Altogether, the bill was as favorable to the Center's interests as was possible. The question was, how could it be sold to the People's party, staunch advocates of community schools? The DVP delegation had been annoyed at the Center's refusal to accept Julius Curtius as chancellor but had been so anxious to take part in a rightist coalition that they had consented to serve under Marx, in spite of protests from the liberal press about a "clerical conspiracy" for a school bill. But as the parliamentary committee began its consideration of the Keudell draft the party's representatives grew more and more uncomfortable with it, and their misgivings came to focus on the question of the

19. Grünthal, p. 190.
20. Ibid., p. 294.

retention of the "simultaneous" schools of Baden and Hesse. Curtius himself, the minister of economics, was from Baden and like most of its citizens was proud of its school system. There had been little or no agitation for change in recent years even from the Baden Center party, until a recent campaign by Dr. Ernst Föhr, and most of the community schools in the state were exclusively of one denomination anyway because of the residence patterns, except in a few large cities.[21] The Keudell draft not only threatened to disrupt the existing system by permitting change by parental petition but opened the way for the introduction of secular schools in the southwest, and possibly even into Bavaria, for the first time.

DVP committee members inevitably brought up again the constitutional statement, so troublesome for the Center, that the community school was to be "the rule," and they proposed that no special petition be necessary to establish one, giving it preference over the other two types of schools. The Democratic party strongly supported the DVP in this. The Social Democratic party, as shown when the bill became the subject of public debate, was divided on the question, with very many of its fraction more inclined to support community schools, as being more democratic and less socially divisive, than to continue to be pacified by the provision for secular schools as a kind of third "denomination." If the Center had continued the tactics used by its representatives in effecting the First Weimar School Compromise in 1919, it might have worked out a reasonable compromise with the Socialists, as it had done informally in Prussia, but a bill sponsored by the Marx-Keudell coalition was sure to be opposed by the SPD.

The bill was sent to the Reichsrat at the end of the summer and met with great resistance from the state representatives. Prussia presented its own counterdraft, but it was defeated partly because of objections from the provincial delegates from Silesia and the Rhineland. No final decision was taken by the Reichsrat because the Reichstag committee reached an impasse, making it impossible for the bill to survive. A DVP motion to exempt Baden, Hesse, and Nassau from the provisions of the bill was accepted by a majority in the committee but absolutely vetoed by the Center.

Such stubbornness on this one seemingly minor point baffled

21. Ibid., p. 213.

many observers, including Stresemann, who wrote later that he could not understand why the Center would not agree to compromise rather than see the bill meet certain defeat. Heinrich Köhler, Centrist minister of finance and former president of Baden, also wrote later that he did not believe that this single issue could have been the sole reason for the failure of the bill and the subsequent breakup of the cabinet.[22] The reason behind the refusal of the Centrists on the committee to compromise probably lay in Article 174 of the constitution. If a new law could not improve upon the "existing legal situation" it was not worth having, in the minds of Kaas, Schreiber, Rheinländer, and Föhr, the education specialists in the party, three of whom were clerics. The Center had been trying to introduce true denominational schools into the southwestern states for decades; to concede an exception in their case would be to admit defeat and court bitter recrimination from the Catholic School Organization and the Nationalist Catholics. It was true that it was hard to imagine a more auspicious opportunity of achieving a satisfactory school bill than this, *within the Weimar parliamentary system*, but the Nationalist Catholic Committee had been saying all along that Catholic goals would be more attainable in an authoritarian regime, and Monsignor Kaas openly agreed with them at the Catholic Congress in Dortmund in 1927. Marx's sincere efforts to explain the difficulties of a Catholic minority in a democratic state met with deaf ears.

The school bill could not be passed unamended, and the Center would not agree to the People's party's amendment. Each party blamed the other for the failure of the bill and for the breakup of the government. Only Hindenburg's urgent plea to Marx to conclude vital current business held the cabinet together for a few more weeks. The Center fraction was actually delighted to see an end to this government because it had been extremely unpopular with a large section of the voters and with many fraction members themselves. The party had been continually embarrassed by belligerent foreign policy pronouncements by Nationalists, who had by the end of the year broken most of the terms of the "manifesto" they had agreed to at the time the coalition was formed.

In addition, Brauns as labor minister was constantly at odds with

---

22. Köhler, p. 265; Stresemann, from Sutton, 3:293–95.

Curtius and other People's party leaders on questions of social policy;[23] and Centrist labor delegates in the Reichstag were growing increasingly dissatisfied with the government's labor policy. They had been hotly opposed to the law passed that year providing generous raises in civil servants' salaries. Stegerwald had regained favor with his old rival Imbusch over this issue, and he no longer believed that the DNVP was an ideal political partner for the Center. He may even have hoped to win over some of the membership of the Socialist unions to his own movement by contesting the civil servants' raises, since the Social Democratic party had supported them.[24]

The labor representatives in the Center fraction broke party discipline to vote against the civil servants' raises, but they did not go so far as to refuse to support the coalition itself, as some of them had done in 1925. Wirth, however, launched a second "crusade" against it, and he carried on a vigorous speaking campaign in the spring and summer of 1927, visiting local organizations of the *Reichsbanner* throughout the country. He declared that "I am not traveling through Germany in order to found a new party. . . . I am leading a fight for the honor of the German Center party." He accused the Nationalist party of leading the Center astray by pretending to support the Center's *Kulturpolitik*. The Nationalist press was infuriated by a speech he made in Königsberg on May 15, in which he said "if the monarchists vote for [prolongation of the Law for the Protection of the Republic enacted in 1922 to combat right-wing terrorism] that will be a disgrace from the monarchists' point of view. That kind of behavior is understandable, though, if shoddy, rubbishy ideas are elevated to the status of political principles."[25] On another occasion Wirth exhorted his listeners to "see to it that the republican government in Prussia remains and that the antirepublican government in the Reich disappears as soon as possible. The next Reichstag must decide that." These speeches so angered Chancellor Marx that he wrote a letter sharply reprimanding Wirth, which the latter promptly published in his magazine, *Deutsche Republik*. Marx referred in his letter to official protests he had received from the Nationalist party. It was unheard of, he wrote, for a member of one party in a coalition to accuse another co-

23. Stürmer, p. 240.
24. Köhler, p. 259.
25. *Deutsche Republik* 1 (1927): 293.

alition party of having rubbishy convictions. It was "inconceivable" that Wirth should demand that the present government be fought and that it be broken up as soon as possible. The government had done nothing to warrant attack on the grounds of antirepublicanism. Marx concluded, "I must ask you whether you actually said these things. If it is so, then I must ask for a statement of explanation. If none is forthcoming, I must regret that I may have to take appropriate measures against you, in the interests of the Center party."[26]

This was unprecedented severity coming from a chairman of the Center, for the party had never in its history attempted to maintain party discipline in the usual sense of the words. Wirth's group of young followers were shocked by the tone of Marx's letter and rallied to his defense. His prestige with this group rose still higher in July, when Marx abruptly resigned his membership, always nominal, in the *Reichsbanner*, an organization for the support of the republic which had originally been intended to unite young people from the three Weimar Coalition parties but had been in fact largely run by Social Democrats. Marx's resignation was a gesture of protest against a speech by the Socialist head of the *Reichsbanner* strongly condemning the Austrian Christian Social government. The Centrist members of the *Reichsbanner*, many of whom were also prominent in the *Windthorst-bund*, were defiantly critical of Marx's resignation, although it had the effect of bringing about a conference of *Reichsbanner* leaders who agreed to ensure in future that Centrist members would be more fully informed about the organization's official pronouncements. In spite of rightists' predictions that Marx's move would bring about a general resignation of Center party members from the *Reichsbanner*, this did not occur, and that summer it appeared more likely that they would join Wirth in a withdrawal from the Center and its coalition policy.

In the fall, Wirth, undaunted by the threat of undefined party discipline, proceeded to make public criticism of the school bill. Immediately, the resentment against him which already existed in conservative Catholic circles increased enormously. The fact that his objections to the bill were political rather than religious made no difference, since the issue was considered to be by definition entirely religious. Wirth's opinion, as expressed at a meeting of the Westphalian

26. Ibid., pp. 293–94; Stehkämper, 3:329.

Windthorst League in September, was that the school issue was being exploited by the Nationalists in order to draw the Center closer to the Right and away from its former partners in the Weimar Coalition; that they were attempting to state the issue as one of the "Christian" Right against the "Unbelieving" Left, which was a false proposition, and one which might very well end in the creation of an anticlerical bloc like the one in France.[27] (In fact, the Nationalists had in their ranks not only "Christians" but also violent anti-Catholics and a number of "pagans" and "Wotan-worshippers.")

There were implications in this speech that Wirth favored the social effects of community schools, which prevented the clear-cut divisions between denominations and, hence, often between social and occupational classes, which a confessional system created. He did not actually say as much at the time, and he firmly maintained that he stood for denominational schools in principle. However, in an earlier article in the Democratic paper the *Berliner Tageblatt*, Wirth had taken a stronger line and had appeared to be defending the schools in Baden (his home state) on *federalist* grounds, though on most issues he was a decided advocate of centralization.

Wirth's critics pounced on this admission and claimed that his objection to the school bill could not merely be tactical, as he insisted, but that he must really be in favor of community schools. Prelate Schofer, chairman of the Baden Center party, accused him outright of treason to the party and declared that the more a man belonged to an extreme "wing" on other questions, the more that man must stand firmly in the "center" on cultural questions.[28] The Catholic Congress in Dortmund that September passed a resolution to the effect that whoever dissented on the school question "placed himself outside the ranks of the Center." At the same meeting, Kaas spoke in favor of a stricter authoritarianism within the church, which could compel Catholics to obey its leaders on matters, such as this one, which concerned religion.[29] These statements were clearly aimed directly at Wirth, who continued to insist that he *did* agree with the party's stand on religious matters and opposed the school bill simply as part of his general opposition to the Marx-Keudell coalition. When he was asked

27. *Frankfurter Zeitung*, 6 Aug. 1927.
28. *Kölnische Volkszeitung*, 9 Aug. 1927; Stehkämper, 3:332–34.
29. *Frankfurter Zeitung*, 5 Sept. 1927.

to confer with Schofer concerning the lack of confidence of the Baden party in him, he did not attend the scheduled meeting but stayed on vacation in Switzerland while his case was under discussion by the Executive Council of the state party.[30]

Wirth's rudeness and offhand manner toward Schofer created such resentment that in the next election the state party refused to put Wirth's name at the head of its list of candidates, a position it had held ever since the war. Wirth was evidently considerably chastened by this unexpected move but blamed it on personal antagonisms.

The cabinet of the Blue-Black Bloc, which had had the effect of alienating Wirth and his followers from the Center, had the opposite effect upon the Bavarian People's party, which was pleased and relieved by the Center's change in orientation and was consequently amenable to a formal reconciliation with the party. The agreement was brought about on the initiative of the Center, however, and only with considerable sacrifice on its part. The Bavarian party made virtually no concessions and did not appear to value the settlement very highly.

Terms were agreed upon in November 1927, the conditions being: the closest cooperation was to exist between the two Reichstag fractions and in parliamentary committees, but there were to be no combined meetings of the fractions except in unusual circumstances; there was to be no election campaign rivalry, and election campaigns were to be coordinated between the two parties; the Centrist deputy from the Palatinate who sat in the Bavarian *Landtag* was to become a member of the BVP; and a combined list was to be presented in national elections in the Palatinate, with a BVP candidate as the first name on the list. This last condition, upon which the Bavarians were adamant, was equivalent to the Center's giving up all claims in that province, since the votes for the two parties combined had never been enough to elect more than one candidate.[31]

The Center thus allowed itself to be, for all practical purposes, pushed out of the Palatinate entirely, while the only sacrifice on the part of the Bavarian party was its acquiescence in the idea of reconciliation. This was the meager result of years of patient courtship of

---

30. Köhler, pp. 176–77. Köhler reports that Wirth fell out with him when as finance minister he refused to sanction government subsidies for a company with which Wirth was associated.

31. Stehkämper, 3:233–37; Schönhoven, pp. 182–90; *Frankfurter Zeitung*, 24 Nov. 1927.

the BVP by the Center. Just how much the BVP modified its program in order to enjoy the blessings of parliamentary cooperation with the Center is revealed by the fact that when the Center fraction head Guerard made a mildly republican speech in the Palatinate in January 1928, the *Korrespondenz*, a BVP paper, complained loudly and declared that the Bavarian People's party would never be a republican party.[32]

Most Centrists expressed great satisfaction with the reconciliation, except for the left-wing *Westdeutsche Volksblatt* and the Wirth circle, who felt that unity was not worth obtaining at the expense of political and social goals. Some labor representatives, on the other hand, approved the union, particularly Stegerwald, who as a native Bavarian had been anxious to bring about an agreement with the Bavarian party ever since its secession.[33]

The relationship between the two parties continued to be an unequal one; the BVP exercised great influence over the Center and almost formed a voteless branch of the national party, while the Center never succeeded throughout the Weimar period in influencing the BVP in any significant manner whatever. Later efforts to conclude a closer union of the parties proved fruitless.

32. *Deutsche Republik* 2 (1928): 525.
33. Schreiber, *Politisches Jahrbuch, 1927/28*, p. 146.

17
THE LAST NORMAL YEARS, 1928–1929

The Marx-Keudell cabinet broke up in February 1928 amid mutual recriminations by the Center and the People's party, each blaming the other for the hopeless impasse over the school bill. Schreiber, the Center's recordkeeper, singled out the "fanatical obstinacy" of the People's party as the sole reason for the fall of the government, while Stresemann wrote that the one factor which made compromise impossible was "Herr Schreiber's excessive zeal" in the education committee.[1] Actually, the bill was only one of many reasons for the collapse of the coalition. Contrary to the expectations of the liberal press, the Center did not even make an election issue of the school bill in the spring campaign. The violent quarrels with the People's party seemed to be forgotten, and the party's campaign was fought against the Nationalist party, whose ministers had fully supported the school bill. Martin Spahn and other Nationalist Catholics wanted very much to see the two "Christian-national" parties enter the campaign together on the school issue (as they had campaigned in the Blue-Black partnership of 1912), but Marx rejected the idea, preferring to be "without ties."[2] The reason for the new line was plain: the Center had nothing to hope from the elections so far as the school bill was concerned, and the serious disaffection of the left wing of the party had to be counteracted by a reversion to Weimar slogans.

Republican and social-minded members of the fraction and party committees were given a prominent position during the election campaign. On the national party list, the name of Joseph Wirth appeared second, after Marx's. Although Wirth had persisted to the end in op-

---

1. Schreiber, p. 150; On Stresemann, Sutton 3:293.
2. *Deutsche Republik* 2 (1927) :165.

posing the cabinet and had voted with the Socialists for a no-confidence motion in the Reichstag in December, the party leadership felt that his prestige with the younger and more radical groups in the party was high enough to warrant his being placed in the first rank of party candidates. The swing to the Right in 1927 was to be balanced by a swing to the Left in 1928.

But the united front in the party hierarchy had come too late and was too obviously contrived. The disaffection of the Left was too strong to be halted so soon after the Center's participation in the unpopular Marx government. Besides the opposition of Wirth's followers, who were not won back so quickly as Wirth himself, there was deep resentment in the Christian trade unions about the party's coalition policy. Large numbers of the rank and file of Catholic labor had come to feel that the Center's claim to be a social party was a fraud, and that their demands would be better satisfied by some other party—by the Social Democratic party, or by the splinter groups springing up in the Rhineland, or even by the Communist party.

Even Adam Stegerwald had become disillusioned about the Nationalist party and had led the unions in protesting the government's bill granting large raises to civil servants. He and Imbusch had condemned Finance Minister Köhler, a man who had risen to the top from the lower ranks of the civil service himself, for granting the raises while continuing to insist that the economy could not afford either wage raises or the eight-hour day for industrial workers. Marx had indicated in January 1928 that he disapproved of Stegerwald's objecting to the bill (which was passed into law by a large majority, including the SPD). The two labor leaders resented what they interpreted as a reprimand from Marx and made criticisms of him which were more personal and vituperative than any previous references to a chairman of the Center party by members of his own party. Imbusch declared in a public speech that Marx had no right to try to quiet Stegerwald, and in a private letter to Marx that he (Marx) had "no heart for the distress of the poor man." Stegerwald resigned his position as deputy chairman of the party, saying that he could no longer work with Marx. The whole affair was patched up at the end of January in meetings of the Executive Council and the National Committee, where Marx regretted any "misunderstanding" and said that the original letter of reprimand to Stegerwald was supposed to have been confidential and should not have been revealed to the press.[3] The National Committee then passed a resolution which contained many pledges for the party's future social policy, including the obtaining of wage raises, better housing, and efforts to decrease the rate of unemployment; but it was wishful thinking to suppose that labor resentment could be cleared up so easily before a national election. Furthermore, the social promises which formed the platform for this election were essentially the same as those in the "manifesto" of the previous year which had turned out to mean little so far as achievements of the coalition were concerned.

For these reasons the Center suffered what amounted to a crushing defeat in the elections of May 1928. The results showed a condemnation of the Marx-Keudell cabinet, since those parties which had participated in it showed the most severe losses. The Center ordinarily relied upon a stable bloc of votes and did not expect much fluctuation in its support, yet the party lost eight seats in the Reichstag, dropping from sixty-nine to sixty-one, and nine seats in the Prussian *Landtag*, dropping from eighty-one to seventy-two. Its share of the popular vote was reduced to 12 percent, and its total vote was smaller than it had been at any time during the republican period, in spite of the continued rise in population. The party received 400,000 fewer votes than in December of 1924.

The losses occurred in those areas where the Center had normally a large following, while those areas with small Catholic minorities were less affected (possibly because these areas had a greater stake in the school bill). The party's percentage of the popular vote in individual districts declined in every single district in the west and south of Germany.[4] The Bavarian People's party showed similar losses: a low total vote and a decline of two seats in the Reichstag. The recent agreement with the Center over the Palatinate resulted in a slightly larger vote there, however, since there was no division between the two parties. The German Nationalist party lost thirty seats in the Reichstag and the two liberal parties continued their steady decline, while the elections saw a resurgence of the Social Democratic party, which gained twenty-one seats.

3. Morsey, *Protokolle*, 1:170–72; *Frankfurter Zeitung*, 16 Jan. 1928; Stehkämper, 3: 341–53.
4. Cuno Horkenbach, *Das deutsche Reich von 1918 bis heute* (Berlin, 1931), pp. 456–70.

The Center's leadership and press were deeply concerned about the results of the elections and for almost a year afterward showed the effect of uncertainty and demoralization. The party leaders were cautious and hesitant because they did not want to draw the conclusions that had to be drawn. It was clear from the election results that the Center could attract the greatest number of voters by following a policy oriented to the Left, but the Center did not evaluate its supporters solely in terms of numbers. If by changing policy in a leftward direction in order to attract thousands of industrial workers they would thereby lose the support of hundreds of educated, *bürgerliche* Catholics, the change would not be worth it: would be, in fact, disastrous. Many felt that the party should simply resign itself to the loss of more and more voters among industrial workers, arguing that the pull of socialism was so strong in this class that no amount of coddling the labor unions would prevent the Center from losing votes here, while too many concessions to labor might alienate more highly valued supporters.

Numerous analyses of the 1928 elections in the Centrist press illustrate unwillingness to draw the obvious conclusions from the results. Joos, in an article in the *Kölnische Volkszeitung*, cited the need for more vivid personalities and blamed defeat on the effect of proportional representation and the lack of effective party organization at the local level. Stegerwald, in an article for *Germania*, listed as reasons for the loss a lighter turnout, the loss of young people, and defections to the Christian Social Reich party and the Economic party.[5] There is little evidence to support his contention that the growth of the Economic party, which claimed to speak for the lower middle classes, was at the expense of the Center, since it kept its strength after the 1930 elections while the Center regained its losses in that year, and it seems probable that the Economic party took votes from the fading liberal parties rather than from the Center.

The Christian Social Reich party of Vitus Heller *was* an important factor in the Center's losses. This splinter group, professedly Catholic but sharply critical of some church doctrines, accounted for about 40 percent of the Center's losses in three districts, Hesse, Cologne-

---

5. *Kölnische Volkszeitung,* 24 May 1928; Stegerwald's article cited in *Frankfurter Zeitung,* 31 May 1928; Wachtling, pp. 122–24.

Aachen, and Koblenz-Trier, which fell away strikingly from the Center. The party did not succeed in capturing any seats in the Reichstag and had little following outside a small area in the west, but it was naturally of great concern to the Center because its voters were nearly all former Center voters or young Catholics belonging to radical groups which rejected the Center's program. Its platform had become more radical since the early 1920s and now was closer to the KPD than to the SPD. The CSRP even formed a coalition with the Communists in a small town near Düsseldorf. The party "approved of the idea of a dictatorship and also advocated vocational groups"; its publication, *Neues Volk*, declared that "a dictatorship, if it is exercised by persons of the highest standards of morality and honor, is absolutely to be preferred to formal and powerless democracy and barren parliamentarianism."[6]

Much of the youth vote in the Catholic population had gone to the CSRP in those urban areas where it was organized, but equally many votes had been diverted from the Center directly to the Socialists and Communists and "it seems likely that the agitation of Heller's party may only have served to increase the Catholic vote for the SPD and KPD."[7] It would seem that if the Catholic working-class voter leaving the Center had favorable attitudes to the parliamentary system he moved in sympathy toward Social Democracy, and if unfavorable, to the Communists or to one or another of the splinter groups of which the CSRP was the most important. But in either case, in 1928 the reason for leaving the Center was the party's recent coalition policy and its apparent abandonment of the goal of being a social party. To be sure the party lost votes because people stayed home, because young people did not support it, because many people were attracted to the splinter groups, but behind all of these reasons lay strong dissatisfaction with the Center's political orientation.

The liberal press pointed out that the long struggle over the law to raise the salaries of civil servants cost the Center "tens of thousands" of votes, and that the protracted opposition by Wirth also had an effect even though Wirth himself had been reconciled before the election.[8] But most obvious to outside observers was the fact that

6. Knapp, "The Red and the Black," p. 402; Grebing, p. 239, and App., p. 16.
7. Knapp, p. 403.
8. *Frankfurter Zeitung*, 31 May 1928.

nearly all of the defections from the Center occurred in the industrial areas of the west and were to the parties of the Left, and that if the Center wanted to regain the numerical strength which it had in the years 1919 and 1920 it would have to return to its policies of those years, of cooperating with Social Democracy and taking a stand against the Right. Inside the party this was not only not clearly recognized, but it was not aways assumed that numerical strength was worth the measures necessary to acquire it.

The substantial victory of the Social Democratic party in the election made it appropriate that the party should lead the next government, and Hermann Müller was chosen to form a cabinet of the Great Coalition (with all major parties in the spectrum from SPD on the Left to DVP on the Right-center). The Center at first gave every indication of being very willing to cooperate. The conditions which the party spokesmen made in the early stages of negotiations were not insurmountable. The first condition was that the Center could not enter any government that did not also include the Bavarian People's party, in accord with the recent reconciliation of the two parties. Acceptance of this condition would mean a certain restriction of program but no more so than was the case with the People's party, and the Bavarians were prepared to enter a Great Coalition.

The second condition made by the Center was that the party receive assurances from Müller that in the matter of education the government would make no move to "worsen the situation." That is, the Center wanted a guarantee that the Socialists and liberals would not try either to present their own education bill to the Reichstag or to change the present legal interpretation of the constitution by encouraging judicial decisions favorable to the liberal-Socialist conceptions of public education.

The most serious obstacle to the formation of a Great Coalition at this stage came from the DVP, which was insistent that the Prussian cabinet be "adjusted" to admit its representatives into a Great Coalition there, if there was to be one in the Reich. The Center refused to consider this; it was anxious to ensure the continuance of the Weimar Coalition in Prussia in order to maintain the favorable situation in the school system there, and in order to smooth the current negotiations for a concordat between Prussia and the Vatican. Müller's original efforts to form a Reich government therefore foundered. A Weimar Coalition in the Reich was equally impossible, since the BVP declared that the very words "Weimar Coalition" were offensive to it, and the Center held to its condition of joining a government only in conjunction with the BVP. An impasse was reached, one more in the long series of parliamentary crises that were strangling the republic.

Müller was finally able to put together a "camouflaged" Great Coalition, a government which was theoretically without party ties but actually differed from an ordinary cabinet only in that no program was agreed upon in advance. But after this apparent settlement, made to placate the DVP and BVP, surprisingly unreasonable demands from the Center held up the final naming of the ministers for some days.

Originally, it had been planned that Brauns would continue as labor minister, and that the party would also fill the ministries of Transport and Occupied Territories, for which the fraction had tentatively approved Guerard and Wirth. The fraction had agreed with the other parties that the office of vice-chancellor was an unnecessary one. It then suddenly developed that Wirth was unwilling to enter the cabinet as minister of transport or occupied territories because these were "unpolitical" posts and lacking in prestige. He would agree only if he could also have the title of vice-chancellor or, if not that, then a "political" ministry, hinting at the Ministry of the Interior, which had never been held by a Centrist. His attitude obliged the Center fraction to reverse its former decision and demand that there either be a vice-chancellor or that Wirth be given the Interior. The Social Democrats considered that their election victory made the Interior post their prerogative. Hindenburg also had strong personal objections to Wirth as vice-chancellor.[9] The Center then astounded the other parties by withdrawing Brauns from the Labor Ministry, where he had appeared to be almost a permanent fixture, and keeping only one man in the cabinet, Guerard, who took the combined ministries of Transport and Occupied Territories. The party called the arrangement a temporary expedient and said the representation would be increased in the autumn. Brauns's vacant position was filled by the Socialist Rudolf Wissell.

Brauns himself seems to have been surprised and hurt by this maneuver, which was instigated by Wirth and Stegerwald and the labor unions, partly in the belief that the Social Democrats should take over

9. Morsey, *Protokolle*, 1:221–22.

the responsibility for social policy instead of being in a position always to criticize the actions or inactions of the minister. It was also true, however, that Brauns had been closely associated with the right wing of the party which was then under fire from the unions. He had always been somewhat isolated from other fraction members because his cold, abrupt manner prevented his acquiring a personal following, and his departure from the ministry also signaled an end to his political influence; he spent the next years in a futile attempt to resolve the financial difficulties of the *Volksverein*.[10]

The Socialist and liberal papers were highly critical of the part played by their erstwhile hero Wirth in this unnecessary crisis. *Vorwärts*, the Social Democratic paper, remarked that Wirth's "tactical abilities do not keep in step with his talents as a speaker." An editorial in the *Frankfurter Zeitung* blamed the crisis on the "morally weak" position of the Center and on intrigues within its fraction, some of which were actually aimed at Wirth and at the destruction of his reputation.[11] It was plain that Wirth was no longer the shining crusader of the year before; his reputation had been tarnished, whether deliberately or not, by his apparently childish behavior. In a speech to the Reichstag that November, Wirth declared, "Whatever else happens, there must be a final clearing-up of the poisoned political atmosphere, because we are afraid that this present situation has in it the dangerous possibility of a lingering governmental crisis." At this point he was interrupted by Goebbels of the National Socialist delegation, who shouted out "Because *you* want to be vice-chancellor!" and was rewarded with laughter from all parts of the house.[12]

Only a few weeks after the election, the Center's leaders had shown, by their extraordinary obstinacy in the negotiations with Müller, that there was not likely to be any decisive turn to the Left or to the policies of the Weimar Coalition. The election campaign had been merely a tactical maneuver, and the only discernible change in party policy had been a retreat from the unsatisfactory partnership of 1927 with the German Nationalists.

10. Mockenhaupt, "Heinrich Brauns," in Morsey, *Zeitgeschichte*, p. 157.
11. *Frankfurter Zeitung*, 29 June 1928.
12. *Verhandlungen des Reichstags* 423: (16 Nov. 1928): 364–65. Köhler describes Wirth as having always been consumed by personal ambition (Köhler, p. 175). For Marx's views, see Stehkämper, 1:490, 498.

The results of the elections of May 1928 were as unfavorable for the Center in Württemberg and Bavaria as in the Reich, but in these states the local parties' strong preference for rightist coalitions overcame all pressures for any adjustments in accordance with the outcome of the vote. In Württemberg, the Center lost only one seat in the *Landtag*, but its coalition partner the *Bürgerpartei und Bauernbund*, the state branch of the DNVP, lost five seats and the Social Democrats gained nine.[13] The vote was an obvious response to the abysmal record of Nationalist Minister-President Bazille. In his role as education minister he had succeeded in having a year cut off the school requirements, reducing them from eight to seven years, thus pleasing his farmer constituents but penalizing the urban students. The farmers had also been courted by a one-sided tax policy and were exempted from the building tax not only for their barns and other outbuildings but also for their residences. Industry had been ignored; and, as might have been expected, the votes lost by the Nationalists had nearly all been from their minority wing, the *Bürgerpartei*.

The election results appeared to dictate the formation of a Great Coalition or a Weimar Coalition, either of which could command a substantial majority in the eighty-seat *Landtag*. The Center until 1924 had cooperated fully in a Weimar Coalition in the state, but it now refused to join one or to participate in any coalition at all in which the Social Democrats were included. The People's party would not join a government unless Bazille resigned; he was detested by both the liberal parties and the Socialists because of his clericalism and agrarian bias. The Center absolutely refused to consider Bazille's resignation, and the cabinet that was finally formed was still supported only by the Center and the Nationalists, in spite of the fact that they controlled only thirty-seven out of eighty seats. It was necessary to contrive a majority by securing limited support from a splinter party, the *Christliche Volksdienst*, and to persuade the People's party delegation to abstain from voting on the Socialists' motion of censure. Both of the small parties had campaigned against Bazille but were willing to grant this measure of toleration. Since the opposition was divided on all legislative issues, the government was able to continue in power indefi-

13. Information on Württemberg from Keil, pp. 1214–17; Fischer, "Die Rechtsregierung," pp. 28–29, and "Das politische Gesicht," pp. 349–51; *Frankfurter Zeitung*, 1 June 1928.

nitely. Bazille did resign his position as minister-president, remaining minister of education. Eugen Bolz, the Centrist minister of the interior, became the new minister-president.

In 1929 the coalition in Württemberg was threatened by a decision of the Court of Appeals in Leipzig, which had been investigating the elections of the previous year. The court now ordered that three seats in the *Landtag* be given to the Nazi and "People's Rights" parties. Two of the seats were at the expense of the Center and the Nationalists, thus reducing still further their percentage of the house. When the *Landtag* next convened in the fall of 1929, the SPD began immediately to challenge the government (this time because of support given to Hugenberg and Hitler by Bazille). The fall of the cabinet seemed inevitable, when it was unexpectedly saved in November by the decision of first the People's party and then the Democratic party to support it, surprisingly in the light of these parties' long and violent hostility to Bazille and his reactionary policies. In fact, the state's best-known Democrat, Friedrich von Payer (vice-chancellor of the Second Reich in 1917 and 1918), resigned from his party when the decision was made. Apparently, the Democrats had agreed to support the regime in order to preserve the friendship of the People's party which had, on its part, come round in order to assist the business interests in the state. It was a further example of the degeneration of German political parties into economic pressure groups. In the long run, the Center's obstinacy had won out over liberal principles.

The party's motives in sticking with Bazille and the Nationalist partnership were its basic distrust of the Socialists and its need to keep the vote of Catholic farmers who would otherwise have turned to the Nationalist *Bauernbund*. Similar motives kept the Bavarian People's party on its reactionary course in that state. *Landtag* elections of May 1928 did not reduce the BVP representation but did greatly increase that of the Social Democrats and the Bavarian *Bauernbund*.

The *Bauernbund*, a party somewhat to the Left of the BVP, had been represented in the state government, but was becoming increasingly dissatisfied with its policies, and its leader Anton Fehr called the coalition "a not very happy marriage of convenience."[14] Georg Heim had forged the link between the two parties in his role as head of the

14. Schönhoven, pp. 201–6.

Christian *Bauernverein*, but his influence was waning (he had been ill a good deal in recent years), and the Farmers' League supported Fehr over Heim when the two men clashed in the autumn of 1927, thus forcing Heim's resignation. The *Bauernbund* also came into conflict with the BVP over the Reich law raising the salaries of civil servants and finally threatened to leave the Bavarian cabinet and call for a vote of confidence in the government.

A showdown was postponed until after the 1928 elections, but in spite of the gains made in the elections by the *Bauernbund* and the Social Democrats, the BVP refused to consider any concessions to the Left. The result was another long governmental crisis like that in 1924. After two months of negotiations and the combining and relabeling of several ministries, the former coalition of Bavarian People's party, Nationalists, and *Bauernbund* was again installed. Heinrich Held was reelected minister-president and the Nationalist Gürtner remained minister of justice. The reorganization of the government combined the Labor Ministry and the Ministry of Agriculture, giving the new post to the *Bauernbund* and demoting the former labor minister to the subordinate office of state secretary. The eight labor representatives in the BVP *Landtag* fraction opposed the reorganization, but the concession was considered essential by the party's leaders in order to avoid cooperating in any way with the Social Democratic party in Bavaria.[15]

The controversy between clericals and liberals in Baden proved nearly as disruptive to good government in that state as inflexible hostility to Social Democracy was in the other two southern states.[16] When in the fall of 1929 *Landtag* elections brought a substantial victory to the Center, a gain of six seats with a total of thirty-four out of eighty-eight seats, the one concern of the party was to rid the cabinet of the anticlerical Democrats without thereby forming another uncomfortable exclusive partnership with the Social Democrats as in 1925 and 1926. Schofer hoped to replace the Democrats with the DVP, thus forming a kind of hybrid between Weimar and Great coalitions, with the understanding that the Center would receive the important Ministry of Education and Religion. The two liberal parties, however,

15. Ibid., p. 213.
16. Information on Baden from Otto Leers, "Badische Politik," *Die Hilfe* 35: (1 Dec. 1929): 568.

stood firmly together in rejection of the plan, and for the second time during the republican years the Center was obliged to form a cabinet alone with the Social Democrats. The solution was equally unsatisfactory to the Social Democratic party in Baden, which made it a condition that one of its own men should take the *Kultus* ministry. In the cabinet as finally organized, there were two Centrists in the ministries of Finance and the Interior, one Socialist, Adam Remmele, who combined the *Kultus* Ministry and the Ministry of Justice, and an extra "state's councillor," also a Socialist. It was well known that Remmele, though a Social Democrat, would prove more amenable to clerical interests than would any representative from either of the two liberal parties. After a month of squabbling, Josef Schmitt, the Center's minister of finance, was chosen minister-president.

The most important project for the Center, in organizing this government, was the conclusion of a state concordat with the Vatican. The concordat was concluded in 1932, but in order to secure its passage in the *Landtag* its wording had to avoid any reference to the vital subject of education. The Center had failed both on the national and the state level to make any change whatever in the Baden system of community schools.

Internal party conflict in the Center had, after all, been exacerbated rather than healed by the Marx-Keudell government of 1927, and it was not resolved by the breakup of that government. Marx had found himself at the heart of the controversy, under intemperate attack from both sides; in the fall of 1927 the labor leader Imbusch had accused him of having "no understanding whatever for social and economic matters"[17] and the Catholic School Organization refused to comprehend his reasoned explanations of the failure to obtain a satisfactory school law. Marx suffered nervous exhaustion and illness as a result and resolved as early as January 1928 to resign as party chairman, making this officially known at a meeting of the party's Executive Council in October.

There was consequently ample time for discussion, proposals, and counterproposals before the election of a new chairman by the party congress in December, the first to be held in three years. No obvious candidate emerged from preliminary discussions, but two distinct

17. Stürmer, pp. 239–40 for Imbusch; Wachtling, p. 125.

preferences were discernible. Many of the members of the Executive Council favored the choice of a labor representative as chairman, in order to win back this disaffected wing of the party. Stegerwald had expressed his intention of giving up his union positions and devoting himself entirely to politics. In the past year, during the long period of Marx's illness, Stegerwald had served as acting head of the Reichstag fraction, and he now hoped to combine the two offices of fraction head and party chairman. As a labor leader, Stegerwald would please the unions; as a conservative and a nationalist he would please the conservatives. Furthermore, his resignation as head of the Christian trade unions and promotion to chairman would please those among his union followers who had clashed with him repeatedly in the past and permit them to choose a more congenial leader.[18] The arguments in favor of Stegerwald's candidacy were persuasive.

Another labor leader frequently mentioned as an alternative to Stegerwald was Joseph Joos, the affable Alsatian journalist from the workers' associations who had worked so hard to reconcile West German Catholics to the republic. Joos had criticized Wirth for his self-imposed exile from the party in 1927 and had criticized Stegerwald and Imbusch for their belligerent opposition to the civil servants' raises; yet he was a well-liked man who could perhaps heal the rifts within the left wing as well as help to reconcile the left wing with the Right.

There were others on the Executive Council who did not believe that either of these men could perform the necessary healing function for the party and preferred the selection of a member of the clergy for chairman. The national Center party had never elevated a cleric to its top office, but the state and regional organizations had frequently been led by clergy. Possible candidates under consideration were Brauns, the former minister of labor; Ulitzka, the Silesian party head; Schofer, chairman of the Baden Center; and Kaas, the university professor, papal household prelate, foreign policy expert, and *Kulturpolitiker* from the Rhineland. Brauns, however, was lacking in the personal qualifications required in a chairman: he was neither conciliatory nor widely popular and in any case was urgently needed as financial adviser to the

---

18. Morsey, "Die Zentrumspartei," in Matthias and Morsey, eds., *Das Ende der Parteien 1933*, p. 419.

Volksverein. Ulitzka was a shade too radical, and a Silesian might not be acceptable to the western sections of Germany which dominated the party. Schofer was also too closely tied to a particular region. Marx himself was aligned with those who were opposed to the choice of any priest as chairman.

When the congress opened in Cologne on December 8, no consensus had been reached, and so the Executive Council voted to decide the nomination by written ballot instead of by acclamation as in the past. Stegerwald's name received the majority of votes and it was then sent on to the National Committee, which according to past precedent should automatically have seconded it. But the nomination met with strong resistance from the committee, particularly from the large delegation of civil servants who deeply resented Stegerwald's vociferous objection to their raises. His plan to unite the two offices of fraction head and party chairman was also criticized. At the very moment when Stegerwald was observed confidently composing a gracious speech of acceptance and thanks, the committee was voting to reject him by a vote of 120 to 40.[19]

The Executive Council then considered an alternative, and rather hastily fixed upon Joos. The committee enthusiastically endorsed the choice and the matter appeared to be settled, when Joos, after conferring with other labor delegates, refused to serve as chairman. His refusal "fell like a bomb" on the committee and created such an uproar that for a time it was impossible for anyone to be heard. Joos had found that the labor representatives would not back him and he personally regarded his election as a betrayal of Stegerwald. He may well also have felt inadequate to the task, as he was not an assertive or self-confident man.

Joos suggested that the committee recommend to the congress a three-man collegium on which both he and Stegerwald could serve. After much heated discussion, the committee accepted the suggestion. But when the proposal for a collegium of Joos, Stegerwald, and Kaas was put before the general meeting of the congress, there was hearty objection to the idea. The loudest protests came from the representatives of youth groups and particularly from the Windthorst League which demanded a single strong "leader" for the party. A civil

19. Schorr, p. 132.

servant warned that if Stegerwald served on a three-man collegium he would be sure to "elbow his way into control." The collegium scheme was abandoned, and instead, the entire congress voted by secret ballot for the three candidates. The results were decisive and surprising. Stegerwald received 42 votes, Joos 92, and Kaas an overwhelming majority of 182 votes.[20]

While the labor delegates had been wrangling among themselves, the clericals had pushed through the candidacy of Kaas with single-minded fervor. Professor Schreiber had personally gone from group to group whispering Kaas's name into the delegates' ears. A priest who was not identified with any socioeconomic group might be able to restore unity to the party and to German Catholics.

If Kaas's victory was the result of resurgent clericalism in the Center, Stegerwald's defeat can also be attributed to this factor, although his intense unpopularity with the civil servants and his position as labor leader were equally important. He himself said later that his well-known opposition to political activity by the clergy was a major reason for his defeat and in 1946 asserted that "events proved *me* right, not the party congress."[21] This helps to explain the fact that Wirth, though personally friendly to Joos, supported Stegerwald, his former great rival, for the chairmanship. (His own name had, of course, been conspicuously absent from all lists of candidates.) Since the confrontation of the two men at the party congress of 1925, Stegerwald had mellowed somewhat toward the republic and had become disillusioned with the DNVP. Wirth on his part had become more aware, during the debate on the school bill in 1927, of the divisive dangers of increased emphasis on religious and cultural questions. Although they had different concepts of what the Center should be, they were agreed about what it should not be. Joos, on the other hand, was as much a defender of clerical interests as any priest, and the future of the party would probably not have been very different if he had been chosen instead of Monsignor Kaas.[22]

After the election, Wirth wrote a sympathetic article in his magazine in which he stated "It is . . . an irony and a paradox of party history in Germany that a political figure like Adam Stegerwald, at the

20. *Frankfurter Zeitung*, 8 Dec. 1928.
21. Adam Stegerwald, *Von deutschen Zukunft* (Würzburg, 1946), p. 3.
22. Wachtling, pp. 24, 136.

very moment when he has at long last broken out of the trade union faction to become an active party leader, is thrust back again by bourgeois circles, and then . . . still has to defend himself to his labor associates regarding his political advances."[23]

Stegerwald's own paper, *Der Deutsche*, charged that the election demonstrated antilabor bias in the Center, and Stegerwald issued a personal statement which, although it stressed his complete indifference to the outcome of the election, actually revealed his deep disappointment in it. He denied, in this statement, that he had ever actively sought the chairmanship; he had simply agreed to serve as acting head of the Reichstag fraction and had not thought it worthwhile to give up his union work in order to become permanent head unless the offices of party chairman and fraction head were combined. Therefore, since he had not after all been elected party chairman, he now intended to resign his post as acting fraction head.[24] His bitterness was considerably lessened during the next month when he was unanimously elected permanent head of the fraction. Immediately after this, he resigned both of his posts as head of the German Federation of Unions and head of the League of Christian Industrial Unions. Thus the goal desired by so many of his union followers of "promoting" him out of the union movement was achieved even though he had not won the party chairmanship.

Stegerwald was the first Center Reichstag fraction head without a university education. His election and his subsequent reconciliation with the party were said to have been due to the personal efforts of Dr. Kaas.[25] Kaas seemed at that stage to possess the necessary ability to heal conflict within the Center. Whether he had the physical strength and the determination of character to deal with the national crises Germany was sure to face was doubtful. More ominous than any personal inadequacy, however, was the fact that the election of Kaas as party chairman was the manifestation of a return to an emphasis upon Catholic religious and educational issues; yet events had shown that the Weimar Constitution represented the utmost in concessions in this area that the rest of Germany was willing to grant within a democratic parliamentary system. Thus the new emphasis must prove to

23. Joseph Wirth, "Parteirevolution—der Fall Stegerwald," *Deutsche Republik* 3 (1928): 387.
24. *Kölnische Volkszeitung*, 11 Dec. 1928.
25. Heinrich Teipel, "Kaas und Stegerwald," *Deutsche Republik* 3 (1928): 550.

be at best a waste of effort and very probably a positive danger to republican institutions. How could the Center hope to carry out a program favored only by the Catholic minority in a nation where the majority ruled? As Marx had written in 1925, "It becomes more and more evident that in these *Kultur* questions we stand *completely alone*."[26]

Early in 1929 negotiations began again among the parties to transform Müller's cabinet into a genuine Great Coalition with party ties. It was imperative to have a strong, effective government behind Germany's delegation to the reparations conference which was scheduled to take place in The Hague later in the year. The negotiations resulted in yet another impasse between Center and People's party, with the Center demanding two additional seats in the cabinet and the DVP insisting upon admittance into the Prussian coalition. Kaas was personally anxious to reach an accommodation with the DVP and had promised to use his influence to persuade Hess, the Prussian Center fraction head, to accept that party's demand, but just at the point when a compromise seemed to have been worked out, the Center Reichstag fraction gave Müller an ultimatum demanding *three* ministries, and when this was refused, withdrew its single minister (Guerard) from the government.

The reason behind this move was that Hess had convinced Kaas and the Reichstag fraction that the People's party wanted to join the Prussian government in order to sabotage a proposed state concordat with the Vatican, and had even been demanding the Ministry of Religion and Education. Stresemann's strong desire to admit his party to the Prussian cabinet was ascribed to his personal hostility to the idea of a concordat.[27] Otto Braun, the Socialist minister-president, was prepared to steer the concordat through the *Landtag* if the Weimar Coalition remained undisturbed. Kaas agreed to this, but rather than be obliged to renege on his verbal commitments to the People's party in Prussia, he had preferred to make difficulties for Müller in the Reich government. These convoluted reasons for the withdrawal of Guerard from the Reich cabinet were not made clear to the public and it seemed to be just one more example of the breakdown of the parlia-

26. Stehkämper, 2:378.
27. Brüning, pp. 145–46; Braun, p. 273.

mentary system, as indeed it was. Müller did not attempt to find a replacement for Guerard.

There were few regrets in Center circles about the incident. An editorial in *Germania* expressed relief that the party was now free from the "liberal-Socialist bloc" (hardly an accurate description considering that the BVP was still represented in the cabinet). A statement of justification from the Reichstag fraction spoke of the party's "ten long years of sacrifice" and said that it was intolerable that the party should now be obliged to play a "Cinderella role"; the Center was not renouncing responsibility but wanted responsibility in proper proportion to its numerical strength; the People's party was to blame for the entire crisis.[28]

Two months later a Great Coalition was formed at last. The People's party agreed to postpone consideration of changes in the Prussian cabinet on condition that alterations be made in the national budget for the year. The other parties accepted the condition, and a settlement was made in April, when the Center entered the government with three ministers: Wirth for Occupied Territories, Stegerwald for Transport, and Guerard for Justice. The coalition was made binding upon all parties. Wirth was willing this time to settle for less than he had demanded the previous spring, and nothing more was heard of Cinderella, in spite of the fact that none of the three ministries was "political." Another unnecessary crisis was over, and the postponement of the Prussian question by the DVP enabled the Center to claim a victory.

The way was then clear for the waging of *Kulturpolitik* in Prussia, and the concordat was concluded in July with the cooperation of the three parties of the Weimar Coalition under the astute leadership of Braun. Relations between the Prussian state and the Catholic church had formerly been regulated by the terms of the papal bull *De Salute Animarum* of 1821. After the war it had been decided that the bull was still legally in effect, but its terms were clearly inadequate for modern Prussia, with its larger and more widely distributed Catholic population. Papal Nuncio Pacelli had discussed the possibilities of a concordat with the minister-president on several occasions since the war. As long as there seemed to be some chance of a national treaty,

28. *Kölnische Volkszeitung*, 7 Feb. 1929.

the actual drafting of one for Prussia had been postponed, but when hope of this faded in 1927, work began in earnest on a state treaty.

Braun was determined that the concordat should not mention education. Even the word "education" appearing in the draft, he maintained, would be enough to ensure its failure in the *Landtag*. Pacelli pleaded that he could not take a draft back to Rome that did not mention education. Braun wrote: "The tenacity and mental elasticity with which he championed the interests of Rome afforded me, now and then, a real aesthetic pleasure."[29] But in spite of Pacelli's protests, he was willing to accept an "incomplete" concordat rather than none at all, in order to obtain a written, legally binding mutual recognition between church and state. Braun, on his part, sent a note to Pacelli assuring him of the Prussian government's continued intention of protecting the religious rights laid down in the constitution and promising that religious instruction in the schools would be in no way jeopardized by the omission of the subject from the concordat.[30]

The final treaty was an innocuous document. Its most important provisions were those which arranged for a redistribution of dioceses to conform to the Catholic population of modern Prussia. The concordat gave Berlin a bishop for the first time. Other clauses resembled those in the Bavarian treaty and the national concordat of 1933: independence of the church was guaranteed; the church was given a veto over state appointments to theological faculties and in return promised to ensure that its priests, bishops, and teachers were German in citizenship and education.[31] In all respects the position of the church was improved over its former status.

The government had some difficulty in obtaining a majority for the treaty, because the Nationalist party objected that a simultaneous treaty with the Evangelical church was not concluded, as had been done in Bavaria. (A satisfactory treaty with the Evangelical church was eventually worked out in 1931.) Consequently Braun was obliged to call for a unanimous vote from the Social Democratic fraction and to invoke party discipline against the anticlerical impulses of some of its members. When the final vote was taken, the entire Social Demo-

29. Braun, p. 278.
30. Robert Lieber, "Das preussische Konkordat," *Stimmen der Zeit* 118 (1929): 26–28.
31. Johannes V. Bredt, "Das preussische Konkordat," *Preussische Jahrbücher* 217 (1929): 140–41.

cratic delegation voted for the concordat, giving the measure a large majority.

The passage of the Prussian concordat was of advantage to those in the Center who wanted to prove that cooperation with Social Democrats need not mean the sacrifice of an active Catholic program. The treaty's acceptance also showed that the republic continued to provide a more favorable climate for Catholic interests than the empire had done. But the example was not enough to convince the anti-republicans in the party: the concordat had not mentioned education, the most vital interest of the defenders of the Church in political life, and its passage had not solved the problem of how to reconcile the other parties of the middle to clerical measures.

18
THE BRÜNING ERA, 1930–1932

In 1929, when lengthy and heated debates over the Young Plan occurred in the Reichstag, the Center, after a year of inactivity, showed a surge of energy in national policy-making. Kaas seemed to be providing the strong leadership demanded by the party congress. He did not miss an opportunity to demonstrate to the other parties that the Center was independent and was not bound by any special ties of loyalty to the Müller government. On October 18, in a speech in Dortmund, he called for parliamentary reform, saying that in his opinion a government which had once been approved by parliament should not be inhibited by any change of mood in one of the government parties, and that a "greater independence from the unpredictable contingencies of changes in parliamentary weather" ought to be guaranteed. He pronounced the Center ready for "basic reforms" to attain this goal.[1] Although it is true that Kaas had previously shown a general desire for a more authoritarian state, this particular statement suggests strongly that he was echoing the thoughts of Heinrich Brüning, who had recently become acting head of the Reichstag fraction after Stegerwald was named minister of transport. If Brüning's own account is to be believed, he had in the course of 1929 become the alter ego of the party chairman, substituting for him in all matters Kaas did not want to handle personally, which included "practically everything" except religious and educational issues. "The most burdensome things were done for him right from the beginning."[2] Allowing for Brüning's hind-

1. *Frankfurter Zeitung*, 18 Oct. 1929.
2. Brüning, 1:143. Rudolf Morsey has questioned the accuracy and authenticity of Brüning's memoirs and believes them to have been heavily edited by his secretary (Morsey, "Zur Entstehung, Authentizität und Kritik von Brüning's *Memoiren, 1918–1934," Proceedings of the Rheinische-Westfälische Akademie der Wissenschaften* [Opladen, 1975]). They must certainly be used with caution.

sight and his natural bitterness toward Kaas because of the subsequent events of 1933, it is difficult to avoid concluding that for the years 1929 through 1931 the nominal chairman of the Center party was steadily guided by the stronger personality and will of Brüning. The fact that Kaas's health was delicate, and that he spent long periods away from Berlin at various resorts trying to improve it, supports this assumption.

Brüning had begun his career in politics in 1924 as the protégé of Stegerwald, whom he had served for several years after the war as secretary and as editor of *Der Deutsche*, but he had never been fully committed to the trade union movement. By 1929 he had dissociated himself from it and was rapidly rising in the parliamentary party as an expert on finance. He was by temperament an intellectual and had spent many years before the war preparing for, but never entering upon, an academic career. Brüning had been born in Münster, in Westphalia, but unlike most Centrist leaders he seems to have felt no strong regional affections but to have identified with Prussian nationalism, a feeling "intensified still more during his long residence at the border University of Strassburg under the influence of Martin Spahn."[3] When the war broke out, he abandoned his university studies to volunteer for the army, and served with distinction as an officer in spite of poor eyesight and lack of any previous military training. In the war years he acquired a permanent deep respect for, and even awe of, the German officer corps, which was to prove a "fateful predisposition for his later relationship to Hindenburg, Groener, and Schleicher."[4]

Apart from his union contacts and Kaas himself, Brüning's closest colleagues were not in the Center party but in the moderate wing of the German Nationalist party, particularly in the circle around the former naval officer Gottfried Treviranus, soon to lead a secession from that party. Brüning also valued highly his connections with the *Reichswehr*, and ever since his retirement from military duty after the war he had kept up acquaintance with individuals in the army command. These connections led him inevitably to an introduction to Gen. Kurt von Schleicher, the army's political representative in the War Ministry and good friend to President Hindenburg.

3. Morsey, "Heinrich Brüning," in *Zeitgeschichte*, p. 251.
4. Ibid., p. 252.

Brüning and Schleicher held their first conversation in the spring of 1929. They found they shared a similar distaste for ineffectual parliamentary politics and a desire to see the monarchy restored, but Brüning expressed scruples about the use of authoritarian methods. He was "astonished" when Schleicher pointed out that Article 48 of the constitution provided a legal means of carrying out needed change through a presidential dictatorship.

After this illuminating talk, Brüning discreetly discussed the possibilities of such a government with several Centrists, evidently including Kaas, thus inspiring the Dortmund speech on "parliamentary reform."[5] Whether or not Brüning was aware at that time that he himself might be the initiator of "reform" is not clear, and his first meeting with President Hindenburg did not take place until February 1930. The continued existence of the Müller government was of course an obstacle in the path of plans for a presidential cabinet, but it proved unnecessary to plot its overthrow because Müller's own supporters were rapidly undermining him.

Brüning attended the Hague Conference with Wirth in the summer of 1929 and returned with the recommendation that the Center support the Young Plan, as it was a distinct improvement over the Dawes Plan. But he became convinced that the Reich could not afford to continue international reparations payments without a reform of its own finances, and he succeeded in persuading the Center delegation that the party's acceptance of the Hague agreements must be made contingent upon a reform of Reich finances.

The urgent need for reform was an unforeseen consequence of the Law for Unemployment Insurance passed in 1927, the major social legislation of Marx's third cabinet. The funding of unemployment benefits had been expected to be derived from increased tax revenues in an expanding economy. This optimistic assumption had proved to be totally in error. In the two years since the law had been passed, German production had not expanded sufficiently to provide adequate funding for the program, in spite of a temporary upswing in 1928, and the number of unemployed eligible to receive benefits was far larger than expected, even before the world depression began at the end of 1929. As a result, government subsidies to the unemployment service

5. Brüning, 1:148–55.

were necessary and seemed likely to be steadily increasing in the future.

Brüning and other German financial experts believed that expenditures should be cut by lowering payments and revenues should be increased by a rise in the percentage of contributions by employers and workers. Although a temporary increase in contributions was proposed by the Reichsrat in September 1929, any agreement to this by the Reichstag was made impossible by the diametrically opposed stands taken by the People's party, as representative of German manufacturers and employers, and the Social Democratic party, as representative of the hard-pressed workers and their unions.

Stresemann as leader of the DVP managed until the day of his death, on October 3, to prevent his party from clashing so violently with the Socialists on this issue as to endanger the passage of the Young Plan and the existence of the coalition. His successor as foreign minister, Julius Curtius, also from the DVP, was a man of far less strength of will. He found it difficult enough to hold his party to the Young Plan and did not try to restrain it in the matter of unemployment insurance, while the party chairman, Ernst Schulz, was firmly on the side of the employers. Chancellor Müller was equally ineffective in controlling his own parliamentary delegation, which was strongly influenced by union representatives pledged not to decrease benefits or to increase workers' contributions. The breakup of the Great Coalition was thus foreseeable months before the chancellor's resignation on 27 March 1930. However satisfactory this outcome may have been in presidential circles, there is no reason to believe that the government's fall was due to any other factor than this collision course of the two wing-parties over insurance benefits, as investigation has shown.[6]

It is not remarkable, therefore, that the Center's Reichstag delegation was prepared for a new cabinet or that Brüning should have pursued his efforts to obtain financial reform with an eye to presidential assistance. A Great Coalition could not be re-created, and he knew, as he told the Center fraction, that Hindenburg would never accept a

6. See Timm, *Die deutsche Sozialpolitik und der Bruch der grossen Koalition im März 1930* (Düsseldorf, 1952).

Weimar Coalition.[7] A presidial cabinet of the minority was predictable and the Center leadership seemed prepared to accept it.

The party was also anxious to prevent a possible liberal and Socialist collaboration in legislation concerning education and religion. In November the Centrist members had walked out of a meeting of a Reichstag committee considering reform of the divorce laws, and the party made it clear that it would tolerate no liberalizing moves in this direction by the Müller government. A possible Socialist-liberal school bill had only been forestalled by direct pressure on the chancellor when the coalition had first been formed. The parties of the middle had proved as unreliable as partners for a clerical party as the left was assumed to be.

In December 1929 and January 1930 a sequence of events took place which was of great interest to the Center and which particularly encouraged Brüning and Kaas in their calculations about the future. First was the secession of twelve Reichstag deputies from the German Nationalist party. Among the twelve were several representatives of the Christian trade unions, Walter Lambach of the Clerks' Union, Franz Behrens of the Christian industrial unions, and several heirs to Adolf Stöcker's prewar Christian Social party. Brüning's friend Treviranus and Walter von Keudell, the former interior minister in Marx's cabinet and sponsor of the ill-fated school bill, were also among those resigning.

Several of the dissidents joined a Christian Social splinter group from the southwest to form the Christian Social People's Service (*Christliche Soziale Volksdienst*, or CSVD). Treviranus and his friends organized themselves as a People's Conservative party. An earlier exodus from the DNVP had resulted in the creation of yet another conservative splinter group, the Agrarian party (*Deutsches Landvolk*). The new parties were free from the radicalism and anti-Catholicism of Hugenberg's followers in the DNVP. Although they were small, they might in the future combine forces and provide for the Center the conservative Protestant partner which the German Nationalist party had never been. An alliance of the Center with such a Protestant conservative group could greatly strengthen its position and approach the

7. Morsey, *Protokolle*, 2:426–27.

ideal of the Essen Program which Brüning had helped to create in 1920.

The Catholic hierarchy in Germany had been showing signs of distaste for Hugenberg's direction of Nationalist policy, and the bishops were particularly annoyed at the Nationalists' refusal to support the Prussian Concordat. They were now more inclined to favor the Center, especially since the election of Kaas as its chairman. Martin Spahn's Catholic Committee in the DNVP Reichstag fraction had defied Hugenberg on the Young Plan and it seemed possible that he might bring them into Treviranus's new party. (Actually, this hope was disappointed, and Spahn eventually joined the National Socialist party in 1933 after the breakup of the Catholic Committee.) If the new parties attracted large numbers of former Nationalist voters in the next elections they might provide a really congenial "friend on the Right" for the Center and set it "free from Social Democratic pressure," as Kaas put it.[8] The party faced the imminent fall of the Great Coalition with no regret in the spring of 1930.

Brüning had been elected chairman of the Center Reichstag fraction in December, an extraordinarily rapid rise for a man of forty-four in a party which had traditionally been led by much older and more experienced men.[9] He persuaded the fraction that it should not accept the Young Plan until financial reform measures had been carried out, and the fraction rejected any idea of granting Müller an enabling act to bypass the parties. On March 8, Brüning gave Müller an ultimatum that his party could not accept the Hague Agreements before financial reform. Müller and Curtius were equally determined to push the Young Plan bills through the Reichstag before the expected showdown on unemployment insurance. A solution to the impasse was provided in a private interview between Brüning and Hindenburg on March 11, the day of the second reading of the Young Plan bills. The president gave Brüning the assurance that he would use "all constitutional means" to accomplish the prompt "adjustment of finances."[10] With such an assurance behind it the Center could give up its uncompro-

---

8. Wirth, "Die Ereignisse und ihre Bedeutung," and Teipel, "Die Parteipolitik des katholischen Klerus," *Deutsche Republik* 4 (1929): 393–98.
9. Morsey, "Brüning," in *Zeitgeschichte*, p. 255.
10. Timm, p. 174.

mising position and vote for the Young Plan, and the bills were passed on March 13. Neither the Bavarian People's party nor the new People's Conservatives supported the Young Plan bills.

Concerning the financial "adjustment," the possibility of a temporary use of Article 48 was fully recognized. An editorial in *Germania* said that "although it is the earnest wish of the Center that the financial program be carried out by parliamentary means, we believe that we now have a guarantee that in the failure of Parliament and the parties to act, all constitutional means may be used."[11] Assuming no new elections were held, this meant that if the Socialists refused to compromise on the question of unemployment insurance (as seemed certain) the Center would support a minority cabinet formed to deal with the situation by extra-parliamentary means.

Immediately after the passage of the Young Plan, the government parties again began to argue about unemployment insurance. On March 27, Oscar Meyer, a Democratic legal expert, proposed a compromise draft bill, which Brüning accepted, that provided for an immediate loan to the insurance fund but kept the employers' contributions fixed at 3½ percent instead of the 4 percent asked by the Socialists. In effect, the compromise proposal postponed the most vital decisions until a later date.[12] The People's party leadership finally agreed to accept the Meyer-Brüning compromise. But to the majority of the Social Democratic fraction, a postponement meant that if the economic depression in Germany continued, as it seemed likely to do, the bargaining position of the labor unions would be weakened and that of the industrialists correspondingly strengthened. For that reason the Socialists rejected the compromise and that same day Chancellor Müller notified the president of the cabinet's resignation.

President Hindenburg requested Brüning to form a new cabinet and he was able to accomplish this within three days. There were rumors that the government had been planned long in advance and that Brüning had in some way conspired in Müller's fall. There seems to be no basis for the former charge, and as for the latter, there was no reason to overthrow a government which was openly disintegrating for rea-

11. Ibid., p. 175.
12. Ibid., p. 181.

sons evident to all. Eight of the ministers in Brüning's cabinet were simply held over from Müller's cabinet, with Stegerwald moving from Transport to Labor and Wirth from Occupied Territories to the coveted post of the Interior, never before held by a Centrist. The choice of the three new men reflected Brüning's desire to forge stronger ties with the nonradical Right: Treviranus became minister for occupied territories; Johann Viktor Bredt of the Economic party, minister of justice; and Martin Schiele, minister of agriculture. Schiele, an agrarian who had also served in Marx's 1927 cabinet, was Hindenburg's personal choice.[13] Although he gave up his seat in the Nationalist Reichstag delegation, his ties with that party and his agrarian background prevented the DNVP from opposing the new government as vigorously as it might otherwise have done. Against Hugenberg's real inclinations, the Nationalists voted to defeat the motion of no-confidence introduced by the Social Democrats, and the government was permitted to survive.

In personnel and in program the new government was at least as conservative as that of 1927, yet it was accepted by the Center with equanimity. The fraction did not question Brüning's explanation that Hindenburg "doesn't want a liberal government . . . in the last years of his life." The seemingly great influence of Center party members in the cabinet certainly did much to reconcile possible critics. Wirth was evidently completely tamed by having obtained a "political" ministry and was content to be the "bridge" to the Left that Brüning expected him to be. He was repeatedly used by the chancellor to explain or justify unpalatable legislation to labor. He stopped publishing his journal *Deutsche Republik* in 1930 and cut his formerly close ties with the *Reichsbanner*.[14] Since 1928, as one historian has put it, "he had gradually poured [water] into his democratic wine."[15]

The reaction of the Christian trade unions was favorable to the new regime because they identified Brüning and Stegerwald with their interests, even though both men had dropped their union affiliations. The *Westdeutsche Arbeiterzeitung*, on behalf of the workers' associations, asserted that Wirth, Brüning, and Stegerwald were better repre-

13. Brüning, 1:170–71.
14. Knapp, "The German Center Party and the *Reichsbanner*," p. 176.
15. Eyck, 2:329.

sentatives of workers' interests than the Social Democrats,[16] and Joos wrote that a presidial regime need not mean the end of democracy and would save the country from dangerous "experiments."[17] Stegerwald himself, however, worried that the government might radicalize the Social Democratic party and the Free unions.[18]

By July, the government had drawn up a rigorous financial program involving heavy tax increases and special aid to agriculture. Although the reforms were acknowledged by all of the moderate parties to be necessary, each party and each interest group within the parties presented objections to particular details of the plan. Finance Minister Paul Moldenhauer was forced to resign after failing to persuade his party, the DVP, to accept his program, and his replacement, former Economic Minister Hermann Dietrich, was repudiated by his delegation from the Democratic party. The Bavarian People's party, Economic party, and Social Democratic party all complained of special hardships for their constituents, and the Agrarian party was not satisfied with the extensive aid provided to agriculture.

It is nonetheless probable that Brüning could have made a few compromises and steered a revised bill through the Reichstag.[19] Instead, he preferred to cut through parliamentary entanglements and put the reforms into effect through the use of Article 48. The opportunity to use presidential emergency decrees had been one of the reasons for forming the cabinet in the first place, and the urgency of the financial crisis seemed justification enough to Brüning. The Center fully supported him, and Wirth defended the move to the Reichstag. The Social Democrats then sought to nullify the emergency decrees, as was permitted by the constitution. Their motion received a majority of votes from a combination of Social Democrats, Communists, National Socialists, and Hugenberg's Nationalists.

Brüning might still have effected a compromise, but chose instead to dissolve the Reichstag in order to oppose "sterile parliamentarianism" with a plebiscite from a "healthy democracy."[20] Never was a de-

16. Grebing, "Zentrum und katholische Arbeiterschaft," pp. 285–86.
17. Wachtling, p. 153.
18. Morsey, *Protokolle*, 2:428.
19. Eyck, 2:267–71.
20. Brüning, 1:192.

cision so wrongly calculated as this one. The German democratic plebiscite produced a result that was anything but healthy and a Parliament that was far more sterile than the one elected in 1928.

A few days after the dissolution, the financial reforms were again issued as an emergency decree, with some modifications reducing the tax burden for lower incomes. The absence of the Reichstag allowed the chancellor to act directly in the crisis. He hoped that the elections scheduled, as late as possible, for September would strengthen the moderate Right and relieve him of the necessity of cooperating with the Socialists.

The election campaign provided a perfect arena for extremists of both Right and Left. The National Socialists received huge increases in support, raising their number of Reichstag delegates from 12 to 107, most of them totally without political experience, bringing the behavior of the streets into the previously sedate proceedings of Parliament. The Communists also made heavy gains among the unemployed working class, increasing their number of seats from 54 to 77, and the Social Democrats lost 10 seats from the same electorate, dropping from 153 to 143. Hugenberg's Nationalists declined from 73 to 41, as Brüning had hoped, but the defectors did not transfer their allegiance to the small conservative splinter groups; neither had the splinter parties amalgamated. They received insignificant representation in the Reichstag (Conservative People's party 4, Christian People's Service 14, Agrarians 19). This was a serious blow to Brüning's long-term plan of forging a strong Protestant-conservative partnership for the Center. The middle parties of the DVP and the State party (the reorganized form of the German Democratic party) continued to atrophy and comprised little more than splinter groups themselves in the new Reichstag, with only 44 seats between them.

The Center and the Bavarian People's party did well in the election, recouping their 1928 losses. The Center gained 6 seats, rising to 68, and the BVP 3, rising to 19. The Center had campaigned much more actively than usual: in Düsseldorf, for example, over 700,000 pamphlets were circulated, cars with loudspeakers broadcast Kaas's election speech all over the city, and an airplane with streaming banners exhorted the voters in this heavily Catholic district to vote for the Center. In spite of this, the Communist party for the first time received more votes than the Center in Düsseldorf. The Nazis did less well than either Center or KPD in the city, but gained in those parts of town where civil servants lived, evidence perhaps of continued resentment against Brüning's and Stegerwald's stand on their salary raises.[21]

Several statistical analyses of the 1930 election have been made, examining the reason for the great increase in National Socialist support. Participation in the election was high, 82 percent of eligible voters, and one analyst concluded that about 32 percent of Nazi support came from new voters, primarily the newly enfranchised young people but also formerly apathetic nonvoters. As many as 38 percent of the votes for the Nazis came from defectors from the DNVP and other traditional rightist groups. About 23 percent came from former voters for other "non-Catholic parties." "The decrease in the Socialist vote and increases in the Catholic and Communist votes bore no statistical relationship to the increase in the Nazi vote."[22] This agrees with other analyses which show that the Center's vote held firm against the Nazis through the elections of 1933, and that, in general, those who left the Center were more likely to be industrial workers who turned to the Communists (as in Düsseldorf) than converts to the extreme Right. This was scant comfort to the party in the fall of 1930, however, since the Center alone could never be more than an impotent minority if the non-Catholic middle collapsed.

After the elections, the chancellor did not seriously consider the formation of a normal parliamentary regime, as this would have meant coalition either with the Socialists or the National Socialists. He told the Center fraction that any cabinet containing National Socialists would provoke "serious economic consequences [internationally]" and told Wirth as interior minister to make a radio speech announcing that the government would continue in office and would not carry on coalition negotiations "of the old kind." Joos defended the government's stand to the Reichstag. Such assistance from members of the Center's democratic Left was helpful, mollifying the Socialists and, equally important, Hess's Prussian Center delegation.[23]

Brüning told the fraction that he expected the National Socialists to be in sharp opposition, and in fact, he welcomed this and made use

21. Stump, pp. 80–81.
22. Karl O'Lessker, "Who Voted for Hitler? A New Look at the Class Basis of Naziism," *American Journal of Sociology* 74 (1969): 63–69.
23. Brüning, 1:197; Morsey, *Protokolle*, 2:479–84.

of Nazi agitation to put pressure on the Allies in the hope of winning reduction or cancellation of reparations. Not only did the foreign policy of Brüning's government become markedly more nationalistic after the elections, to the dismay of Curtius, the foreign minister, who wanted to continue Stresemann's policies, but Brüning even naïvely assured Hitler, in a meeting October 5, that his exclusion from government for a year or so longer would reap benefits for German nationalism in the long run.[24]

Brüning was urged by a number of his colleagues, among them Treviranus, Schiele, and Kaas, to admit National Socialists to his cabinet. Monsignor Ignaz Seipel, the Austrian chancellor, also recommended cooperation, but Stegerwald agreed with Brüning that such a move would have disastrous effects on Germany's foreign relations. A second meeting with the National Socialist leadership was held at Treviranus's house, but their demand for the ministries of the Interior and Defense was unacceptable. Mediation between Centrists and Nazis in these months was often performed by members of the employees' branch of the Christian trade unions, the Clerks' Union, for example, by Albert Krebs, *Gauleiter* of Hamburg and editor of a National Socialist newspaper, who was also an official in the DHV. This link to the supposedly more "tamable" labor wing of the NSDAP was valued both by rightist Centrists and later by General Schleicher. It was probably of little real significance, and simply served as a "convenient stratagem" for its disparate proponents, who "permitted the rumor mills to exaggerate their contacts principally in order to silence or win over opponents in their respective camps."[25]

Although dislike of National Socialism was very strong within the Center, many Centrists were more worried about continued presidial dictatorship than about Nazi participation in the government. Brüning's regime violated the Weimar Constitution in spirit if not in letter. A coalition of the Center with the NSDAP would restore parlia-

24. Julius Curtius, *Sechs Jahre Minister der deutsche Republik* (Heidelberg, 1948), p. 171; Brüning, 1:197–217; Gerhard Schulz, "Erinnerungen an eine misslungene Restauration: Heinrich Brüning und seine Memoiren," *Der Staat* 2 (1972): 69.

25. Peter Hayes, "'A Question Mark with Epaulettes?' Kurt von Schleicher and Weimar Politics," *Journal of Modern History* 52 (1980): 51–55. See William Sheridan Allen, ed., *The Infancy of Nazism: The Memoirs of Ex-Gauleiter Albert Krebs, 1923–1933* (New York, 1976), for the tie between the DHV and Strasser's following.

mentary rule and perhaps, so the reasoning went, responsibility would tame the Nazi leadership. In the Reichstag fraction, Kaas, Thomas Esser (vice-president of the Reichstag and leader of white-collar workers in the Christian trade unions), Johannes Bell, and Ludwig Perlitius (the ineffectual fraction chairman) all belonged to this school of thought, and in 1932 even Joseph Joos wished to return to legitimate parliamentary government in this improbable way.[26] Brüning, on the other hand, continued to find the National Socialists more useful as enemies than as possible partners and they played only a peripheral role in his long-term plans to restore the monarchy and transform his government into one of the responsible Right.

During these years the continued existence of the Weimar Coalition in Prussia posed a difficult problem for the Center. Hess's personality and the Center's position in the *Landtag* were largely responsible for Minister-President Braun's success in maintaining a stable regime, but demands were continual for a broadening of the coalition, and as the months passed, for new elections to the *Landtag*, last chosen in 1928. Brüning had promised the DNVP in the spring of 1930 to use his influence to try to admit that party to the Prussian government if it would support his financial program, but the offer had been rejected. After the September elections, Braun had been of invaluable aid to Brüning in staving off extremist demands and the two men had become allies. On several occasions it was suggested that Braun's office be coordinated more closely with the Reich government; Hirtsiefer, Centrist union man in the Prussian cabinet, urged that Brüning strengthen his connections with the SPD by offering Braun the post of vice-chancellor without portfolio in the Reich government. Late in 1930 and again in November 1931, Braun offered to hand over the Prussian minister-presidency to Brüning, reviving the imperial tradition, which would have helped the chancellor's situation greatly. Hess, Kaas, Brüning, and Severing discussed the possibility, but President Hindenburg was unalterably opposed to the suggestion, considering it an infringement of his own prerogative.[27] Since Braun's government had a majority and was perfectly legitimate, more so than Brüning's,

---

26. Morsey in *Das Ende der Parteien*, pp. 302–3; Wachtling, p. 162.
27. Brüning, 1:260–61; Severing, 2:303; Knapp, "Heinrich Brüning in Exil: Briefe an Wilhelm Sollmann, 1940–1946," *Vierteljahrshefte für Zeitgeschichte* 22 (1971): 99.

the strange partnership of Left-democratic coalition in Prussia and conservative-autocratic presidial cabinet in the Reich continued until state elections were held in April, 1932.

Brüning's relations with the smaller states were less satisfactory than with Prussia. Most of them found it impossible to maintain financial solvency in the deepening depression and their governments expected aid from the Reich which Brüning was not anxious to provide. Relations with Bavaria were particularly poor. The BVP, now heading a minority regime at home, was mildly approving of Brüning's government for political reasons, but Held and Fritz Schäffer, the dynamic younger man who had been chairman of the party since 1929, fought the chancellor's economic program every step of the way and ordered the Reichstag fraction to resist it, to the distress of Prelate Leicht. Schäffer was on friendly personal terms with Brüning, but he was determined to prove himself as dedicated a federalist as Heim and Held. The party eventually agreed to support the first laws of July 1930, in spite of the fact that they included a rise in the hated beer tax, but later, in January 1931, it threatened an appeal to the courts if modification in the laws' application to Bavaria could not be obtained otherwise. Brüning was able to effect a compromise before the suit was actually completed, and the state withdrew its complaint.

When Brüning formed his second cabinet in October 1931, the BVP tried to obtain special conditions for the state, including direct financial aid, hardly a very "federalist" request. There was some fear in Bavaria that the chancellor might use Article 48 to alter the relations between Reich and Länder in some fundamental way, and it says much for Brüning's self-restraint that he did not take this way out of a highly provoking situation. Very little had come of the much-acclaimed "reunion" of Center and BVP in 1927.

The governments of Baden and Hesse, both headed by Centrists, also were in serious financial difficulty and needed Reich assistance, while at the same time resisting (under Bavarian influence, according to Brüning) the effects of the emergency decrees on their autonomy. The government of Eugen Bolz in Württemberg, in contrast, maintained impeccable finances, winning the chancellor's praise. Bolz, who sat in the Center Reichstag fraction as well as serving as minister-president of his state, approved the presidial government and its authoritarian methods and became a close friend to Brüning.

Brüning's first cabinet included five ministers from the Catholic parties, and it was free from the need to bargain with the other parties, yet the Center's goals in *Kulturpolitik* were not furthered in any way during his term of office. Kaas had said on several occasions that a more authoritarian form of government could achieve more for Catholicism than the parliamentary system, but if he expected Brüning to make use of his powers to enact Catholic legislation, he was disappointed. When Brüning was criticized by other Centrists for his inaction, he indicated that he did not feel it was appropriate for a Catholic chancellor to take the initiative in this field (though Fehrenbach, Wirth, and Marx had all agreed to their governments' introduction of bills on education and other issues important to Catholics). The real reason for his obvious reluctance to deal openly in any way with Catholic programs was probably Hindenburg's known prejudice against Catholics, which has been attested to in several sources. Brüning had acquired Hindenburg's favor as an ex-army officer and the president was willing to overlook the fact that his chancellor was a "Cathlist" (as he pronounced the word), but there was no point in unnecessarily reminding him of it.[28]

In any case, the prospects for the success of another school bill had decidedly worsened since the elections of 1930. The National Socialists, as Marx reported to the Vatican in a letter of December of that year, favored community schools and opposed private schools altogether, even though a great many of their Reichstag deputies were Catholics. He estimated that a tentative Nationalist proposal for a school bill, essentially similar to the Keudell bill of 1927, would have obtained at most 180 of 577 votes in the Reichstag.[29] Chances for a *Reichskonkordat* were equally remote. The Vatican itself in these years seemed to be looking away from the political arena and favoring nonparliamentary means of achieving Catholic objectives. Pius XI's call for Catholic Action appealed to the initiative of private individuals and undermined efforts at political activity.[30]

---

28. Dorpalen, pp. 174, 235, and 226 for Hindenburg's pronunciation; John W. Wheeler-Bennett, *The Wooden Titan*, p. 340; Brüning, 2:471–82.
29. Grünthal, pp. 286–87.
30. Becker, "Das Ende der Zentrumspartei und die Problematik des politischen Katholizismus in Deutschland," *Die Welt als Geschichte*, 23 (1963): 164; see also Stehkämper, 2:363–68.

The Lateran treaty of 1929 between the Vatican and Mussolini's government abandoned the Catholic party in Italy in return for direct guarantees from the Fascist regime. The papal encyclical *Quadrigesimo Anno*, issued in 1931 by Pius XI on the fortieth anniversary of *Rerum Novarum*, was far more favorable to corporativism than the earlier social encyclical had been, and its recommendation of the organization of society into vocational groups could be interpreted as approval of Mussolini's corporative state and, hence, as a rejection of the parliamentary system and conventional labor unions. The Austrian Christian Social party took *Quadrigesimo Anno* as justification for its formation of an authoritarian and vaguely corporate government in that country. Germany's Center party seemed more and more to be an anachronism on the European scene whose future role was uncertain.

The years of Brüning's chancellorship saw a steady deterioration in the Center's ability to function as a political party. Although in the Weimar era an elaborate organizational structure had been achieved for the party, the site of most real political decision-making and communication had continued to be the parliamentary delegations in the Reichstag and the state legislatures. The National Committee itself was led by the men who directed their fractions in the capitals. Brüning's presidial regime, coupled with the impossibility of conducting orderly business in the Reichstag after the extremists' victory in the 1930 elections, had resulted in a steep decline of parliamentary activity and consequently in the frequency and significance of fraction meetings. The Reichstag was adjourned for weeks, sometimes months, at a time, and the records of the Center's delegation reveal a corresponding drop in the number of fraction meetings.

When the delegation did meet, moreover, it was not to decide policy but to listen to the chancellor, who literally came to deliver speeches to his colleagues as if he were addressing a public gathering. Occasionally Kaas or Stegerwald would report on government business, though Kaas was away so often, at health resorts or visiting in Rome, that there were complaints about his neglect of the party. In 1931, and in the two years following, the party attempted to make up for the absence of parliamentary life by holding fraction meetings outside Berlin, in cities around the country, where Centrists from the state parties could attend as guests; for example, a meeting was held in August 1931 in Stuttgart at which the Centrist ministers from the governments of Baden, Württemberg, and Hesse participated. But this kind of peripatetic rallying merely emphasized the abnormal political conditions.

In former years, a serious political or economic crisis had been able to call forth effective leadership in the party but from 1930 to 1933 there appears to have been an extraordinary reluctance among the experienced men in the party to take on the responsibility of leadership. Kaas was never really interested in party affairs, and whatever energy he could summon was expended in private intrigues carried on without consultation with the party or even, after the autumn of 1931, with Brüning. Wirth had lost his old spirit, following Brüning loyally but refusing even to exercise the power he might have wielded in the Interior Ministry. In the spring of 1930 he surprised his former friends on the Left by declining to move against National Socialist penetration of the Thuringian police until overruled by the Supreme Court.[31] Stegerwald had also ceased to be interested in leadership and he had become increasingly alienated from the labor wing of the party because of the harsh policies carried out by his Labor Ministry, which he defended in an insensitive manner and with disregard for any political effects they might have. Marx had permanently stepped down from responsibility, and Guerard and Perlitius were personally incapable of assuming it. The deaths of Hess in Prussia, February 1932, and Schofer in Baden, December 1930, left those two state parties without guidance. Hirtsiefer was indecisive, and others in the Prussian fraction, Albert Lauscher and Fritz Grass, were early converts to accommodation with National Socialism.

All looked to Brüning, but Brüning aspired to lead the country, not a political party or a parliamentary delegation. He regarded the fraction as a compliant sounding-board and valued his contacts with the People's Conservatives, the Clerks' Union, and the Agrarians more highly than those with the Center.[32] He refused for a long time to see the evidence of Kaas's inadequacy as party chairman, and even when

31. Severing, 2:241–42; Eyck, 2:261.
32. Schulz, p. 72.

disillusioned on this score, did not choose to act as his replacement until more or less forced to do so in the summer of 1933.

For many in the party, especially the young, Brüning became the object of a kind of *Führer* cult, unlikely as this may seem considering his personality and inclination. The Windthorst League, which had demanded a *Führer* at the party congress of 1928, found one in Brüning. Joos was a conscious promoter of the cult, seeing Brüning as the symbol of resistance to National Socialism.[33] Brüning himself told the Reichstag fraction at the end of 1930 that the party should accommodate its youth movement by permitting them to wear uniforms and to carry small-caliber weapons.[34] Members of the Windthorst League began dressing alike in 1931, though not in military uniforms. By 1933, many local branches of the Center had organized defense corps to protect their meetings—a strange metamorphosis for the antimilitarist Center party.

Unlike the *Führer* of the National Socialist movement, Brüning derived his power not from a mass following, since the young Centrists alone could not provide that, but from the president, and this support was already beginning to erode by the fall of 1931. "He became dependent upon [Hindenburg] in the same degree that he sought to make himself independent from democratic party politics. Partly consciously, partly unconsciously, he thus evolved from the supposed rescuer of the republic into the first of its liquidators."[35] The president could not be induced to sponsor Brüning's plan to restore stability in the Reich by putting the grandson of William II on the throne, because Hindenburg would not pass over William himself; and he would not agree to Brüning's choice of a moderate conservative as his successor because he preferred his own aristocratic friends. If William could rid himself of a Bismarck, Hindenburg could much more easily rid himself of a Brüning.

In October 1931 Brüning was forced by the president (on the advice of General Schleicher) to drop Curtius, the foreign minister, from the cabinet, after his failure to create a customs union between Ger-

---

33. Wachtling, p. 155.
34. Morsey, *Protokolle*, 2:502.
35. Karl Dietrich Bracher, "Die Brüning-Memoiren," *Vierteljahrshefte für Zeitgeschichte* 19 (1971): 118.

many and Austria. At the same time, Hindenburg indicated that five Catholics in a cabinet of nine (now eight, as Brüning himself replaced Curtius as foreign minister) were far too many, and demanded that Guerard and Wirth (whom he had always disliked) be dropped also.[36] Schätzel, the post office minister, was retained, even before he had been officially confirmed in the post by the Bavarian People's party leadership in Munich. One source has implied that Schätzel was favored by Hindenburg because his technical knowledge of communications enabled the president to keep himself informed about conversations in the chancellory.[37] Stegerwald was also allowed to remain, although a few months later he was to be accused by Hindenburg of being an "agrarian Bolshevik" who intended to send Catholic workers to settle in eastern Germany.

Brüning was humiliated by this high-handed action and offered to resign at that time, and again in January and February; but he wanted to stay in office long enough to ensure the evacuation of Allied troops from the Rhineland and to carry through the reelection of Hindenburg as president. The reelection seemed to him to be the only security against a victory of the National Socialists, and the Center, strongly backed by the Windthorst League, followed his lead; in fact the party campaigned more vigorously for Hindenburg's second election than it had worked to prevent his first. In ironic reversal of the situation in 1925, the chairman of the Bavarian People's party, Fritz Schäffer, was at first opposed to the candidacy, saying that he preferred Brüning to run, and that Hindenburg would soon make terms with Hitler;[38] but the BVP electorate, like the Center's, loyally returned the president to office.

As soon as his reelection was certain, Hindenburg expressed his gratitude for Brüning's efforts by suggesting that he resign, but was persuaded to accept a delay for the sake of appearances. The immediate reason for the abrupt dismissal was the cabinet's plan to investigate the *Osthilfe*, the aid to agrarians in east Germany, with the goal of reforming its finances. Schlange-Schöningen, the minister in charge

36. Morsey, *Protokolle*, 2:542–44; On Schleicher, Hayes, p. 45.
37. Gottfried Treviranus, *Das Ende von Weimar* (Düsseldorf, 1963), pp. 141–42.
38. Schwend, "Die Bayrische Volkspartei," in Matthias and Morsey, *Das Ende der Parteien 1933*, p. 459.

of the *Osthilfe*, planned to resettle unemployed workers on small farms to be created from unprofitable landed estates in the east. This was denounced as "agrarian Bolshevism" by Hindenburg's friends, and the president, a newly endowed landowner himself, agreed with them. On May 29, he made it clear to Brüning that he was finished, and on the following day the entire cabinet tendered its resignation.

19
"THE END OF THE PARTY"

The Center Reichstag fraction was stunned to learn that Brüning's successor as chancellor was Franz von Papen. To dismiss a leader of the Center party and replace him with another Centrist without consultation with the party was an insult; that Papen should accept the post, again without consultation, was a double insult. There was nearly unanimous agreement that the party could never support Papen's cabinet of aristocrats, and the Center went into opposition for the first time since 1909.

No one was more shocked at the turn of events than Ludwig Kaas, who suffered a total nervous collapse for several days; and yet there is some evidence that he had, perhaps unwittingly, had some hand in the choice of Papen, if not also in Brüning's dismissal. The close relationship between Kaas and Brüning had broken up the previous autumn, when Kaas had asked for Brüning's assistance in rescuing from bankruptcy the *Kölnische Volkszeitung* and its affiliate, the *Görreshaus*. Very many institutions connected with the Center party were experiencing financial difficulties: the banks holding the assets of the Christian trade unions, the *Volksverein*, and several newspapers of which the *Kölnische Volkszeitung* was one. Directors of these institutions expected government help, but the chancellor was reluctant to reward what he considered to be the result of inefficiency, waste, and corruption. He was especially anxious to avoid the charge of favoring Catholic enterprises, and had little respect for the competence of the Cologne banks run by Catholics.[1] Kaas was on the board of directors of the *Kölnische Volkszeitung* and hence should have been supervising the paper's finances, but apparently he had been totally negligent. Eventually, the paper received some assistance, a good deal of it from

1. Brüning, 2:471–76.

Center party funds, but relations between Kaas and Brüning were never the same after the incident, and Kaas's position in the party was weakened.

Already in late 1931 and on several occasions after that, Kaas was meeting in friendly fashion with Papen. Their discussions ranged over several subjects, including their mutual interests in Rome, the possibility of a *Reichskonkordat*, and the question of a change in the government. Kaas indicated his distress that Brüning had done nothing to eliminate the Socialist-democratic coalition in Prussia (which was much disliked at the Vatican) or to coordinate that state with the Reich. The inclusion of National Socialists in the *Länder* governments and the theoretical possibility of a more Rightist presidial cabinet were probably also discussed. Kaas must have known that Papen was an intimate of Hindenburg's, but it is not clear that he actually aided in Brüning's overthrow or that he made any commitments on behalf of his party.[2] Papen seems to have boasted that he could split the Center and bring at least substantial numbers of its delegates to the support of his government, but it is fairly evident from eyewitness accounts of Kaas's astonishment and dismay that he did not expect Papen himself to be named chancellor.[3] Whatever commitments were made or were thought to have been made, the party was not split, but united against Papen.

Papen had failed in his effort to break up the Prussian democratic coalition in 1925, but his activities in the Center had not ended then. He failed to win reelection to the *Landtag* in 1928, because the party ranked him much lower than before on the district list of candidates, but this did not discourage him from trying, unsuccessfully, to have himself appointed to the national Executive Council of the Center at the party congress of December 1928. He regained a seat in the *Landtag* after the resignation of his friend Roeingh, but took little part in parliamentary life and did not seek election in 1932.[4]

Papen's goal of directing Center policy through his control of the *Germania* press was not much more successful than his parliamentary career. Purchase of the majority block of shares in 1924 had enabled him to become chairman of the board of directors in 1925 and to make

2. Becker, "Brüning, Prälat Kaas," pp. 103–5.
3. Morsey in *Das Ende Der Parteien*, pp. 306–7.
4. Ibid., pp. 287–88.

some changes on the board, replacing a number of moderate and republican Centrists with his aristocratic friends, but it had not ensured a significant change in editorial policy, because the paper was committed to reflecting official Center party views; any major change would have resulted in the paper's being repudiated by the party leadership.

In 1927, Karl Spiecker, who had bought Erzberger's shares from his widow but had left the board of directors of the paper before Papen had acquired control, published an article revealing the extent to which *Germania* had by that time become an aristocratic preserve. He named two princes, five counts, and six barons among the shareholders, most of whom were openly monarchist. Erzberger's efforts to bring the paper under the direction of republicans had been thoroughly undermined.

Spiecker subsequently sold his shares to the *Kölnische Volkszeitung*, and at the end of 1927, with the approval of the Center party, an *Interessengemeinschaft* was formed between the publishing concern of the *Kölnische Volkszeitung* and the *Germania* press for the expressed purpose of obtaining a "unified representation of the Center program and the interests of the Catholic population." Members of the boards of directors were exchanged and the feature writer of *Germania*, Bernhard Orth, changed positions with the head of the Berlin bureau of the *Kölnische Volkszeitung*. A few months later it was revealed that the consolidation had also affected local Catholic papers from towns and districts all over the Rhineland and Westphalia: a local Cologne paper and papers from Gelsenkirchen, Osnabrück, Koblenz, Duisburg, Krefeld, Hamm, and München-Gladbach. All of these were now bound to the *Germania* press. The cartelization had apparently been motivated partly by a desire to minimize Papen's role in the press, but it had the inevitable effect of further diluting the distinctively republican, metropolitan flavor of the postwar *Germania*.[5]

As a newspaper magnate, Papen was frustrated politically and hard-pressed financially (he tried to sell his shares to a suitable buyer in 1927), and he complained that his editors "refused to allow me any expression at all of my political convictions,"[6] but in fact he did use the paper as a vehicle for his opinions in special articles, for example,

5. Information on the cartelization from *Kölnische Volkszeitung*, 13 Nov. 1927; *Frankfurter Zeitung*, 13 Nov. 1927, 21 Nov. 1927, and 3 Jan. 1928; Bach, pp. 194–315.
6. Papen, p. 112.

"The Center's Course," which appeared in June of 1925 and advocated an authoritarian form of government. Wirth and his friends regularly boycotted *Germania* in the late 1920s, preferring to submit material to Democratic papers like the *Berliner Tageblatt*. It was not until May of 1932, however, just before he became chancellor, that Papen made a serious attempt to alter the editorial content of *Germania*. He tried to appoint a new editor in chief, but his choice, Emil Ritter, was so much opposed both in the party and by the rest of the staff of the press that after Kaas threatened a general Center boycott of the paper Ritter was dismissed. During his term as chancellor, Papen resigned as chairman of the board of the press, but he resumed the position after his fall and in July 1933, he brought Ritter back as editor in chief and was then finally able to see the paper reflect his own convictions.[7]

Papen's chancellorship was short-lived and his government had few positive objectives, but one of them was to end the anomalous position of the Prussian government. State elections in April 1932 had brought a great increase in National Socialist representation in the *Landtag* and Braun's government lost its scant majority. But the *Landtag*, polarized as it now was between the extremes of Left and Right, would not and could not elect a new minister-president. According to the constitution, in these circumstances the existing cabinet was expected to carry on until a new one was chosen, but naturally this was violently opposed by the extremist parties. Braun, exhausted by years of controversy, took an extended leave of absence in June and never served as minister-president again. His post was filled by the senior minister, Welfare Minister Hirtsiefer, a Centrist who did not measure up to the standards of responsible leadership set by Porsch and Hess. The parties of the Right demanded that a Reich commissioner be appointed, to end the impasse and to coordinate the state with the Reich government.

Rumors of a possible Reich commissioner alarmed the governments of the southern states, and in June, the minister-presidents of Bavaria, Württemberg, and Baden—Held, Bolz, and Schmitt—came personally to Berlin and met first with Papen and then with Hindenburg, to discover if such a move was planned. They received assurances that no act against Prussia or any other state was contemplated.

7. Bach, pp. 304–6; Morsey in *Das Ende der Parteien*, pp. 305–6.

Nevertheless, on July 20, before the scheduled national elections, Papen made use of presidential emergency powers and made himself Reich commissioner to Prussia.

He attempted to explain his move to the southern minister-presidents at a meeting in Stuttgart on July 24, but they would not be pacified, and Held and Schäffer, in particular, turned implacably against him. The BVP had been wavering on the question of supporting Papen until this time, but the Prussian coup aligned it firmly with the opposition. The governments of the southern states all strongly supported the legal steps taken to restore the previous Prussian regime, but the equivocal nature of the Supreme Court's decision, which upheld the legal right of Braun's government but at the same time recognized the legitimacy of the commissioner, gave them little satisfaction.[8]

Papen's chief deputy in the Prussian government, Franz Bracht, was a former member of the right wing of the state Center, and he may have been chosen in a further attempt to split the party, but the Prussian fraction like the Reich fraction was united in its opposition to Papen's regime. Hirtsiefer, however, made no serious protest at being ousted from his post as acting head of the cabinet and offered little cooperation with the Social Democratic ministers.[9] Without the firm guidance of Hess, the Prussian delegation floundered. Like many in the national party, the Prussian fraction under its new head, Prelate Lauscher, tried to seek accommodation with the NSDAP as a means of returning to normal parliamentary conditions and ridding themselves of Papen's illegitimate rule.

Because Papen had practically no parliamentary support, he dissolved the Reichstag in June 1932 and scheduled elections for July 31. The Center's election campaign was directed both against the National Socialists and against Papen, with the stated objective of restoring Brüning to the chancellorship. The party slogan was "Brüning is the name of the leader, Center is the name of the party, freedom is the name of the goal!" Brüning's name was at the head of the national list, and he made a triumphant tour through Germany, speaking to huge crowds; as he pointed out, it was the most successful election for the Center since the septennate election of 1887. The party won 6 new

8. Eyck, 2:421–25.
9. Severing, 2:334–40.

seats, making a total of 75, with 22 seats for the equally victorious BVP, and seems to have received a number of votes from Protestants and Jews, especially in Berlin.[10] Papen's hopes of splitting the party had no basis in reality. The electorate supported the party, but what the party would do with its mandate was problematical.

The tremendous victory of the National Socialists, who increased their seats to 230, meant that the NSDAP and Center between them controlled a majority of seats in the Reichstag. This inspired hope in the Center of a return to normal coalition government. In the last half of 1932, a confusing series of negotiations were carried on between members of the Nazi party and individual Centrists, with the only consistent party policy being the desire to get rid of Papen. Effective leadership was lacking: Kaas had been absent from Berlin during most of the summer and in the fall he not only failed to call the party's National Committee into session but often did not attend meetings of the Reichstag fraction; Brüning refused to fill the vacuum or even to take much part in public relations, because he believed himself to be too closely associated with unpopular economic measures to be of much service.[11] (This self-confessed diffidence does not accord with the adulation which he received from the large gatherings on the summer campaign tour.)

In August, in the absence of guidance from Berlin, a party meeting in Cologne decided to delegate to a committee composed of Joos, Bolz, and Hugo Mönnig, chairman of the Rhenish Center party, the task of trying to form a constitutional government of Centrists and National Socialists. Fritz Schäffer of the Bavarian People's party also took part in the meeting and spoke out enthusiastically in favor of a coalition "from Frick to Kaas." Talks continued in September, but the Nazis did not take them seriously and continued to demand not only the chancellorship but the use of presidential emergency powers. Since the Center's prime motivation was to dispense with presidential decree and return to parliamentary government, the talks came to nothing.

Similar negotiations were held in Prussia, led by Fritz Grass of the *Landtag* fraction. Here the Nazis demanded the office of minister-

---

10. Morsey, pp. 312–14; Brüning, 2:664.
11. Brüning, 2:665.

president and the ministries of the Interior, Finance, and Religion and Education, which the Center refused even to consider.

Some Centrists hoped for eventual accommodation with Hitler; others expected to split the Nazis and work out a satisfactory arrangement with Gregor Strasser, who led a more moderate group in the NSDAP and had good contacts with the Christian trade unions. Even at this date, in the fall of 1932, there was more anger and mistrust directed against Papen and Hugenberg than against the less-known and underestimated Nazi danger. But the party's mandate from the voters had very plainly not been an invitation to give power to Hitler. Heinrich Krone, head of the Windthorst League, warned party leaders that the talks with the National Socialists were unacceptable to the league and hurt the Center's reputation.[12]

Several Center fraction members were attracted to the Nazi proposal to indict Hindenburg for breach of the constitution. Professor Schreiber, rather surprisingly, was one of those who thought the legal grounds perfectly sufficient for such a move. But Bolz, Kaas, and Wirth argued that it would solve nothing and would be playing into Hitler's hands. The plan was abandoned when the parties discovered that Papen did not intend to let the Reichstag hold a session at all. In the ludicrous scene on September 12, when Goering as president of the Reichstag tried to push through a vote on a Communist motion of no-confidence before Papen could produce the order to dissolve the house which he had already obtained from Hindenburg, the Center delegation was caught between a deep desire to express its genuine lack of confidence in Papen's government and a feeling of dismay at joining Communists and National Socialists in a vote on anything whatever. As so often in the last months, neither Brüning nor Kaas was present to give direction. Perlitius, the indecisive fraction head, had intended to direct the delegation to abstain, but instead, they followed the lead of Leicht, the BVP fraction head, in voting yes.[13] The no-confidence vote would have passed even without their votes, and it was nullified, in fact if not in law, by Papen's dissolution order, but the incident is

12. Morsey, p. 322; Schönhoven, "Zwischen Anpassung und Ausschaltung: die Bayerische Volkspartei in der Endphase der Weimarer Republik 1932/33," *Historische Zeitschrift* 224 (1977): 348–51.
13. Brüning, 2:663–64.

significant as a glimpse into the confusion and loss of bearing in the Center.

In the elections of November 1932, the representation of the Center and the BVP was slightly reduced (the Center to seventy seats and the BVP to twenty) because of a smaller turnout of voters than in July. The Nazis lost substantially, but their loss appeared to have benefited only Hugenberg's Nationalists and the Communist party. Parliamentary arithmetic now made a coalition between Center and NSDAP alone impossible, and discussions between the two parties ended.

Papen's base of support was only slightly less minuscule after the election than before it, but for a while he hoped to keep the chancellorship. Kaas and Joos informed him that under no circumstances would the Center agree to prop up his government. His trip to Munich before the election to woo the Bavarian People's party had failed to convince that party to give him its support.[14] Kaas was asked by President Hindenburg to try his own hand at forming a cabinet but he met with total resistance from Nationalists and National Socialists alike. The president then reluctantly let Papen go and appointed General von Schleicher as chancellor, with no other change in the cabinet.

The Center, from its perspective of continuing resentment against the renegade Centrist Papen, viewed Schleicher's government not as one more step into disorder but as a distinct improvement over its predecessor. The Reichstag fraction was favorable to his program of December 15, although its executive council refused to accept more than a week's postponement of the scheduled opening date for the Reichstag of 24 January 1933. Schleicher returned again to his old plan of securing a broad base of support from the unions and the more tamable of the National Socialists. He was on good terms with the Clerks' Union and hoped through it to reach most of the Christian trade unions and the Socialist Free unions. It was even rumored that Gregor Strasser and Stegerwald would be given posts in the cabinet. (Imbusch of the Christian Miners' Union had been working to arrange a Hitler-Schleicher-Stegerwald cabinet in the fall of 1932.)[15] But Strasser's sudden resignation of all his posts in the Nazi party showed what a weak reed he had been to lean upon. The National Socialist movement had

14. Werner Braatz, "Franz von Papen und die Frage der Reichsreform," *Politische Vierteljahresschrift* 16 (1975): 319–36; Schönhoven, pp. 356–58.
15. Hayes, pp. 51–53, 61; Eyck, 2:460.

always derived its real strength from its loyalty to one man, not from any particular platform, and to talk of appealing to "moderates" in the movement was to misunderstand its nature.

The illusory prop of Strasser and the moderates in the NSDAP was knocked from under Schleicher, and his hope of support from the Free unions was probably just as much an illusion. He had little chance to discover this, however, because those very signs of social and economic progressiveness which had at first persuaded the Center to consider cooperating with him were exactly the indications which persuaded Hindenburg to drop him. The general proposed to revive plans to resettle unemployed workers on the eastern estates. The whole question of misuse of funds in the *Osthilfe* administration was to be raised again, and the Center delegate Joseph Ersing was expected to open an investigation into the scandal in the Reichstag. Schleicher thus laid himself open, like Schlange-Schöningen, Stegerwald, and Brüning before him, to the charge of "agrarian Bolshevism."

An opening was there for Papen's intrigues and the frustrated former chancellor did not hesitate to take advantage of it. If he could not regain power on his own he hoped to do so through Hitler and his mass following. After enticing Hugenberg into his plot, he was able to induce the president to name Hitler as chancellor and himself as vice-chancellor. The inauguration ceremonies on January 30 were followed by demonstrations of joy by tens of thousands of Nazi supporters.

For several days after Hitler's appointment, Kaas and Perlitius expected to secure at least one seat in the cabinet for the Center. They met with Hitler and Frick and were given vague words of encouragement, but no ministry was actually forthcoming. The Bavarian People's party was not even consulted about representation in the cabinet, which angered Schäffer, who had been urging for some time that the National Socialists be included in the government. He blamed the omission of the BVP upon Papen, and upon Hugenberg's prejudice against Catholics and sent President Hindenburg a telegram offering the cooperation of his party in a national government.[16]

In the Center, there was still a tendency to underestimate the sig-

16. Morsey, "Hitlers Verhandlungen mit der Zentrumsführung am 31. Januar 1933," *Vierteljahrshefte für Zeitgeschichte* 9 (1961): 183–94; Brauns, "Abbau des Reichsarbeitsministerium?" in Mockenhaupt, *Katholische Sozialpolitik*, p. 181; Schönhoven on Bavaria, pp. 363–64.

nificance of Hitler's appointment (Brauns referred to the "Hitler-Hu-genberg-Papen" government in February), but a distinct change in mood can be detected in accounts of the next two months. Greater issues of policy and the restoration of national order and unity give way in precedence to the lesser but much more urgent question of the personal security of individual party members and their constituents. Would the National Socialists dismiss Centrists from their hard-won positions in the civil service? Continued opposition to the new regime might bring this about; the clergy were also vulnerable to reprisals through the government's control over their stipends. The very success of the Center in integrating Catholics into German society had made its members much more reluctant to become martyrs than in Windthorst's day, and Hitler's methods would obviously be more painful than Bismarck's. The violence attending the March elections made that abundantly clear. Center rallies were broken up, speakers regularly intimidated, and Stegerwald physically beaten. The price of continued resistance would be very high.

On their part, the Nazi leaders were anxious to persuade the Center to voluntary cooperation. Socialists and Jews could be safely isolated and treated like enemies, but it was unwise and unnecessary to antagonize the one-third of Germany's population which was Catholic. Some way had to be found, also, to bring about the withdrawal of the ban on membership in the National Socialist party which had been imposed upon Catholics in 1931 by the bishops. From the early days of the Nazi movement, Hitler had determined not to repeat the mistake of Georg von Schönerer, whose alienation of the Catholic church in Austria and Bohemia had brought about the eclipse of his Pan-German party in the prewar era.[17] German Catholics must, at least for a time, be conciliated. But the March elections showed that the Center's voters were still holding back from support of the regime. The Center actually increased its Reichstag delegation by three seats, and its vote was needed in order to pass the Enabling Act which was to grant dictatorial powers to the new government. Accordingly, just before the Enabling Act was to be voted upon by the Reichstag, Hitler made overtures to Kaas, agreeing to guarantee certain conditions limiting the Enabling Act and to deliver a written declaration of these conditions

17. See Adolf Hitler, *Mein Kampf* (New York, 1940), pp. 128, 150–58, 825–30.

to the Center Reichstag fraction before the vote was taken on March 22. If Brüning's account is to be believed, the possibility of a *Reichskonkordat* was also brought up at this time, and Kaas was "entranced" at the idea.[18] The conditions were

1. The *Länder* were to remain and no constitutional changes were to be introduced except through normal legislative processes. [This assurance ignored the fact that Reich Commissioners had been imposed upon Hesse in February and Bavaria on March 9.]
2. All laws were to be submitted to a working committee for consideration.
3. Equality of all before the law was to be maintained.
4. Existing rights of Christian confessions in the schools and elsewhere were to be maintained.
5. Existing treaties with the churches were to be kept.
6. The judiciary was to remain independent.
7. The professional civil service was to be retained if possible, and if financial exigency demanded a reduction in staff, there was to be objective treatment of all.
8. All presidential rights were to be upheld and nothing was to be done without the consent of the president.[19]

In the lengthy and emotional fraction meetings on March 21 and March 22, Kaas discussed these conditions and clarified them. He admitted that protection for religious freedom applied only to Christians, not to Jews, who were to be classified as aliens; and that "equality before the law" was not to apply to aliens or to "internal criminals" whom Hitler had defined as including Communists and "Marxists." Kaas defended the arrest of leading Socialists because they were or might become coconspirators with the Communists in an attempt at revolution.

Stegerwald voiced approval of moves against "Marxists" in the unions. Brüning cut through the discussion of the content of the conditions to point out that there was no way whatever to ensure that the conditions would be kept, and that the "guarantees" were in fact guaranteed by nothing. A preliminary oral vote was taken in the fraction on whether or not to accept the Enabling Act, with the conditions. No

---

18. Brüning, 2:693.
19. Morsey, Protokolle, 2:624–29. Morsey, *Das "Ermächtigungsgesetz" vom 24. März 1933* (Göttingen, 1968), pp. 15–83; Brüning, 2:694–96.

records were kept of the vote, and individual recollections vary, but evidently only a dozen, or fewer, out of seventy-two in the fraction (with one absent) followed Brüning in his vote of no. Among these were Wirth, Joos, Bolz, Dessauer, Weber, and Fritz Bockius (head of the Hessian Center). Stegerwald's vote is disputed, but Kaas unquestionably led and influenced the majority vote of yes.[20] The fraction then decided that the party's response should be unanimous in the Reichstag vote.

The written note containing Hitler's guarantees did not, in fact, arrive before the Reichstag session, which disturbed those in the fraction who put faith in it, but his speech to the Parliament enumerated nearly all of the points. The Center delegation was visibly intimidated by the Storm Troopers at the entry to the Opera House where the Reichstag was meeting.[21] Fear for personal safety, for family, for future income, was certainly a key motive for those who wanted to vote for the Enabling Act, as it was for those in all the other "bourgeois" parties who unanimously approved the act. The Bavarian People's party fraction voted yes. Schäffer later said that he had sent a telegram ordering the Reichstag fraction to vote no, but evidently it did not reach them, and for once the Berlin delegation overruled the directives of Munich.[22] In May, the Center fraction of the Prussian Landtag voted for Goering's Enabling Act with only two negative votes.

It has often been stated that the vote for the Enabling Act was meaningless, since Hitler would have acquired dictatorial powers with or without legislation. But the Center's vote made it possible for it to be done with legality and respectability, which greatly eased Hitler's position both in Germany and in his relations with the rest of the world. A unanimous vote of no such as was given by the Social Democratic fraction would probably not have provoked many more acts of reprisal and terrorism than occurred to individual Centrists anyway, and would have denied to the regime the appearance of orderly, legal process.

The vote for the Enabling Act released most Center politicians

---

20. Morsey, *Das "Ermächtigungsgesetz,"* pp. 27–30.
21. See, for example, André François-Poncet, *The Fateful Years* (New York, 1949), pp. 64–66.
22 Schwend in *Das Ende der Parteien*, p. 491.

from national responsibility and allowed them to concentrate on securing satisfactory terms for themselves in the new circumstances. The abrupt turnabout of the German hierarchy on March 24, when the Fulda Bishops' Conference under the direction of Cardinal-Archbishop Bertram of Breslau withdrew its ban on Catholic participation in the NSDAP and even seemed to express approval of the government, was reassuring to some Centrists and distressing to others. Prelate Föhr of the Baden party said that the directive made the cooperation of the Center in the new Reich a "duty."[23] In justification for such rapid accommodation to a movement so recently condemned, the experience of the French church in the nineteenth century was cited, without mention that Leo XIII had waited years, not days, before attempting to "rally" his clergy to the Third Republic. The bishops' action, occurring so soon after the Center had waged a desperately anti-Nazi election campaign, made the party's efforts seem irrelevant and even mistaken. News of an impending treaty between the Third Reich and the Vatican compounded the feelings of irrelevance and uselessness in party circles. The Center began to disintegrate.

The top ranks of the party were further weakened by the disappearance of its chairman. Kaas left Germany on April 7 for what was assumed to be just another of his frequent visits to Rome. It was some time before his colleagues realized that he was not going to return. Only on May 5 was the fact openly recognized and Brüning chosen, much against his will, as the new party chairman. Many branch organizations of the party, including the Windthorst League, continued to express loyalty and evidently hoped that with Brüning as its head the Center could somehow continue to exist, but Brüning felt no more identified with the needs of the party at this perilous moment than he had in better times, and he had even considered resigning his Reichstag seat before he was drafted as chairman.[24]

In the months between April and July, more and more pressure was put on individual Centrists, as on members of other parties, to give up their political affiliations. Intimidations and sudden arrests of prominent party members were coupled with assurances of prompt release if this were done. At the same time, the Nazi government

23. Morsey in *Das Ende der Parteien*, pp. 369–70.
24. Brüning, 2:702.

made revelations of widespread misuse of funds, and even of corruption, in Catholic organizations. Although many of the charges were exaggerated and some actions were alleged to be criminal, which were really only the result of negligence or incompetence, some of the allegations were true. In Bavaria a scandal was revealed concerning the diversion of funds from the Munich Catholic Workers' Association, the *Leohaus*, by the two clerics who ran it. The men were *Landtag* deputies for the BVP and were expelled from the party after the exposure. The financial problems of the *Görreshaus* run by the *Kölnische Volkszeitung* were given wide publicity. Two of the directors of the organization were imprisoned, Hugo Mönnig, head of the Rhenish Center party, was financially ruined, and it is possible that Kaas's flight to Rome was in part motivated by a fear of criminal prosecution for his responsibility in that case. The financial collapse of the *Volksverein* was also vulnerable to accusations of misuse of funds and of corruption. Brauns, Marx, Lammers, Stegerwald, Dessauer, and others were later indicted by the regime in this connection, though charges of criminal liability were not substantiated.[25] These unsavory revelations, true, half-true, or false, brought about further demoralization in the ranks of the Center party.

In June, the pressures increased when several prominent party leaders, Eugen Bolz, Joseph Ersing, and Friedrich Dessauer, were arrested on varying charges, Weber and others were dismissed from positions in the ministries, the Windthorst League was closed down, and the Christian trade unions were disbanded. Franz Wieber, one of the original founders of the unions, died on the day before their dissolution; Imbusch of the miners' union fled to the *Saarland*, and Bernhard Otte, chairman of the unions, was hounded to suicide.[26] The Nazis's target was not merely the "Marxist element" in the unions, as Stegerwald had assumed, but the union movement itself.

Joos hoped that it would be possible for the workers' associations to survive, because their function was religious and educational rather than economic, and this kind of Catholic activity was secured in the concordat, but in the spring of 1934, double membership in the asso-

25. Morsey, pp. 371–72; on Bavaria, Schwend, p. 503; Stehkämper, 3:394, 4:135–36.
26. Brüning, 2:713–14.

ciations and the Nazi Labor Front was forbidden, and the associations consequently dwindled into insignificance.[27]

The Prussian *Landtag* fraction broke apart in June, and Dr. Hackelsberger and Dr. Grass arranged to be received as *Hospitanten* in the NSDAP delegation. A number of local Center organizations dissolved themselves, and some merged with National Socialist organizations. Papen's protégé Emil Ritter became editor in chief of *Germania* on July 2 and brought the paper's editorial policy in line with Nazi dictates. (The *Kölnische Volkszeitung*, on the other hand, retreated into a nonpolitical position, becoming more concerned with religious and cultural issues.) On the evening of July 5, the Center party was officially dissolved by those of its leaders who had not already deserted it.[28]

The dignity of the party's demise was marred by the ensuing haggling over the Reichstag and *Landtag* seats—and salaries—to be assigned to former Center delegates. Albert Hackelsberger, always eager to adapt himself to the new regime, was in charge of this transaction. Original offers from the Nazis implied that virtually all would be welcome to sit as individuals in whatever sessions the former parliaments would hold, but it was then announced that exceptions would be made: no priests, no women, no trade union personnel, and no men over the age of sixty were to be eligible. These exceptions excluded two-thirds of the Center's Reichstag delegation![29] Many delegates, of course, did not care to avail themselves of the privilege of becoming members of National Socialist sounding boards.

The end of the Bavarian People's party was more dramatic than that of the Center. Its leadership had been filled with apprehension since the summer of 1932 not so much of a Nazi dictatorship in Germany but of the loss of autonomy for Bavaria. The plan of restoring the Wittelsbach dynasty to the throne in the person of the popular Crown Prince Rupprecht was seriously revived, and Schäffer believed that this would be no more in violation of the constitution than Pa-

27. For an account of the associations in the National Socialist period, see Jürgen Aretz, *Katholische Arbeiterbewegung und Nationalsozialismus* (Mainz, 1978).
28. Brüning says that the dissolution was on the evening of the sixth, but other sources agree upon the fifth.
29. Morsey, pp. 407–9.

pen's coup in Prussia, particularly if the crown prince could be installed as a kind of special state commissioner, as Kahr had been in 1922. It was even believed that some Social Democrats in Bavaria would accept a restoration under these circumstances. Held and Wohlmuth, however, realized that the state would be helpless to counter the expected move from the Reich government to squash a restoration, because the local *Reichswehr* units would take their orders from Berlin.[30]

Held's minority regime had survived the National Socialist victories in the *Landtag* elections of April 1932, and even after the national elections of 5 March 1933, his government continued in office, in spite of the fact that the NSDAP won a substantial victory in the state, receiving an absolute majority in most of the districts formerly considered permanent BVP strongholds. The local Nazi party, in frustration, was planning a coup to take over the government on March 9, but the plan was made unnecessary by the dispatching of a Reich commissioner from Berlin on that same day. The Bavarian ministers actually sounded out the army to find if the local commanders would help them to resist, but they discovered that these officers were already under orders to do nothing.[31] Held and Schäffer (acting minister of finance in the cabinet) protested to Hindenburg, reminding him of his promise of a month before that no commissioner would be sent. They were referred to Hitler.

Held left for Switzerland, a broken man, but others in the party were quick to accommodate to the new situation. The new fraction head said in a speech to the *Landtag* that the BVP was ready to work with the regime and to "combat materialistic socialism"; circulars were sent out to the party's branches urging cooperation. The long-standing identification of the party with the Bavarian state made it particularly difficult for its leaders to accept their total eclipse, and they expected the party somehow to continue as a participant in the new order, but they were soon disabused of that notion.

Schäffer visited Vienna in May and received a sympathetic hearing from Chancellor Dollfuss of the Austrian Christian Social party. It was

---

30. Schwend, pp. 482–83; Schönhoven, pp. 368–69.
31. Schwend, pp. 487–89; Fritz Schäffer, "Die Bayrische Volkspartei," *Politische Studien* 14 (1963): 62.

perhaps this close tie of geography and cultural affinity between Bavaria and Austria, and a fear that there might be retaliation against the
Austrian Nazi party, that motivated the government's terroristic
moves in Bavaria in June. Many more arrests, an estimated two thousand, were made of BVP politicians and Catholic clergy in the state
than of Centrists elsewhere.[32] The party was finally dissolved on July
4, at a time when Held was still in Switzerland and Schäffer was in
prison. Most of the prisoners were released after the dissolution.

At the time of the disbanding of the Center and the BVP, it was
generally known that the long-sought goal of a concordat between the
Vatican and the German government had been reached. The contents
of the treaty were made public on July 22, and it became law in September. It is understandable that many observers then and in recent
years have suggested a connection between the concordat and the end
of the party: that the treaty represented in some sense an exchange for
the party, or that the acceptance of the Enabling Act and the dissolution of the party were conditions for agreement to a concordat by the
Hitler government.[33] Conclusive evidence of such a bargain is lacking,
and all are agreed that the Center party would have been disbanded in
the same way and at the same time if there had been no concordat. If
the National Socialist regime insisted upon the destruction of its ally
the German Nationalist party, it would certainly never have counte-
nanced the continued existence of a party which had been its opponent. Furthermore, the party as an organization, and the majority of

32. Schwend, pp. 503–6; Schönhoven, pp. 370–76.
33. The debate on the *Reichskonkordat* of 1933 has been prolonged and often acrimoni-
ous. Among those writing on the subject, in addition to the works already cited by
Morsey and Becker, have been Karl Othmar, Freiherr von Aretin, "Kaas, Papen und
das Konkordat von 1933," *Vierteljahrshefte für Zeitgeschichte* 14 (1966): 252–79;
Morsey, *Der Untergang des politischen Katholizismus: Die Zentrumspartei
zwischen christlichen Selbstverständnis und "National Erhebung,"* 1932–33
(Stuttgart, 1977), a revision of his chapter in *Das Ende der Parteien*; Konrad Rep-
gen, *Ermächtigungsgesetz, Zentrumsende, Reichskonkordat* (Mainz, 1979); Klaus
Scholder, *Die Kirchen und das Dritte Reich* (Berlin, 1977); Ludwig Volk, *Das
Reichskonkordat vom 20. Juli 1933* (Mainz, 1972); John Jay Hughes, "The Reich
Concordat 1933: Capitulation or Compromise?" *Australian Journal of Politics and
History* 20 (1974): 164–75; and two collections of documents: Alfons Kupper, ed.,
Staatliche Akten über die Reichskonkordatsverhandlungen 1933 (Mainz, 1969);
and Ludwig Volk, ed., *Kirchliche Akten über die Reichskonkordatsverhandlungen
1933* (Mainz, 1969).

its leadership, took no part in the early negotiations for the treaty; the initiative on the German side did not come from the Center, which was skeptical of the original proposal after the disappointments of the past, but from the Nazi government and from Kaas and Papen acting as individuals.[34]

The feeling that somehow a dishonorable "horse trade" was made probably has two causes. First, the knowledge that a *Reichskonkordat* was being negotiated undoubtedly served to relieve the minds of many party members and supporters and to weaken resistance to pressures from the government.[35] If the Center party since its founding in 1870 had existed primarily for the purpose of defending the interests of the church and the Catholic population in Germany, then its purpose might now be considered to have been fulfilled. The combined protections of the religious clauses in the Weimar Constitution and the terms of the concordat appeared to mean a total victory in the long struggle. At first only a few, Brüning among them, recognized that a treaty without an army to enforce it was of dubious value.[36] The Catholic church in Germany was disarmed in this supposed moment of victory by the loss of the Center party which had served as its defender. This was to become evident very soon; but in the spring and summer of 1933, satisfaction over the "guarantees" in the concordat did much to reconcile Catholics and their representatives to the loss of the party and prevented them from making a more heroic stand at the end. On the very day the concordat was signed, official harassment of Catholic clergy and organizations was ended, and this seemed to be a promising omen for the future.[37]

Second, even though no "horse trade" of party for treaty was made, one man seems to have thought that it had been and was proud to have made it. The behavior and motivation of Ludwig Kaas remain mysterious. He left no memoirs and explained his conduct to no one. The goal of a treaty between the Reich and the Vatican was always very important to him, as it was to many Centrists, and he had become increasingly doubtful that it could be attained within the repub-

34. Aretin, pp. 253–57.
35. This is the argument of Morsey in *Das Ende der Parteien*, p. 406; and Grünthal, p. 263.
36. Brüning, 2:709; Morsey in *Das Ende der Parteien*, p. 406.
37. Hughes, p. 173.

lican parliamentary system. His hopes that Brüning's nonparliamentary government would promote Catholic legislation must have faded by the end of 1931. It is possible, even probable, that his friendly talks with Papen after this time included mention of a concordat. Papen as a good Catholic would certainly have been sympathetic. Relations between the two men were broken off when Papen accepted the chancellorship, but already in July 1932 Kaas had started discussing a treaty with General Schleicher.

Their talks began over a long-standing disagreement between the army and the German hierarchy over the question of a special field bishop for the army (ironically, the same issue which had been one of the precipitating factors in the *Kulturkampf*). In the course of the argument, the former papal nuncio to Germany, Eugenio Pacelli, now cardinal-state secretary to Pope Pius XI, pointed out that a legal treaty like the Lateran treaty in Italy would make a settlement easier, and in October, Pacelli sent a letter to the German government offering to conclude a concordat.[38] Papen's minister of the interior responded discouragingly at first, but Papen's personal reaction was favorable. As in the past, however, the known hostility of the Reichstag to a concordat was the obstacle.

The precedent of the Lateran treaty naturally would recall the sacrifice of the Catholic political party in Italy, the *Partito Popolare*, which it had entailed. Whether or not Kaas contemplated a similar sacrifice of the Center cannot be determined. He published an article in the fall of 1933 praising the Lateran treaty as a model for Germany; the article was presumably written some months before, perhaps as early as the previous November.[39]

At that time, Papen had no opportunity as chancellor to try to make use of this possible leverage over the Center, and Schleicher hoped for the party's support without it. It was Hitler who had both the need for such a lever and the power to wield it. A few casual hints from Papen to Hitler about the background of the concordat proposal and about Kaas's personal obsession would have been all that was nec-

38. Aretin, pp. 256–57; Gunter Lewy, *The Catholic Church and Nazi Germany* (New York, 1964), pp. 57–61.
39. Scholder, "Altes und Neues zur Vorgeschichte des Reichskonkordats (Erwiderung auf Konrad Repgen)," *Vierteljahrshefte für Zeitgeschichte* 26 (1978): 534–70, and p. 556 n. 41.

essary to indicate the key to breaking the Center's resistance as well as that of the German bishops.

Papen and Kaas were reconciled the day after the March elections of 1933, evidently the first time the two had talked directly since the previous May. The guarantees in the note prepared for the Center fraction before the vote on the Enabling Act made it possible for Kaas to persuade the fraction to vote yes to the act, and the Enabling Act itself made it possible for the new German government to negotiate a concordat without concern for parliamentary approval. Several years later, Goebbels said that Kaas had made the Center's yes vote contingent upon a concordat, but this is unsupported by other evidence (certainly not by the minutes of the fraction meetings), and the members of the fraction did not decide to accept the act solely on the recommendation of their chairman.[40]

Kaas went on a diplomatic mission to Rome on March 24, a mission which had been planned for some time and did not concern a concordat. He was recalled by Hitler on March 31 and left for Rome again on April 7, without an invitation from the Vatican. By his own account, Kaas met Papen by accident on the train to Rome and began a discussion about a concordat at this time. Goering was traveling to Rome by a different train on the same day. The three men began fruitful negotiations with Pacelli. Within three months, a draft concordat had been completed. Kaas told no one in the Center party of his intention to remain in Rome. The most damaging piece of evidence to connect him with the end of the party is his telephone call to Joos on July 2 or 3 asking "have you people not disbanded yet?"[41] But this is hardly an indication that he personally helped to bring about the dissolution of the Center, when all political parties were rapidly being destroyed.

Most of the wording of the *Reichskonkordat* was taken from the 1924 draft and resembled the treaties concluded with Bavaria, Prussia, and Baden, but the same clauses which protected the church and activities connected with the practice of the Catholic religion took on much more practical significance in the anticipation of a police state than they had in the republican period. The treaty differed from the

---

40. On Goebbels, Aretin, pp. 259–65. Morsey and Becker refute these implications: Morsey, *Protokolle*, 2:624–29; Becker, "Das Ende der Zentrumspartei," p. 152.
41. Aretin, pp. 263–67; Lewy, pp. 65–76.

earlier draft in two important ways. First the continued existence of Catholic denominational schools was assured. This must have gratified Kaas, considering the previous National Socialist support for community schools. Second, the last clause of the treaty (Article 32 in the final version) forbade members of the clergy to take part in politics. This clause was protested by the German bishops and questioned by Pius XI, but Papen insisted upon it, and Kaas reluctantly followed his lead, though he apparently fought a delaying action on the clause as long as he could. Kaas believed at first that the clause would not apply to those clergy already sitting in the Reichstag and the state legislatures, and Prelate Lauscher expected to become the liaison man in the Prussian *Landtag*; but they were soon informed otherwise.[42] The disarmament program was now complete. The Center party as an organization was dissolved and the Catholic clergy as individuals were depoliticized.

It is hardly necessary to add that the terms of the concordat were repeatedly violated both in spirit and in the letter by the Nazi regime. Many Catholic organizations were merged with Nazi organizations as early as August 1933, and all were eliminated by 1939.[43] The distinction between denominational, community, and secular schools was meaningless when all schools became centers of National Socialist indoctrination. In a final irony, the first effective functioning of the concordat as a legal document occurred only after 1957 when the courts of the postwar democratic republic declared it to be law.

It is fitting that the epitaph for the Center party be given by its historian Carl Bachem, who traced its development from the 1860s to 1932. On July 7 of 1933 he wrote:

> So the Center is formally dissolved. The Center is dissolved by its own decision! It is said that Brüning was sharply opposed, but consideration for Catholic civil servants was decisive. . . . It really is a terrible fate for a party which has existed in good faith for more than sixty years and has accomplished so much. One can only submit patiently and humbly to the decree of divine providence. . . . Would it have been of any use if they had rallied the Catholic people and the entire Center party to a united resistance?

42. For Lauscher, Aretin, pp. 271–73; on Kaas's delaying action, Hughes, p. 171 n. 41; Morsey in *Das Ende der Parteien*, pp. 406–8.
43. Lewy, pp. 127–32.

Such resistance would have revealed immediately the party's lack of physical power and would have been brutally put down. . . . But in spite of everything, it is hard that the Center party after such long and honorable effectiveness is vanishing so ingloriously, without a trace. Perhaps a later age will say: it could quietly leave the stage of history after it had fulfilled its task. But is this task fulfilled for the future as well? From now on, who will provide for looking after religious interests, and for the freedom and well-being of the church? Aren't we now handed over completely to the good will of the National Socialist party? Will the church keep its right if there is no actual political power in existence any more to stand up for this right?[44]

44. Quoted in full in *Das Ende der Parteien*, pp. 442–52.

EPILOGUE: NEW SOLUTIONS TO
OLD PROBLEMS

The Center, the Bavarian People's party, the Social Democratic party, and the Communist party were the four parties of Weimar Germany which kept the loyalty of their voters through the last elections of March 1933. The SPD and KPD were crushed, like all political organizations outside the Nazi movement, but they managed to maintain a shadowy existence throughout the Third Reich by means of communications among party members in exile and even in Germany. After the war, they revived to take up political activity in much the same form as before. The Center party, in contrast, was not merely dormant, but dead; it could perhaps be re-created but not revived. Individual survivors from the old party were as keenly interested in restoring normal political institutions in Germany as the Socialists, but were not at all certain of the desirability of restoring the Center.

Many of the older party leaders did not survive the Third Reich. Heinrich Held died in 1938, Brauns in 1939, Leicht in 1940, Guerard in 1943. Eugen Bolz was executed in 1945 for his part in the plot to assassinate Hitler. Otto Gerig died in Buchenwald in 1944; Imbusch died in prison the same year. Former Reich Minister Andreas Hermes was condemned to death but escaped the carrying out of his sentence. Marx, Bell, Stegerwald, and Carl Bachem were unmolested and all lived a few months after the end of the war, long enough to learn of postwar political plans and to approve of them. Adenauer, the controversial mayor of Cologne, was arrested several times but survived; Joos spent years in Dachau and was deprived of his citizenship because of his Alsatian birth but lived for twenty more years after the war; Professor Schreiber lived until 1963.

Relatively few Centrists spent the Nazi years in exile, voluntary or forced: among those who did were Wirth, Dessauer, Spiecker, and Brüning. Brüning left Germany only weeks before the Nazi purge of 1934, and after visiting in England and Switzerland, spent the years from 1937 to 1951 in the United States, teaching at Harvard University. He consistently refused to cooperate with other emigrants in any sort of government-in-exile or to do anything which he felt might injure Germany. He returned to Germany in the 1950s but never felt comfortable with the Bonn regime and eventually retired to Vermont, where he died in 1970. Wirth left Germany in 1933 and lived in exile in Switzerland; unlike Brüning he had many contacts with resistance groups and Social Democratic exiles. After the war his views moved steadily, if eccentrically to the Left, but he was never able to make a new political career for himself, and he died in 1956 "embittered and hardly noticed by the world."[1]

Kaas never went back to Germany, even for a visit, and spent his first six years in Rome without significant employment. When his friend Cardinal Pacelli became Pope Pius XII in 1939, he was given the more worthy task of supervising the excavations under St. Peter's Basilica, which occupied him until his death in 1952.

Those former Centrists who remained in Germany and survived the war found themselves separated by the Allied zones of occupation in a Germany whose boundaries and demographic makeup had been altered even more than after the First World War. Loss of the lands east of the Oder-Neisse line and continuing separation of the Soviet zone from the three Western zones of occupation meant that in the Western zones, soon to be united in the Federal Republic, the proportion of Catholics in the population was far greater than it had been in the Weimar republic or the Second Reich. Approximately 45 percent of West Germany's population was at least nominally Catholic. Furthermore, the permanent breaking-up of Prussia, which the Allies had insisted upon, gave to the Rhineland and other Prussian provinces the self-rule and self-assertion they had lacked in the past; it also had the effect of giving greater importance to the southern and southwestern states formerly overshadowed by Prussia.

No one would suggest, of course, that the destruction and dis-

---

1. Knapp, "Joseph Wirth," in Morsey, *Zeitgeschichte*, p. 172.

memberment of Germany and its permanent division into two nations, East and West, was in any way desirable or acceptable to German Catholics, but the fact remained that the new geographic and
demographic structure of the country was very much more favorable
to Catholic interests than the old, at both the state and federal levels.
In West Germany, the Catholic population was no longer an underprivileged minority, either in the nation or in the states, for in the new
configuration of states, the northernmost were almost entirely Protestant, while all of the others had a proportion of Catholics great
enough to be politically decisive. A special party to protect Catholic
rights was no longer needed. On the other hand, the percentage of
Catholics within the borders of East Germany was so small that a special party to protect their rights would have little possibility of influence (except in the city of Berlin, where political development paralleled that in West Germany).

The old party was not necessary, but what new party structure
should replace it? Among former Centrists there were at first two different plans for a regrouping of German political life, both involving
the uniting of Catholics with non-Catholics in new parties. One of
these plans was put forth by conservatives who believed that the time
had come to revive the Essen Program of 1920 and to create a genuinely interdenominational "Christian" party whose platform would
provide a common front against socialism, though with less hostility
toward the Left than Stegerwald's original conception had shown. This
was the plan which culminated in the creation of the Christian Democratic Union.

The alternative plan for a new party came from several former
leaders in the Christian trade unions and other left-wing Centrists
who believed that Catholic workers could and should overcome their
antagonism to socialism and unite with all workers in a non-Marxist
labor party, modeled upon the British Labour party. Jakob Kaiser and
Karl Spiecker were two who advocated a labor party and took part in
discussions with former Social Democrats in 1945. They received
some favorable response, notably from Carl Severing, but most Social
Democrats under Kurt Schumacher's strong guidance rejected the plan
and preferred to restore the old Social Democratic party. Although
most of the Marxist platform of the SPD was of purely symbolic and

nostalgic significance, this made it impossible for the Catholics to accept a merger. The labor party plan was thus thwarted by the Socialists.[2]

Kaiser and other union men (Ersing, Andre) then accepted the plan for an interdenominational conservative party and helped in the formation of the Christian Democratic Union which was organized in all parts of Germany by the end of 1945. The word "Union" in the new party's title was important because it implied the cooperation of many different regional organizations, a heritage from the older Center party tradition.

In the 1920s, the Essen Program was never implemented, in spite of the interest shown among Catholics, because there was no corresponding interest in Protestant circles. Protestants had been invited to join Catholics in the Center since its founding in 1870, and in 1919 and 1920 they were invited to join Catholics in a new party. They had been totally unwilling to do so. Practicing Protestants had been imbued by their churches with anti-Catholic sentiments, and nonpracticing Protestants had been steeped in anticlerical tradition. The creation of the CDU in 1945 was made possible less by change in Catholic attitudes than by a decisive change in Protestant attitudes. Anticlerical liberals found a new political home in the Free Democratic party, but conservative, religious Protestants could not, and no longer wanted to, re-create the German Nationalist party which had previously held their allegiance. It was these "politically homeless" former Nationalists and also former National Socialists, who welcomed a chance to shelter under the roof of the CDU.[3] Men like Robert Lehr, the autocratic former Nationalist mayor of Düsseldorf, Kurt Kiesinger, former Centrist leader in Württemberg turned Nazi, and Gunter Gereke, Nationalist agrarian who continued in government in 1933, gave the new party in the early years a rightist coloration it later lost. Some of the Protestant organizers of the CDU came from the former splinter parties which had seceded from the Nationalist party, like Schlange-Schöningen of the Agrarian party and others from the Christian People's Service, thus carrying out the merger which

2. Hans Georg Wieck, *Die Entstehung der CDU und die Wiedergründung des Zentrums im Jahre 1945* (Düsseldorf, 1953), pp. 145–46, 212–13; Bruno Dörpinghaus and Kurt Witt, eds., *Politisches Jahrbuch der CDU/CSU* (Frankfurt, 1950), p. 183.
3. Wieck, p. 137.

Brüning had hoped for fifteen years before. Brüning himself strongly approved of the creation of the CDU and considered it the direct descendant of the Essen Program he had helped to design.[4]

Protestant participation made the creation of a genuine interdenominational party possible, but in the early postwar years, most prominent CDU leaders were Catholics, former Centrists with experience and a commitment to democracy. Leadership of the party at first appeared to be preempted by Hermes, who organized the Berlin branch, but in personality and in location the Rhineland offered greater attractions: Konrad Adenauer not only led the party from 1946 until his death in 1967 but managed to establish the nation's capital at the improbable site of Bonn near his own home.[5]

Bavaria, as would be expected, followed a separate, though parallel, path of development. Fritz Schäffer tried at first to reorganize the Bavarian People's party, but soon consented to the founding of a new interdenominational party. Stegerwald had spent the war years in Bavaria, his home state, and in the months before his death he helped to create the Christian Social Union, frequently reminding his audiences in his speeches that the new parties were delayed implementations of his Essen Program. He rejected the term "Christian Democratic" for the Bavarian party, saying that "democratic" had unfavorable connotations from the past. His favored title of "Christian Social" was adopted instead.[6] (The founders of the CDU had rejected the phrase "Christian Social" because of *its* obviously unfavorable connotations from the past.)

Most former Centrists rallied to the CDU-CSU but there were some who feared that, like Stegerwald's original Essen Program, the new party would be too conservative, too hostile to the Left, and perhaps too nationalistic for their tastes. These men and women distrusted the influence of former Nationalist party members in the CDU, and they decided to re-create the Center party as an alternative for those Catholics who felt uncomfortable with the new organization. The motive for the re-creation of the Center was thus a political one, not any desire to retain the exclusively Catholic nature of the party;

4. Arnold J. Heidenhammer, *Adenauer and the CDU* (The Hague, 1960), pp. 57, 60, 199. On Lehr, Stump, pp. 151–53; on Brüning, Wieck, p. 218.
5. Heidenhammer, pp. 173–74; Prittie, p. 137.
6. Stegerwald, *Von Deutsche Zukunft*, pp. 9–10.

indeed, the postwar Center was officially declared to be interdenominational like the old party. The founders, who met in the town of Soest in October 1945 to refound the Center on the site of its first creation, were members of the former left wing of the Center who were "mistrustful . . . of the former DVP supporters and especially DNVP supporters, who had entered [the CDU] from the Protestant side, who had supported the Harzburg Front which had allied itself with National Socialism and helped it to power."[7] Several of the founders were also advocates of a socialized economy for Germany. Karl Spiecker, former friend to Wirth, was one of these founders (after failing to form a labor party) and Wirth himself, returned from exile like Spiecker, helped to reorganize the Center in Baden, along with Prelate Föhr, the former state party chairman. Johannes Brockmann, former member of the Prussian *Landtag*, re-formed the Center in the Rhineland where it attracted the largest following.

At first, the Center seemed to have some chance of survival as a leftist alternative to the CDU. In 1949 it received 3.7 percent of the West German vote, compared to 31 percent for the CDU-CSU, and 9.8 percent of the vote for the North Rhine-Westphalia *Landtag*. But it soon became apparent that the Centrists' fears concerning the orientation of the CDU were unfounded, and most of their original supporters shifted their allegiance to the larger party, including Spiecker, who tried unsuccessfully to merge the two parties. By 1957 the Center party had lost all representation in the *Bundestag* and was reduced to splinter-party status even in its home state of North Rhine-Westphalia.[8]

The new spirit of interdenominationalism in West Germany did not succeed without a certain amount of self-conscious effort. As one observer has written: "within [the CDU] as in the allocation of positions elsewhere, proportionality of denominations is often the guiding principle: where there are two positions, both denominations have to be represented; if there is but one chairman, the vice chairman has to belong to the other denomination."[9] As in contemporary Switzerland

7. Ludwig Bergstrasser, *Geschichte der politischen Parteien in Deutschland* (Munich, 1955), pp. 337–38; Buchheim, pp. 431–38.
8. Uwe W. Kitzinger, *German Electoral Politics: A Study of the 1957 Campaign* (Oxford, 1960), pp. 6–7.

and the Netherlands, religious affiliation is still not simply a private concern but very much a form of political group-identity.

The successful merger of Catholic and Protestant Germans in the CDU-CSU was paralleled by a merger of the former Christian trade unions and the Free trade unions in the nonpolitical German Federation of Unions. This was not accomplished without dissension and it proved to be less successful than the political unification, but the old divisions in Germany between Christian and anticlerical, Catholic and Protestant, were not restored.

The one institution in the new federal republic in which the interdenominational spirit did not prevail was the school system. The Catholic preponderance in West Germany had resulted in the natural breakdown of the Center tower of defense, but it also resulted in effective resistance to the idea of community schools. The school issue was the principal reason for claiming the continued validity of the concordat of 1933 after the war. The United States military government recognized its provisions in the American zone, and in 1957, after its legality was challenged, the Supreme Court of the federal republic declared it to be valid for all of West Germany. On the other hand, the court's ruling said that the provisions of the concordat did not affect the autonomy of the states in matters of education, so that the community schools in the districts formerly in the old *Länder* of Hesse and Baden, and in Nassau and the city of Frankfurt, still could not be altered into denominational schools. Elsewhere in the country, Catholic schools were preserved and, in effect, restored, since the National Socialist regime had hardly permitted Catholic education to be carried on. In 1959, therefore, in North Rhine-Westphalia, 95.6 percent of Catholic children attended Catholic elementary schools, 77.9 percent in Rhineland-Palatinate, and 92.4 percent in Bavaria. In West Germany 40 percent of all elementary schools were Catholic. A much smaller percentage of Protestant children attended Protestant denominational schools, and the process of changing these into community schools, which had begun in the days of Prussian Minister Falk, continued. Private Catholic schools, which Weimar Parliaments had refused to sanction, were now permitted and received public funds.[10]

9. Ralf Dahrendorf, *Society and Democracy in Germany* (New York, 1969), p. 111.
10. Ernst Christian Helmreich, *Religious Education in German Schools: An Historical Approach* (Cambridge, Mass., 1959), pp. 237–42; Spotts, p. 219.

The persistence of Catholic denominational education is not only attributable to Catholic efforts but also to a greater feeling of tolerance on the part of non-Catholics in Germany and to a decline in the dogmatic anticlericalism that characterized so many liberals and Socialists in the past. But the exclusively Catholic elementary school, so often in rural areas a "dwarf" school, too small and poorly staffed to be educationally effective, has held back Catholic children from equal opportunity in higher education and hence from equal opportunity in adult careers. One observer has called Catholics still an underprivileged group in their lack of access to higher education.[11] This has been increasingly acknowledged in Germany and there are signs that in the future more Catholic parents may be coming to accept the idea of community schools (which offer denominational religious instruction as a subject in the curriculum) as one more step in the direction of attaining true "parity" for Catholics.

The Center party was in existence for sixty-three years of German history. Its purpose was not simply to serve the interests of the Catholic church, but rather to represent the interests of the Catholic population, whether these interests were religious, social, or political. In its early years after 1870, the immediate Catholic interest was the defense of the church in the *Kulturkampf*, but underlying this was a need to represent the defeated *grossdeutsch* sentiments of the south and the Catholic provinces of Prussia. In defending these minority elements, the Center became a party which championed the civil rights of other minorities as well: of Poles and Alsatians who were discriminated against not primarily as Catholics but as aliens; of Protestant groups like the Danes and Hanoverians; and even the rights of Marxists and Jews threatened by exceptional legislation of the type condemned by the Center. Thus this essentially conservative party was led to a surprisingly liberal position on civil rights in general.

By a similar process, the claim of the Center party to represent all German Catholics and not just those who were "bourgeois" led the party to recognize the social needs of small farmers and industrial workers, and to advocate social reforms. Though remaining autocratic

11. R. B. Tilford and R. J. Preece, *Federal Germany: Political and Social Order* (London, 1969), pp. 49–54; Dahrendorf, "The Crisis in German Education," *Journal of Contemporary History* 2 (1967): 142.

in its organization, the Center became in some sense of the word a democratic party in its outlook. At the same time, the leaders of this party of the masses did not altogether identify with the program of civil rights and social reform, did not admire either democracy or parliamentarianism as a political system, and greatly desired to be accepted as members of the governing classes in Wilhelmine Germany. The goal of integration into German society was as powerful as the goal of protecting Catholic rights and interests.

The First World War and subsequent revolution removed much of the reason for the Center's existence. Civil rights were guaranteed in the Weimar Constitution, and social reform was championed much more vigorously by the Social Democrats. Entry into the ruling classes was a meaningless goal now that the Wilhelmine social system had been destroyed. Regional resentments were lessened, the federal system was modified, and Prussia was democratized. These changes further reduced the Center's platform. Only inertia and a lack of welcome on the part of other elements in the political spectrum prevented the Center from dissolving into its component socioeconomic groups. The Center, while never fully accepting the republic or the parliamentary system, became par excellence the party of parliamentary accommodation, the perfect coalition partner, existing for its own sake.

When in the final years of the republic a totalitarian movement threatened to destroy democracy and violate the individual rights of hundreds of thousands of German citizens with a ruthlessness far surpassing that of Bismarck, the Center's leaders did not identify themselves with other minorities or threatened persons and made no effort to unite with them, in spite of evidence that the party's voters wanted and expected a strong stand of resistance. In Windthorst's day, he led the Center in opposing exceptional legislation not only against Jesuits but also against Jewish immigrants and Marxist revolutionaries. In 1933 the party's chairman was content to accept assurances of continued rights for Catholics, assurances which explicitly did not apply to Jews or Marxists.

The ultimate "guarantee" which was to justify and compensate for the destruction of the party itself was the concordat. If this document did indeed sum up all the important goals of the sixty-three-year existence of the party, it would have been a fair exchange, always supposing that it could be enforced. A similar treaty could have terminated the need for a Catholic political party at any time since 1870. But the Center had historically been much more than a defender of specific rights and privileges of the Catholic church, and its greater role of representing all the interests of the Catholic people of Germany, and those of other minority groups, could not be replaced by any list of guarantees or legal documents. The Center party could not have survived in 1933 any more than any other political organization outside the National Socialist movement, but it could have made a braver end. The ignoble nature of the party's demise was a powerful reason for the decision not to re-create it but instead to found a new political structure unburdened by the past.

BIBLIOGRAPHY
INDEX

BIBLIOGRAPHY

PRIMARY SOURCES: DOCUMENTS, MEMOIRS AND OTHER CONTEMPORARY ACCOUNTS

BEBEL, AUGUST. *Abrechnung mit dem Zentrum.* Cologne, 1974.

BERGSTRÄSSER, LUDWIG. *Der politische Katholizismus: Dokumente.* 2 vols. Munich, 1923.

BEYERLE, KONRAD. *Föderalistische Reichspolitik.* Munich, 1924.

BISMARCK, OTTO VON. *Reflections and Reminiscences.* New York and Evanston, Ill., 1968.

BRAUN, OTTO. *Von Weimar zu Hitler.* New York, 1940.

BRAUNS, HEINRICH. "Das Zentrum." *Volk und Reich der Deutschen.* 2 vols. Berlin, 1929.

BRECHT, ARNOLD. *Federalism and Regionalism in Germany.* New York, 1945.
———. *The Political Education of Arnold Brecht: An Autobiography, 1884–1970.* Princeton, 1970.
———. *Prelude to Silence.* New York, 1944.

BREDT, JOHANNES VIKTOR. "Das preussische Konkordat." *Preussische Jahrbücher* 217 (1929): 137–45.

BRÜNING, HEINRICH. *Memoiren, 1918–1934.* 2 vols. Munich, 1972.
———. "Ein Brief." *Deutsche Rundschau* 70 (1947): 4–8.

BÜLOW, BERNHARD VON. *Imperial Germany.* New York, 1917.
———. *Memoirs.* 4 vols. Boston, 1931–32.

CONSTABEL, ADELHEID, ed. *Die Vorgeschichte des Kulturkampfs: Quellenveröffentlichung aus dem Deutschen Zentralarchiv.* Berlin, 1957.

CURTIUS, JULIUS. *Sechs Jahre Minister der deutsche Republik.* Heidelberg, 1948.

DEUERLEIN, ERNST, ed. *Briefwechsel Hertling-Lerchenfeld, 1912–1917.* 2 vols. Boppard am Rhein, 1973.

Deutsche Republik. 1924–30.

DOHM, ERNST, ed. *Zentrums-Album des Kladderadatsch, 1870–1910.* Berlin, 1912.

ERZBERGER, MATTHIAS. *Das deutsche Zentrum*. Amsterdam, 1910.

———. *Erlebnisse im Weltkriege*. Stuttgart, 1920.

Flugschriften des deutschen Zentrumspartei, 1924. Berlin, 1924.

FORSTHOFF, ERNST. *Deutsche Geschichte von 1918 bis 1938 in Dokumenten*. Stuttgart, 1943.

Frankfurter Zeitung. 1924–30.

GILSON, ETIENNE, ed. *The Church Speaks to the Modern World: The Social Teachings of Leo XIII*. Garden City, N.Y., 1954.

HEILBRON, EDUARD, ed. *Die Deutsche Nationalversammlung im Jahre 1919*. 2 vols. Berlin, 1919–20.

HELLPACH, WILLY. "Kulturpolitik." *Die neue Rundschau* 38 (1927): 449–64.

Die Hilfe. 1924–30.

Hochland. 1924–30.

HOHENLOHE-SCHILLINGSFÜRST, CHLODWIG VON. *Memoirs*. 2 vols. New York and London, 1906.

HUBER, ERNST RUDOLF, ed. *Dokumente zur deutschen Verfassungsgeschichte*. 3 vols. Stuttgart, 1961.

JOOS, JOSEPH. "Die politisches Ideenwelt des Zentrums." *Wissen und Wirken*. Karlsruhe, 1928.

———. *Am Räderwerk der Zeit*. Augsburg, 1948.

KEUDELL, WALTER VON. "Unser Kampf um das Reichsschulgesetz." In *Der Nationale Wille: Werden und Wirken der DNVP, 1918–1928*, edited by Max Weiss. Leipzig, 1928.

KÖHLER, HEINRICH. *Lebenserinnerungen des Politikers und Staatsmannes, 1878–1949*. Stuttgart, 1964.

Kölnische Volkszeitung. 1924–30.

LUTZ, RALPH HASWELL. *Fall of the German Empire, 1914–1918*. 2 vols. Stanford, Calif., 1932.

MATTHIAS, ERICH, and MORSEY, RUDOLF, eds. *Der Interfraktionelle Ausschuss, 1917–1918*. 2 vols. Düsseldorf, 1959.

———. *Die Regierung des Prinzen Max von Baden*. Düsseldorf, 1962.

MOCKENHAUPT, HUBERT, ed. *Heinrich Brauns: Katholische Sozialpolitik im 20. Jahrhundert: Ausgewählte Aufsätze und Reden*. Mainz, 1976.

MORSEY, RUDOLF, ed. *Die Protokolle der Reichstagsfraktion und des Fraktionsvorstands der deutschen Zentrumspartei, 1926–1933*. 2 vols. Mainz, 1969.

Offizieller Bericht des Zweiten Reichsparteitages der deutschen Zentrumspartei. Berlin, 1922.

PAPEN, FRANZ VON. *Appell an das deutsche Gewissen*. Oldenburg, 1933.

———. *Memoirs*. London, 1952.

SALOMON, F. *Die deutschen Parteiprogramme*. 2 vols. Leipzig, 1912.

SCHÄFFER, FRITZ. "Die Bayerische Volkspartei." *Politische Studien* 14 (1963): 46–63.

SCHREIBER, GEORG. *Politisches Jahrbuch, 1925*. München-Gladbach, 1925.

———. *Politisches Jahrbuch, 1926*. München-Gladbach, 1926.

———. *Politisches Jahrbuch, 1927/28.* München-Gladbach, 1928.

———. *Regierung ohne Volk.* Cologne, 1932.

———. *Zentrum und deutsche Politik.* Berlin, 1924.

———. *Zwischen Demokratie und Diktatur.* Münster, 1949.

SEVERING, CARL. *Mein Lebensweg.* 2 vols. Cologne, 1950.

SPAHN, MARTIN. *Das deutsche Zentrum.* Mainz, 1907.

STEGERWALD, ADAM. *Von deutschen Zukunft.* Würzburg, 1946.

———. *Wo Stehen Wir?* Würzburg, 1946.

STEHKÄMPER, HUGO, ed. *Der Nachlass des Reichskanzlers Wilhelm Marx.* 4 vols. *Mitteilungen aus dem Stadtarchiv von Köln,* pp. 52–55. Cologne, 1968.

Stenographische Berichte über die Verhandlungen des deutschen Reichstages. Berlin, 1870–1933.

Stenographische Berichte über die Verhandlungen des Reichstages des Norddeutschen Bundes im Jahre 1867. Berlin, 1867.

Stenographische Berichte der Verhandlungen der verfassunggebenden Deutschen Nationalversammlung 1919. Berlin, 1919.

Stimmen der Zeit. 1924–30.

SUTTON, ERIC, ed. *Gustav Stresemann: His Diaries, Letters, and Papers.* 3 vols. London, 1935–40.

TREVIRANUS, GOTTFRIED. *Das Ende von Weimar.* Düsseldorf, 1963.

Die Ursachen des Deutschen Zusammenbruchs im Jahre 1918: Das Werk des Untersuchungsausschusses der Verfassunggebenden Deutschen Nationalversammlung und des Reichstages, 1919–1926. 12 vols. Berlin, 1925–29.

Die Verfassung des deutschen Reichs vom 11 August 1919. Berlin, 1929.

WETTERLÉ, ABBÉ EMILE. *Behind the Scenes in the Reichstag.* New York, 1918.

WIRTH, JOSEPH. *Reden während der Kanzlerschaft.* Berlin, 1925.

SECONDARY SOURCES: BOOKS

ACHENBACH, HERMANN. *Die konfessionale Arbeitervereins-Bewegung unter besonderer Berücksichtigung ihrer sozialen und sozialpolitischen Problematik.* Giessen, 1935.

ALEXANDER, THOMAS. *The Prussian Elementary Schools.* New York, 1919.

———, and Parker, Beryl. *The New Education in the German Republic.* New York, 1929.

ANDERSON, MARGARET L. *Windthorst: A Political Biography.* Oxford, 1981.

ARETZ, JÜRGEN. *Katholische Arbeiterbewegung und Nationalsozialismus.* Mainz, 1978.

BACH, JÜRGEN A. *Franz von Papen in der Weimarer Republik.* Düsseldorf, 1977.

BACHEM, KARL. *Vorgeschichte, Geschichte und Politik der deutschen Zentrumspartei, 1815–1914.* 9 vols. Cologne, 1927–32.

BALFOUR, MICHAEL. *The Kaiser and His Times.* London, 1964.

Bibliography

BECKER, JOSEF. *Liberalerstaat und Kirche in der Aera von Reichsgründung und Kulturkampf (1860–1876)*. Mainz, 1973.

BEER, RÜDIGER ROBERT. *Heinrich Brüning*. Berlin, 1931.

BERGSTRÄSSER, LUDWIG. *Geschichte der politischen Parteien in Deutschland*. Munich, 1955.

BERTRAM, JÜRGEN. *Die Wahlen zum deutschen Reichstag vom Jahre 1912*. Düsseldorf, 1964.

BÖHME, THEODOR. *Die christlich-nationale Gewerkschaft*. Stuttgart, 1930.

BORN, KARL ERICH. *Staat und Sozialpolitik seit Bismarcks Sturz*. Wiesbaden, 1957.

BOSL, KARL, Ed. *Bayern im Umbruch*. Munich, 1969.

BOURCERET, ALBERT. *Les associations professionelles ouvrières en Allemagne*. Paris, 1932.

BOWEN, RALPH H. *German Theories of the Corporative State*. New York, 1947.

BRACHER, KARL DIETRICH. *Die Auflösung der Weimarer Republik*. Stuttgart and Düsseldorf, 1955.

BRUNET, RENÉ. *The New German Constitution*. New York, 1922.

BUCHHEIM, KARL. *Geschichte der christlichen Parteien in Deutschland*. Munich, 1953.

CASSAU, JEANETTE *Die Arbeitergewerkschaften*. Halberstadt, 1927.

CLARK, R. T. *The Fall of the German Republic*. London, 1935.

CROTHERS, GEORGE D. *The German Elections of 1907*. New York, 1941.

DAHL, ROBERT A., ed. *Political Oppositions in Western Democracies*. New Haven, 1966.

DAHRENDORF, RALF. *Society and Democracy in Germany*. New York, 1969.

DAWSON, W. H. *The German Empire, 1867–1914*. 2 vols. London, 1919.

DEMETER, KARL. *The German Officer Corps in Society and State, 1650–1945*. New York, 1965.

DEUTZ JOSEF. *Adam Stegerwald: Gewerkschaftler-Politiker-Minister, 1874–1945*. Cologne, 1952.

DOEBERL, MICHAEL. *Entwicklungsgeschichte Bayerns*. 3 vols. Munich, 1931.

DORPALEN, ANDREAS. *Hindenburg and the Weimar Republic*. Princeton, 1964.

DÖRPINGHAUS, BRUNO, and WITT, KURT. *Politisches Jahrbuch der CDU/CSU*. Frankfurt, 1950.

DUVERGER, MAURICE. *Political Parties: Their Organization and Activity in the Modern State*. London, 1954.

EPSTEIN, KLAUS. *Matthias Erzberger and the Dilemma of German Democracy*. Princeton, 1959.

ESCHENBURG, THEODOR. *Matthias Erzberger: Der grosse Mann des Parlamentarismus und der Finanzreform*. Munich, 1973.

EVANS, RICHARD J., ed. *Society and Politics in Wilhelmine Germany*. London, 1978.

EYCK, ERICH. Bismarck: *Leben und Werk*. 3 vols. Erlenbach-Zurich, 1941–44.

————. *A History of the Weimar Republic.* 2 vols. New York, 1967.

————. *Das Persönliche Regiment Wilhelms II.* Zurich, 1948.

EYCK, FRANK. *The Frankfurt Parliament, 1848–1849.* New York, 1968.

FISCHER, FRITZ. *Germany's Aims in the First World War.* New York, 1961.

FOERSTER, ERICH. *Adalbert Falk: Sein Leben und Wirken.* Gotha, 1927.

FOGARTY, MICHAEL P. *Christian Democracy in Western Europe, 1820–1953.* Notre Dame, Ind., 1957.

FRANZ, GEORG. *Kulturkampf.* Munich, 1954.

FRANZ-WILLING, GEORG. *Kulturkampf gestern und heute: Eine Säkularbetrachtung, 1871–1971.* Munich, 1971.

FREY, LUDWIG. *Die Stellung der christlichen Gewerkschaften Deutschlands zu den politischen Parteien.* Berlin, 1931.

FRICKE, DIETER, ed. *Die Bürgerlichen Parteien in Deutschland.* 2 vols. Berlin, 1968.

GENGER, LUDWIG FRANZ. *Die deutsche Monarchisten 1919 bis 1925.* Kulmbach, 1932.

GILLIS, JOHN R. *The Prussian Bureaucracy in Crisis, 1840–1860.* Stanford, Calif., 1971.

GREBING, HELGA. *Geschichte der deutschen Parteien.* Wiesbaden, 1962.

————. "Zentrum und katholische Arbeiterschaft 1918–1933." Ph.D. dissertation, Free University of Berlin, 1952.

GRÜNTHAL, GÜNTER. *Reichsschulgesetz und Zentrumspartei in der Weimarer Republik.* Düsseldorf, 1968.

GUNDLACH, GUSTAV. *Zur Soziologie der katholischen Ideenwelt und des Jesuitenordens.* Freiburg, 1924.

HACKER, RUPERT. *Die Beziehungen zwischen Bayern und dem heiligen Stuhl in der Regierungszeit Ludwigs I (1825–1845).* Tübingen, 1967.

HALPERIN, S. WILLIAM. *Germany Tried Democracy.* New York, 1946.

HAMEROW, THEODORE S. *Restoration, Revolution, Reaction: Economics and Politics in Germany, 1815–1871.* Princeton, 1958.

————. *The Social Foundations of German Unification, 1858–1871.* 2 vols. Princeton, 1969–72.

HECKART, BEVERLY. *From Bassermann to Bebel: The Grand Bloc's Quest for Reform in the Kaiserreich.* New Haven, 1974.

HEIDENHAMMER, ARNOLD J. *Adenauer and the CDU.* The Hague, 1960.

HELMREICH, ERNST CHRISTIAN. *Religious Education in German Schools: An Historical Approach.* Cambridge, Mass., 1959.

HÖFFNER, JOSEPH. *Wilhelm Emmanuel von Ketteler und die katholische Sozialbewegung im 19. Jahrhundert.* Wiesbaden, 1962.

HOLBORN, HAJO. *A History of Modern Germany,* 3 vols. New York, 1969.

HOPE, NICHOLAS MARTIN. *The Alternative to German Unification: The Anti-Prussian Party: Frankfurt, Nassau and the Two Hesses, 1859–1867.* Wiesbaden, 1973.

HORKENBACH, CUNO. *Das deutsche Reich von 1918 bis heute.* Berlin, 1931.

HUBER, ERNST. *Deutsche Verfassungsgeschichte seit 1789.* 5 vols. Stuttgart, 1978.

HÜSGEN, EDUARD. *Ludwig Windthorst.* Cologne, 1911.

ILLICH, HANS. *Ueber die Haltung der Zentrumspresse zu Parlamentarizierung, 1917–1918.* Würzburg, 1932.

JARAUSCH, KONRAD H. *The Enigmatic Chancellor: Bethmann-Hollweg and the Hubris of Imperial Germany.* New Haven, 1973.

KAUFMANN, WALTER H. *Monarchism in the Weimar Republic.* New York, 1953.

KENT, GEORGE O. *Arnim and Bismarck.* Oxford, 1968.

———. *Bismarck and His Times.* Carbondale and Edwardsville, Ill., 1978.

KESSLER, RICHARD. *Heinrich Held als Parlamentarier: Eine Teilbiographie, 1868–1924.* Berlin, 1971.

KITCHEN, MARTIN. *The German Officer Corps, 1890–1914.* Oxford, 1968.

KITZINGER, UWE W. *German Electoral Politics: A Study of the 1957 Campaign.* Oxford, 1960.

KLEMPERER, KLEMENS VON. *Germany's New Conservatism.* Princeton, 1957.

———. *Ignaz Seipel: Christian Statesman in a Time of Crisis.* Princeton, 1972.

KOEVES, TIBOR. *Satan in Top Hat.* New York, 1941.

KOSCH, WILHELM, ed. *Das katholische Deutschland.* 2 vols. Augsburg, 1933.

KREMER, WILLY. *Der sociale Aufbau der Parteien des deutschen Reichstages von 1871–1918.* Emsdetten, 1934.

KUPISCH, KARL. *Die deutschen Landeskirchen im 19. und 20. Jahrhundert.* Göttingen, 1966.

LEVY, RICHARD S. *The Downfall of the Anti-Semitic Political Parties in Imperial Germany.* New Haven and London, 1975.

LEWY, GUNTER. *The Catholic Church and Nazi Germany.* New York, 1964.

LILL, RUDOLF. *Die Wende im Kulturkampf.* Tübingen, 1973.

LOHE, EILERT. *Heinrich Brüning: Offizier-Staatsmann-Gelehrter.* Göttingen, 1969.

LOWIE, ROBERT H. *Toward Understanding Germany.* Chicago, 1954.

LUTZ, RALPH HASWELL. *The German Revolution, 1918–1919.* Stanford, Calif., 1922.

MACARTNEY, C. A. *The Habsburg Empire, 1790–1918.* London, 1968.

MACFARLAND, CHARLES S. *The New Church and the New Germany.* New York, 1934.

MASON, JOHN BROWN. *Hitler's First Foes.* Minneapolis, 1936.

MATTERN, JOHANNES. *Bavaria and the Reich.* Baltimore, 1923.

MATTHIAS, ERICH, and MORSEY, RUDOLF, eds. *Das Ende der Parteien 1933.* Düsseldorf, 1960.

MEIER, HANS. *Revolution and Church: The Early History of Christian Democracy, 1789–1901.* London, 1965.

MAY, ARTHUR. *The Hapsburg Monarchy, 1867–1914.* Cambridge, Mass., 1951.

MEERFELD, J. *Die deutsche Zentrumspartei.* Berlin, 1918.

MENNE, BERNHARD. *The Case of Dr. Brüning.* London, 1942.

MEYER, MAX H. *Die Weltanschauung des Zentrums in ihren Grundlinien.* Munich, 1919.

MICKLEM, NATHANIEL. *National Socialism and the Roman Catholic Church, 1933–1938.* London, 1939.

MITTMANN, URSULA. *Fraktion und Partei: Ein Vergleich von Zentrum und Sozialdemokratie im Kaiserreich.* Düsseldorf, 1976.

MOMMSEN, WILHELM. *Bismarcks Sturz und die Parteien.* Stuttgart, 1924.

MORSEY, RUDOLF. *Die deutsche Zentrumspartei 1917–1923.* Düsseldorf, 1966.

———. *Das "Ermächtigungsgesetz" vom 24 März 1933.* Göttingen, 1968.

———, ed. *Zeitgeschichte in Lebensbildern.* Mainz, 1973.

MOSSE, GEORGE L. *The Crisis of German Ideology.* New York, 1964.

MULCAHY, RICHARD E. *The Economics of Heinrich Pesch.* New York, 1952.

NAUMANN, FRIEDRICH. *Die politischen Parteien.* Berlin, 1911.

NELL-BREUNING, OSWALD VON. *Reorganization of Social Economy.* New York, 1937.

NEUMANN, SIGMUND. *Die deutsche Parteien.* Berlin, 1932.

NICHOLS, J. ALDEN. *Germany after Bismarck: The Caprivi Era, 1890–1894.* New York, 1968.

NIPPERDEY, THOMAS. *Die Organization der deutschen Parteien vor 1918.* Düsseldorf, 1961.

NOBEL, ALPHONS. *Brüning.* Leipzig, 1932.

OPPENHEIMER, HEINRICH. *The Constitution of the German Republic.* London, 1922.

PATEMANN, RICHARD. *Der Kampf um die preussische Wahlreform im Ersten Weltkrieg.* Düsseldorf, 1964.

PEHL, HANS. *Die deutsche Kolonialpolitik und das Zentrum 1884–1914.* Limburg, 1934.

PFLANZE, OTTO. *Bismarck and the Development of Germany.* Princeton, 1963.

PINSON, KOPPEL S. *Modern Germany.* New York, 1954.

POIS, ROBERT. *The Bourgeois Democrats of Weimar Germany.* Philadelphia, 1976.

POWER, MICHAEL. *Religion in the Reich.* London, 1939.

PRITTIE, TERENCE. *Konrad Adenauer, 1876–1967.* Chicago, 1971.

PRÜM, EMILE. *Pan-Germanism versus Christendom.* New York, 1916.

PULZER, PETER G. J. *The Rise of Political Anti-Semitism in Germany and Austria.* New York, 1964.

RAUH, MANFRED. *Föderalismus und Parlamentarismus in Wilhelminischen Reich.* Düsseldorf, 1973.

REAL, WILLY. *Der deutsche Reformverein: Grossdeutsche Stimmen und Kräfte zwischen Villafranca und Königgrätz.* Lübeck, 1966.

RICH, NORMAN. *Friedrich von Holstein.* 2 vols. Cambridge, Mass., 1965.

RITTER, EMIL. *Die katholisch-soziale Bewegung Deutschlands im neunzehnten Jahrhundert und der Volksverein.* Cologne, 1954.

ROBERTSON, C. GRANT. *Bismarck.* London, 1947.

Bibliography

RÖHL, JOHN C. G. *Germany without Bismarck*. Berkeley, Calif., 1967.

ROSENBERG, ARTHUR. *A History of the German Republic*. London, 1936.

———. *Imperial Germany: The Birth of the German Republic, 1871–1918.* Boston, 1964.

ROSS, RONALD J. *Beleaguered Tower: The Dilemma of Political Catholicism in Wilhelmine Germany.* Notre Dame, Ind., 1976.

SCHAUFF, JOHANNES. *Die deutschen Katholiken und die Zentrumspartei: Eine politisch-statistische Untersuchung der Reichstagswahlen seit 1871.* Cologne, 1928.

SCHEELE, GODFREY. *The Weimar Republic*. London, 1946.

SCHMIDT, ERICH. *Bismarcks Kampf mit dem politischen Katholizismus.* Hamburg, 1942.

SCHMIDT-VOLKMAR, ERICH. *Der Kulturkampf in Deutschland, 1871–1890.* Göttingen, 1962.

SCHÖNHOVEN, KLAUS. *Die Bayerische Volkspartei, 1924–1932.* Düsseldorf, 1972.

SCHORR, HELMUT J. *Adam Stegerwald.* Recklinghausen, 1966.

SCHUMANN, FREDERICK L. *Germany since 1918.* New York, 1937.

SCHÜSSLER, WILHELM. *Bismarcks Kampf um Süddeutschland, 1867.* Berlin, 1929.

SCHWEND, KARL. *Bayern zwischen Monarchie und Diktatur.* Munich, 1954.

SENGER, GERHARD. *Die Politik der deutschen Zentrumspartei zur Frage Reich und Länder von 1918–1928.* Hamburg, 1932.

SHANAHAN, WILLIAM O. *German Protestants Face the Social Question.* Notre Dame, Ind., 1954.

SHEEHAN, JAMES J., ed. *Imperial Germany.* New York, 1976.

SILVERMAN, DAN P. *Reluctant Union: Alsace-Lorraine and Imperial Germany, 1871–1918.* University Park, Pa., 1972.

SPANN, OTHMAR. *The History of Economics.* New York, 1930.

SPOTTS, FREDERIC. *The Churches and Politics in Germany.* Middletown, Conn., 1973.

Staatslexikon: Recht, Wirtschaft, Gesellschaft. 6th ed. Freiburg, 1957–63.

STAMPFER, FRIEDRICH. *Die Vierzehn Jahre der Ersten Deutschen Republik.* Karlsbad, 1936.

STEHKÄMPER, HUGO. *Konrad Adenauer als Katholikentagspräsident 1922.* Mainz, 1977.

STEHLIN, STEWART A. *Bismarck and the Guelph Problem, 1866–1890.* The Hague, 1973.

STERN, FRITZ. *The Failure of Illiberalism.* New York, 1972.

———. *Gold and Iron: Bismarck, Bleichröder, and the Building of the German Empire.* New York, 1979.

STUMP, WOLFGANG. *Geschichte und Organization der Zentrumspartei in Düsseldorf, 1917–1933.* Düsseldorf, 1971.

STÜRMER, MICHAEL. *Koalition und Opposition in der Weimarer Republik, 1924–1928.* Düsseldorf, 1967.

————. *Regierung und Reichstag im Bismarckstaat, 1871–1880.* Düsseldorf, 1974.

————, ed. *Das kaiserliche Deutschland: Politik und Gesellschaft, 1870–1918.* Düsseldorf, 1970.

STURMTHAL, ADOLF. *The Tragedy of European Labor.* New York, 1943.

————. *White Collar Trade Unions.* Urbana, Ill., and London, 1966.

TAL, URIEL. *Christians and Jews in Germany: Religion, Politics, and Ideology in the Second Reich, 1870–1914.* Ithaca, N.Y., 1975.

TAYLOR, A. J. P. *Bismarck the Man and the Statesman.* London, 1955.

TILFORD, R. B., and PREECE, R. J. C. *Federal Germany: Political and Social Order.* London, 1969.

TIMM, HELGA. *Die deutsche Sozialpolitik und der Bruch der grossen Koalition im März 1930.* Düsseldorf, 1952.

TIMS, RICHARD WONSER. *Germanizing Prussian Poland.* New York, 1941.

VERKADE, WILLEM. *Democratic Parties in the Low Countries and Germany.* Leiden, 1965.

VIETSCH, EBERHARD VON. *Bethmann-Hollweg.* Boppard am Rhein, 1969.

VOLGELSANG, THILO. *Kurt von Schleicher: Ein General als Politiker.* Göttingen, 1965.

WACHTLING, OSWALD. *Joseph Joos.* Mainz, 1974.

WAHL, ADALBERT. *Deutsche Geschichte von der Reichsgründung bis zum Ausbruch des Weltkrieges, 1871 bis 1914.* 4 vols. Stuttgart, 1926–36.

WALLACE, LILLIAN PARKER. *Leo XIII and the Rise of Socialism.* Durham, N.C., 1966.

————. *The Papacy and European Diplomacy, 1869–1878.* Chapel Hill, N.C., 1948.

WATKINS, FREDERICK MUNDELL. *The Failure of Constitutional Emergency Powers under the German Republic.* Cambridge, Mass., 1939.

WEYMAR, PAUL. *Adenauer, His Authorized Biography.* New York, 1957.

WHEELER-BENNETT, JOHN W. *Brest-Litovsk: The Forgotten Peace, March 1918.* New York, 1971.

————. *The Nemesis of Power: The German Army in Politics, 1918–1945.* New York, 1956.

————. *Wooden Titan.* New York, 1936.

WHITE, DAN S. *The Splintered Party: National Liberalism in Hessen and the Reich, 1867–1918.* Cambridge, Mass., 1976.

WIECK, HANS GEORG. *Die Entstehung der C.D.U. und die Wiedergründung des Zentrums im Jahre 1945.* Düsseldorf, 1953.

WILLIAMSON, JOHN G. *Karl Helfferich, 1872–1924.* Princeton, 1971.

WINDELL, GEORGE C. *The Catholics and German Unity, 1866–1871.* Minneapolis, 1954.

WITT, PETER-CHRISTIAN. *Die Finanzpolitik des Deutschen Reiches von 1903 bis 1913.* Lübeck and Hamburg, 1970.

WRIGHT, J. R. C. *"Above Parties": The Political Attitudes of the German Protestant Church Leadership, 1918–1933.* Oxford, 1974.

ZEENDER, JOHN K. *The German Center Party, 1890–1906.* Philadelphia, 1976.

ZIEGLER, WILHELM. *Die deutsche Nationalversammlung 1919–1920 und ihr Verfassungswerk.* Berlin, 1932.

ZIEKURSCH, JOHANNES. *Politische Geschichte des neuen deutschen Kaiserreiches.* 3 vols. Frankfurt, 1925–30.

ZIMMERMANN, WERNER GABRIEL. *Bayern und das Reich, 1918–1923.* Munich, 1953.

SECONDARY SOURCES: ARTICLES

ARETIN, KARL OTHMAR, FREIHERR VON. "Kaas, Papen und das Konkordat von 1933." *Vierteljahrshefte für Zeitgeschichte* 14 (1966): 252–79.

BECKER, JOSEF. "Brüning, Prälat Kaas und das Problem einer Regierungsbeteilung der N. S. D. A. P. 1930–1932." *Historische Zeitschrift* 196 (1963): 74–111.

———. "Das Ende der Zentrumspartei und die Problematik des politischen katholizismus in Deutschland." *Die Welt als Geschichte* 23 (1963): 149–70.

BERGER, HANS. "Bayerischer Katholizismus zwischen Weimar und Drittem Reich." *Internationale Katholische Zeitschrift* 5 (1976): 448–58.

BERNBACH, UDO. "Aspekte der Parlamentarismus-Diskussion im kaiserlichen Reichstag." *Politische Vierteljahresschrift* 8 (1967): 51–70.

BLACKBOURN, DAVID. "Class and Politics in Wilhelmine Germany: The Center Party and the Social Democrats in Württemberg." *Central European History* 9 (1976): 220–49.

———. "The Political Alignment of the Centre Party in Wilhelmine Germany: A Study of the Party's Emergence in Nineteenth-Century Württemberg." *Historical Journal* 18 (1975): 821–50.

BLANKE, RICHARD. "Bismarck and the Prussian Polish Policies of 1886." *Journal of Modern History* 45 (1973): 211–39.

BOELITZ, OTTO. "Zur Problematik des Reichsschulgesetzes." *Preussische Jahrbücher* 209 (1927): 273–92.

BORNKAMM, HEINRICH. "Die Staatsidee im Kulturkampf." 2 pts. *Historische Zeitschrift* 170 (1950): 41–72; 273–306.

BOYER, JOHN W. "Catholic Priests in Lower Austria: Anti-Liberalism, Occupational Anxiety, and Radical Political Action in Late Nineteenth-Century Vienna." *Proceedings of the American Philosophical Society* 118 (1974): 337–69.

BRAATZ, WERNER. "Franz von Papen und die Frage der Reichsreform." *Politische Vierteljahresschrift* 16 (1975): 319–36.

BRACHER, KARL DIETRICH. "Die Brüning-Memoiren." *Vierteljahrshefte für Zeitgeschichte* 19 (1971): 113–23.

BRAMSTED, E. "The Position of the Protestant Church in Germany, 1871–1933." *Journal of Religious History* 2 (1963): 314–34.

Bibliography

CECIL, LAMAR. "The Creation of Nobles in Prussia, 1871–1918." *American Historical Review* 65 (1970): 757–95.

CONZE, WERNER. "Brüning als Reichskanzler: eine Zwischenbilanz." *Historische Zeitschrift* 214 (1972): 310–34.

DAHM, KARL-WILHELM. "German Protestantism and Politics, 1918–1939." *Journal of Contemporary History* 3 (1968): 29–49.

DAHRENDORF, RALF. "The Crisis in German Education." *Journal of Contemporary History* 2 (1967): 139–47.

DEUERLEIN, ERNST. "Der Gewerkschaftsstreit." *Theologische Quartalschrift* 139 (1969): 40–81.

DILL, MARSHALL, JR. "The Christian Trade Unions during the Last Years of Imperial Germany and the First Months of the Weimar Republic." *Review of Social Economy* 12 (1954): 89–109.

————. "The Christian Trades Union Movement in Germany before World War I." *Review of Social Economy* 11 (1953).

DÜLMEN, RICHARD VAN. "Der deutsche Katholizismus und der Erste Weltkrieg." *Francia* 2 (1974): 355–67.

EPSTEIN, KLAUS. "Adenauer 1918–1924." *Geschichte in Wissenschaft und Unterricht* 19 (1968): 553–61.

————. "Erzberger and the German Colonial Scandals, 1905–1910." *English Historical Review* 74 (1959): 637–63.

————. "Erzberger's Position in the *Zentrumsstreit* before World War I." *Catholic Historical Review* 44 (1958): 553–61.

FISCHER, FRITZ. "Der deutsche Protestantismus und die Politik im 19. Jahrhundert." *Historische Zeitschrift* 171 (1951); 473–518.

FOERSTER, ERICH. "Liberalismus und Kulturkampf." *Zeitschrift für Kirchengeschichte* 47 (1928): 543–59.

FRALEY, J. DAVID. "Reform or Reaction: Dilemma of Prince Hohenlohe as Chancellor of Germany." *European Studies Review* 4 (1974): 317–43.

GIES, HORST. "Die Regierung Hertling und die Parlamentarisierung in Deutschland 1917–1918." *Der Staat* 13 (1974): 471–96.

HARRIS, ABRAM L. "The Scholastic Revival: The Economics of Heinrich Pesch." *Journal of Political Economy* 54 (1946): 38–58.

HAYES, PETER. "'A Question Mark with Epaulettes?' Kurt von Schleicher and Weimar Politics." *Journal of Modern History* 52 (1980): 35–65.

HOLL, KARL. "Konfessionalität, Konfessionalismus und demokratische Republik." *Vierteljahrshefte für Zeitgeschichte* 17 (1969): 254–75.

HUGHES, JOHN JAY. "The Reich Concordat 1933: Capitulation or Compromise?" *Australian Journal of Politics and History* 20 (1974): 164–75.

HUNT, JAMES C. "Peasants, Grain Tariffs, and Meat Quotas: Imperial German Protectionism Reexamined." *Central European History* 7 (1974): 311–31.

JONES, LARRY EUGENE. "Adam Stegerwald und die Krise des deutschen Parteiensystems." *Vierteljahrshefte für Zeitgeschichte* 27 (1979): 1–29.

————. "Between the Fronts: the German National Union of Commercial Employees from 1928 to 1933." *Journal of Modern History* 48 (1976): 462–82.

KNAPP, THOMAS A. "The German Center Party and the *Reichsbanner.*" *International Review of Social History* 14 (1969): 159–79.

———. "Heinrich Brüning in Exil: Briefe an Wilhelm Sollmann 1940–1946." *Vierteljahrshefte für Zeitgeschichte* 22 (1971): 93–120.

———. "The Red and the Black: Catholic Socialists in the Weimar Republic." *Catholic Historical Review* 61 (1975): 386–408.

KOLLMANN, ERIC C. "The Weimar Republic." *Journal of Central European Affairs* 21 (1962): 434–51.

KOONZ, CLAUDIA. "Conflicting Allegiances: Political Ideology and Women Legislators in Weimar Germany." *Signs* 1 (1976): 663–83.

LOEWENSTEIN, KARL. "Occupational Representation and the Idea of an Economic Parliament." *Social Science* 12 (1937): 420–31.

LOUGEE, ROBERT W. "The *Kulturkampf* and Historical Positivism." *Church History* 23 (1954): 219–35.

LUCKAU, ALMA. "Unconditional Acceptance of the Treaty of Versailles by the German Government, June 22–28, 1919." *Journal of Modern History* 17 (1945): 215–20.

MOMMSEN, WILHELM. "Julius Fröbel: Wirrnis und Weitsicht." *Historische Zeitschrift* 181 (1956): 497–532.

MORK, GORDON R. "Bismarck and the 'Capitulation' of German Liberalism." *Journal of Modern History* 43 (1971): 59–75.

MORSEY, RUDOLF. "Bismarck und der Kulturkampf." *Archiv für Kulturgeschichte* 39 (1957): 232–70.

———. "Die deutsche Katholiken und der Nationalstaat zwischen Kulturkampf und Ersten Weltkrieg." *Historisches Jahrbuch* 90: 31–64.

———. "Hitlers Verhandlungen mit der Zentrumsführung am 31. Januar 1933." *Vierteljahrshefte für Zeitgeschichte* 9 (1961): 182–94.

———. "Zur Entstehung, Authentizität und Kritik von Brünings *Memoiren 1918–1934.*" *Proceedings of the Rheinisch-Westfälische Akademie der Wissenschaften.* Opladen, 1975.

MUNCY, LYSBETH W. The Prussian *Landrat* in the Last Years of the Monarchy: A Case Study of Pomerania and the Rhineland in 1890–1918." *Central European History* 6 (1973): 299–338.

O'LESSKER, KARL. "Who Voted for Hitler? A New Look at the Class Basis of Naziism." *American Journal of Sociology* 74 (1968): 63–69.

PIKART, EBERHARD. "Preussische Beamtenpolitik 1918–1933." *Vierteljahrshefte für Zeitgeschichte* 6 (1958): 119–37.

RADEMACHER, ARNOLD. "Die Stellung der katholischen Kirche." In Otto Baumgarten et al., *Geistige und Sittliche Wirkungen des Krieges in Deutschland.* Wirtschafts-und Sozialgeschichte des Weltkrieges: Deutsche Serie, edited by James T. Shotwell, 1: 149–216. Stuttgart, 1927.

REPGEN, KONRAD. "Ueber die Entstehung der Reichskonkordats-Offerte im Frühjahr 1933 und die Bedeutung des Reichskonkordats." *Vierteljahrshefte für Zeitgeschichte* 26 (1978): 499–534.

RÖHL, JOHN C. G. "The Disintegration of the *Kartell* and the Politics of Bis-

marck's Fall from Power, 1887–1890." *Historical Journal* 9 (1966): 60–89.
———. "Higher Civil Servants in Germany, 1890–1900." *Journal of Contemporary History* 2 (1967): 101–21.
———. "Staatsstreichplan oder Staatsstreitbereitschaft?" *Historische Zeitschrift* 203 (1966): 610–24.
ROSENTHAL, HARRY KENNETH. "The Election of Archbishop Stablewski." *Slavic Review* 28 (1969): 265–75.
RUPPEL, EDITH. "Zur Tätigkeit des Eugenio Pacelli als Nuntius in Deutschland." *Zeitschrift für Geschichtswissenschaft* 7 (1959): 297–317.
SCHMITT, HANS A. "Bismarck as Seen from the Nearest Church Steeple." *Central European History* 6 (1973): 363–72.
SCHOLDER, KLAUS. "Altes und Neues zur Vorgeschichte des Reichskonkordats: (Erwiderung auf Konrad Repgen)." *Vierteljahrshefte für Zeitgeschichte* 26 (1978): 534–70.
———. "Die Kapitulation des politisches Katholizismus—die Rolle des Zentrums-Vorsitzenden Kaas im Frühjahr 1933." *Frankfurter Allgemeine Zeitung* 9 (27 Sept. 1977).
SCHOLTES, MATTHIAS. "Katholizismus und deutsche Revolution." *Deutsche Rundschau* 235 (1933): 6–8.
SCHÖNHOVEN, KLAUS. "Zwischen Anpassung und Ausschaltung: Die Bayerische Volkspartei in der Endphase der Weimarer Republik 1932/33." *Historische Zeitschrift* 224 (1977): 340–78.
SCHULZ, GERHARD. "Erinnerungen an eine misslungene Restauration: Heinrich Brüning und seine Memoiren." *Der Staat* 2 (1972): 61–81.
SHEEHAN, JAMES J. "Political Leadership in the German Reichstag, 1871–1918." *American Historical Review* 74 (1968): 511–28.
STEHLE, HANSJAKOB. "Motive des Reichskonkordates." *Aussenpolitik* 9 (1956): 558–64.
STERN, FRITZ. "Adenauer and a Crisis in Weimar Democracy." *Political Science Quarterly* 73 (1958): 1–27.
STÜRMER, MICHAEL. "Bismarck in Perspective." *Central European History* 4 (1971): 291–33.
TRZECIAKOWSKI, LECH. "The Prussian State and the Catholic Church in Prussian Poland, 1871–1914." *Slavic Review* 26 (1967): 619–37.
ULLMANN, HERMANN. "Das Essener Program, November, 1920." *Deutsche Rundschau* 11 (1950): 897–903.
WARD, JAMES E. "Leo XIII and Bismarck: The Kaiser's Vatican Visit of 1888." *Review of Politics* 24 (1962): 392–414.
WARLOSKI, RONALD. "Catholic Students and Revolutionary Germany: the Establishment of *Neudeutschland* in 1918–1919." *Catholic Historical Review* 53 (1968): 600–620.
WEBER, CHRISTOPH. "Der 'Fall Spahn,' die 'Weltgeschichte in Karacterbildern' und die Görres-Gessellschaft I." *Römische Quartalschrift für christliche Altertüm und Kirchegeschichte* 73 (1978): 47–110.
WINDELL, GEORGE C. "The Bismarckian Empire as a Federal State, 1866–1880:

A Chronicle of Failure." *Central European History* 2 (1969): 291–311.

ZANGERL, CARL H. E. "Courting the Catholic Vote: The Center Party in Baden, 1903–1913." *Central European History* 10 (1977): 220–40.

ZEENDER, JOHN K. "German Catholics and the Concept of an Interconfessional Party, 1900–1922." *Journal of Central European Affairs* 23 (1964): 424–39.

———. "The German Catholics and the Presidential Election of 1925." *Journal of Modern History* 35 (1963): 366–81.

———. "The German Center Party during World War I: An Internal Study." *Catholic Historical Review* 42 (1957): 441–68.

ZORN, WOLFGANG. "Student Politics in the Weimar Republic." *Journal of Contemporary History* 5 (1970): 128–43.

INDEX

Abel, Karl von, 15–16

Adenauer, Konrad: at Catholic Congress 1922, 283–84; proposed for chancellorship, 279, 304; and Rhineland separatism, 225, 286–87; after World War II, 397, 401

Agrarian leagues: Baden, 190; Bavaria, 98, 169, 190, 222, 260–61, 345; national, 190, 247; Palatinate, 190; Rhineland, 247, 309; Silesia, 190; Westphalia, 34, 114, 190, 247, 309

Agrarian party (*Deutsches Landvolk*), 359, 363–64, 371, 400

Allekotte, Joseph, 248

Aloisi-Masella, Gaetano, 79

Alsace-Lorraine: Center party in, 34, 49, 109–10, 135, 173–75; discrimination in, 43, 53 142–45, 161, 404; loss of, 227, 241, 262; in World War I, 204, 209

Altenstein, Karl, Freiherr von, 4

Andre, Josef, 252, 313, 400

Anti-Semitism, 40, 69, 114–15, 385–86, 405

Anti-Socialist laws, 79, 83, 86, 125–26, 132, 135

Associations Law of 1908, 105, 160–61, 177, 183

Augusta of Prussia, 47–48, 51, 54, 78, 117

Augustine League, 106, 209

Baader, Franz von, 9, 184–86

Bachem, Carl: as political leader, 102, 124, 129, 152, 156, 197, 204, 214; as party historian, 156, 274, 395–97

Bachem, Joseph, 71

Bachem, J. P., publishing firm, 106, 124

Bachem, Julius, 124, 129, 196–97, 200, 204

Ballestrem, Count Franz von, 96, 103, 112, 123, 148, 191

Bamberger Program of 1922, 270, 288–89

Bassermann, Ernst, 161

Bauer, Otto, 229, 238

Bavarian People's party (BVP): coalition policy, 287–89, 314–15, 344–45; Concordat of 1925, 316–17; dissolution, 389–91; founding, 98, 222; organization, 260–62; in presidential election of 1925, 297–300, 319; reconciliation with Center, 333–34, 337; secession from Center, 267–70, 291; and Papen government, 379–80, 382–38

Bayerische Kurier, 223, 261

Bazille, Wilhelm, 314, 343–44

Bebel, August, 61

Bechly, Hans, 251

Behrens, Franz, 183, 359

Bell, Johannes, 203, 229–30, 304, 367, 397

Benedict XV (pope), 200, 205, 207

Bennigsen, Rudolf von, 27, 49, 69, 77

Berliner Tageblatt, 306, 332, 378

Belrin-Trier orientation, 191–94, 197–201

Bertram, Adolf, 387

Bethmann-Hollweg, Theobald von, 164, 192–94, 204–9, 211–12, 214–15, 270